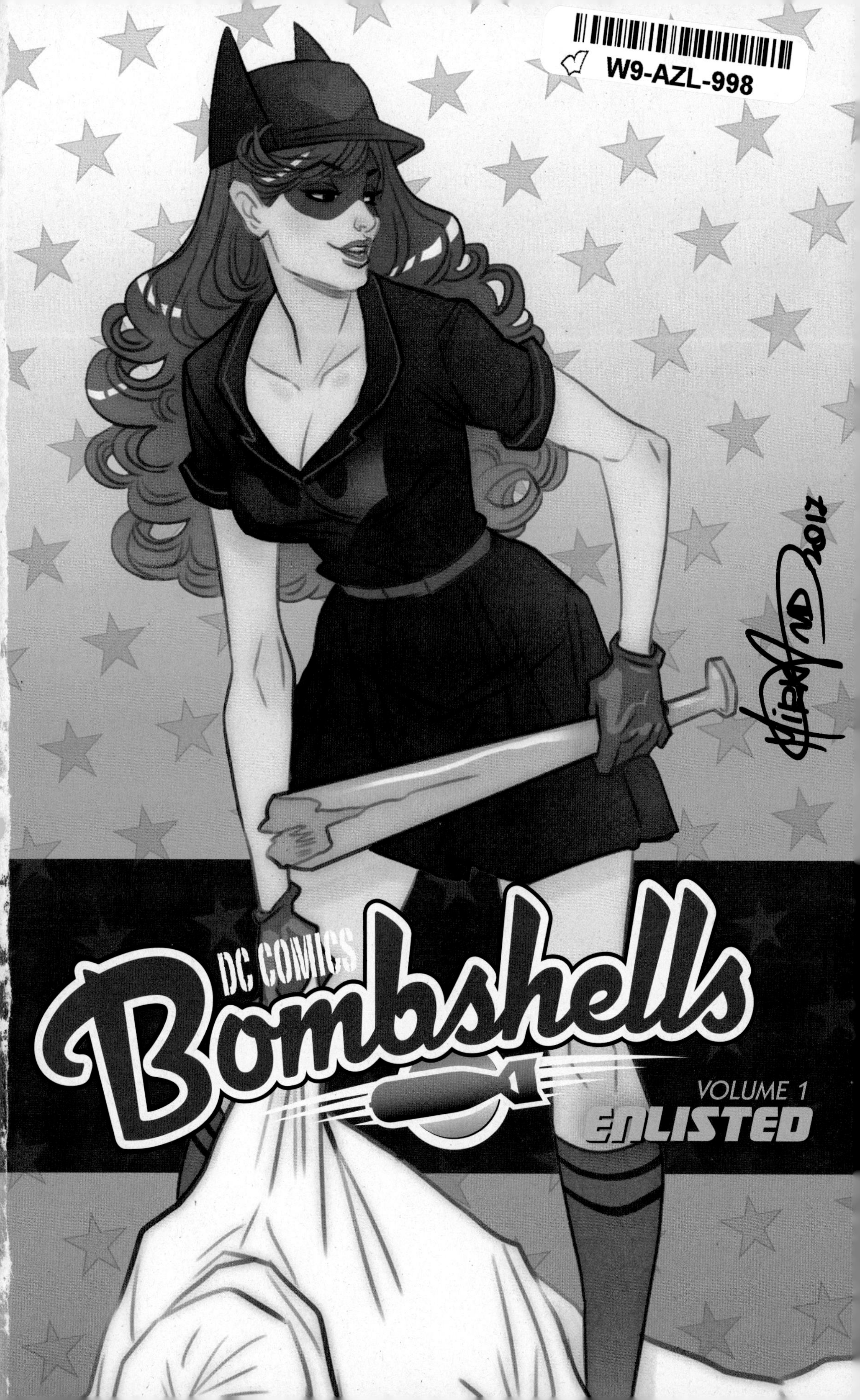
DC COMICS
Bombshells
VOLUME 1
ENLISTED

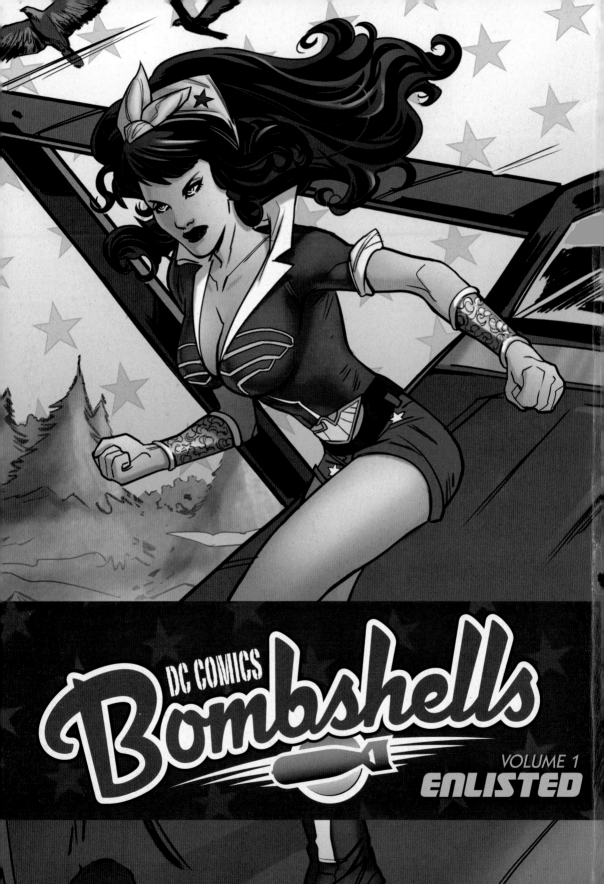

DC COMICS

# Bombshells

VOLUME 1
## ENLISTED

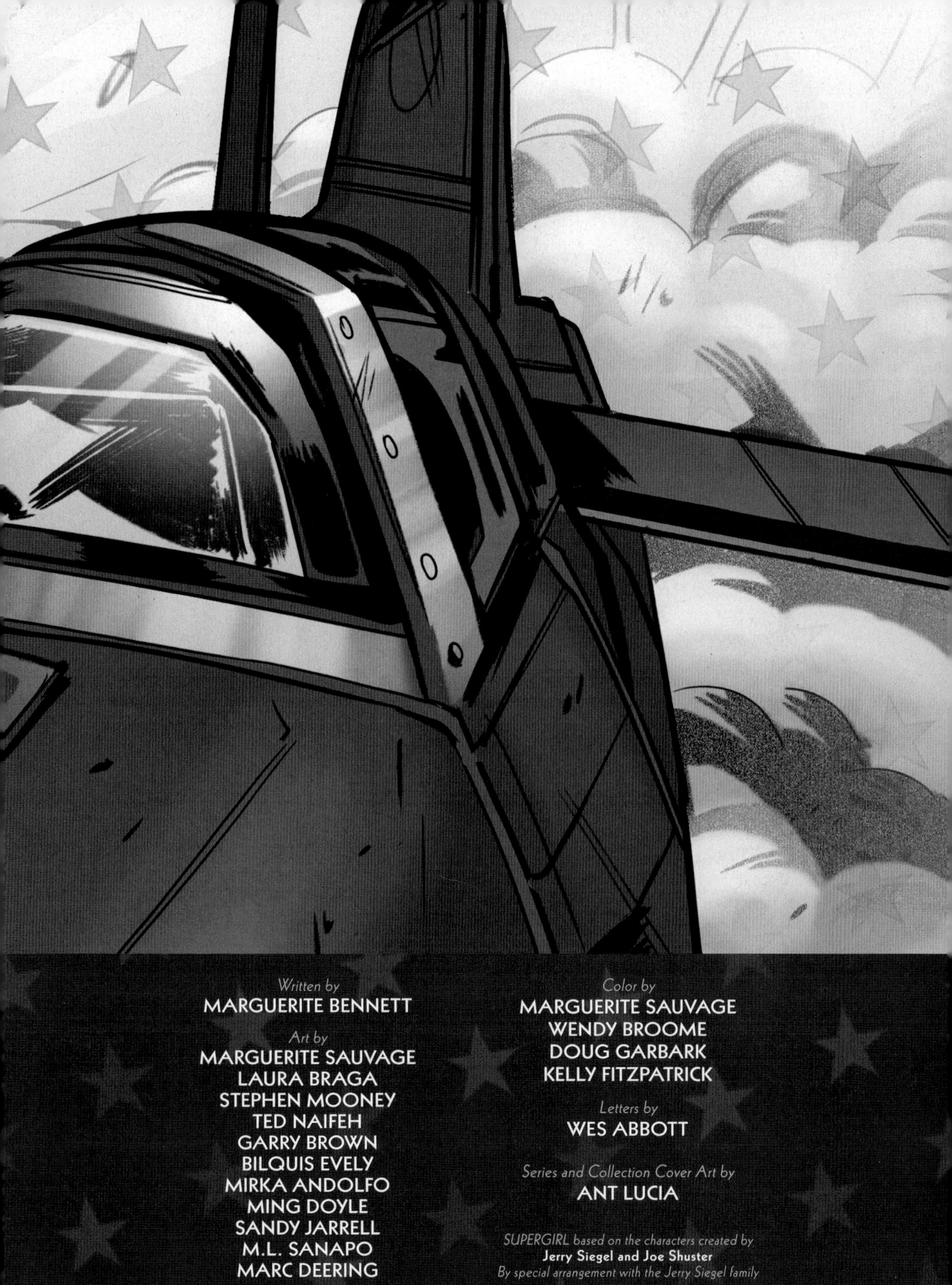

*Written by*
**MARGUERITE BENNETT**

*Art by*
**MARGUERITE SAUVAGE**
**LAURA BRAGA**
**STEPHEN MOONEY**
**TED NAIFEH**
**GARRY BROWN**
**BILQUIS EVELY**
**MIRKA ANDOLFO**
**MING DOYLE**
**SANDY JARRELL**
**M.L. SANAPO**
**MARC DEERING**

*Color by*
**MARGUERITE SAUVAGE**
**WENDY BROOME**
**DOUG GARBARK**
**KELLY FITZPATRICK**

*Letters by*
**WES ABBOTT**

*Series and Collection Cover Art by*
**ANT LUCIA**

*SUPERGIRL based on the characters created by*
**Jerry Siegel and Joe Shuster**
*By special arrangement with the Jerry Siegel family*

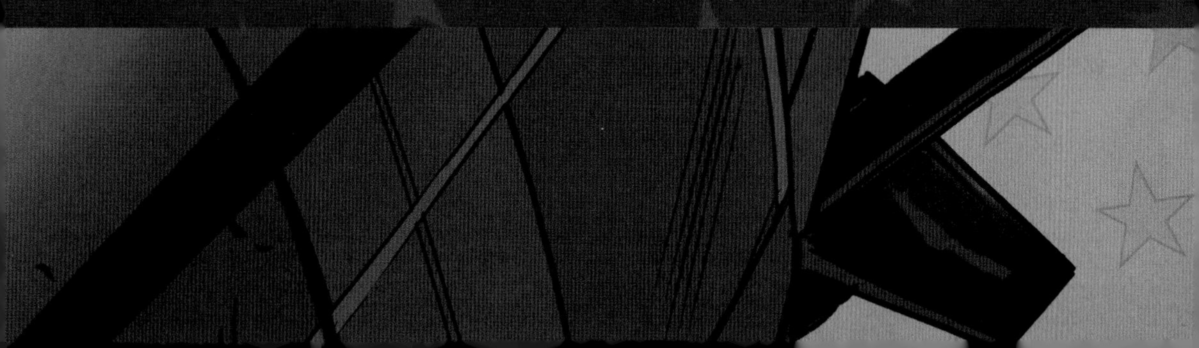

JIM CHADWICK  Editor – Original Series
JESSICA CHEN  Associate Editor – Original Series
JEB WOODARD  Group Editor – Collected Editions
LIZ ERICKSON  Editor – Collected Edition
STEVE COOK  Design Director – Books
CURTIS KING JR.  Publication Design

BOB HARRAS  Senior VP – Editor-in-Chief, DC Comics

DIANE NELSON  President
DAN DiDIO  Publisher
JIM LEE  Publisher
GEOFF JOHNS  President & Chief Creative Officer
AMIT DESAI  Executive VP – Business & Marketing Strategy, Direct to
Consumer & Global Franchise Management
SAM ADES  Senior VP – Direct to Consumer
BOBBIE CHASE  VP – Talent Development
MARK CHIARELLO  Senior VP – Art, Design & Collected Editions
JOHN CUNNINGHAM  Senior VP – Sales & Trade Marketing
ANNE DePIES  Senior VP – Business Strategy, Finance & Administration
DON FALLETTI  VP – Manufacturing Operations
LAWRENCE GANEM  VP – Editorial Administration & Talent Relations
ALISON GILL  Senior VP – Manufacturing & Operations
HANK KANALZ  Senior VP – Editorial Strategy & Administration
JAY KOGAN  VP – Legal Affairs
THOMAS LOFTUS  VP – Business Affairs
JACK MAHAN  VP – Business Affairs
DAN MIRON  VP – Sales Planning & Trade Development
NICK J. NAPOLITANO  VP – Manufacturing Administration
EDDIE SCANNELL  VP – Consumer Marketing
COURTNEY SIMMONS  Senior VP – Publicity & Communications
JIM (SKI) SOKOLOWSKI  VP – Comic Book Specialty & Trade Marketing
NANCY SPEARS  VP – Mass, Book, Digital Sales & Trade Marketing

DC COMICS: BOMBSHELLS VOLUME 1: ENLISTED

Published by DC Comics. Compilation and all new material
Copyright © 2016 DC Comics. All Rights Reserved.

Originally published in single magazine form in DC COMICS: BOMBSHELLS 1-6 and
online as DC COMICS: BOMBSHELLS Digital Chapters 1-18 Copyright © 2015 DC
Comics. All Rights Reserved. All characters, their distinctive likenesses and related
elements featured in this publication are trademarks of DC Comics. The stories,
characters and incidents featured in this publication are entirely fictional. DC Comics
does not read or accept unsolicited ideas, stories or artwork.

DC Comics
2900 West Alameda Ave., Burbank, CA 91505
Printed by Transcontinental Interglobe, Beauceville, QC, Canada.
1/6/17. Third Printing.
ISBN: 978-1-4012-6132-0

Library of Congress Cataloging-in-Publication Data is available.

*For my parents,
John, Joan, and Barbara.*
—Marguerite Bennett

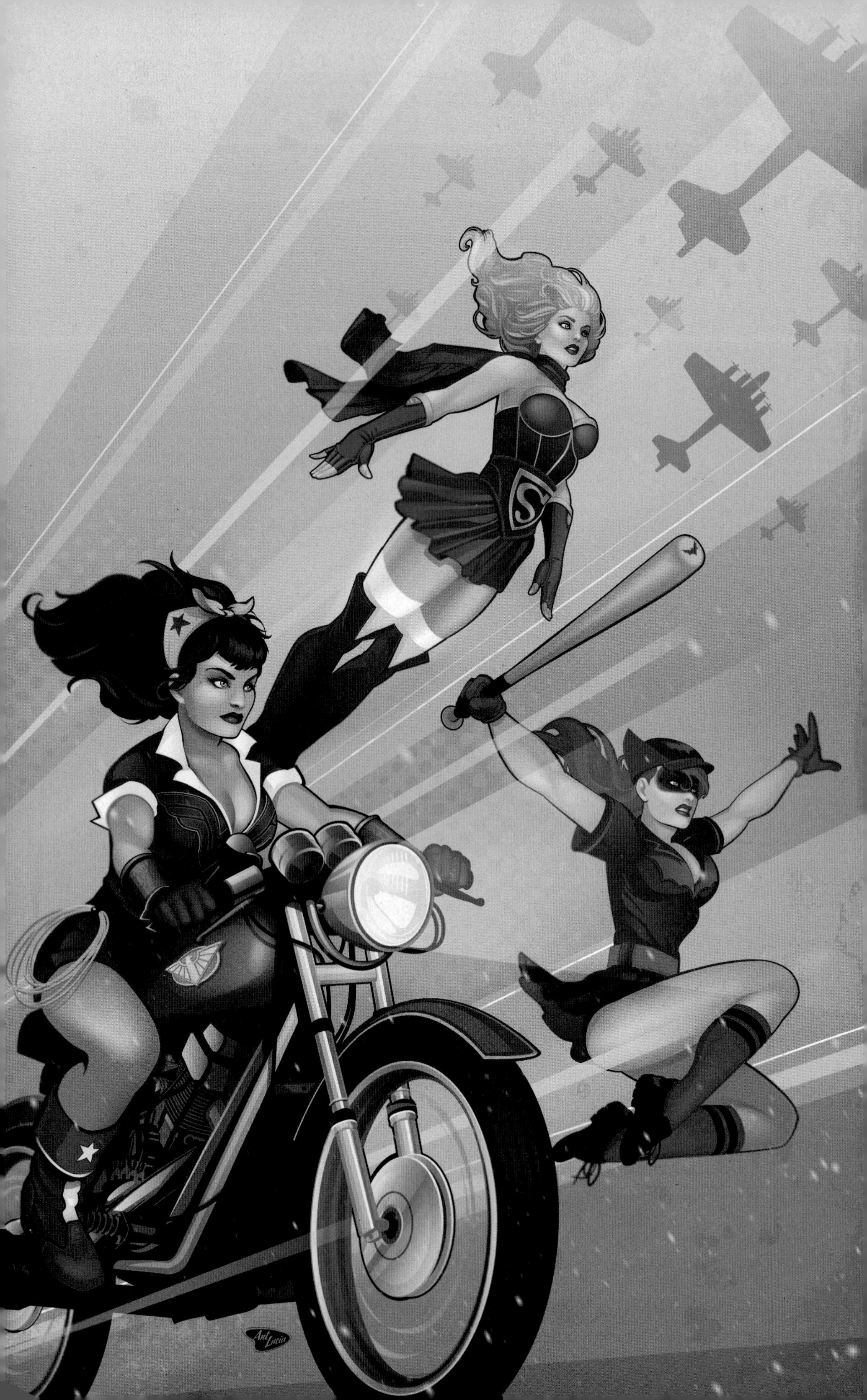

# ENLISTED
## PART ONE

**MARGUERITE BENNETT**
*Writer*

**MARGUERITE SAUVAGE**
*Artist*

**WES ABBOTT**
*Letterer*

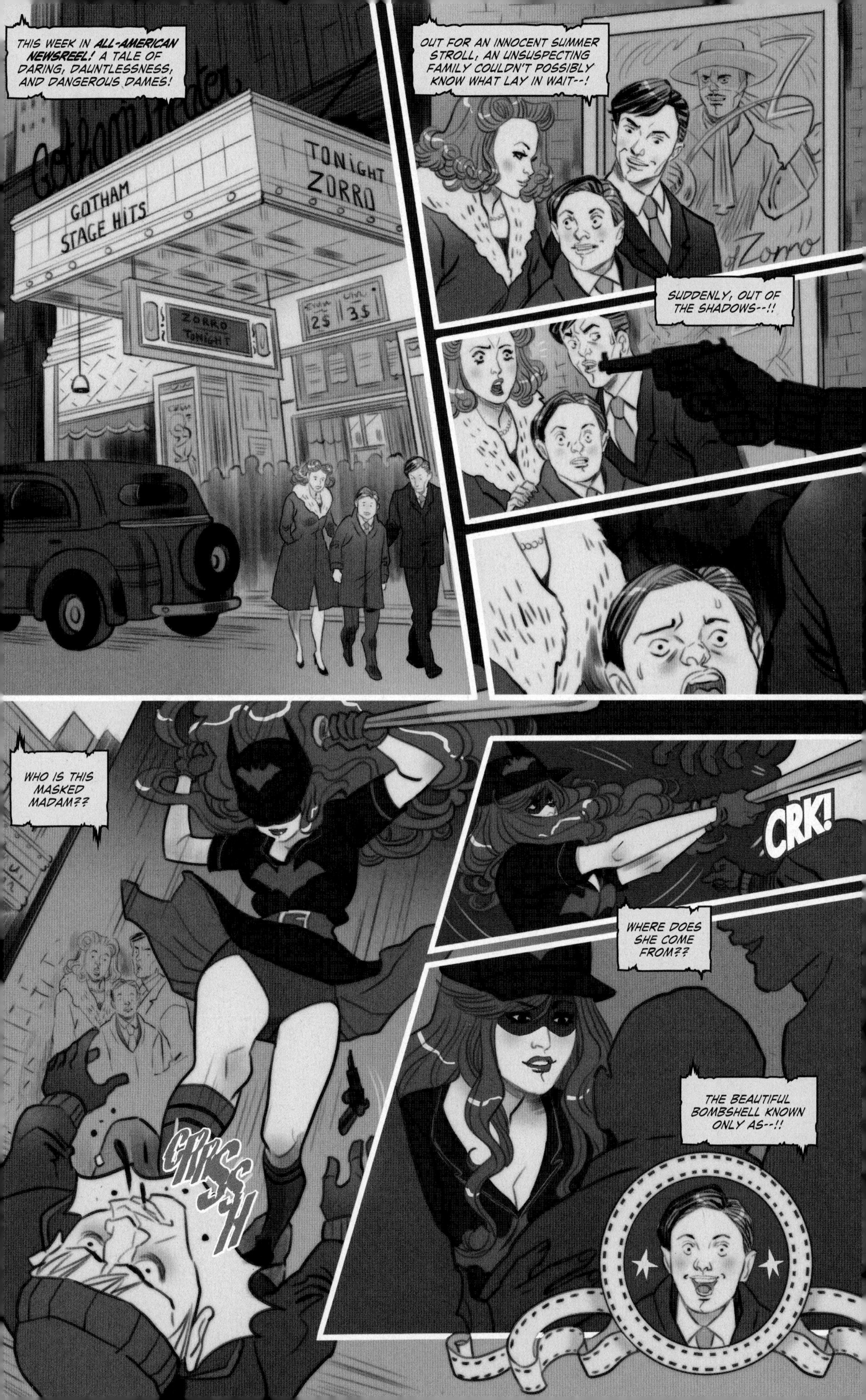
THIS WEEK IN ALL-AMERICAN NEWSREEL! A TALE OF DARING, DAUNTLESSNESS, AND DANGEROUS DAMES!
GOTHAM STAGE HITS
TONIGHT ZORRO
ZORRO TONIGHT
OUT FOR AN INNOCENT SUMMER STROLL, AN UNSUSPECTING FAMILY COULDN'T POSSIBLY KNOW WHAT LAY IN WAIT--!
SUDDENLY, OUT OF THE SHADOWS--!!
WHO IS THIS MASKED MADAM??
CRK!
WHERE DOES SHE COME FROM??
THE BEAUTIFUL BOMBSHELL KNOWN ONLY AS--!!

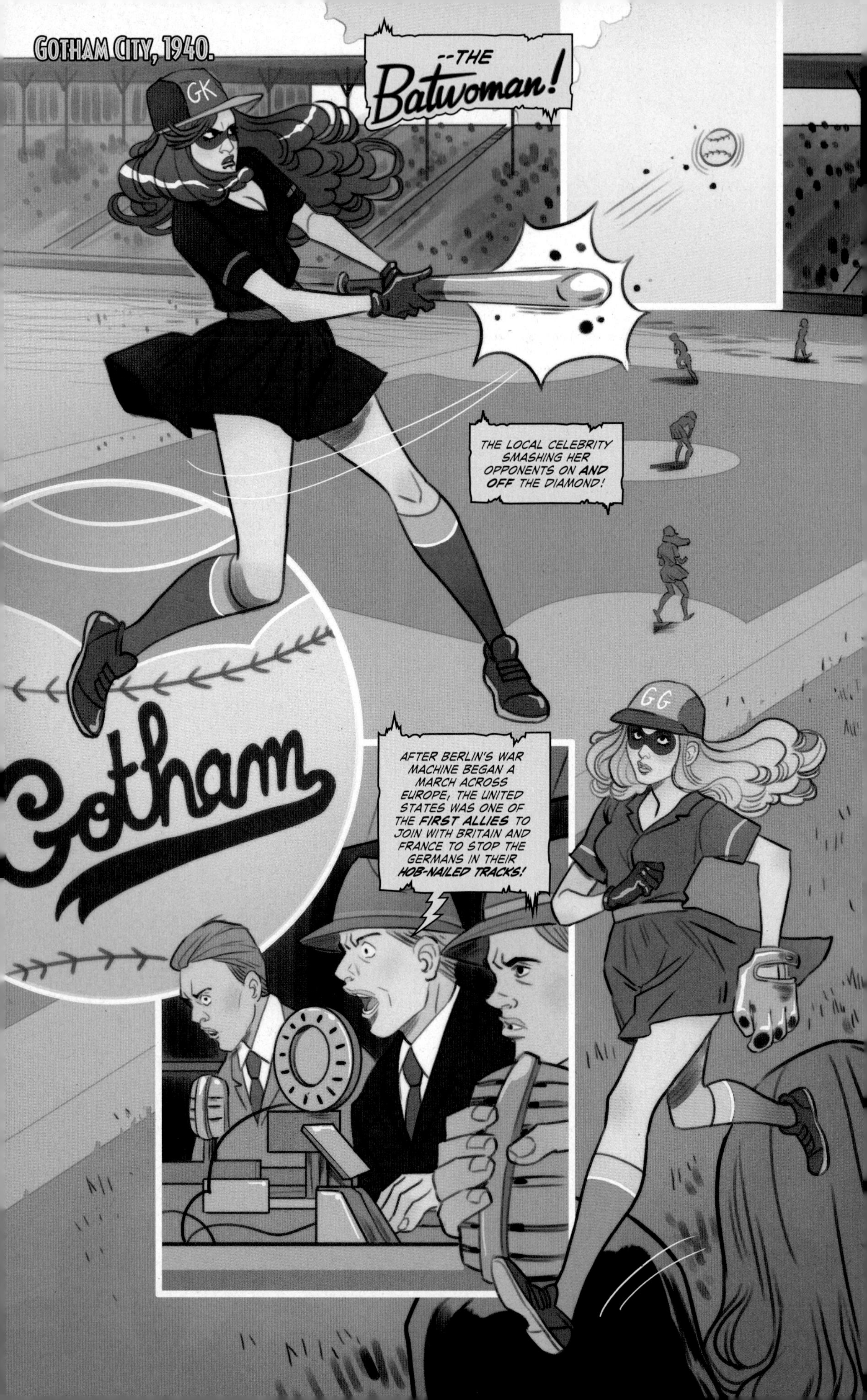

GOTHAM CITY, 1940.
--THE Batwoman!
GK
THE LOCAL CELEBRITY SMASHING HER OPPONENTS ON AND OFF THE DIAMOND!
Gotham
GG
AFTER BERLIN'S WAR MACHINE BEGAN A MARCH ACROSS EUROPE, THE UNITED STATES WAS ONE OF THE FIRST ALLIES TO JOIN WITH BRITAIN AND FRANCE TO STOP THE GERMANS IN THEIR HOB-NAILED TRACKS!

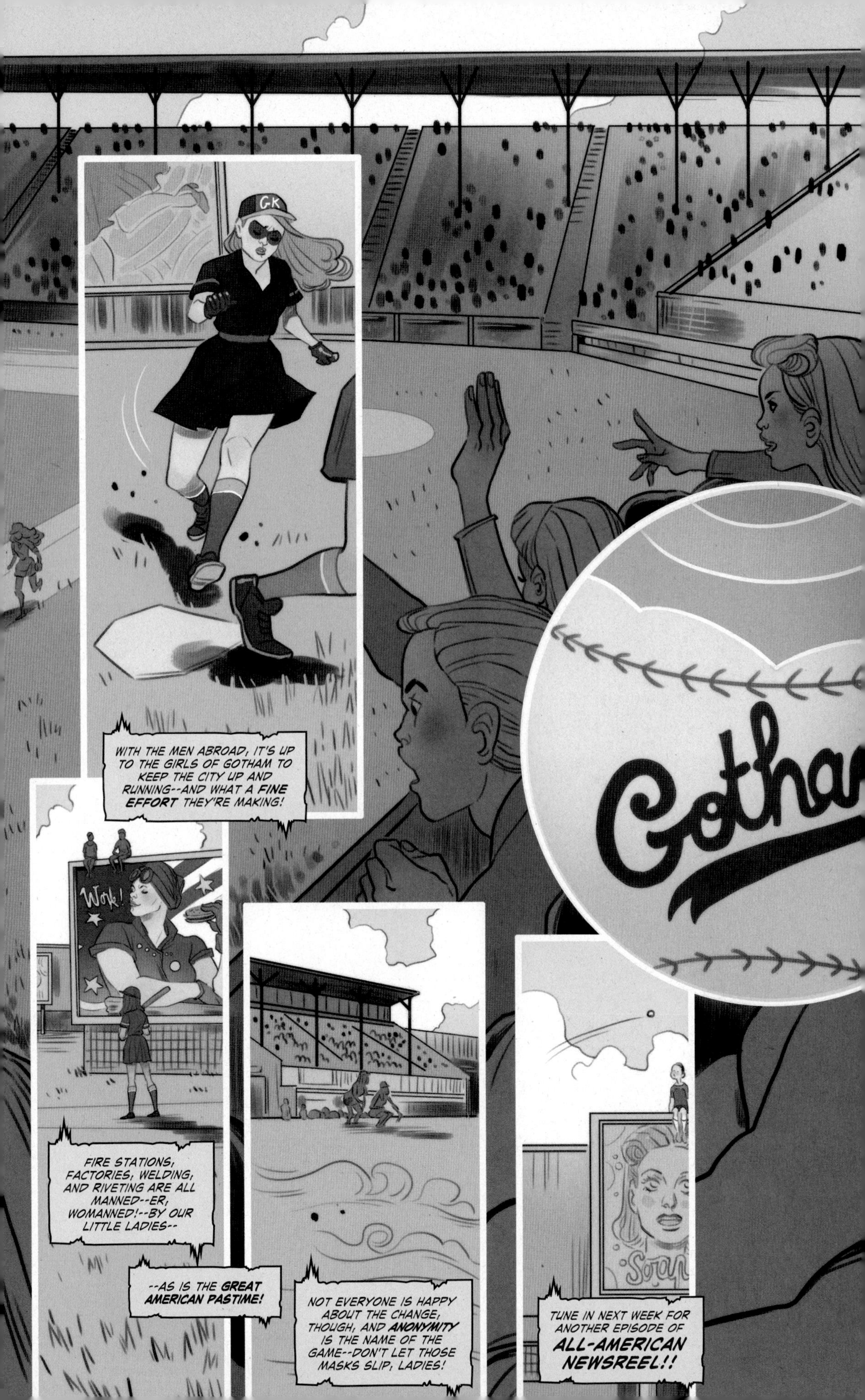
GK
WITH THE MEN ABROAD, IT'S UP TO THE GIRLS OF GOTHAM TO KEEP THE CITY UP AND RUNNING--AND WHAT A FINE EFFORT THEY'RE MAKING!
Gotham
Work!
FIRE STATIONS, FACTORIES, WELDING, AND RIVETING ARE ALL MANNED--ER, WOMANNED!--BY OUR LITTLE LADIES--
--AS IS THE GREAT AMERICAN PASTIME!
NOT EVERYONE IS HAPPY ABOUT THE CHANGE, THOUGH, AND ANONYMITY IS THE NAME OF THE GAME--DON'T LET THOSE MASKS SLIP, LADIES!
TUNE IN NEXT WEEK FOR ANOTHER EPISODE OF ALL-AMERICAN NEWSREEL!!

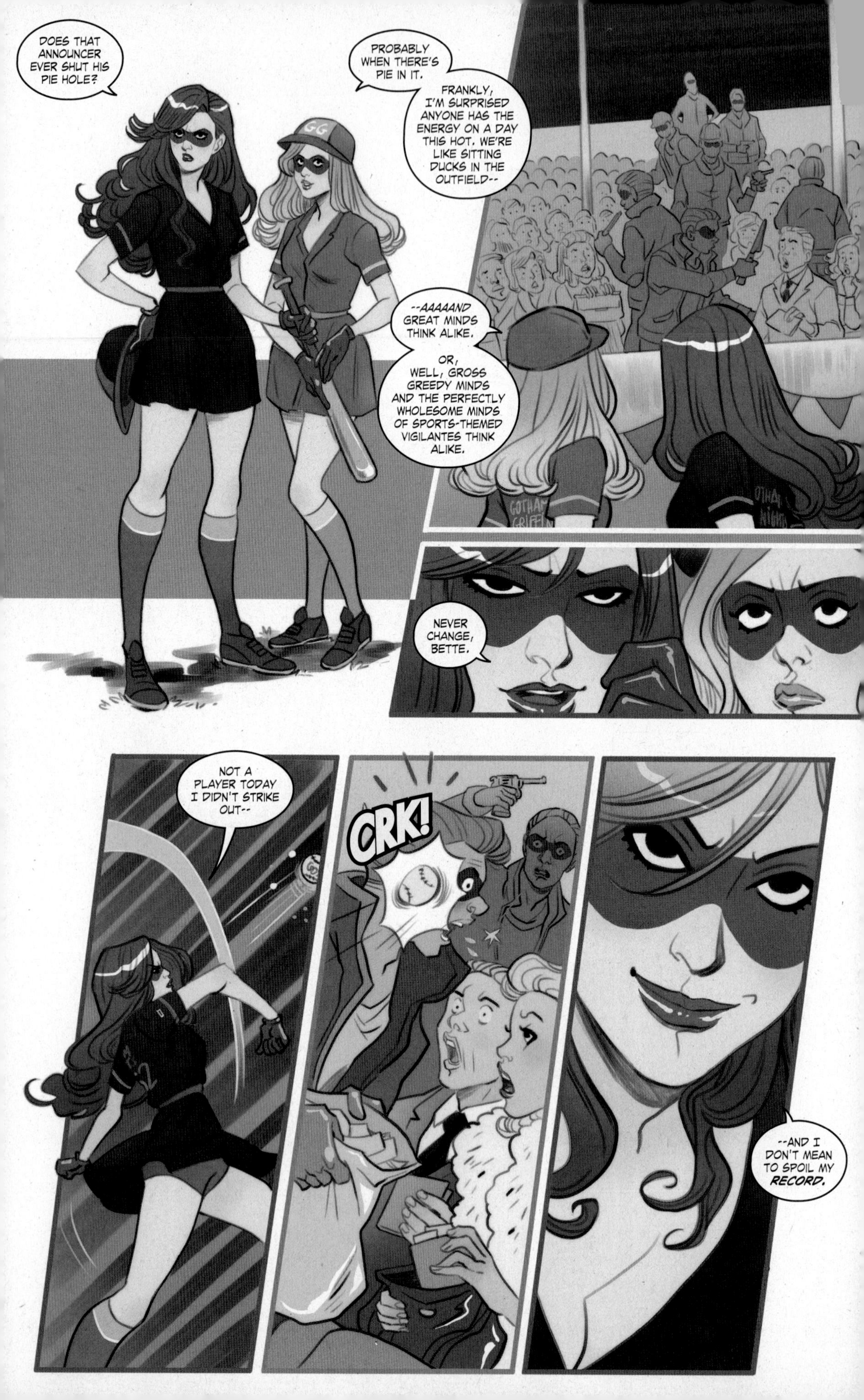
DOES THAT ANNOUNCER EVER SHUT HIS PIE HOLE?
PROBABLY WHEN THERE'S PIE IN IT.
FRANKLY, I'M SURPRISED ANYONE HAS THE ENERGY ON A DAY THIS HOT. WE'RE LIKE SITTING DUCKS IN THE OUTFIELD--
--*AAAAAND* GREAT MINDS THINK ALIKE.
OR, WELL, GROSS GREEDY MINDS AND THE PERFECTLY WHOLESOME MINDS OF SPORTS-THEMED VIGILANTES THINK ALIKE.
NEVER CHANGE, BETTE.
NOT A PLAYER TODAY I DIDN'T STRIKE OUT--
CRK!
--AND I DON'T MEAN TO SPOIL MY ***RECORD.***

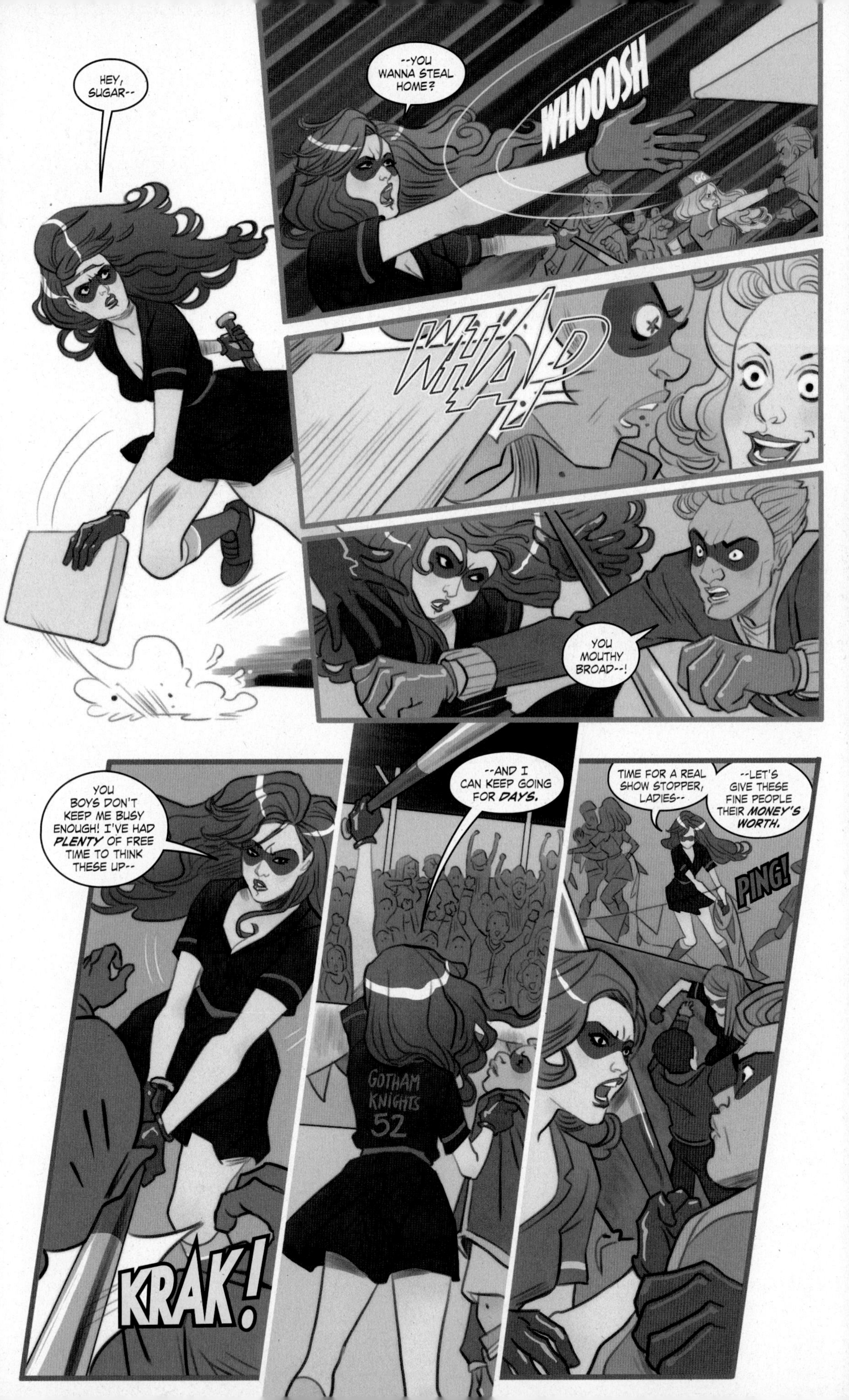
HEY, SUGAR--
--YOU WANNA STEAL HOME?
WHOOOSH
WHAP
YOU MOUTHY BROAD--!
YOU BOYS DON'T KEEP ME BUSY ENOUGH! I'VE HAD PLENTY OF FREE TIME TO THINK THESE UP--
KRAK!
--AND I CAN KEEP GOING FOR DAYS.
GOTHAM KNIGHTS 52
TIME FOR A REAL SHOW STOPPER, LADIES--
--LET'S GIVE THESE FINE PEOPLE THEIR MONEY'S WORTH.
PING!

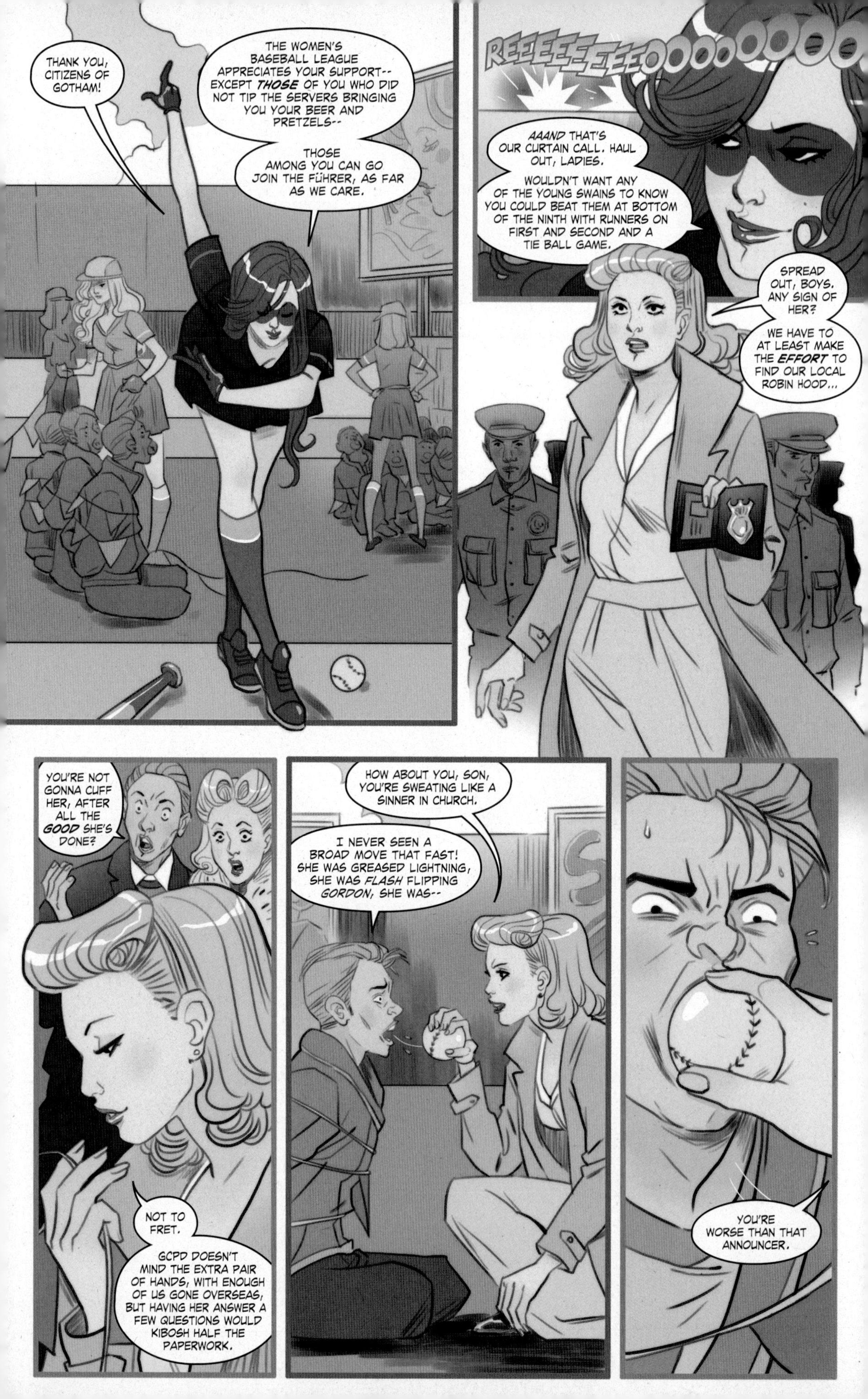
THANK YOU, CITIZENS OF GOTHAM!
THE WOMEN'S BASEBALL LEAGUE APPRECIATES YOUR SUPPORT-- EXCEPT *THOSE* OF YOU WHO DID NOT TIP THE SERVERS BRINGING YOU YOUR BEER AND PRETZELS--
THOSE AMONG YOU CAN GO JOIN THE FÜHRER, AS FAR AS WE CARE.
REEEEEEEEOOOOOOOO
*AAAND* THAT'S OUR CURTAIN CALL. HAUL OUT, LADIES.
WOULDN'T WANT ANY OF THE YOUNG SWAINS TO KNOW YOU COULD BEAT THEM AT BOTTOM OF THE NINTH WITH RUNNERS ON FIRST AND SECOND AND A TIE BALL GAME.
SPREAD OUT, BOYS. ANY SIGN OF HER?
WE HAVE TO AT LEAST MAKE THE *EFFORT* TO FIND OUR LOCAL ROBIN HOOD...
YOU'RE NOT GONNA CUFF HER, AFTER ALL THE *GOOD* SHE'S DONE?
NOT TO FRET.
GCPD DOESN'T MIND THE EXTRA PAIR OF HANDS, WITH ENOUGH OF US GONE OVERSEAS, BUT HAVING HER ANSWER A FEW QUESTIONS WOULD KIBOSH HALF THE PAPERWORK.
HOW ABOUT YOU, SON, YOU'RE SWEATING LIKE A SINNER IN CHURCH.
I NEVER SEEN A BROAD MOVE THAT FAST! SHE WAS GREASED LIGHTNING, SHE WAS *FLASH* FLIPPING *GORDON*, SHE WAS--
YOU'RE WORSE THAN THAT ANNOUNCER.

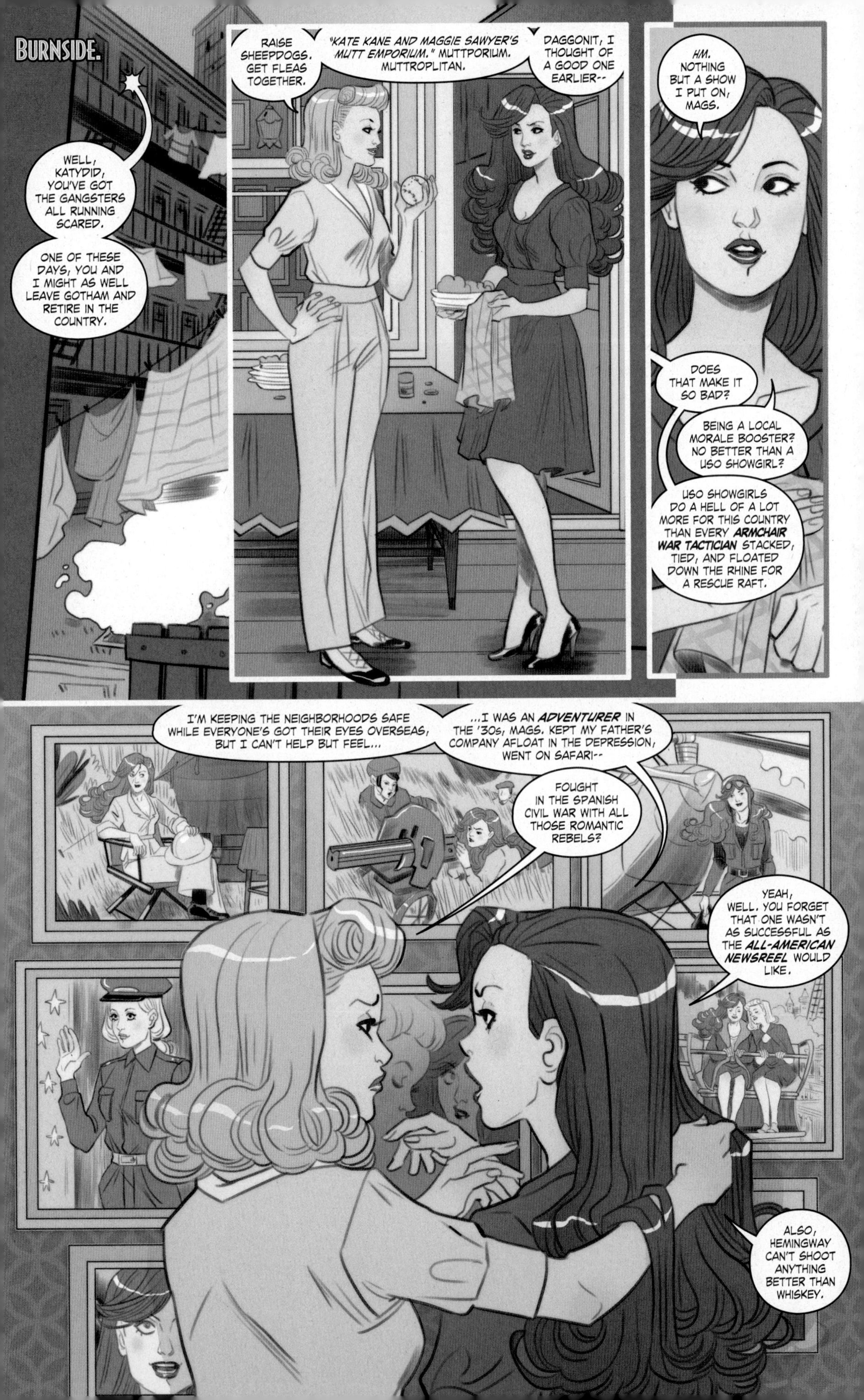
BURNSIDE.
WELL, KATYDID, YOU'VE GOT THE GANGSTERS ALL RUNNING SCARED.
ONE OF THESE DAYS, YOU AND I MIGHT AS WELL LEAVE GOTHAM AND RETIRE IN THE COUNTRY.
RAISE SHEEPDOGS. GET FLEAS TOGETHER.
"KATE KANE AND MAGGIE SAWYER'S MUTT EMPORIUM." MUTTPORIUM. MUTTROPLITAN.
DAGGONIT, I THOUGHT OF A GOOD ONE EARLIER--
HM. NOTHING BUT A SHOW I PUT ON, MAGS.
DOES THAT MAKE IT SO BAD?
BEING A LOCAL MORALE BOOSTER? NO BETTER THAN A USO SHOWGIRL?
USO SHOWGIRLS DO A HELL OF A LOT MORE FOR THIS COUNTRY THAN EVERY ARMCHAIR WAR TACTICIAN STACKED, TIED, AND FLOATED DOWN THE RHINE FOR A RESCUE RAFT.
I'M KEEPING THE NEIGHBORHOODS SAFE WHILE EVERYONE'S GOT THEIR EYES OVERSEAS, BUT I CAN'T HELP BUT FEEL...
...I WAS AN ADVENTURER IN THE '30s, MAGS. KEPT MY FATHER'S COMPANY AFLOAT IN THE DEPRESSION, WENT ON SAFARI--
FOUGHT IN THE SPANISH CIVIL WAR WITH ALL THOSE ROMANTIC REBELS?
YEAH, WELL. YOU FORGET THAT ONE WASN'T AS SUCCESSFUL AS THE ALL-AMERICAN NEWSREEL WOULD LIKE.
ALSO, HEMINGWAY CAN'T SHOOT ANYTHING BETTER THAN WHISKEY.

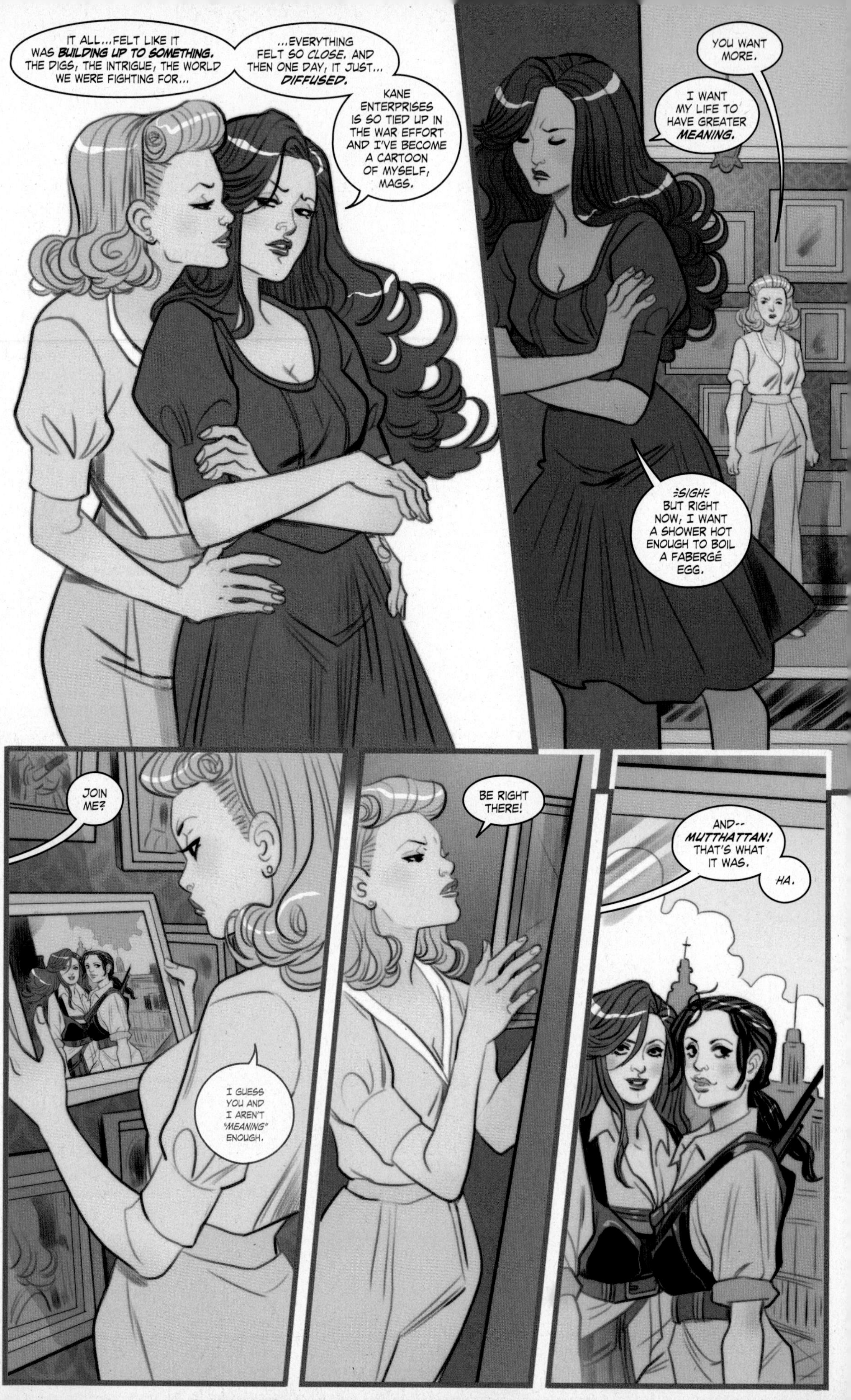
IT ALL...FELT LIKE IT WAS BUILDING UP TO SOMETHING. THE DIGS, THE INTRIGUE, THE WORLD WE WERE FIGHTING FOR...
...EVERYTHING FELT SO CLOSE. AND THEN ONE DAY, IT JUST... DIFFUSED.
KANE ENTERPRISES IS SO TIED UP IN THE WAR EFFORT AND I'VE BECOME A CARTOON OF MYSELF, MAGS.
YOU WANT MORE.
I WANT MY LIFE TO HAVE GREATER MEANING.
SIGH BUT RIGHT NOW, I WANT A SHOWER HOT ENOUGH TO BOIL A FABERGÉ EGG.
JOIN ME?
I GUESS YOU AND I AREN'T "MEANING" ENOUGH.
BE RIGHT THERE!
AND-- MUTTHATTAN! THAT'S WHAT IT WAS.
HA.

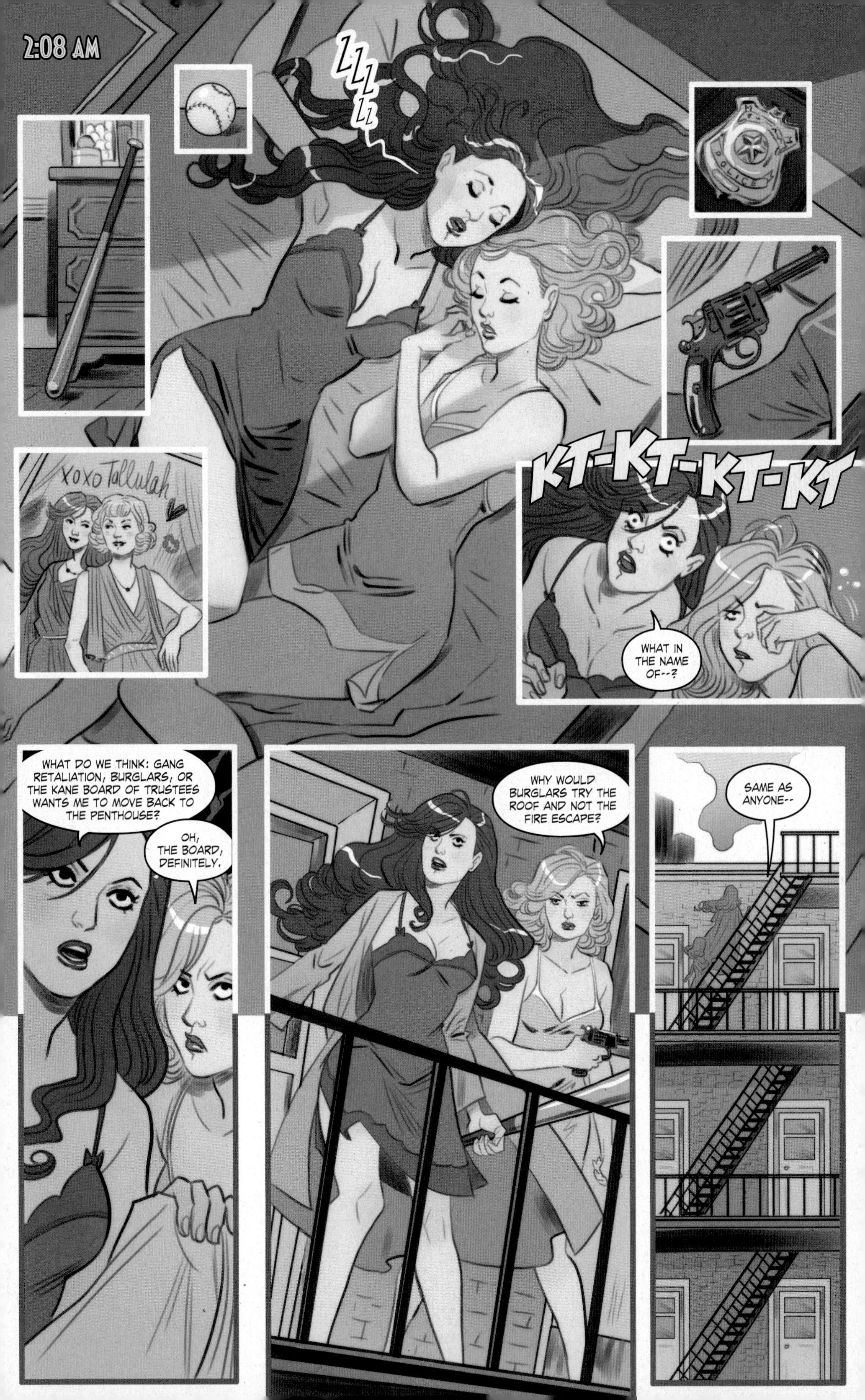
2:08 AM
ZZZZ
POLICE
XOXO Tallulah
KT-KT-KT-KT-KT
WHAT IN THE NAME OF--?
WHAT DO WE THINK: GANG RETALIATION, BURGLARS, OR THE KANE BOARD OF TRUSTEES WANTS ME TO MOVE BACK TO THE PENTHOUSE?
OH, THE BOARD, DEFINITELY.
WHY WOULD BURGLARS TRY THE ROOF AND NOT THE FIRE ESCAPE?
SAME AS ANYONE--

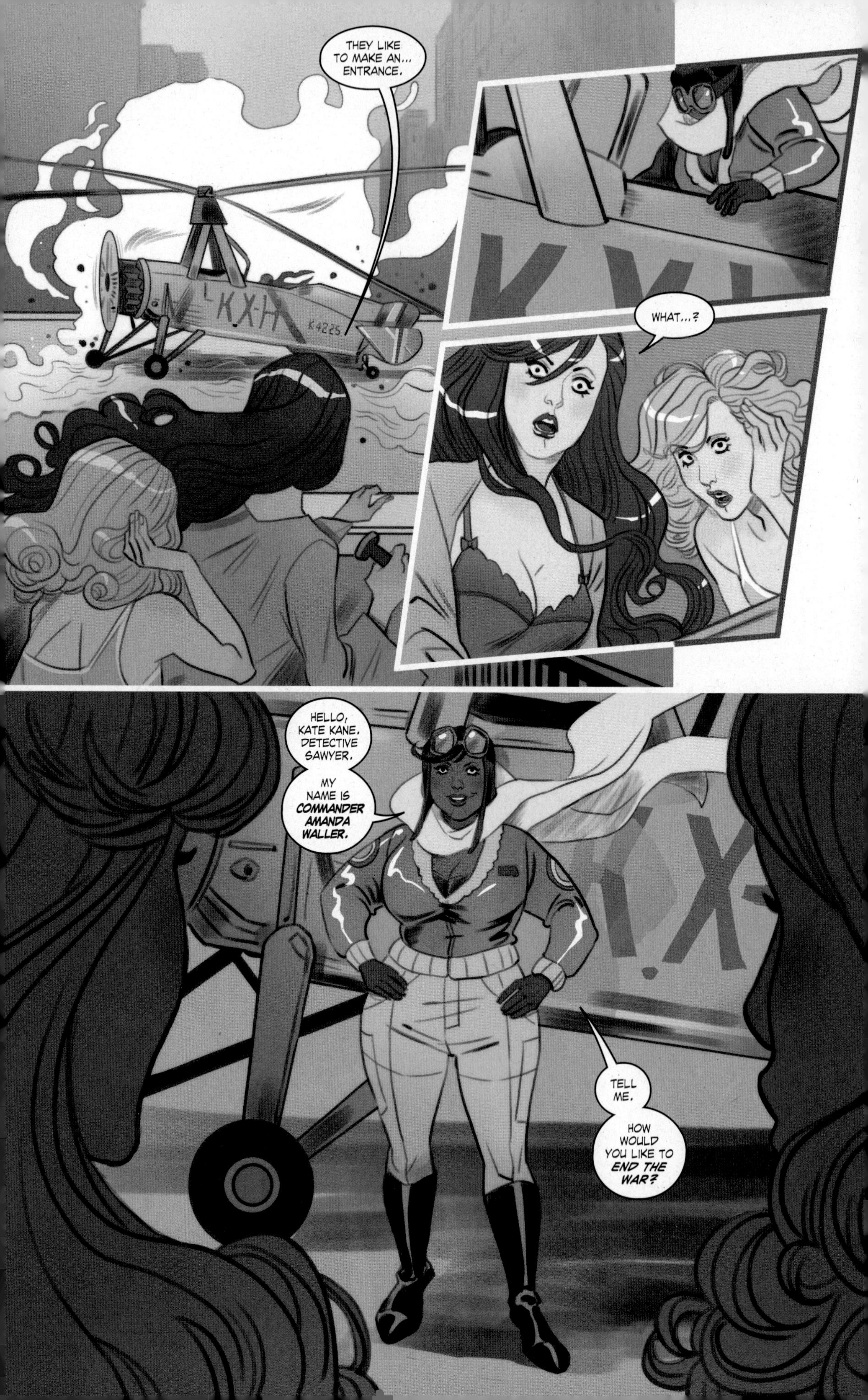
THEY LIKE TO MAKE AN... ENTRANCE.
K4225
WHAT...?
HELLO, KATE KANE. DETECTIVE SAWYER.
MY NAME IS COMMANDER AMANDA WALLER.
TELL ME.
HOW WOULD YOU LIKE TO END THE WAR?

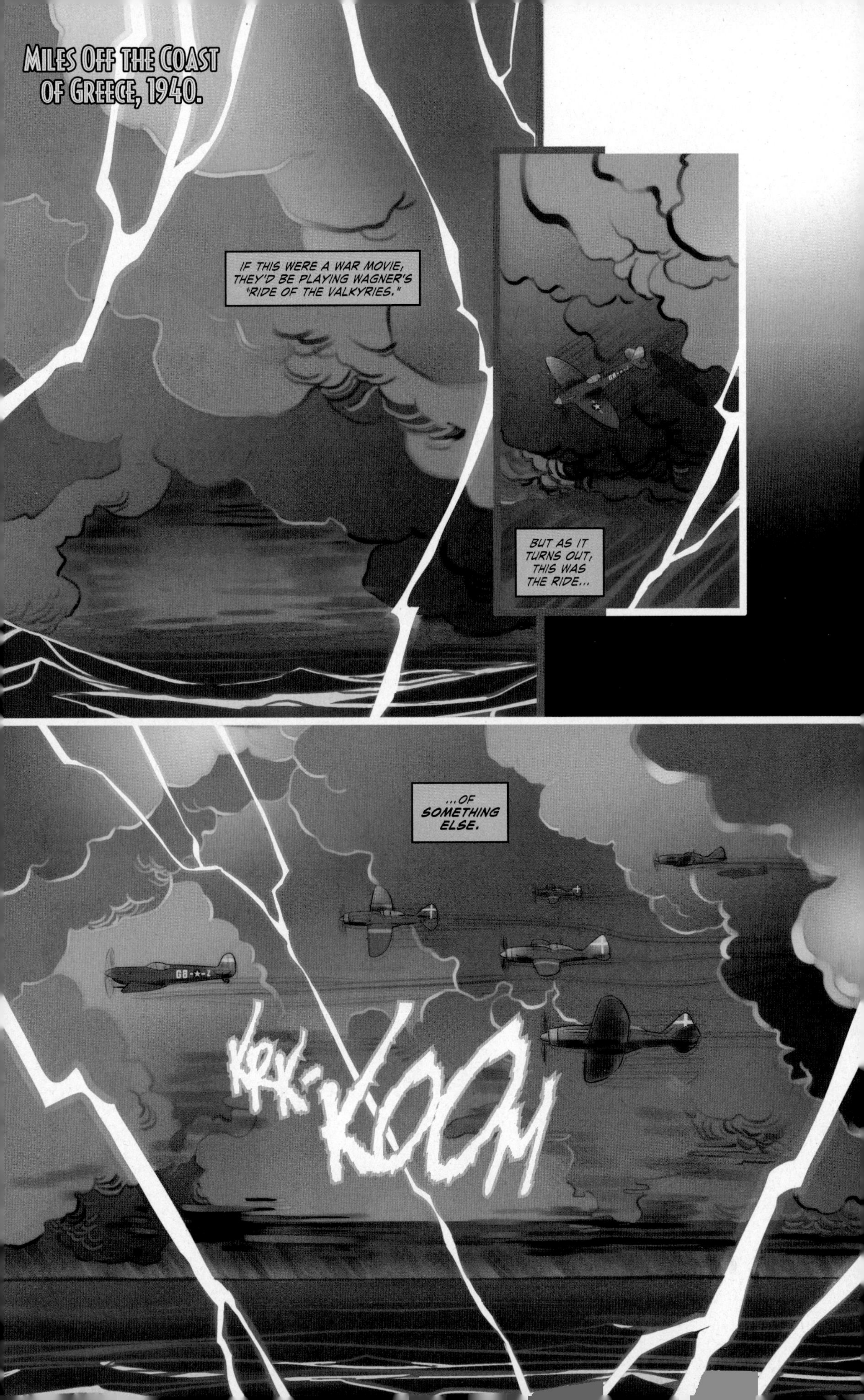
MILES OFF THE COAST OF GREECE, 1940.
IF THIS WERE A WAR MOVIE, THEY'D BE PLAYING WAGNER'S "RIDE OF THE VALKYRIES."
BUT AS IT TURNS OUT, THIS WAS THE RIDE...
...OF SOMETHING ELSE.
KRAK-KOOM

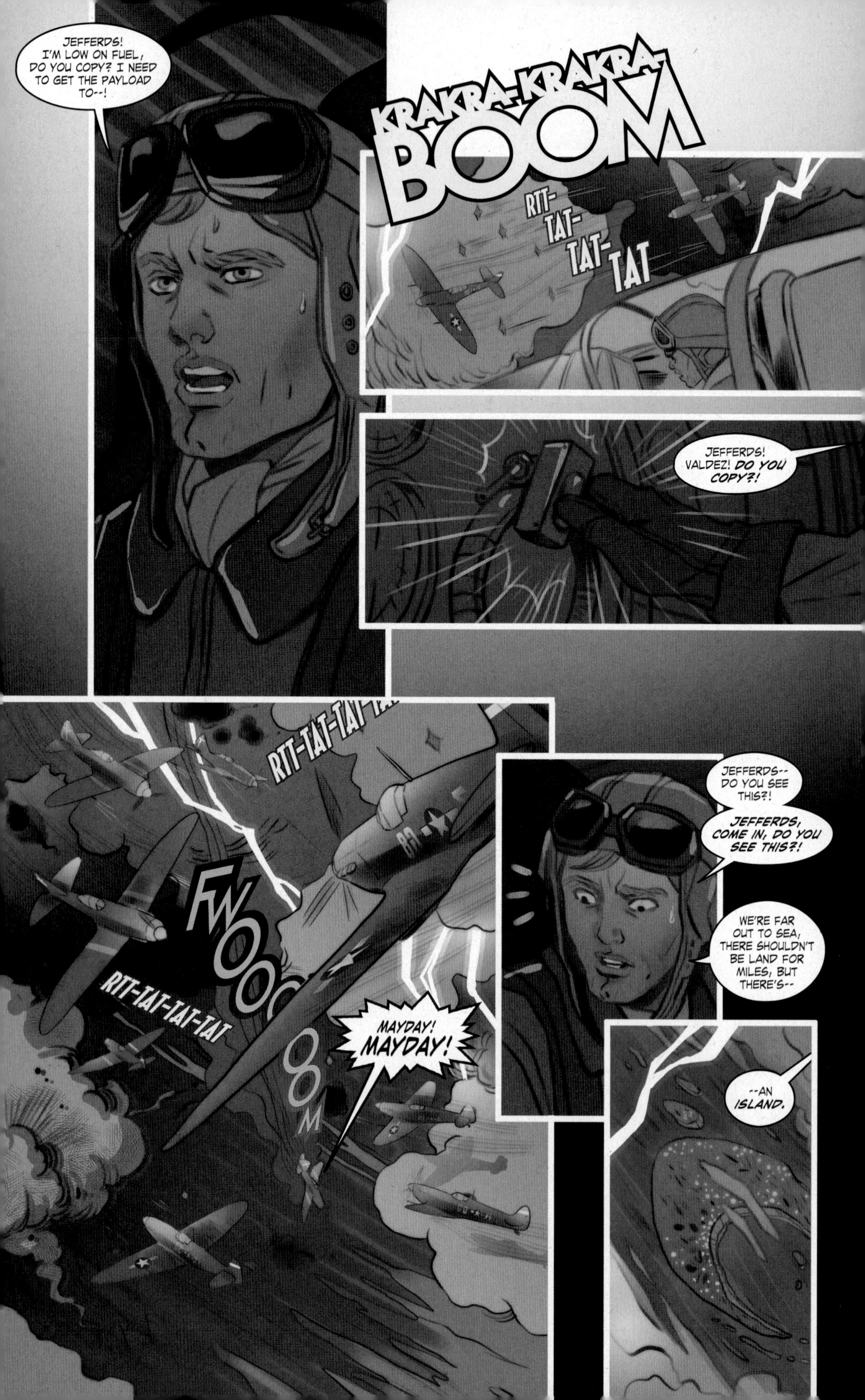
JEFFERDS! I'M LOW ON FUEL, DO YOU COPY? I NEED TO GET THE PAYLOAD TO--!
KRAKRA-KRAKRA-BOOM
RTT-TAT-TAT-TAT
JEFFERDS! VALDEZ! DO YOU COPY?!
RTT-TAT-TAT-TAT
FWOOOOOM
RTT-TAT-TAT-TAT
MAYDAY! MAYDAY!
JEFFERDS-- DO YOU SEE THIS?!
JEFFERDS, COME IN, DO YOU SEE THIS?!
WE'RE FAR OUT TO SEA, THERE SHOULDN'T BE LAND FOR MILES, BUT THERE'S--
--AN ISLAND.

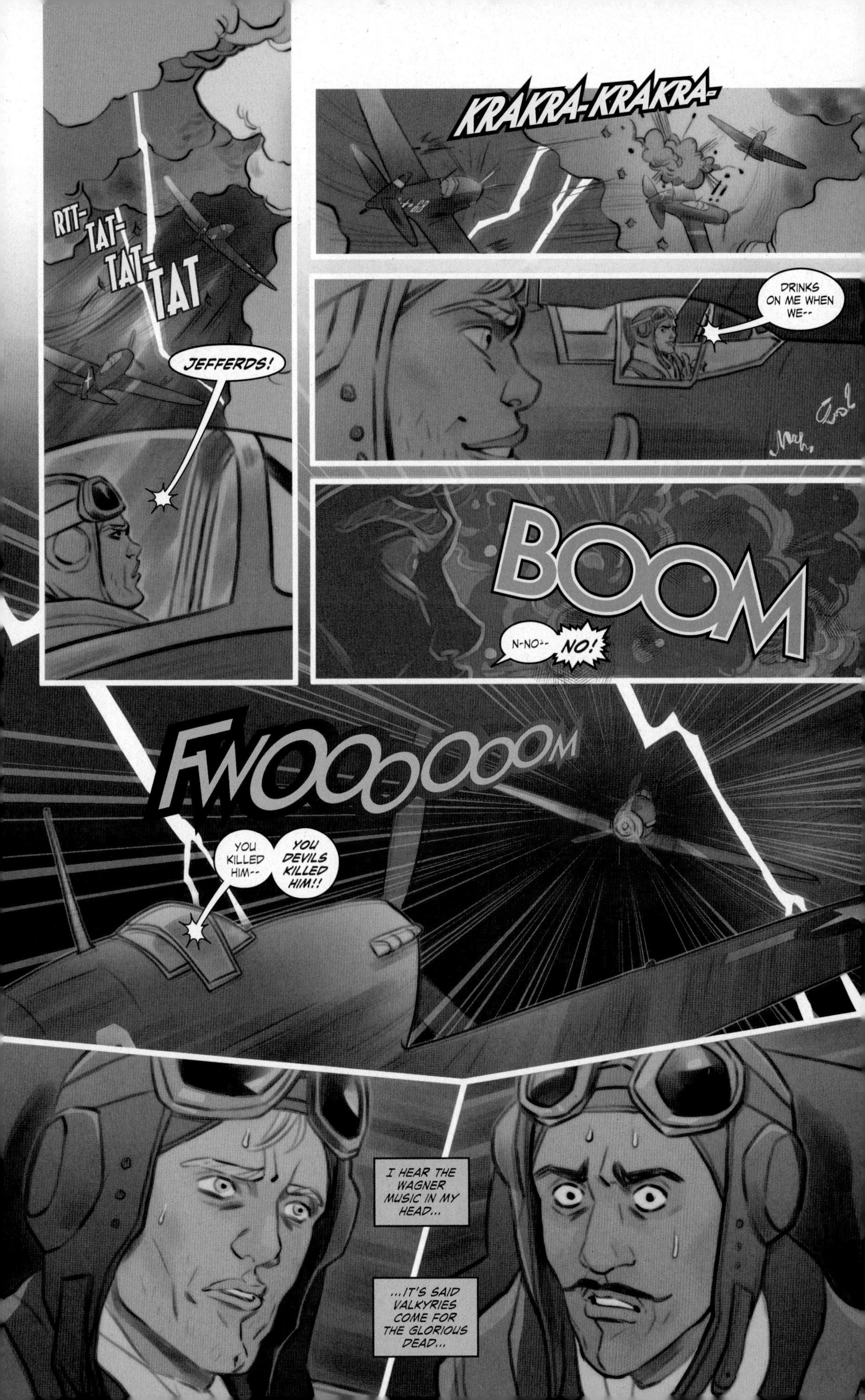
RTT-
TAT-
TAT-
TAT
JEFFERDS!
KRAKRA-KRAKRA-
DRINKS ON ME WHEN WE--
BOOM
N-NO--
NO!
FWOOOOOOOM
YOU KILLED HIM--
YOU DEVILS KILLED HIM!!
I HEAR THE WAGNER MUSIC IN MY HEAD...
...IT'S SAID VALKYRIES COME FOR THE GLORIOUS DEAD...

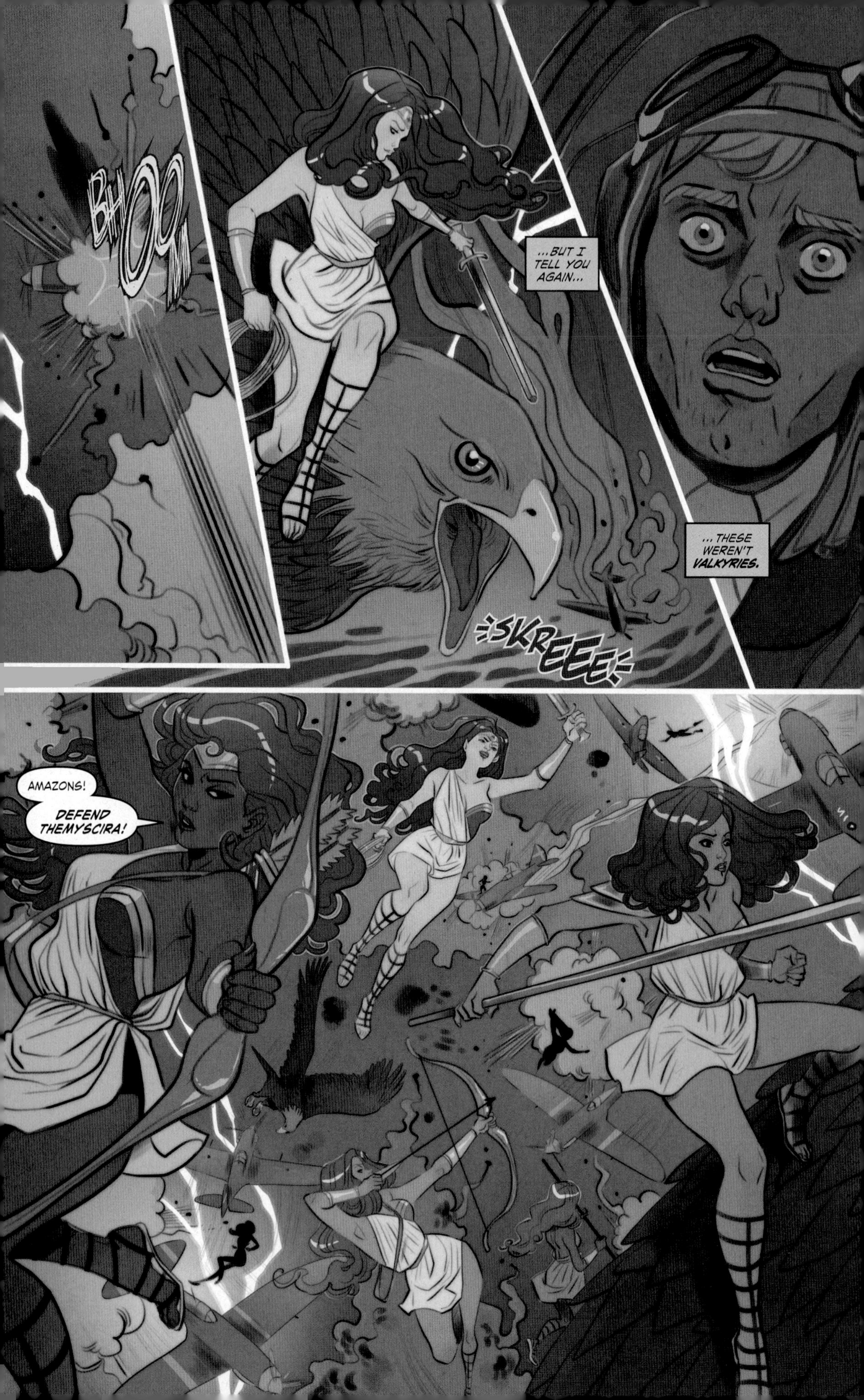

BHOOM
...BUT I TELL YOU AGAIN...
...THESE WEREN'T VALKYRIES.
SKREEEE
AMAZONS!
DEFEND THEMYSCIRA!

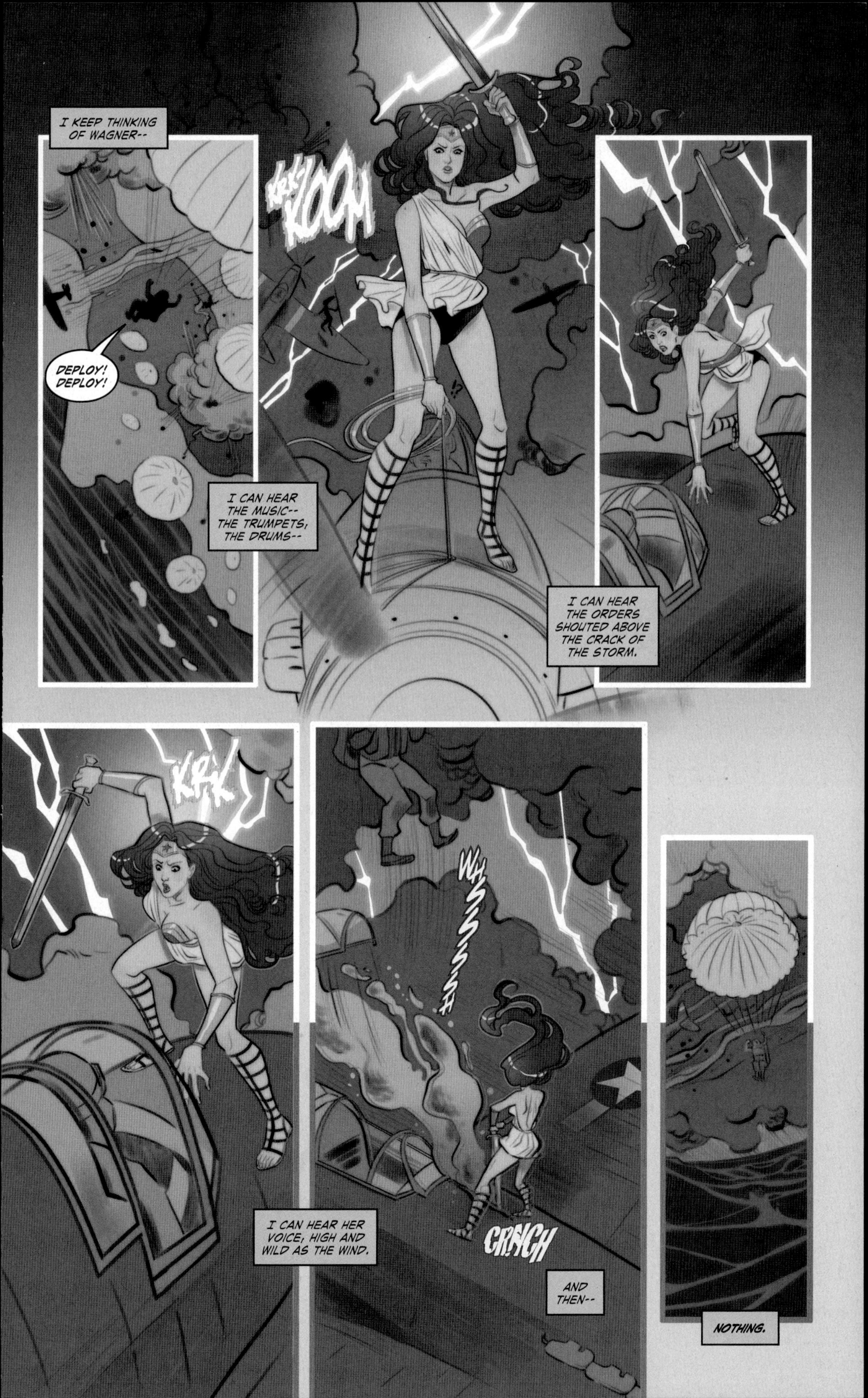
I KEEP THINKING OF WAGNER--
DEPLOY! DEPLOY!
I CAN HEAR THE MUSIC-- THE TRUMPETS, THE DRUMS--
KRK-KOOM
I CAN HEAR THE ORDERS SHOUTED ABOVE THE CRACK OF THE STORM.
KRK
I CAN HEAR HER VOICE, HIGH AND WILD AS THE WIND.
CRNCH
AND THEN--
NOTHING.

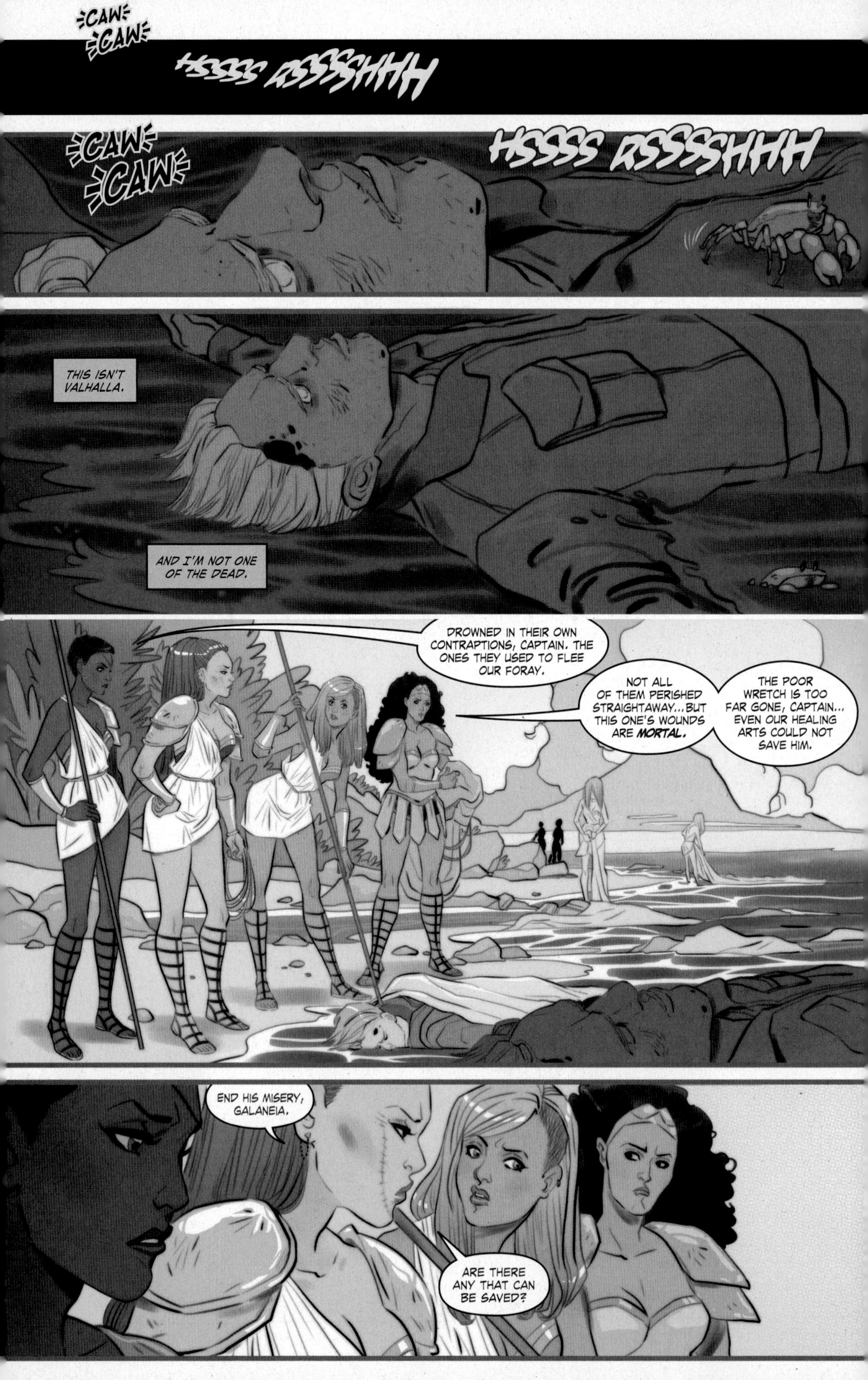
CAW CAW
HSSSS RSSSSHHH
CAW CAW
HSSSS RSSSSHHH
THIS ISN'T VALHALLA.
AND I'M NOT ONE OF THE DEAD.
DROWNED IN THEIR OWN CONTRAPTIONS, CAPTAIN. THE ONES THEY USED TO FLEE OUR FORAY.
NOT ALL OF THEM PERISHED STRAIGHTAWAY...BUT THIS ONE'S WOUNDS ARE *MORTAL.*
THE POOR WRETCH IS TOO FAR GONE, CAPTAIN... EVEN OUR HEALING ARTS COULD NOT SAVE HIM.
END HIS MISERY, GALANEIA.
ARE THERE ANY THAT CAN BE SAVED?

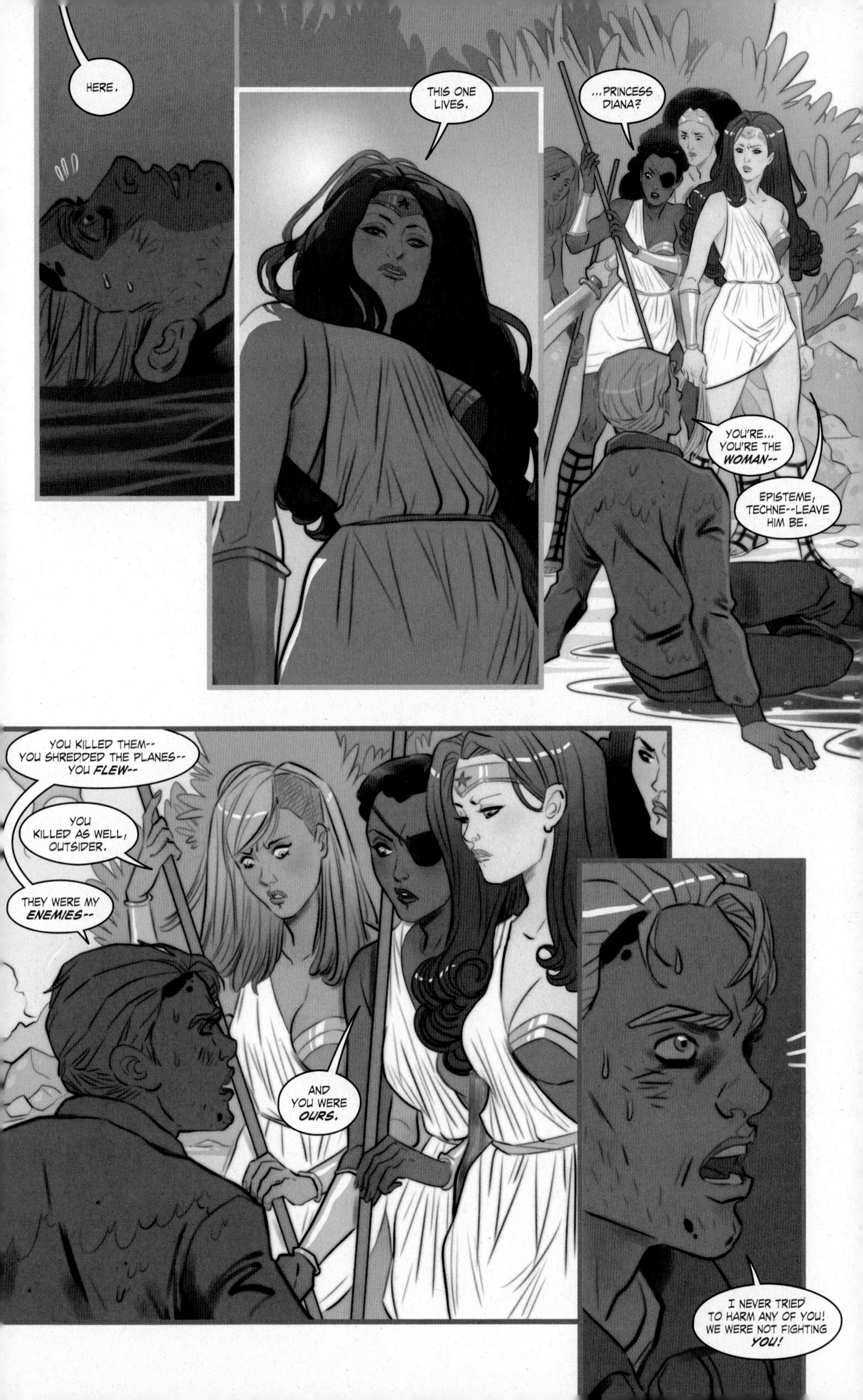
HERE.
THIS ONE LIVES.
...PRINCESS DIANA?
YOU'RE... YOU'RE THE *WOMAN--*
EPISTEME, TECHNE--LEAVE HIM BE.
YOU KILLED THEM-- YOU SHREDDED THE PLANES-- YOU *FLEW--*
YOU KILLED AS WELL, OUTSIDER.
THEY WERE MY *ENEMIES--*
AND YOU WERE *OURS.*
I NEVER TRIED TO HARM ANY OF YOU! WE WERE NOT FIGHTING *YOU!*

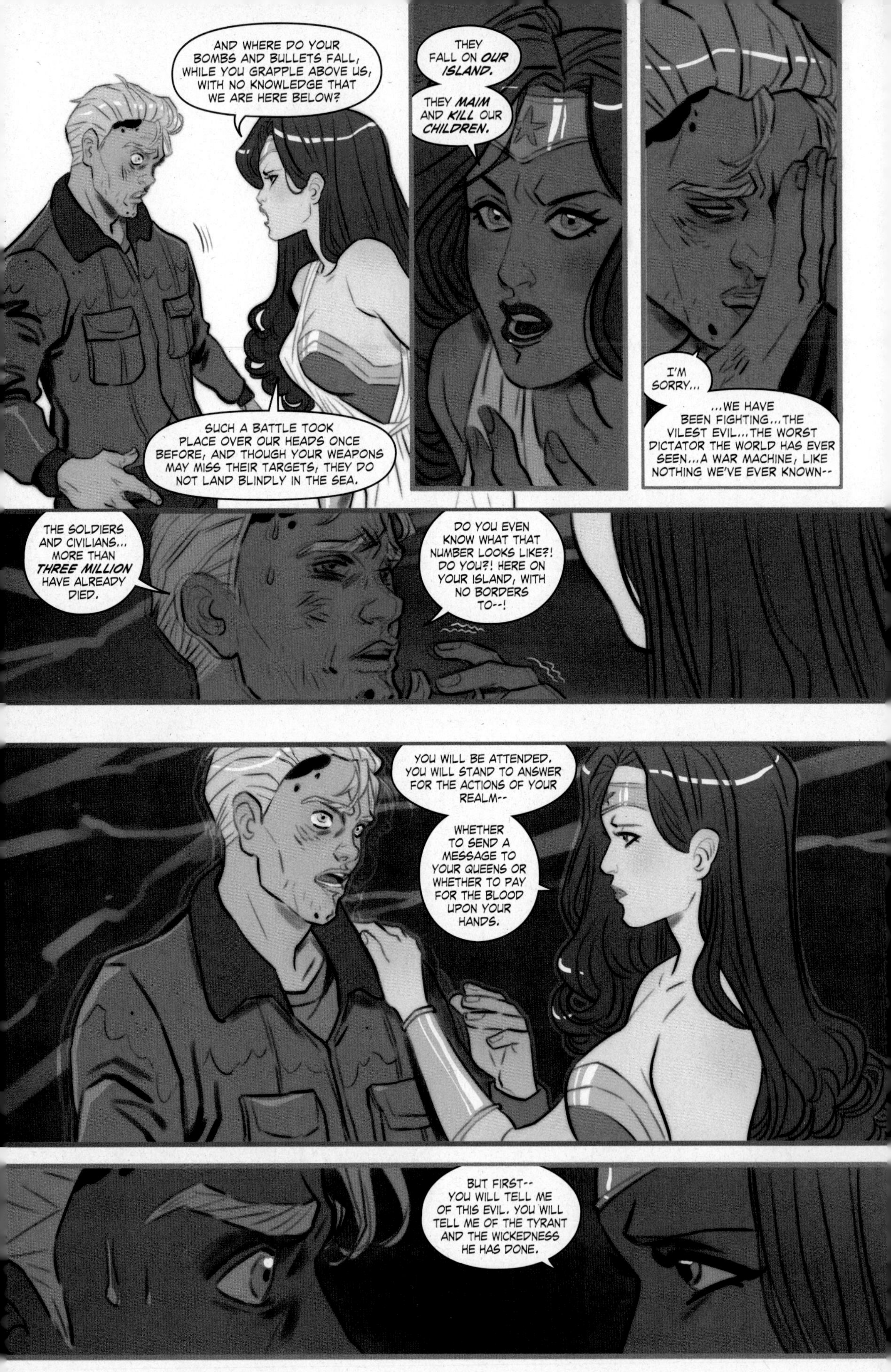
AND WHERE DO YOUR BOMBS AND BULLETS FALL, WHILE YOU GRAPPLE ABOVE US, WITH NO KNOWLEDGE THAT WE ARE HERE BELOW?
SUCH A BATTLE TOOK PLACE OVER OUR HEADS ONCE BEFORE, AND THOUGH YOUR WEAPONS MAY MISS THEIR TARGETS, THEY DO NOT LAND BLINDLY IN THE SEA.
THEY FALL ON OUR ISLAND.
THEY MAIM AND KILL OUR CHILDREN.
I'M SORRY...
...WE HAVE BEEN FIGHTING...THE VILEST EVIL...THE WORST DICTATOR THE WORLD HAS EVER SEEN...A WAR MACHINE, LIKE NOTHING WE'VE EVER KNOWN--
THE SOLDIERS AND CIVILIANS... MORE THAN THREE MILLION HAVE ALREADY DIED.
DO YOU EVEN KNOW WHAT THAT NUMBER LOOKS LIKE?! DO YOU?! HERE ON YOUR ISLAND, WITH NO BORDERS TO--!
YOU WILL BE ATTENDED. YOU WILL STAND TO ANSWER FOR THE ACTIONS OF YOUR REALM--
WHETHER TO SEND A MESSAGE TO YOUR QUEENS OR WHETHER TO PAY FOR THE BLOOD UPON YOUR HANDS.
BUT FIRST-- YOU WILL TELL ME OF THIS EVIL. YOU WILL TELL ME OF THE TYRANT AND THE WICKEDNESS HE HAS DONE.

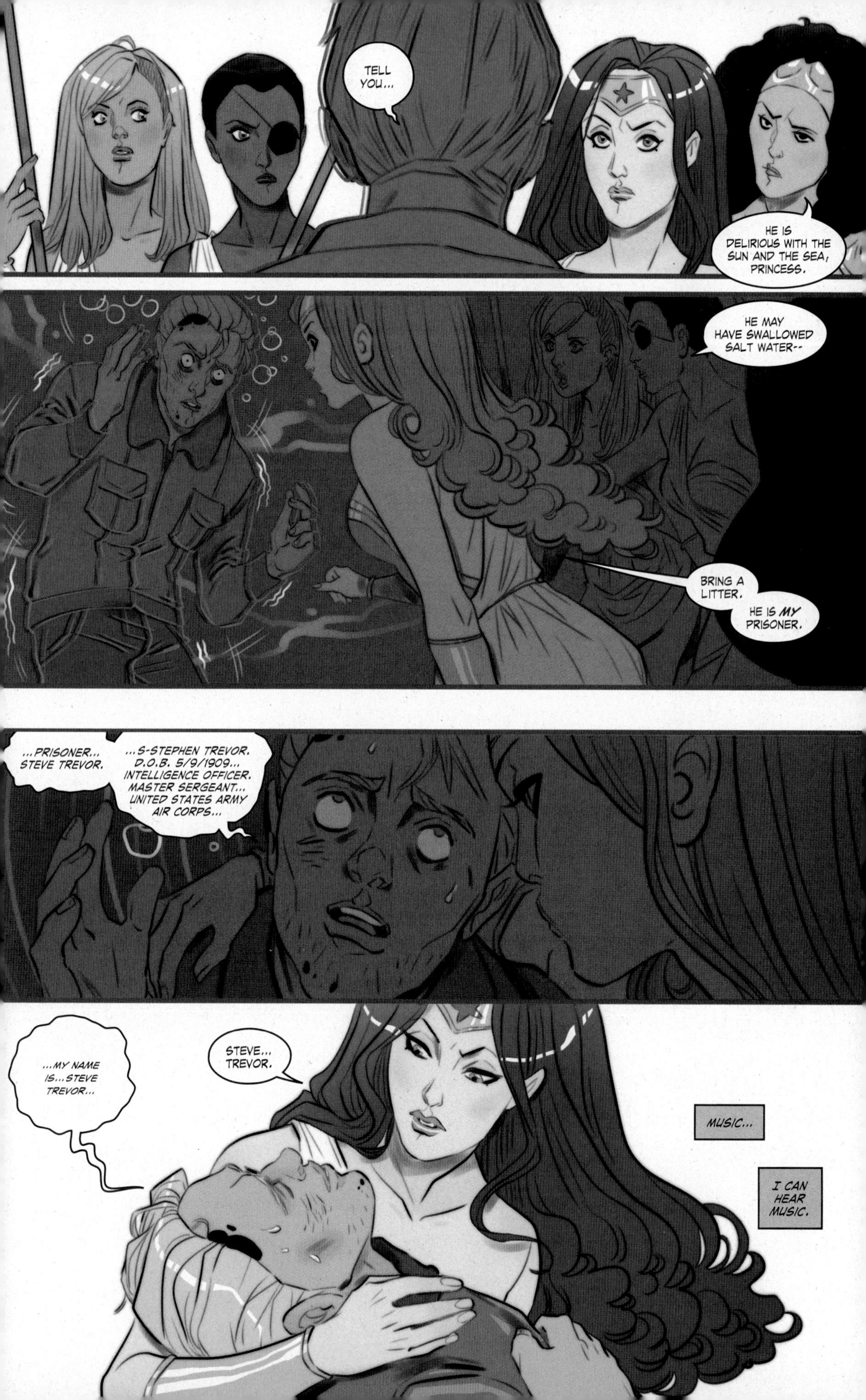
TELL YOU...
HE IS DELIRIOUS WITH THE SUN AND THE SEA, PRINCESS.
HE MAY HAVE SWALLOWED SALT WATER--
BRING A LITTER.
HE IS *MY* PRISONER.
...PRISONER... STEVE TREVOR.
...S-STEPHEN TREVOR. D.O.B. 5/9/1909... INTELLIGENCE OFFICER. MASTER SERGEANT... UNITED STATES ARMY AIR CORPS...
...MY NAME IS...STEVE TREVOR...
STEVE... TREVOR.
MUSIC...
I CAN HEAR MUSIC.

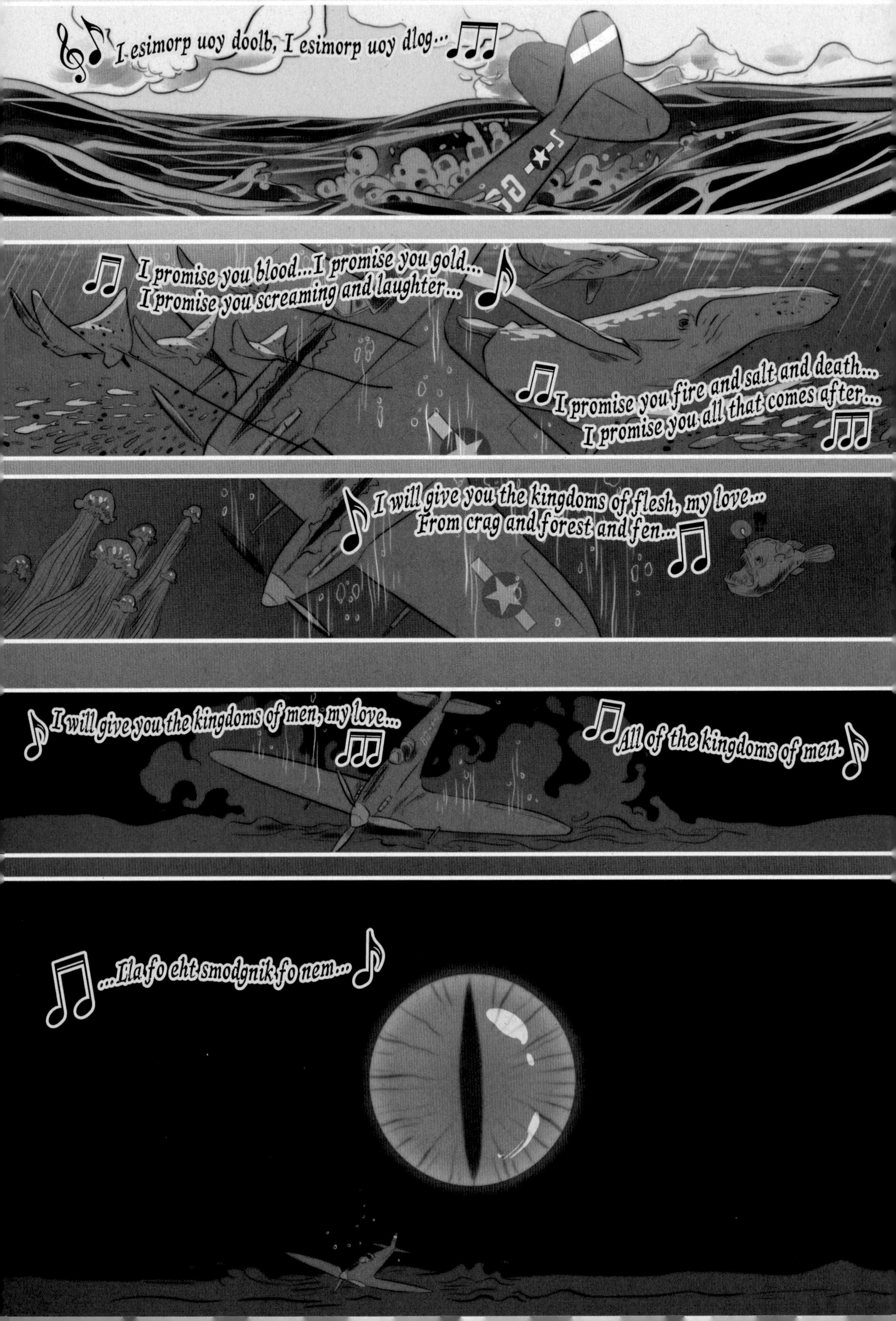
I esimorp uoy doolb, I esimorp uoy dlog...
I promise you blood...I promise you gold...
I promise you screaming and laughter...
I promise you fire and salt and death...
I promise you all that comes after...
I promise you...
I will give you the kingdoms of flesh, my love...
From crag and forest and fen...
I will give you the kingdoms of men, my love...
All of the kingdoms of men.
...Ila fo eht smodgnik fo nem...

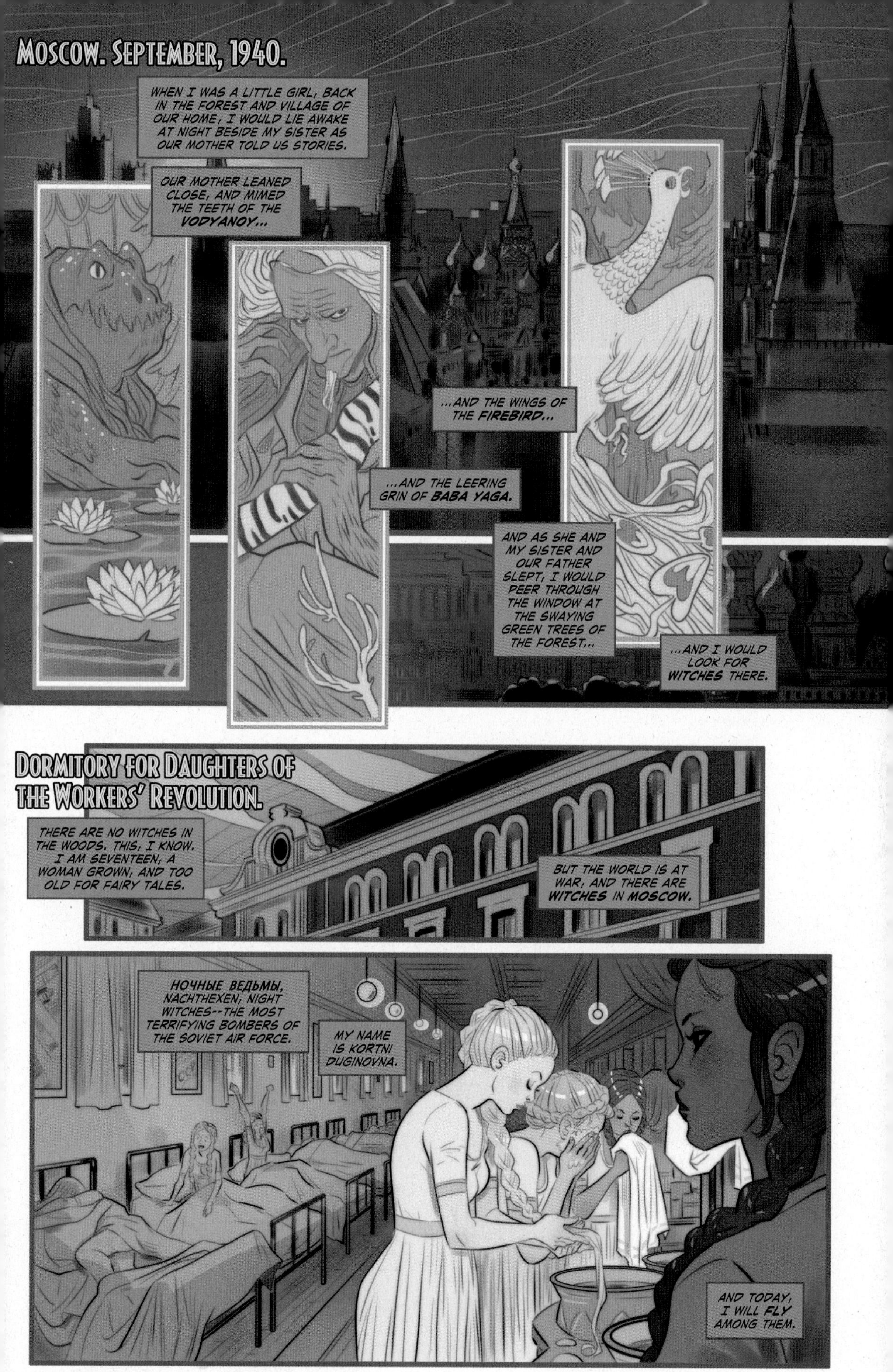
MOSCOW. SEPTEMBER, 1940.
WHEN I WAS A LITTLE GIRL, BACK IN THE FOREST AND VILLAGE OF OUR HOME, I WOULD LIE AWAKE AT NIGHT BESIDE MY SISTER AS OUR MOTHER TOLD US STORIES.
OUR MOTHER LEANED CLOSE, AND MIMED THE TEETH OF THE VODYANOY...
...AND THE LEERING GRIN OF BABA YAGA.
...AND THE WINGS OF THE FIREBIRD...
AND AS SHE AND MY SISTER AND OUR FATHER SLEPT, I WOULD PEER THROUGH THE WINDOW AT THE SWAYING GREEN TREES OF THE FOREST...
...AND I WOULD LOOK FOR WITCHES THERE.
DORMITORY FOR DAUGHTERS OF THE WORKERS' REVOLUTION.
THERE ARE NO WITCHES IN THE WOODS. THIS, I KNOW. I AM SEVENTEEN, A WOMAN GROWN, AND TOO OLD FOR FAIRY TALES.
BUT THE WORLD IS AT WAR, AND THERE ARE WITCHES IN MOSCOW.
НОЧНЫЕ ВЕДЬМЫ, NACHTHEXEN, NIGHT WITCHES--THE MOST TERRIFYING BOMBERS OF THE SOVIET AIR FORCE.
MY NAME IS KORTNI DUGINOVNA.
AND TODAY, I WILL FLY AMONG THEM.

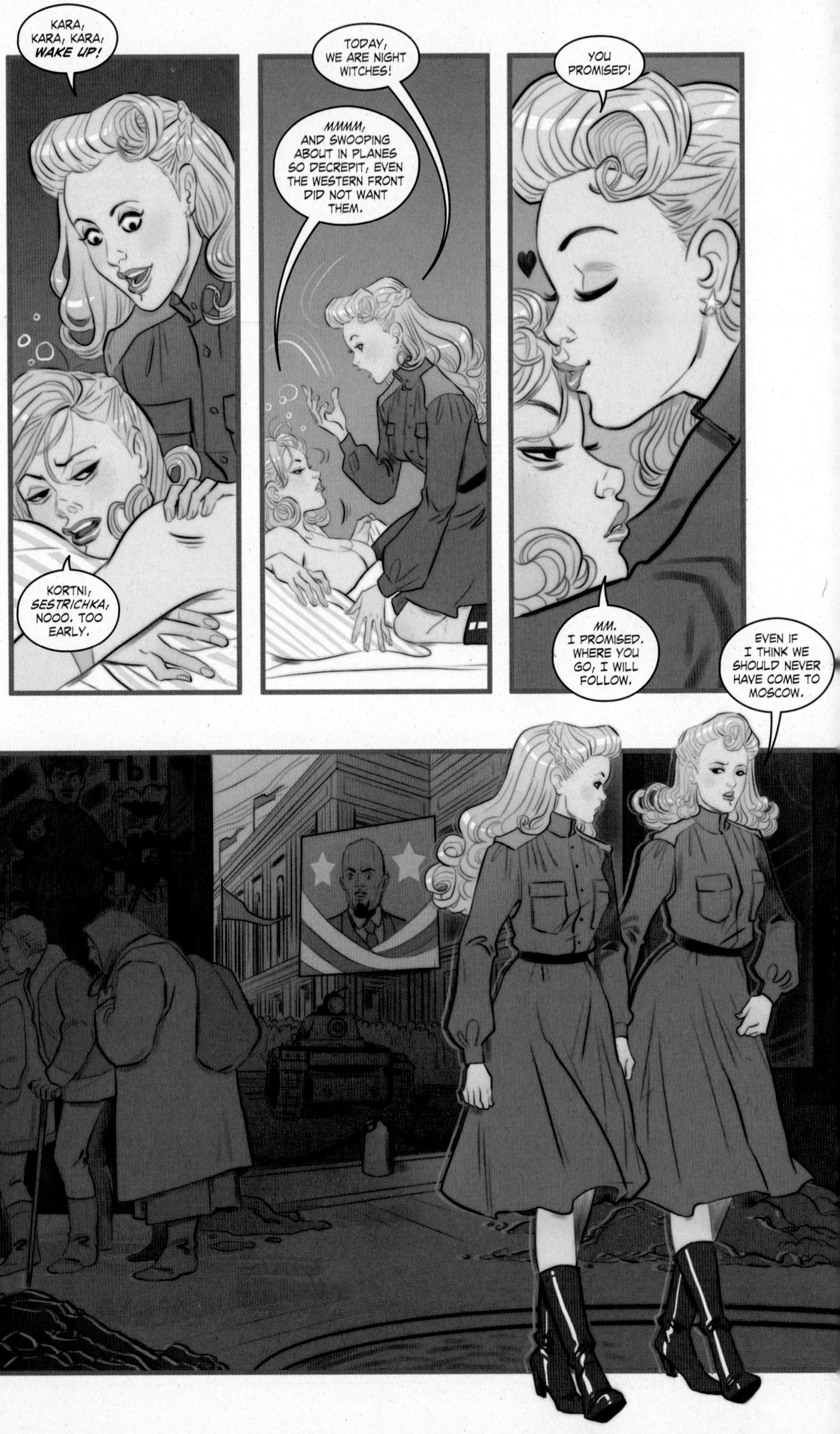
KARA, KARA, KARA, ***WAKE UP!***
KORTNI, *SESTRICHKA*, NOOO. TOO EARLY.
TODAY, WE ARE NIGHT WITCHES!
*MMMM*, AND SWOOPING ABOUT IN PLANES SO DECREPIT, EVEN THE WESTERN FRONT DID NOT WANT THEM.
YOU PROMISED!
*MM.* I PROMISED. WHERE YOU GO, I WILL FOLLOW.
EVEN IF I THINK WE SHOULD NEVER HAVE COME TO MOSCOW.

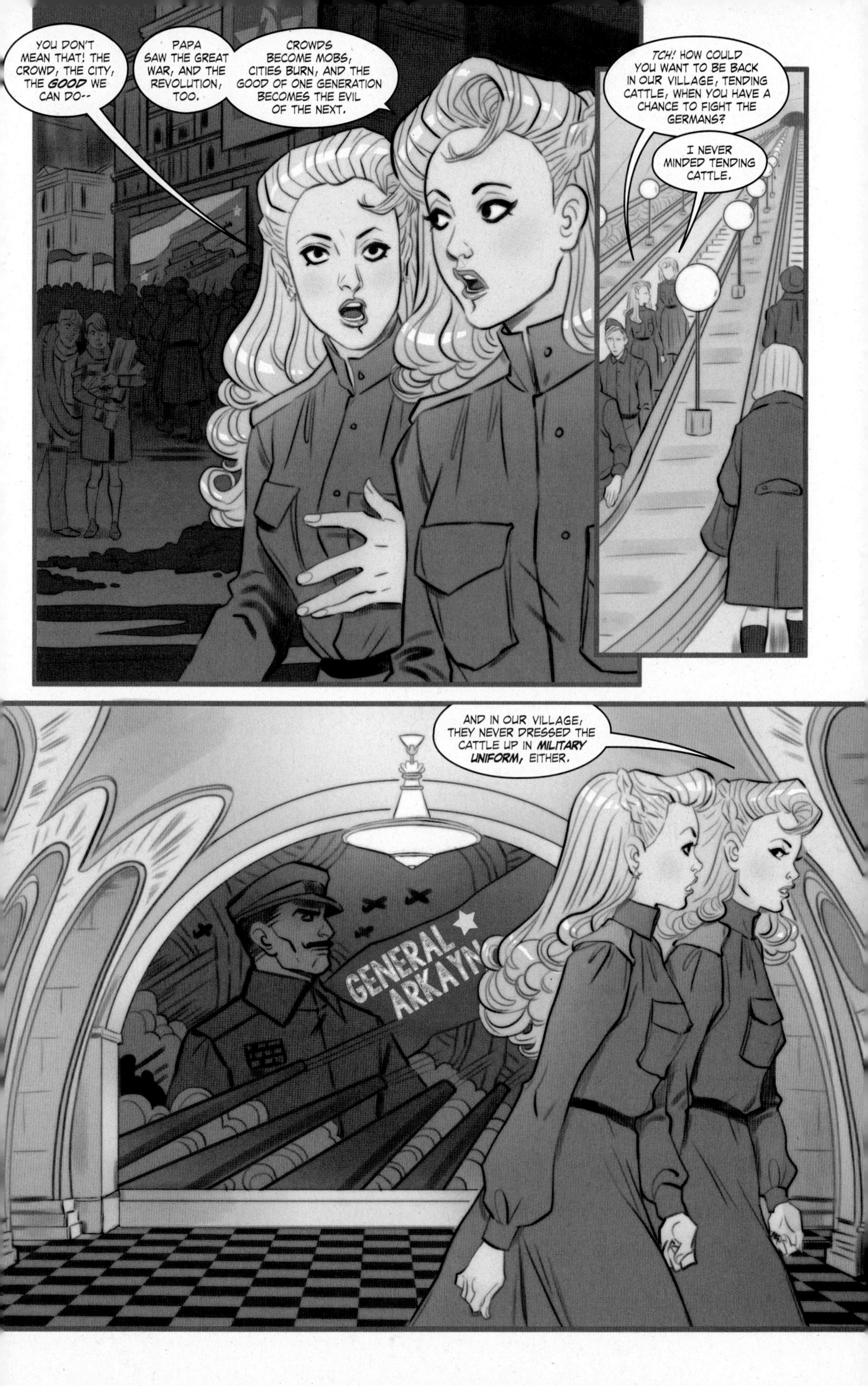
YOU DON'T MEAN THAT! THE CROWD, THE CITY, THE GOOD WE CAN DO--
PAPA SAW THE GREAT WAR, AND THE REVOLUTION, TOO.
CROWDS BECOME MOBS, CITIES BURN, AND THE GOOD OF ONE GENERATION BECOMES THE EVIL OF THE NEXT.
TCH! HOW COULD YOU WANT TO BE BACK IN OUR VILLAGE, TENDING CATTLE, WHEN YOU HAVE A CHANCE TO FIGHT THE GERMANS?
I NEVER MINDED TENDING CATTLE.
AND IN OUR VILLAGE, THEY NEVER DRESSED THE CATTLE UP IN MILITARY UNIFORM, EITHER.
GENERAL ARKAYN

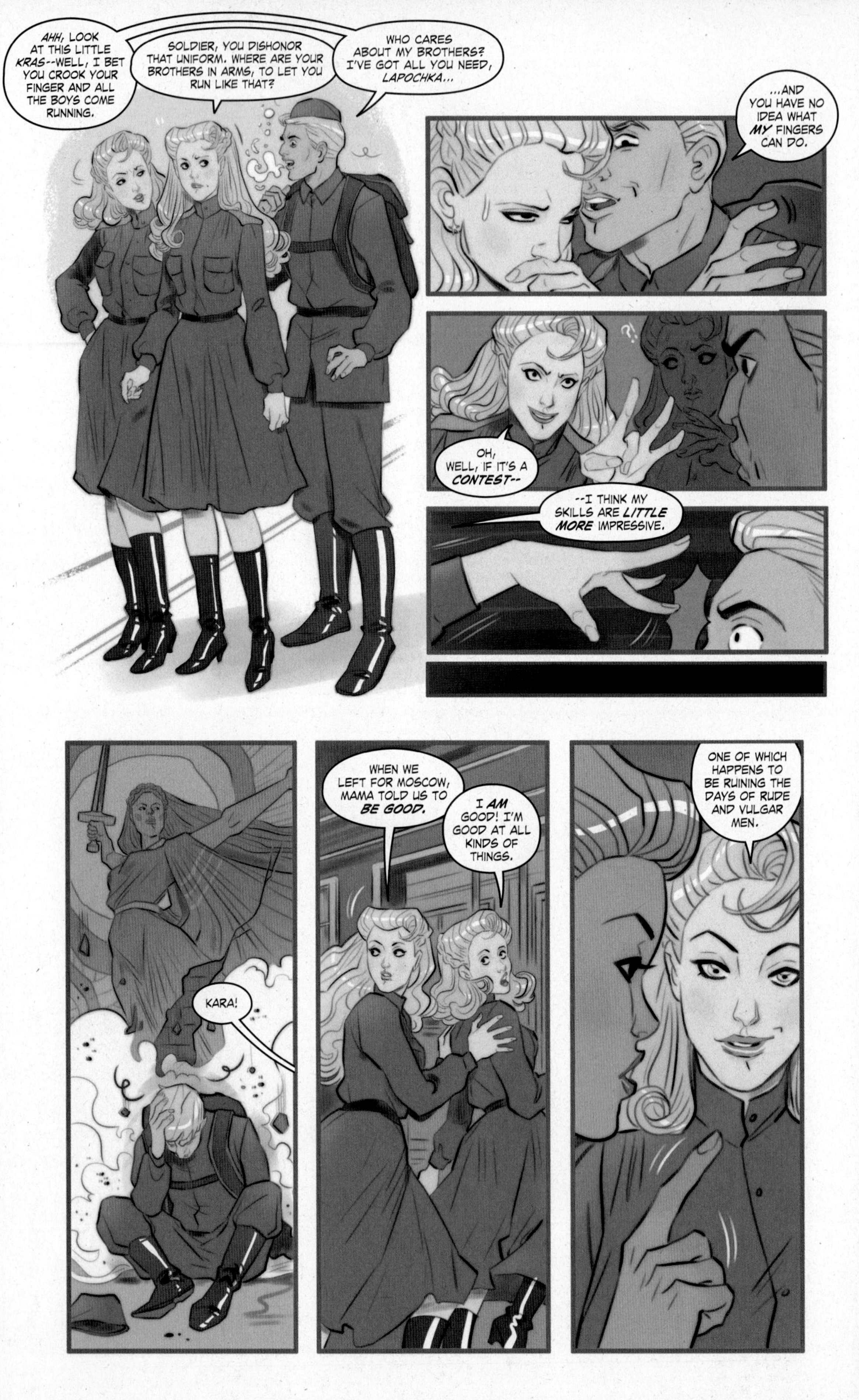
AHH, LOOK AT THIS LITTLE KRAS--WELL, I BET YOU CROOK YOUR FINGER AND ALL THE BOYS COME RUNNING.
SOLDIER, YOU DISHONOR THAT UNIFORM. WHERE ARE YOUR BROTHERS IN ARMS, TO LET YOU RUN LIKE THAT?
WHO CARES ABOUT MY BROTHERS? I'VE GOT ALL YOU NEED, LAPOCHKA...
...AND YOU HAVE NO IDEA WHAT MY FINGERS CAN DO.
?!
OH, WELL, IF IT'S A CONTEST--
--I THINK MY SKILLS ARE LITTLE MORE IMPRESSIVE.
KARA!
WHEN WE LEFT FOR MOSCOW, MAMA TOLD US TO BE GOOD.
I AM GOOD! I'M GOOD AT ALL KINDS OF THINGS.
ONE OF WHICH HAPPENS TO BE RUINING THE DAYS OF RUDE AND VULGAR MEN.

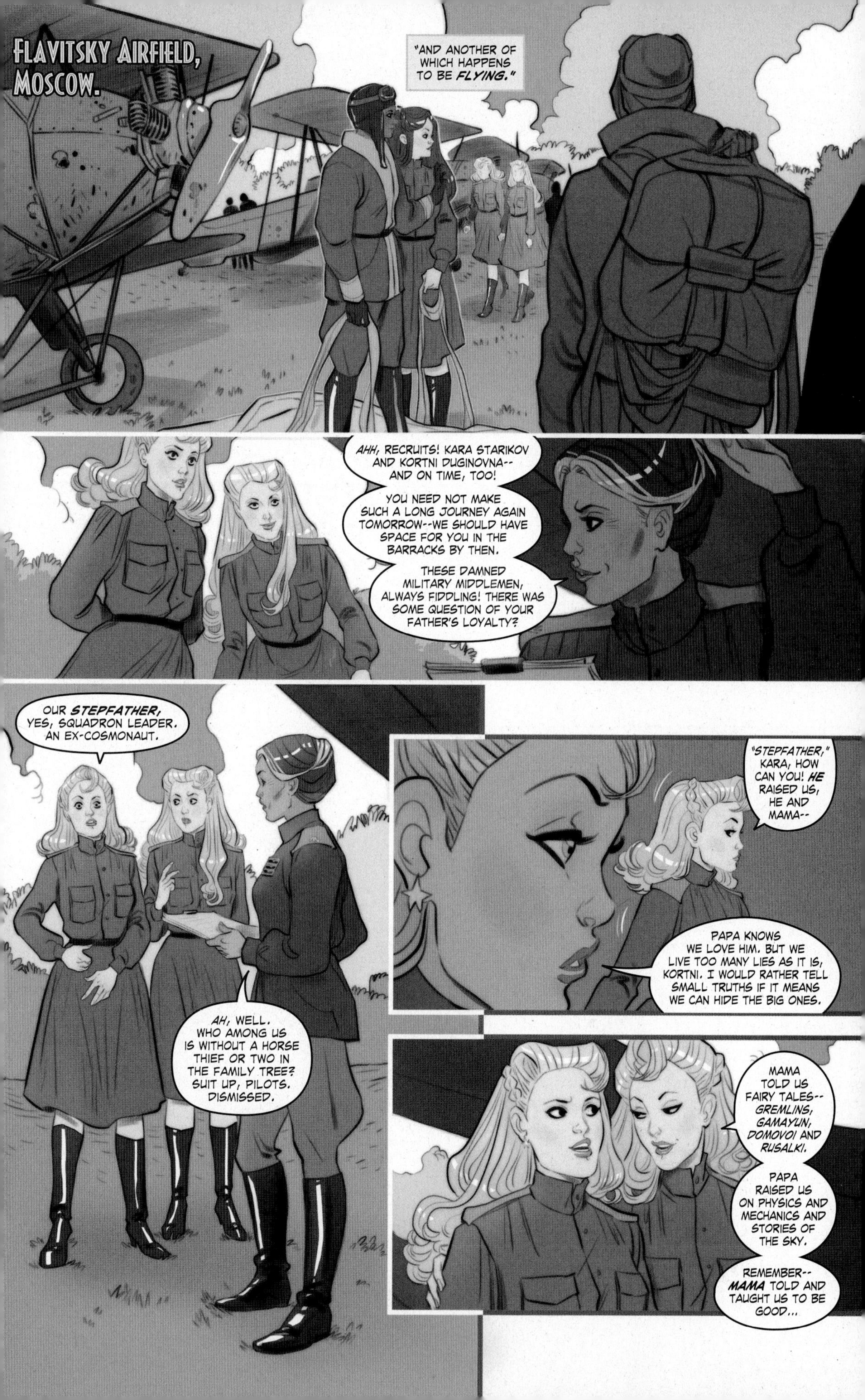
FLAVITSKY AIRFIELD, MOSCOW.
"AND ANOTHER OF WHICH HAPPENS TO BE FLYING."
AHH, RECRUITS! KARA STARIKOV AND KORTNI DUGINOVNA-- AND ON TIME, TOO!
YOU NEED NOT MAKE SUCH A LONG JOURNEY AGAIN TOMORROW--WE SHOULD HAVE SPACE FOR YOU IN THE BARRACKS BY THEN.
THESE DAMNED MILITARY MIDDLEMEN, ALWAYS FIDDLING! THERE WAS SOME QUESTION OF YOUR FATHER'S LOYALTY?
OUR STEPFATHER, YES, SQUADRON LEADER. AN EX-COSMONAUT.
AH, WELL. WHO AMONG US IS WITHOUT A HORSE THIEF OR TWO IN THE FAMILY TREE? SUIT UP, PILOTS. DISMISSED.
"STEPFATHER," KARA, HOW CAN YOU! HE RAISED US, HE AND MAMA--
PAPA KNOWS WE LOVE HIM. BUT WE LIVE TOO MANY LIES AS IT IS, KORTNI. I WOULD RATHER TELL SMALL TRUTHS IF IT MEANS WE CAN HIDE THE BIG ONES.
MAMA TOLD US FAIRY TALES-- GREMLINS, GAMAYUN, DOMOVOI AND RUSALKI.
PAPA RAISED US ON PHYSICS AND MECHANICS AND STORIES OF THE SKY.
REMEMBER-- MAMA TOLD AND TAUGHT US TO BE GOOD...

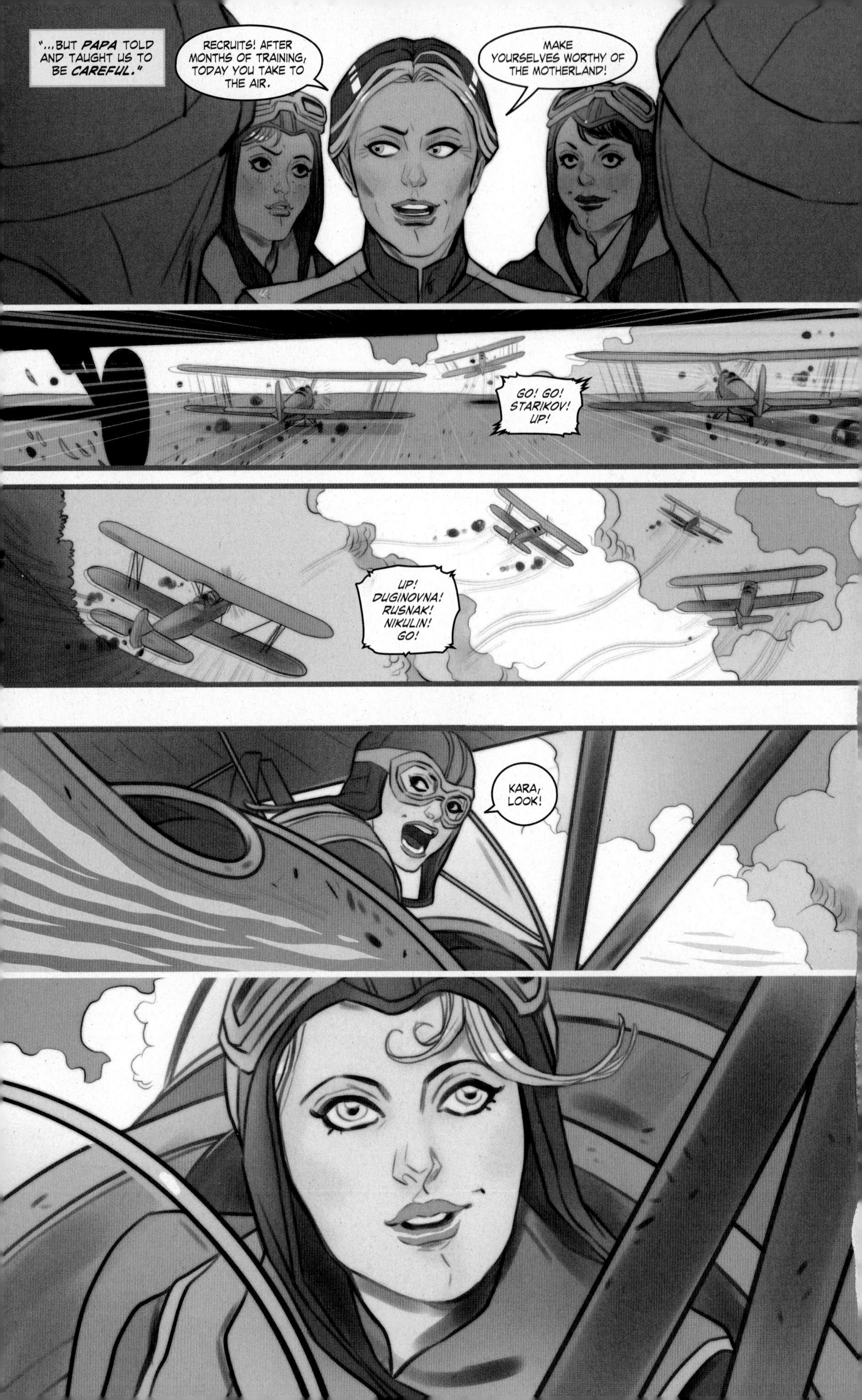
"...BUT PAPA TOLD AND TAUGHT US TO BE CAREFUL."
RECRUITS! AFTER MONTHS OF TRAINING, TODAY YOU TAKE TO THE AIR.
MAKE YOURSELVES WORTHY OF THE MOTHERLAND!
GO! GO! STARIKOV! UP!
UP! DUGINOVNA! RUSNAK! NIKULIN! GO!
KARA, LOOK!

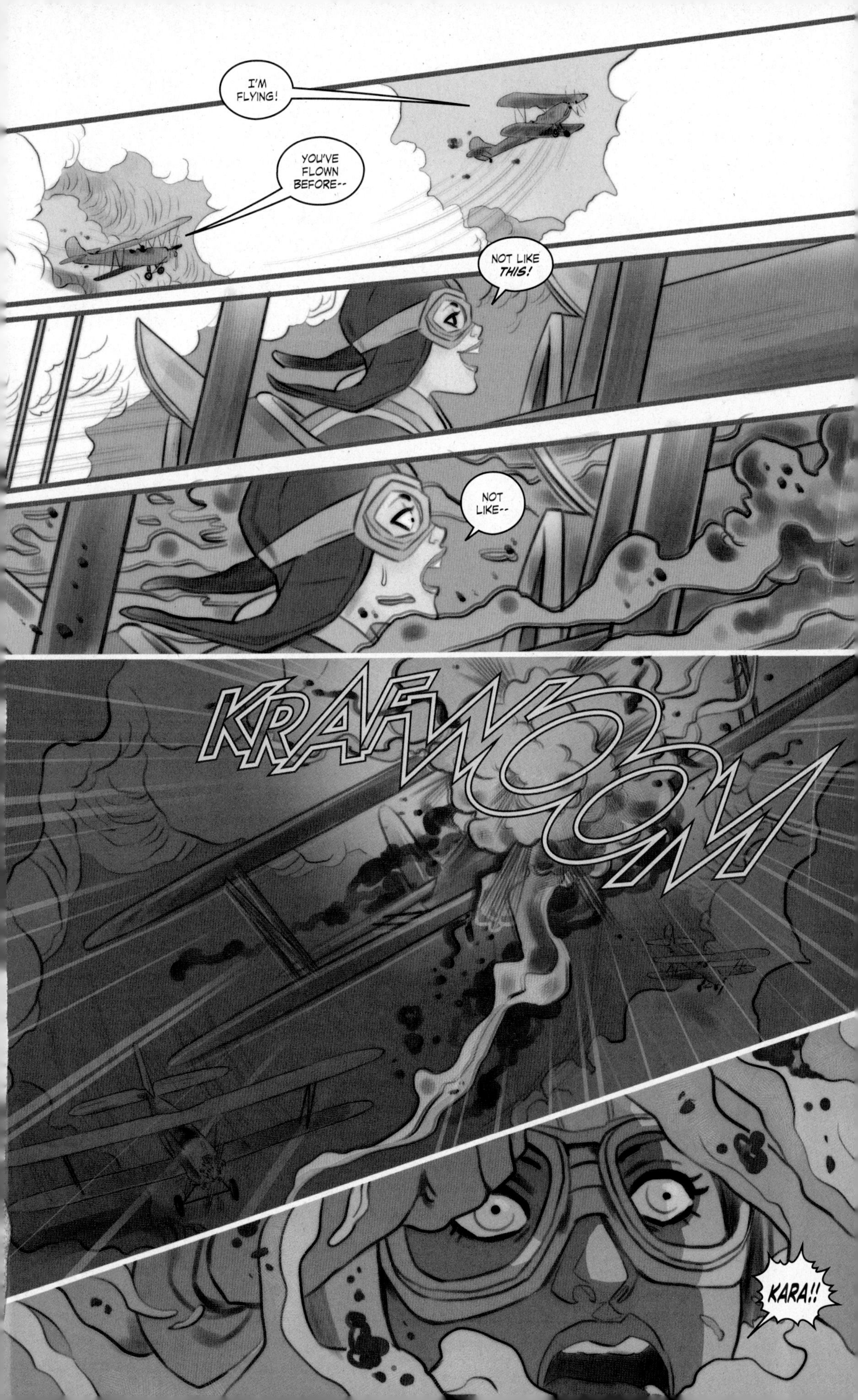
I'M FLYING!
YOU'VE FLOWN BEFORE--
NOT LIKE *THIS!*
NOT LIKE--
KRAFWOOOM
KARA!!

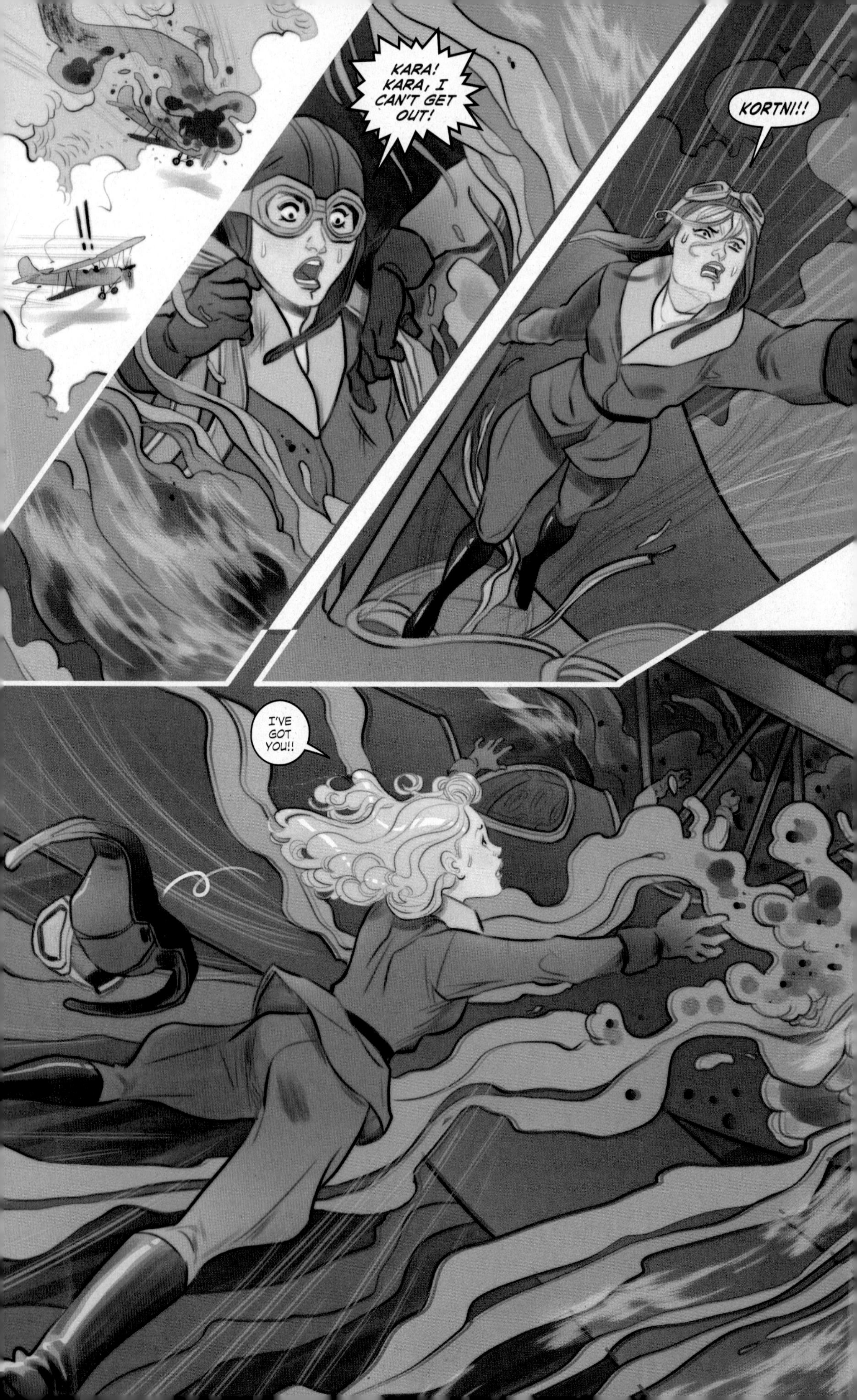
KARA! KARA, I CAN'T GET OUT!
!!
KORTNI!!
I'VE GOT YOU!!

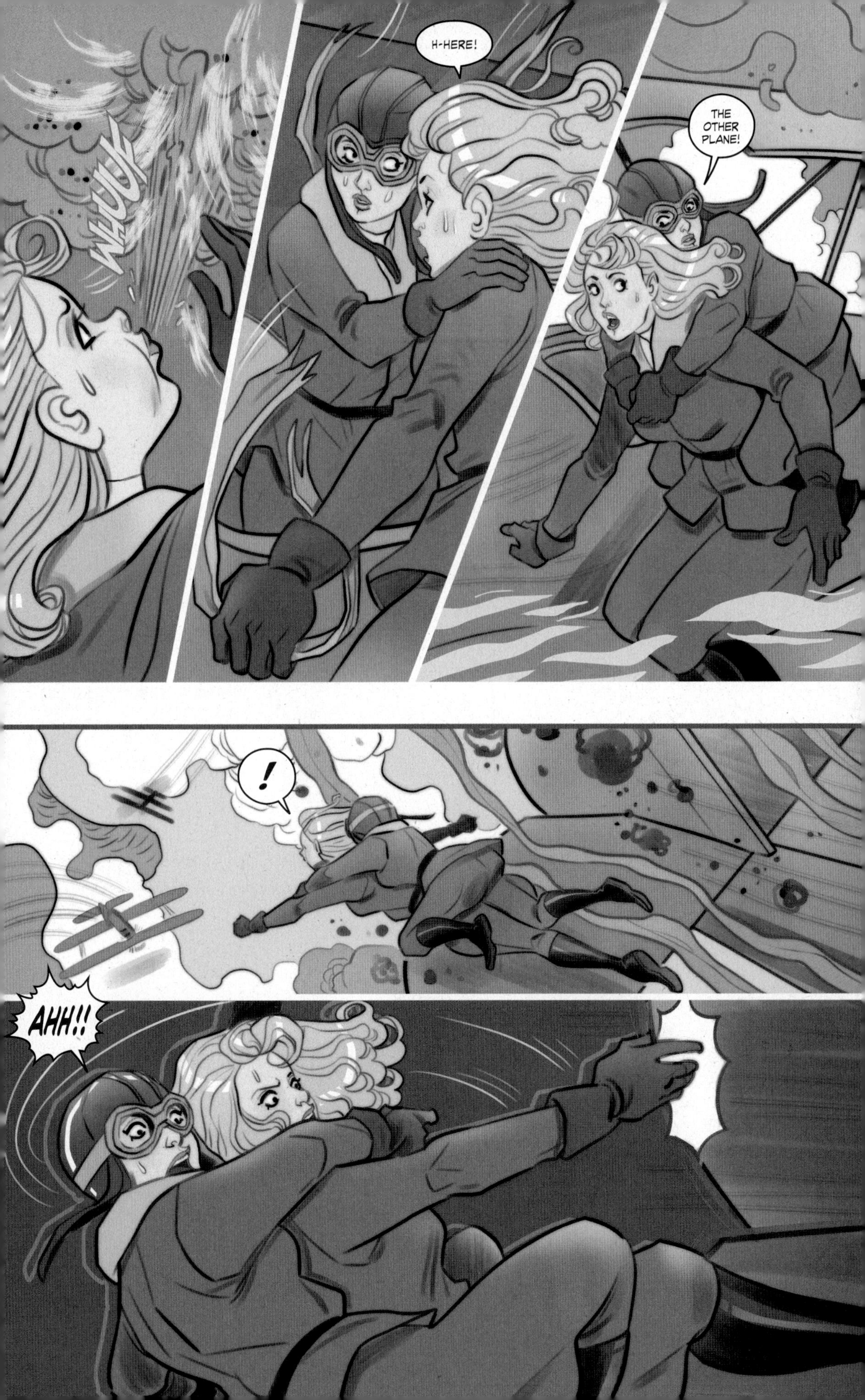
WHUUF
H-HERE!
THE OTHER PLANE!
!
AHH!!

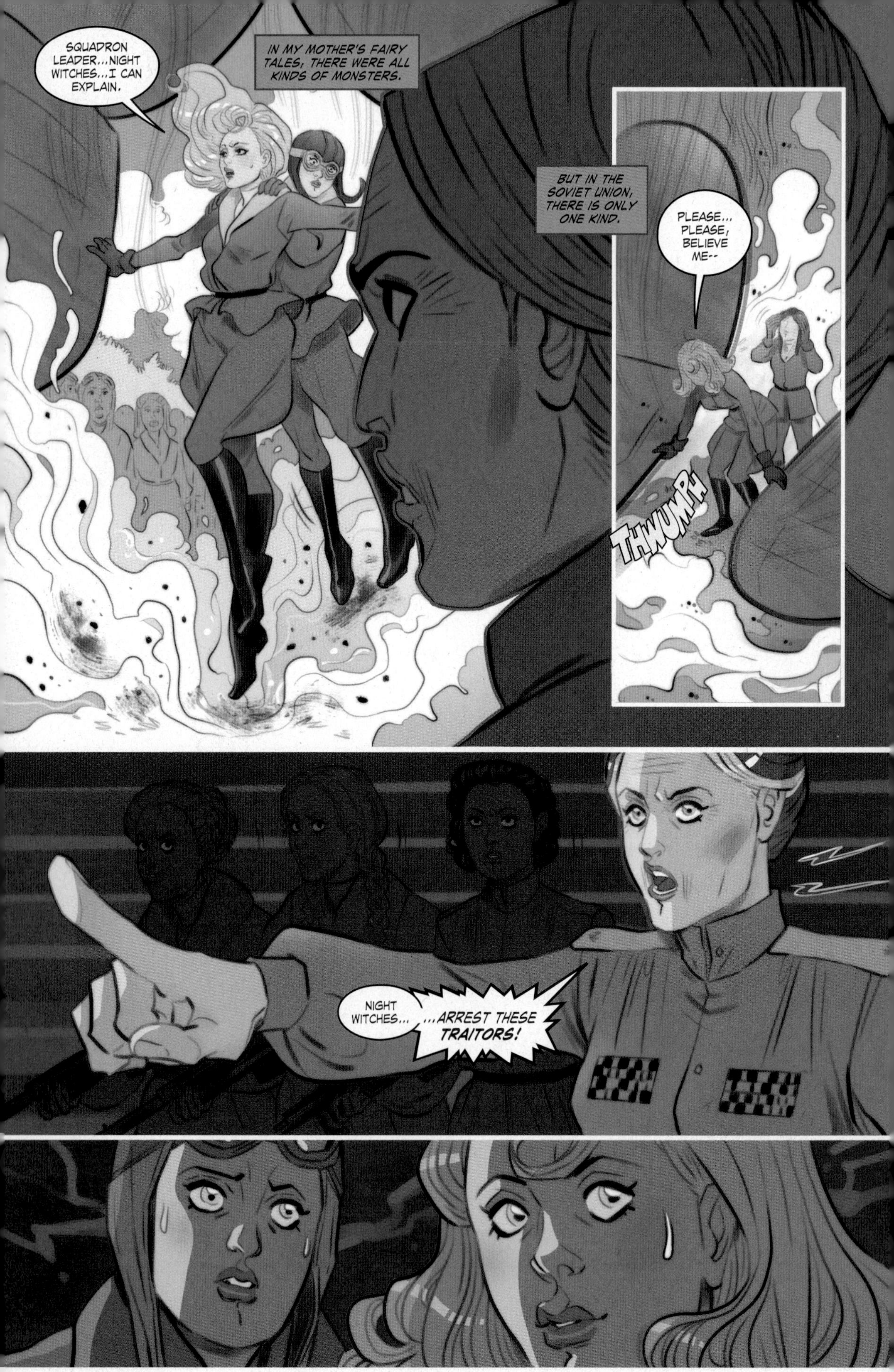
SQUADRON LEADER...NIGHT WITCHES...I CAN EXPLAIN.
IN MY MOTHER'S FAIRY TALES, THERE WERE ALL KINDS OF MONSTERS.
BUT IN THE SOVIET UNION, THERE IS ONLY ONE KIND.
PLEASE... PLEASE, BELIEVE ME--
THWUMPH
NIGHT WITCHES...
...ARREST THESE TRAITORS!

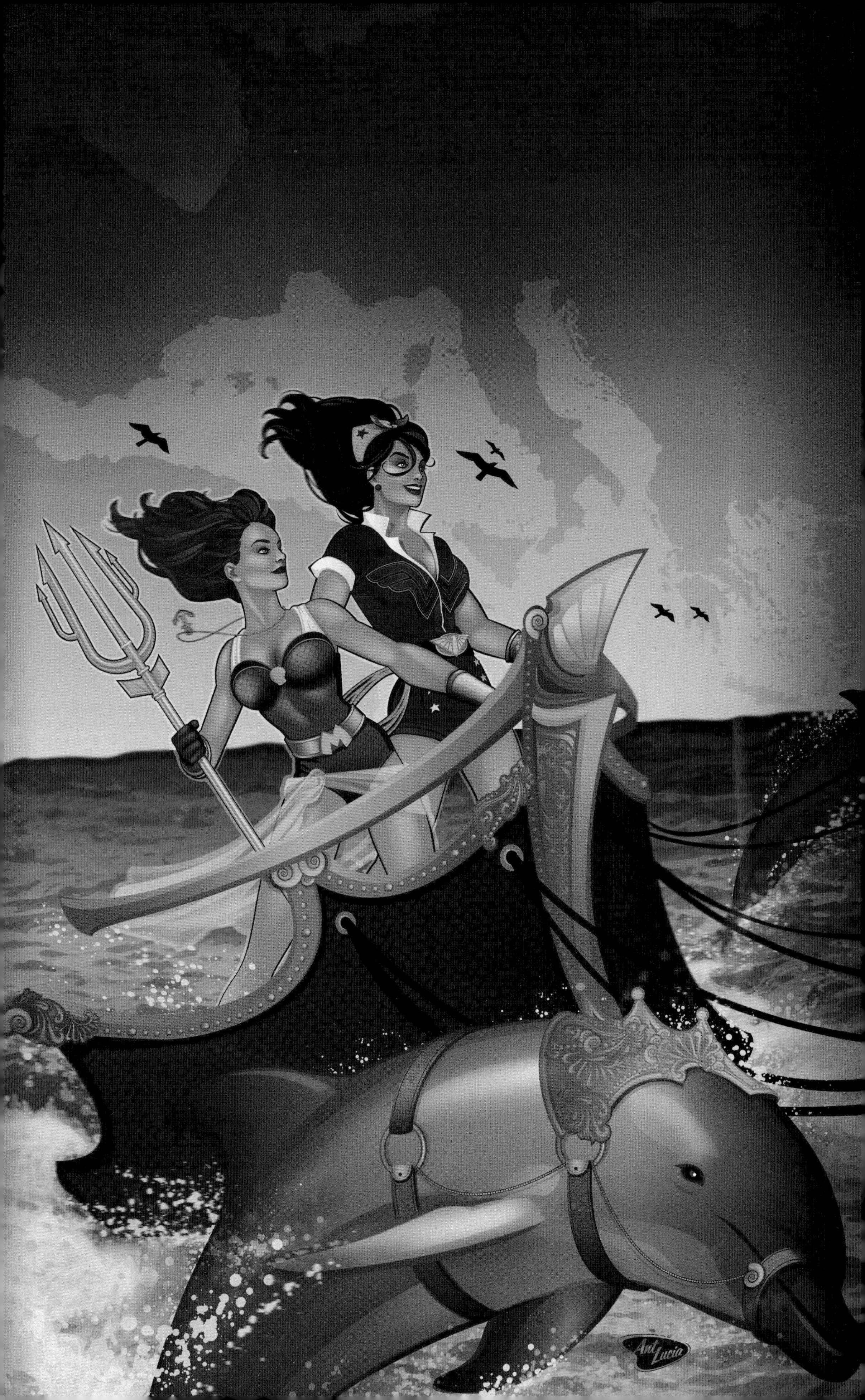
Ant Lucia

# ENLISTED
## PART TWO

**MARGUERITE BENNETT**
*Writer*

**LAURA BRAGA**
**STEPHEN MOONEY**
**TED NAIFEH**
*Artists*

**WENDY BROOME**
**DOUG GARBARK**
*Colorists*

**WES ABBOTT**
*Letterer*

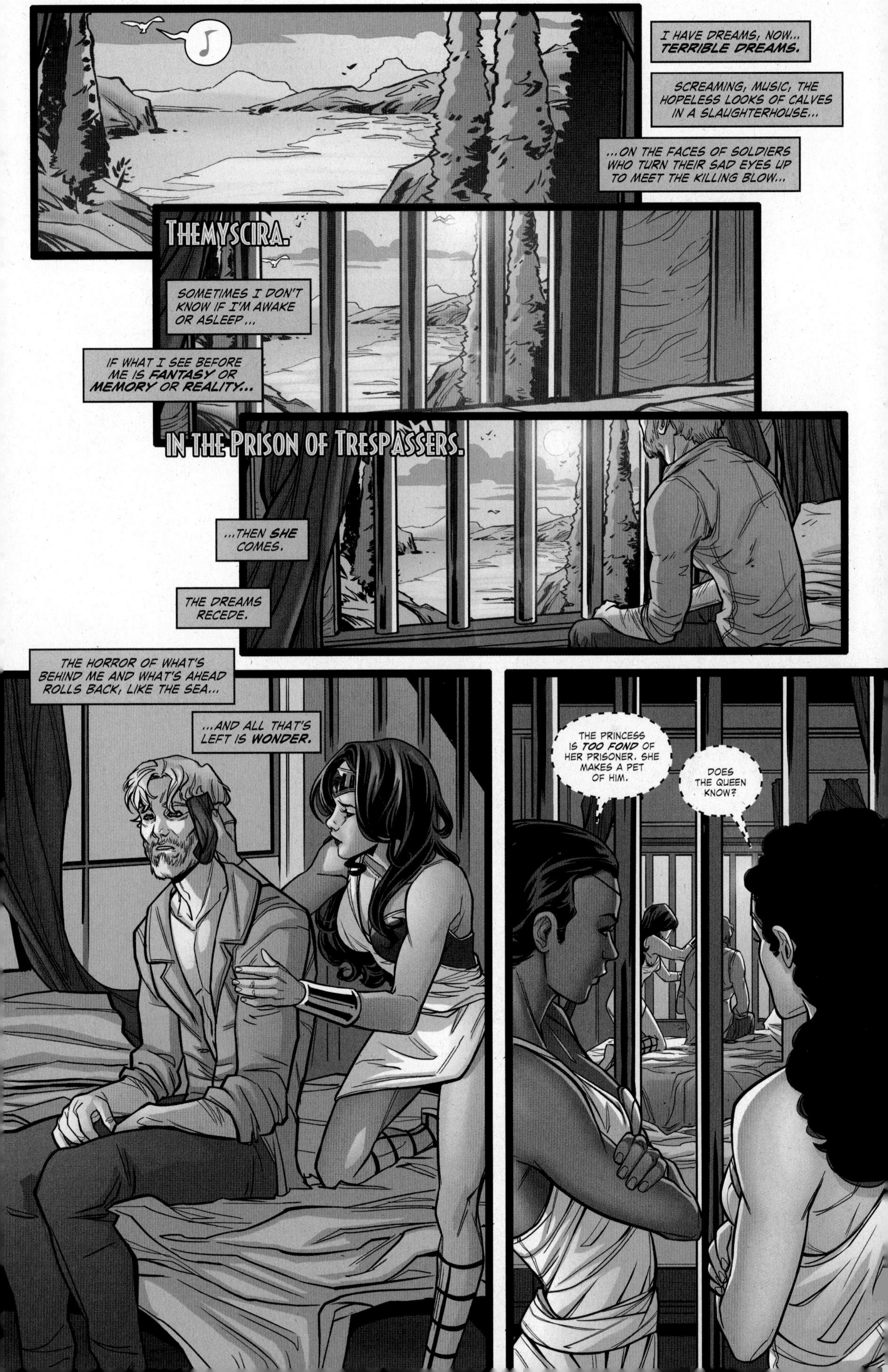

I HAVE DREAMS, NOW... TERRIBLE DREAMS.
SCREAMING, MUSIC, THE HOPELESS LOOKS OF CALVES IN A SLAUGHTERHOUSE...
...ON THE FACES OF SOLDIERS WHO TURN THEIR SAD EYES UP TO MEET THE KILLING BLOW...
THEMYSCIRA.
SOMETIMES I DON'T KNOW IF I'M AWAKE OR ASLEEP...
IF WHAT I SEE BEFORE ME IS FANTASY OR MEMORY OR REALITY...
IN THE PRISON OF TRESPASSERS.
...THEN SHE COMES.
THE DREAMS RECEDE.
THE HORROR OF WHAT'S BEHIND ME AND WHAT'S AHEAD ROLLS BACK, LIKE THE SEA...
...AND ALL THAT'S LEFT IS WONDER.
THE PRINCESS IS TOO FOND OF HER PRISONER. SHE MAKES A PET OF HIM.
DOES THE QUEEN KNOW?

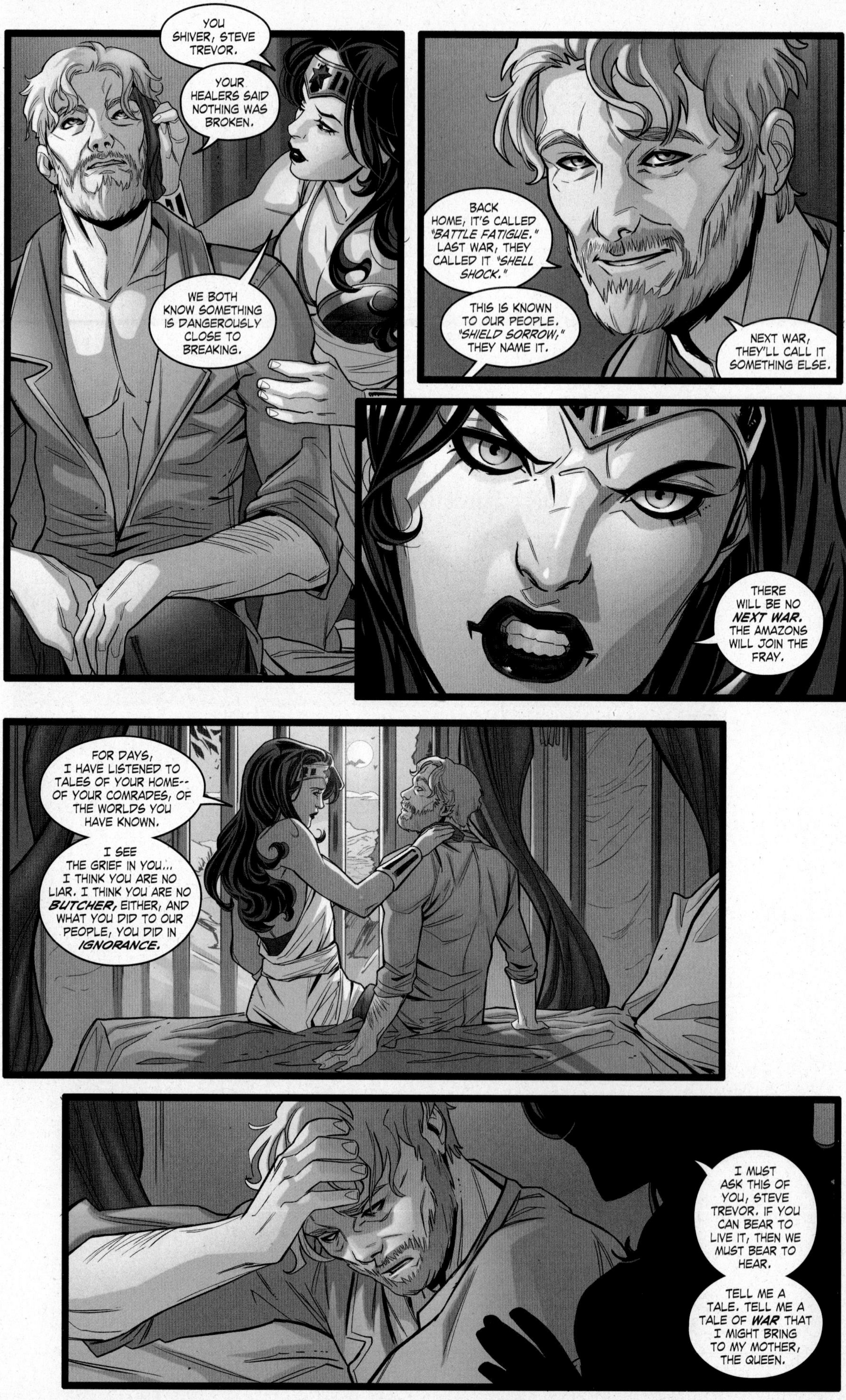
YOU SHIVER, STEVE TREVOR.
YOUR HEALERS SAID NOTHING WAS BROKEN.
WE BOTH KNOW SOMETHING IS DANGEROUSLY CLOSE TO BREAKING.
BACK HOME, IT'S CALLED "BATTLE FATIGUE." LAST WAR, THEY CALLED IT "SHELL SHOCK."
THIS IS KNOWN TO OUR PEOPLE. "SHIELD SORROW," THEY NAME IT.
NEXT WAR, THEY'LL CALL IT SOMETHING ELSE.
THERE WILL BE NO NEXT WAR. THE AMAZONS WILL JOIN THE FRAY.
FOR DAYS, I HAVE LISTENED TO TALES OF YOUR HOME--OF YOUR COMRADES, OF THE WORLDS YOU HAVE KNOWN.
I SEE THE GRIEF IN YOU... I THINK YOU ARE NO LIAR. I THINK YOU ARE NO BUTCHER, EITHER, AND WHAT YOU DID TO OUR PEOPLE, YOU DID IN IGNORANCE.
I MUST ASK THIS OF YOU, STEVE TREVOR. IF YOU CAN BEAR TO LIVE IT, THEN WE MUST BEAR TO HEAR.
TELL ME A TALE. TELL ME A TALE OF WAR THAT I MIGHT BRING TO MY MOTHER, THE QUEEN.

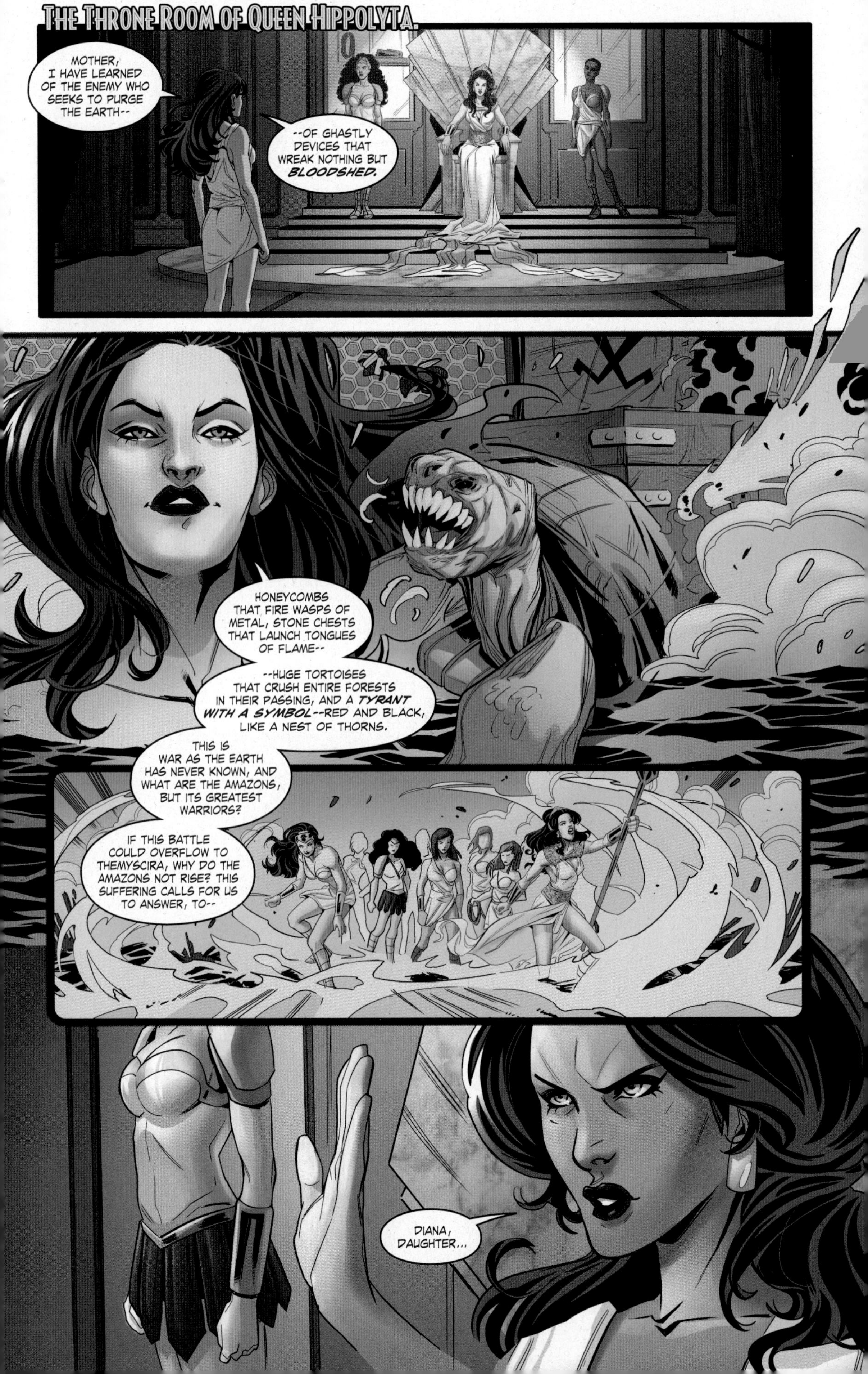
THE THRONE ROOM OF QUEEN HIPPOLYTA.
MOTHER, I HAVE LEARNED OF THE ENEMY WHO SEEKS TO PURGE THE EARTH--
--OF GHASTLY DEVICES THAT WREAK NOTHING BUT BLOODSHED.
HONEYCOMBS THAT FIRE WASPS OF METAL, STONE CHESTS THAT LAUNCH TONGUES OF FLAME--
--HUGE TORTOISES THAT CRUSH ENTIRE FORESTS IN THEIR PASSING, AND A TYRANT WITH A SYMBOL--RED AND BLACK, LIKE A NEST OF THORNS.
THIS IS WAR AS THE EARTH HAS NEVER KNOWN, AND WHAT ARE THE AMAZONS, BUT ITS GREATEST WARRIORS?
IF THIS BATTLE COULD OVERFLOW TO THEMYSCIRA, WHY DO THE AMAZONS NOT RISE? THIS SUFFERING CALLS FOR US TO ANSWER, TO--
DIANA, DAUGHTER...

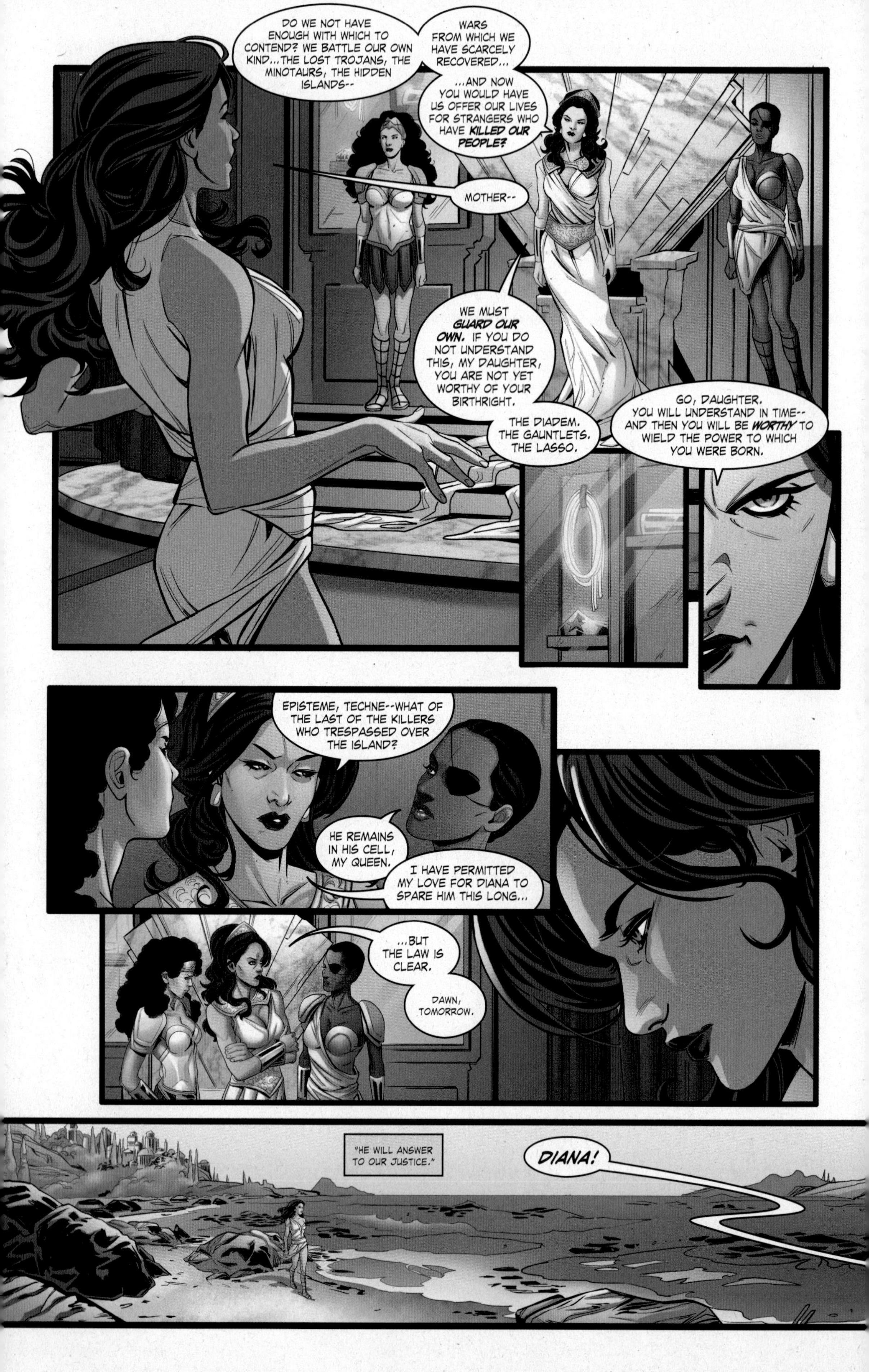

DO WE NOT HAVE ENOUGH WITH WHICH TO CONTEND? WE BATTLE OUR OWN KIND...THE LOST TROJANS, THE MINOTAURS, THE HIDDEN ISLANDS--
WARS FROM WHICH WE HAVE SCARCELY RECOVERED...
...AND NOW YOU WOULD HAVE US OFFER OUR LIVES FOR STRANGERS WHO HAVE KILLED OUR PEOPLE?
MOTHER--
WE MUST GUARD OUR OWN. IF YOU DO NOT UNDERSTAND THIS, MY DAUGHTER, YOU ARE NOT YET WORTHY OF YOUR BIRTHRIGHT.
THE DIADEM. THE GAUNTLETS. THE LASSO.
GO, DAUGHTER. YOU WILL UNDERSTAND IN TIME-- AND THEN YOU WILL BE WORTHY TO WIELD THE POWER TO WHICH YOU WERE BORN.
EPISTEME, TECHNE--WHAT OF THE LAST OF THE KILLERS WHO TRESPASSED OVER THE ISLAND?
HE REMAINS IN HIS CELL, MY QUEEN.
I HAVE PERMITTED MY LOVE FOR DIANA TO SPARE HIM THIS LONG...
...BUT THE LAW IS CLEAR.
DAWN, TOMORROW.
"HE WILL ANSWER TO OUR JUSTICE."
DIANA!

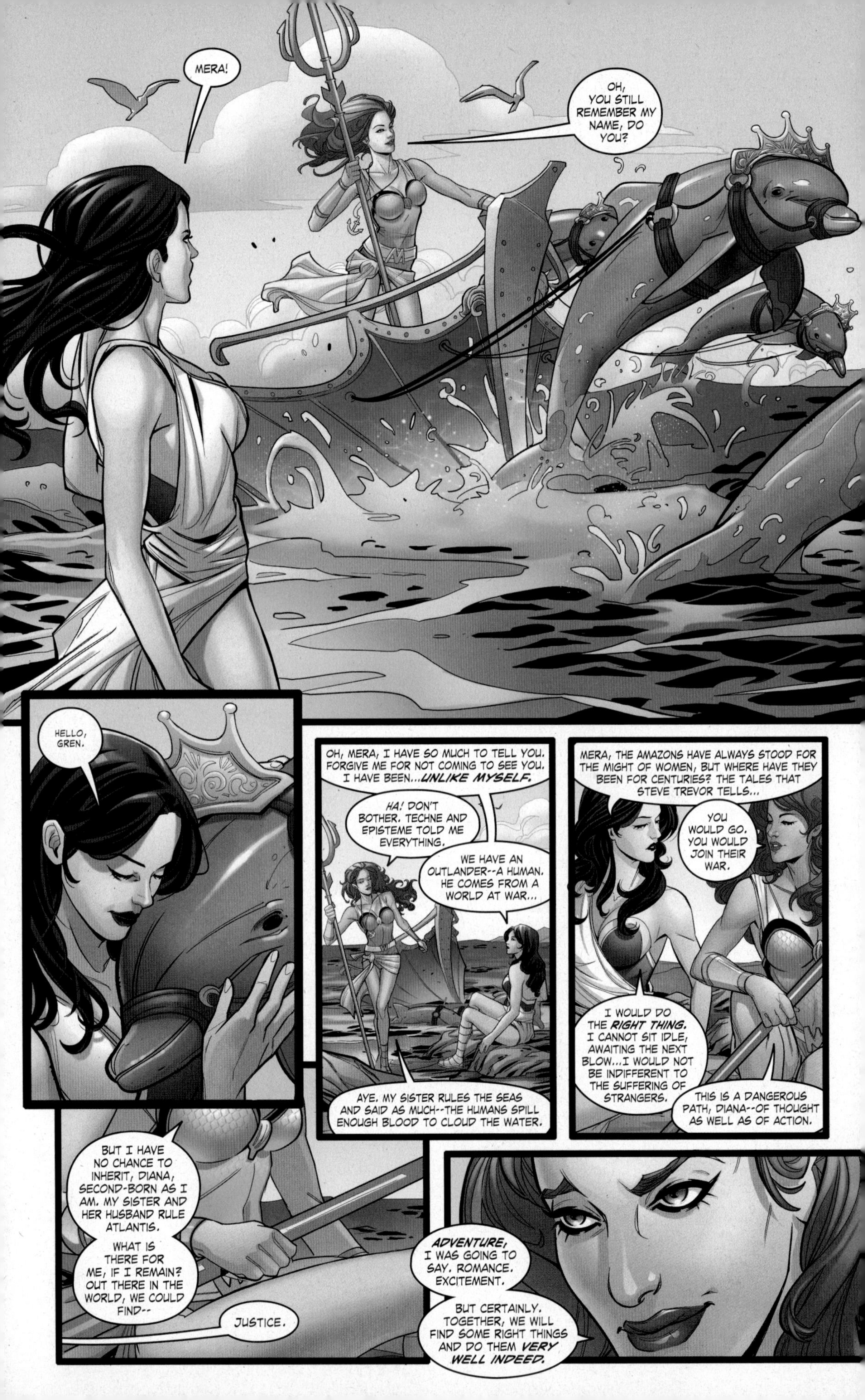
MERA!
OH, YOU STILL REMEMBER MY NAME, DO YOU?
HELLO, GREN.
OH, MERA, I HAVE SO MUCH TO TELL YOU. FORGIVE ME FOR NOT COMING TO SEE YOU. I HAVE BEEN...UNLIKE MYSELF.
HA! DON'T BOTHER. TECHNE AND EPISTEME TOLD ME EVERYTHING.
WE HAVE AN OUTLANDER--A HUMAN. HE COMES FROM A WORLD AT WAR...
AYE. MY SISTER RULES THE SEAS AND SAID AS MUCH--THE HUMANS SPILL ENOUGH BLOOD TO CLOUD THE WATER.
MERA, THE AMAZONS HAVE ALWAYS STOOD FOR THE MIGHT OF WOMEN, BUT WHERE HAVE THEY BEEN FOR CENTURIES? THE TALES THAT STEVE TREVOR TELLS...
YOU WOULD GO. YOU WOULD JOIN THEIR WAR.
I WOULD DO THE RIGHT THING. I CANNOT SIT IDLE, AWAITING THE NEXT BLOW...I WOULD NOT BE INDIFFERENT TO THE SUFFERING OF STRANGERS.
THIS IS A DANGEROUS PATH, DIANA--OF THOUGHT AS WELL AS OF ACTION.
BUT I HAVE NO CHANCE TO INHERIT, DIANA, SECOND-BORN AS I AM. MY SISTER AND HER HUSBAND RULE ATLANTIS.
WHAT IS THERE FOR ME, IF I REMAIN? OUT THERE IN THE WORLD, WE COULD FIND--
JUSTICE.
ADVENTURE, I WAS GOING TO SAY. ROMANCE. EXCITEMENT.
BUT CERTAINLY. TOGETHER, WE WILL FIND SOME RIGHT THINGS AND DO THEM VERY WELL INDEED.

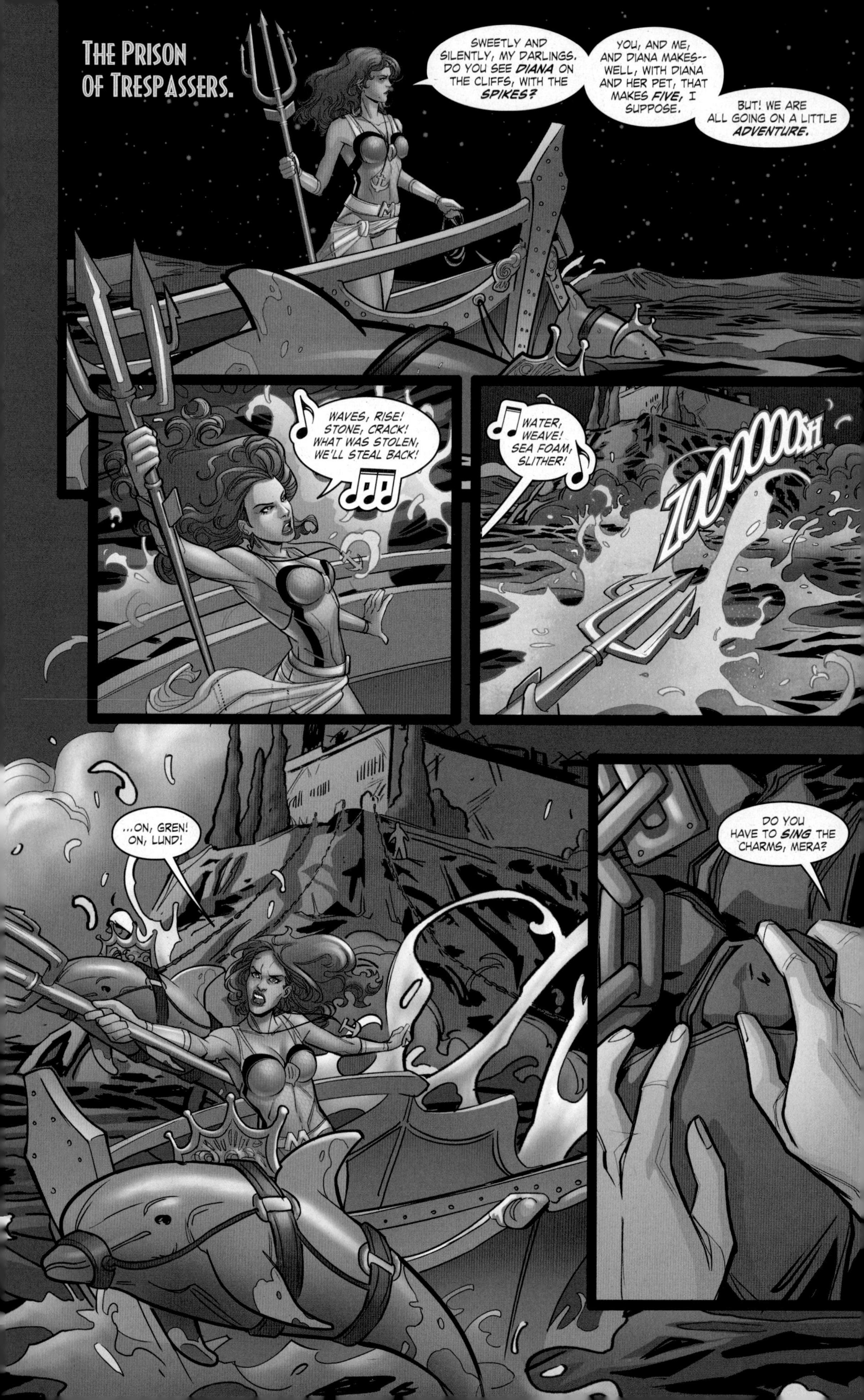
THE PRISON OF TRESPASSERS.
SWEETLY AND SILENTLY, MY DARLINGS. DO YOU SEE DIANA ON THE CLIFFS, WITH THE SPIKES?
YOU, AND ME, AND DIANA MAKES-- WELL, WITH DIANA AND HER PET, THAT MAKES FIVE, I SUPPOSE.
BUT! WE ARE ALL GOING ON A LITTLE ADVENTURE.
WAVES, RISE! STONE, CRACK! WHAT WAS STOLEN, WE'LL STEAL BACK!
WATER, WEAVE! SEA FOAM, SLITHER!
ZOOOOOOSH
...ON, GREN! ON, LUND!
DO YOU HAVE TO SING THE CHARMS, MERA?

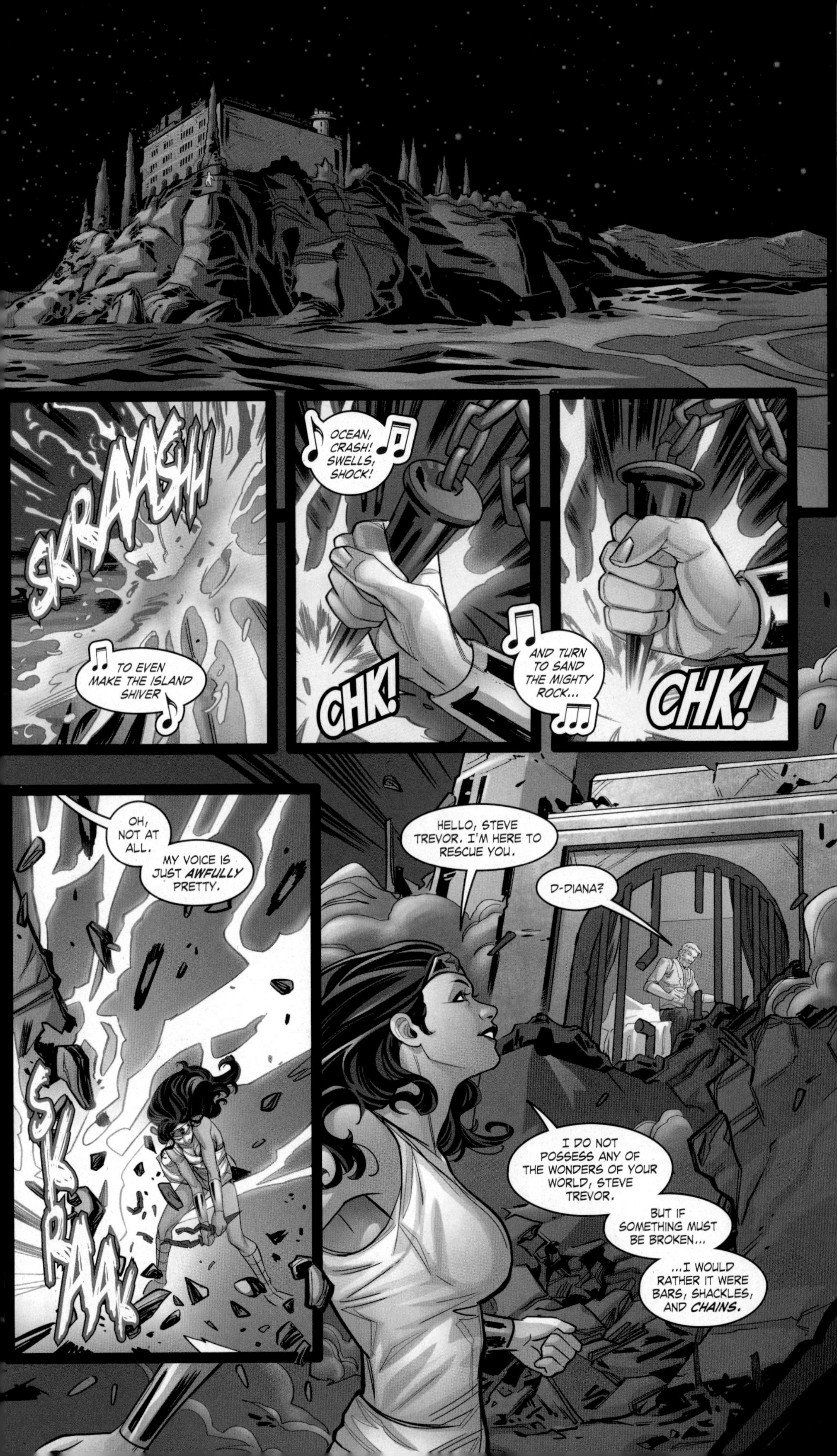
SKRAASHH
TO EVEN MAKE THE ISLAND SHIVER
OCEAN, CRASH! SWELLS, SHOCK!
CHK!
AND TURN TO SAND THE MIGHTY ROCK...
CHK!
OH, NOT AT ALL.
MY VOICE IS JUST AWFULLY PRETTY.
HELLO, STEVE TREVOR. I'M HERE TO RESCUE YOU.
D-DIANA?
I DO NOT POSSESS ANY OF THE WONDERS OF YOUR WORLD, STEVE TREVOR.
BUT IF SOMETHING MUST BE BROKEN...
...I WOULD RATHER IT WERE BARS, SHACKLES, AND CHAINS.

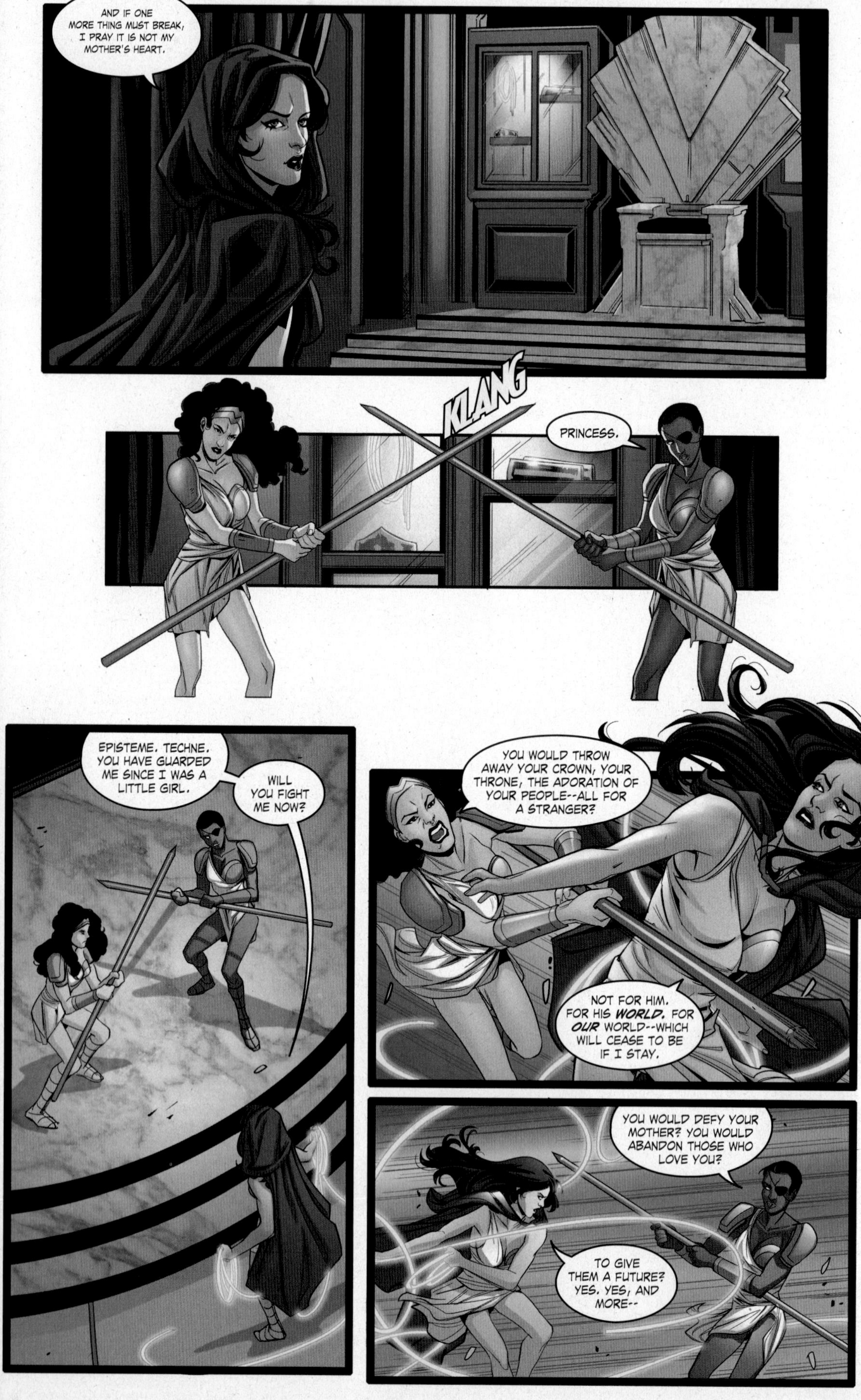
AND IF ONE MORE THING MUST BREAK, I PRAY IT IS NOT MY MOTHER'S HEART.
KLANG
PRINCESS.
EPISTEME. TECHNE. YOU HAVE GUARDED ME SINCE I WAS A LITTLE GIRL.
WILL YOU FIGHT ME NOW?
YOU WOULD THROW AWAY YOUR CROWN, YOUR THRONE, THE ADORATION OF YOUR PEOPLE--ALL FOR A STRANGER?
NOT FOR HIM. FOR HIS **WORLD.** FOR ***OUR*** WORLD--WHICH WILL CEASE TO BE IF I STAY.
YOU WOULD DEFY YOUR MOTHER? YOU WOULD ABANDON THOSE WHO LOVE YOU?
TO GIVE THEM A FUTURE? YES. YES, AND MORE--

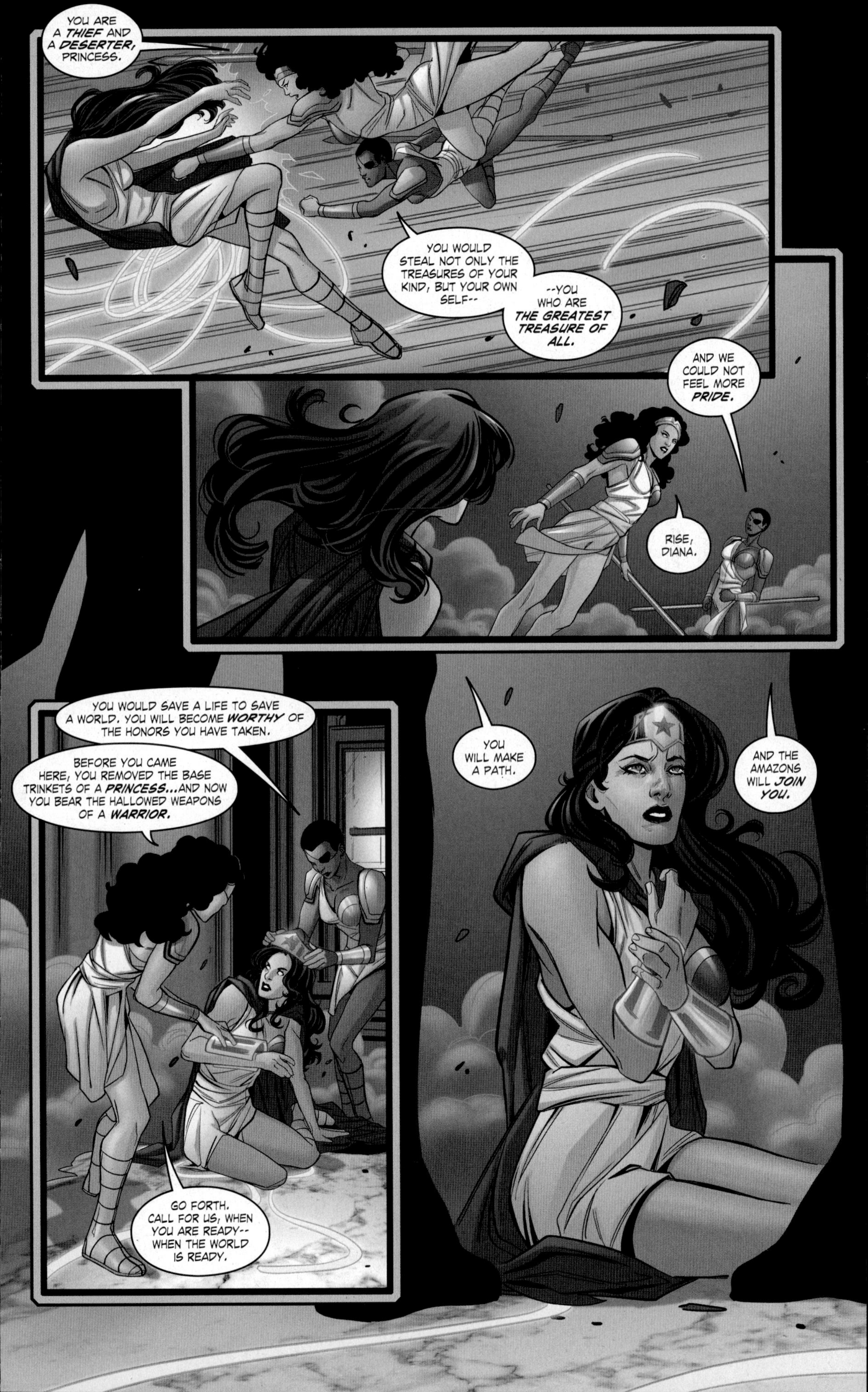
YOU ARE A THIEF AND A DESERTER, PRINCESS.
YOU WOULD STEAL NOT ONLY THE TREASURES OF YOUR KIND, BUT YOUR OWN SELF--
--YOU WHO ARE THE GREATEST TREASURE OF ALL.
AND WE COULD NOT FEEL MORE PRIDE.
RISE, DIANA.
YOU WOULD SAVE A LIFE TO SAVE A WORLD. YOU WILL BECOME WORTHY OF THE HONORS YOU HAVE TAKEN.
BEFORE YOU CAME HERE, YOU REMOVED THE BASE TRINKETS OF A PRINCESS...AND NOW YOU BEAR THE HALLOWED WEAPONS OF A WARRIOR.
GO FORTH. CALL FOR US, WHEN YOU ARE READY-- WHEN THE WORLD IS READY.
YOU WILL MAKE A PATH.
AND THE AMAZONS WILL JOIN YOU.

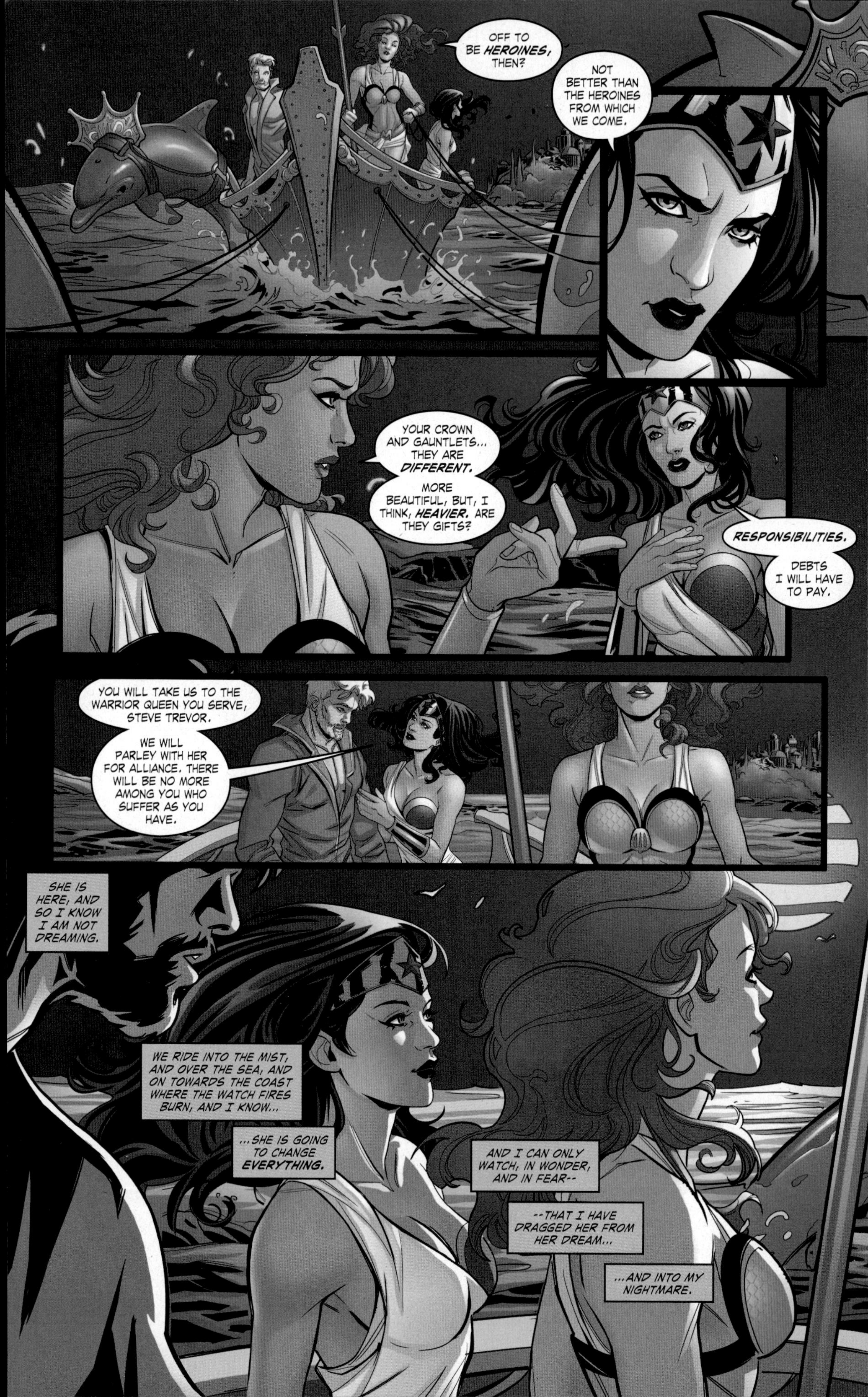
OFF TO BE HEROINES, THEN?
NOT BETTER THAN THE HEROINES FROM WHICH WE COME.
YOUR CROWN AND GAUNTLETS... THEY ARE DIFFERENT.
MORE BEAUTIFUL, BUT, I THINK, HEAVIER. ARE THEY GIFTS?
RESPONSIBILITIES.
DEBTS I WILL HAVE TO PAY.
YOU WILL TAKE US TO THE WARRIOR QUEEN YOU SERVE, STEVE TREVOR.
WE WILL PARLEY WITH HER FOR ALLIANCE. THERE WILL BE NO MORE AMONG YOU WHO SUFFER AS YOU HAVE.
SHE IS HERE, AND SO I KNOW I AM NOT DREAMING.
WE RIDE INTO THE MIST, AND OVER THE SEA, AND ON TOWARDS THE COAST WHERE THE WATCH FIRES BURN, AND I KNOW...
...SHE IS GOING TO CHANGE EVERYTHING.
AND I CAN ONLY WATCH, IN WONDER, AND IN FEAR--
--THAT I HAVE DRAGGED HER FROM HER DREAM...
...AND INTO MY NIGHTMARE.

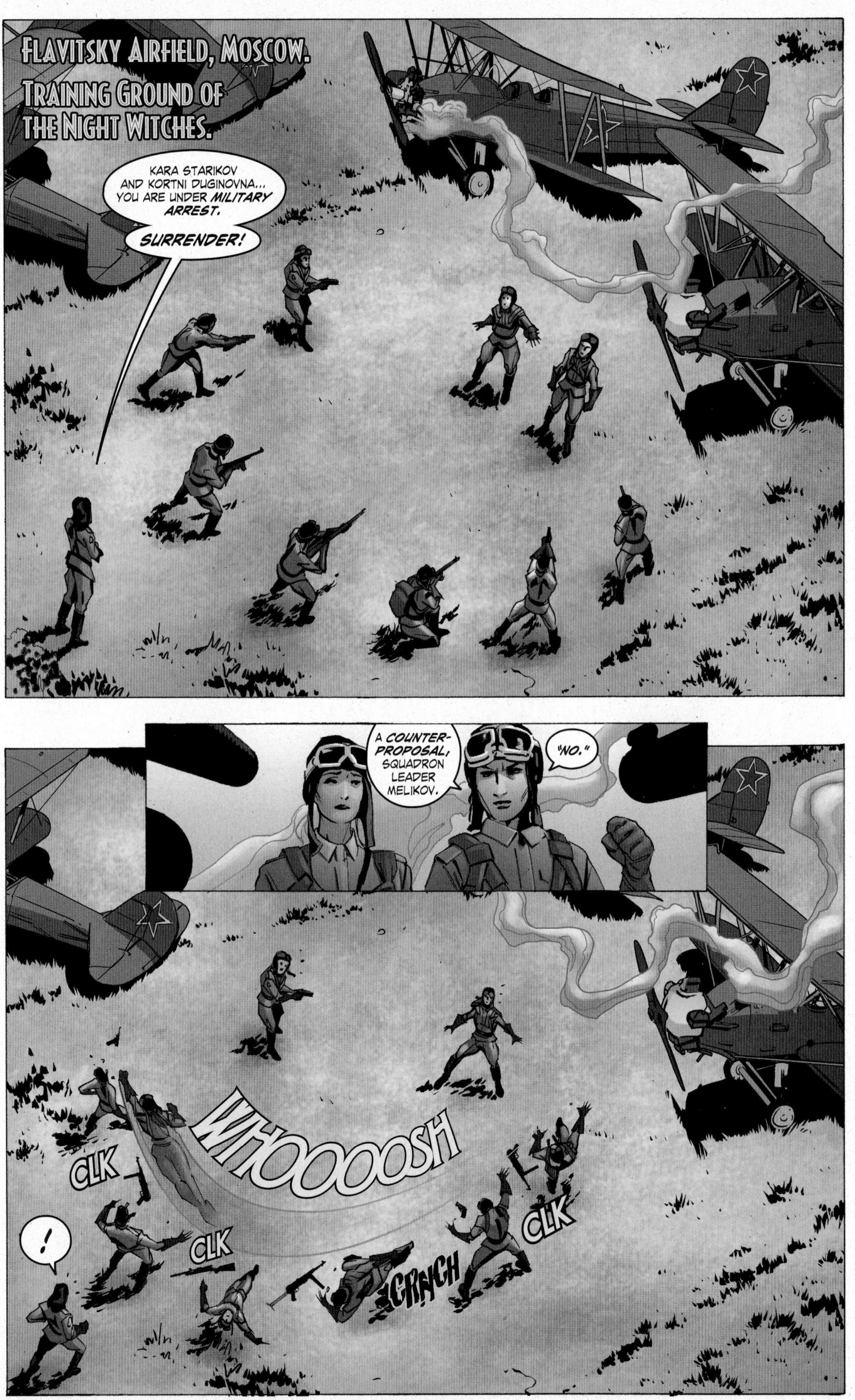
Flavitsky Airfield, Moscow.
Training Ground of the Night Witches.
KARA STARIKOV AND KORTNI DUGINOVNA... YOU ARE UNDER MILITARY ARREST.
SURRENDER!
A COUNTER-PROPOSAL, SQUADRON LEADER MELIKOV.
"NO."
WHOOOOOSH
CLK
CLK
CLK
CRNCH
!

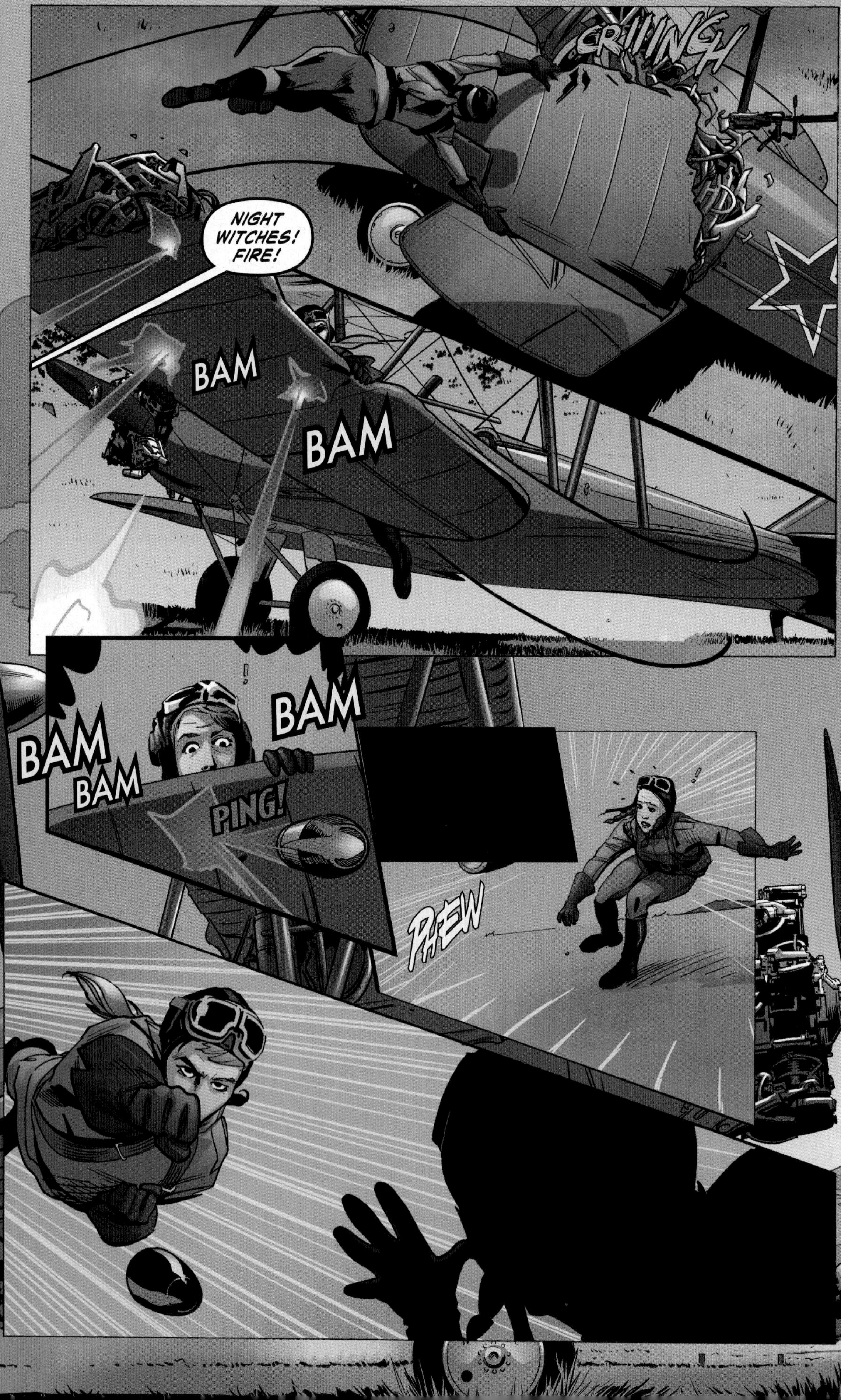
CRIIINCH
NIGHT WITCHES! FIRE!
BAM
BAM
BAM
BAM
BAM
PING!
PHEW

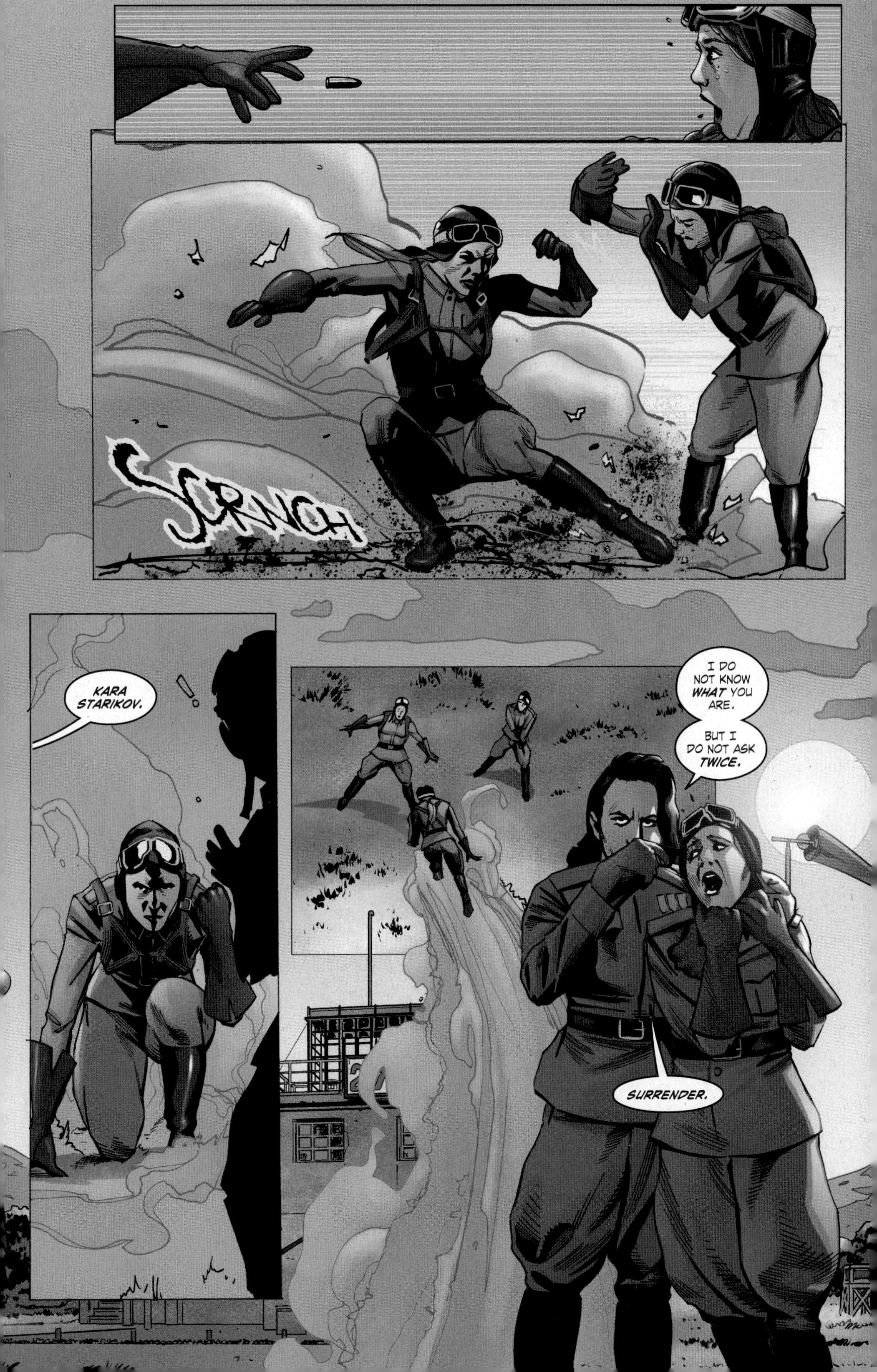
SCRUNCH
KARA STARIKOV.
!
I DO NOT KNOW WHAT YOU ARE.
BUT I DO NOT ASK TWICE.
SURRENDER.

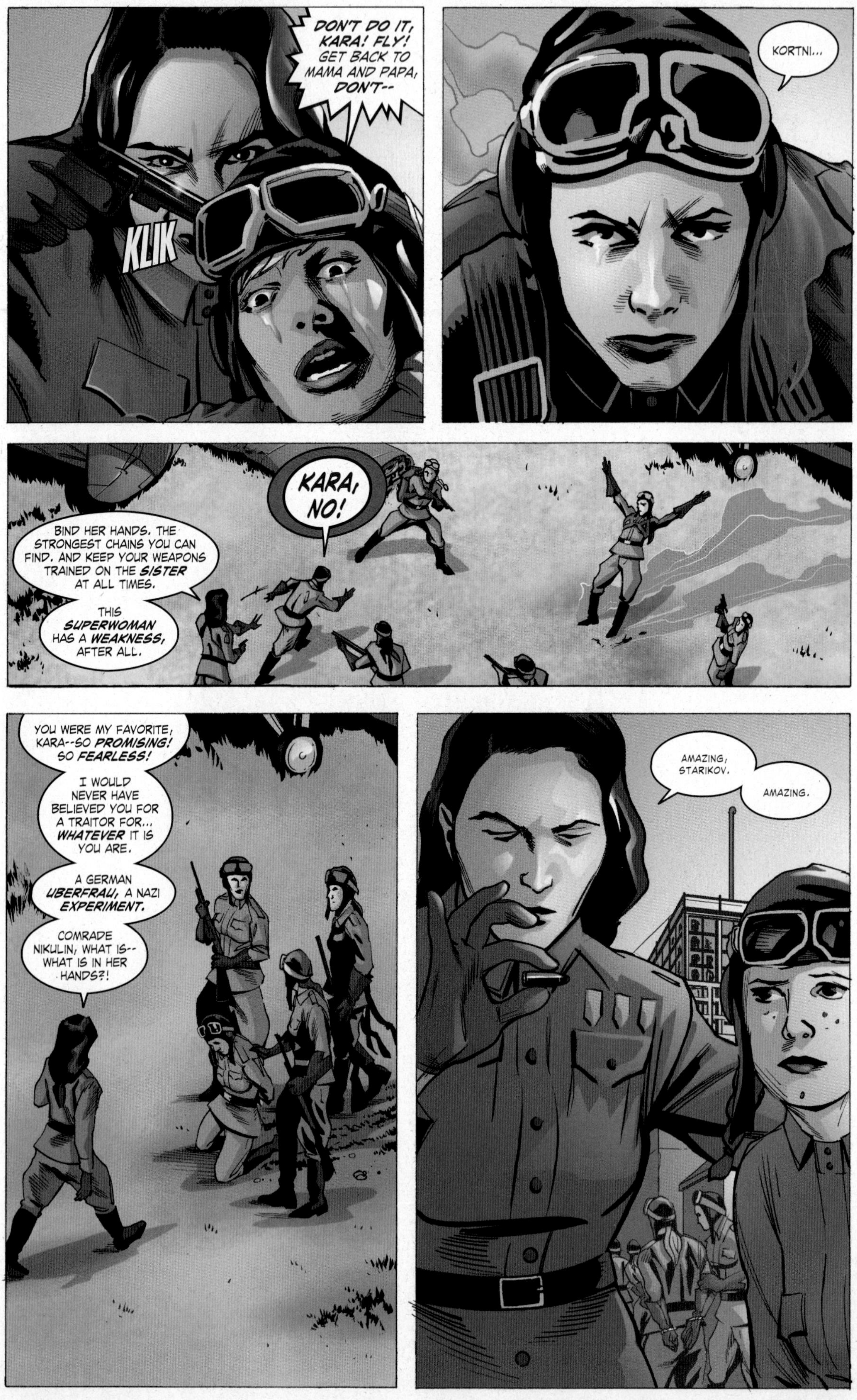
DON'T DO IT, KARA! FLY! GET BACK TO MAMA AND PAPA, DON'T--
KLIK
KORTNI...
KARA, NO!
BIND HER HANDS. THE STRONGEST CHAINS YOU CAN FIND. AND KEEP YOUR WEAPONS TRAINED ON THE SISTER AT ALL TIMES.
THIS SUPERWOMAN HAS A WEAKNESS, AFTER ALL.
YOU WERE MY FAVORITE, KARA--SO PROMISING! SO FEARLESS!
I WOULD NEVER HAVE BELIEVED YOU FOR A TRAITOR FOR... WHATEVER IT IS YOU ARE.
A GERMAN UBERFRAU, A NAZI EXPERIMENT.
COMRADE NIKULIN, WHAT IS--WHAT IS IN HER HANDS?!
AMAZING, STARIKOV.
AMAZING.

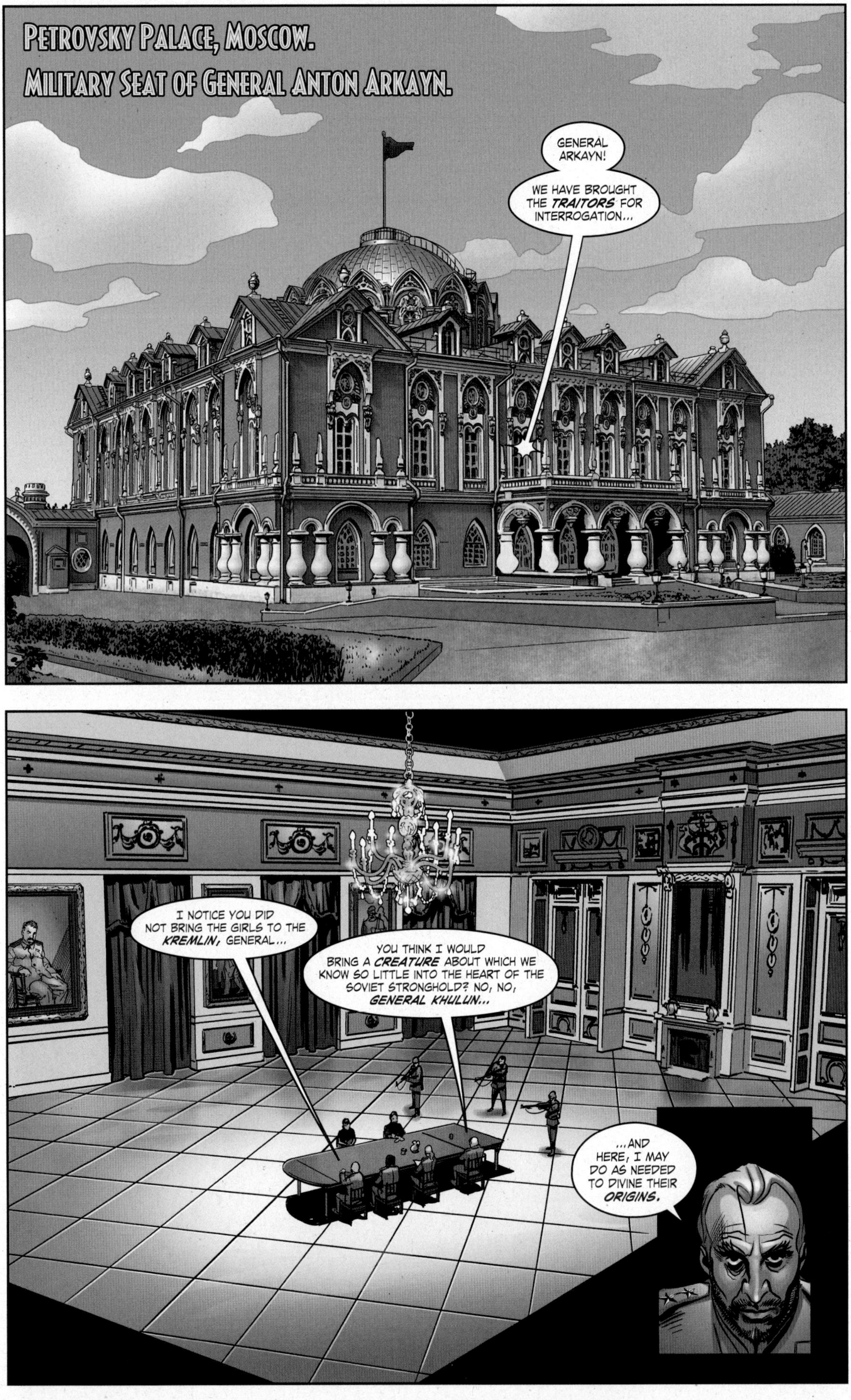

PETROVSKY PALACE, MOSCOW.
MILITARY SEAT OF GENERAL ANTON ARKAYN.
GENERAL ARKAYN!
WE HAVE BROUGHT THE TRAITORS FOR INTERROGATION...
I NOTICE YOU DID NOT BRING THE GIRLS TO THE KREMLIN, GENERAL...
YOU THINK I WOULD BRING A CREATURE ABOUT WHICH WE KNOW SO LITTLE INTO THE HEART OF THE SOVIET STRONGHOLD? NO, NO, GENERAL KHULUN...
...AND HERE, I MAY DO AS NEEDED TO DIVINE THEIR ORIGINS.

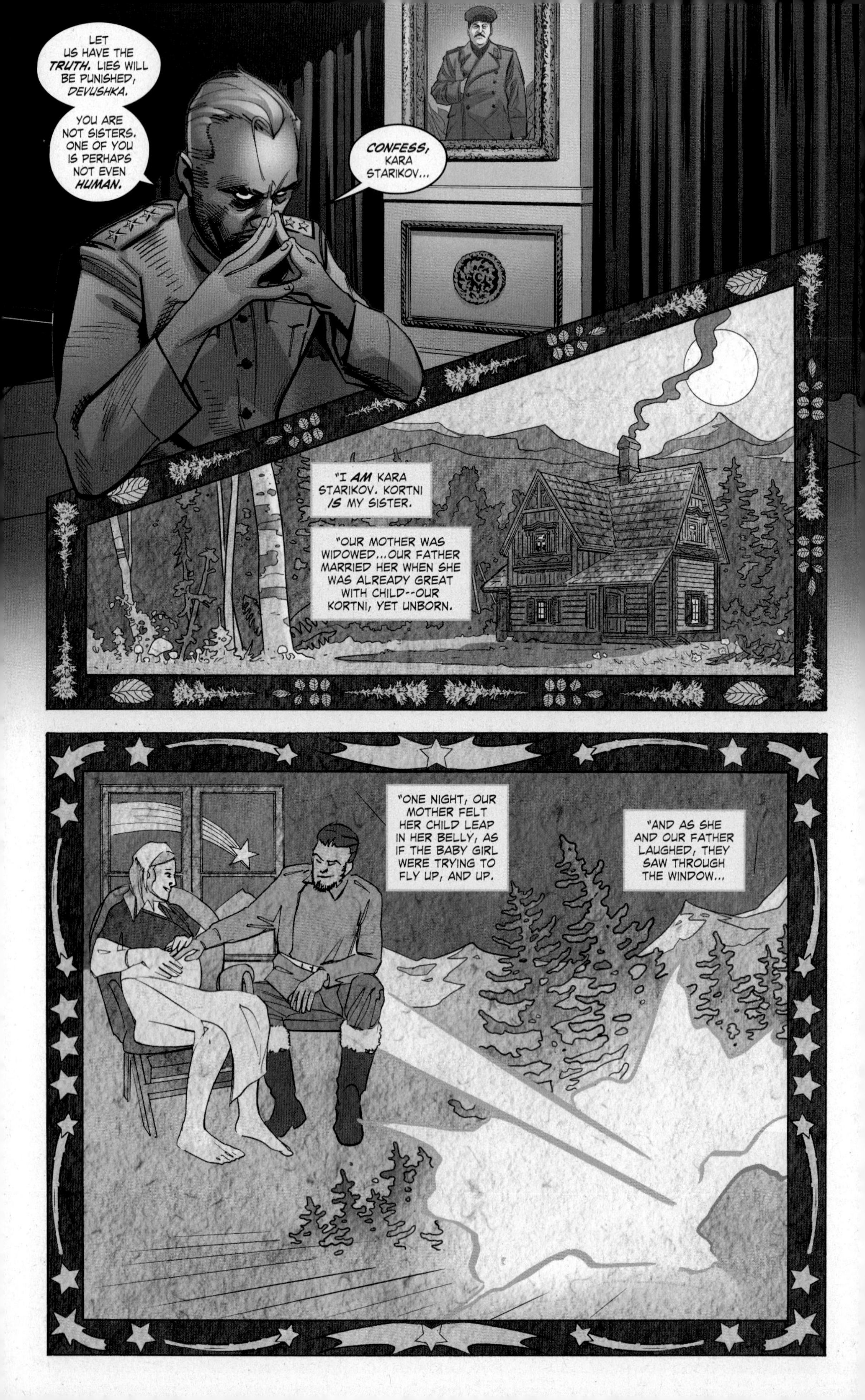
LET US HAVE THE TRUTH. LIES WILL BE PUNISHED, DEVUSHKA.
YOU ARE NOT SISTERS. ONE OF YOU IS PERHAPS NOT EVEN HUMAN.
CONFESS, KARA STARIKOV...
"I AM KARA STARIKOV. KORTNI IS MY SISTER.
"OUR MOTHER WAS WIDOWED...OUR FATHER MARRIED HER WHEN SHE WAS ALREADY GREAT WITH CHILD--OUR KORTNI, YET UNBORN.
"ONE NIGHT, OUR MOTHER FELT HER CHILD LEAP IN HER BELLY, AS IF THE BABY GIRL WERE TRYING TO FLY UP, AND UP.
"AND AS SHE AND OUR FATHER LAUGHED, THEY SAW THROUGH THE WINDOW...

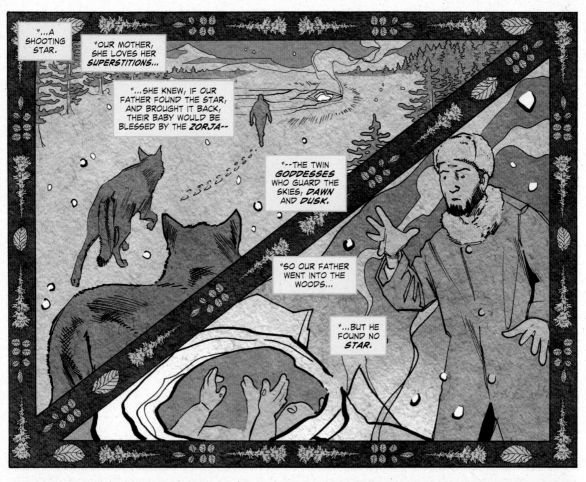

"...A SHOOTING STAR.

"OUR MOTHER, SHE LOVES HER *SUPERSTITIONS*...

"...SHE KNEW, IF OUR FATHER FOUND THE STAR, AND BROUGHT IT BACK, THEIR BABY WOULD BE BLESSED BY THE *ZORJA*--

"--THE TWIN *GODDESSES* WHO GUARD THE SKIES, *DAWN* AND *DUSK*.

"SO OUR FATHER WENT INTO THE WOODS...

"...BUT HE FOUND NO *STAR*.

"MY SISTER AND I SHARED A CRADLE. WE SHARED A HEARTH.

"MAMA, SHE SAYS WE ARE LIKE THE TWIN GODDESSES--MADE WHERE THE SKY MET THE EARTH--

"WE ARE BLESSED BY THE CREATURES OF THE FOREST AND THE CREATURES OF THE SKY, SHE SAYS.

"*HER LITTLE FALLEN STARS.*"

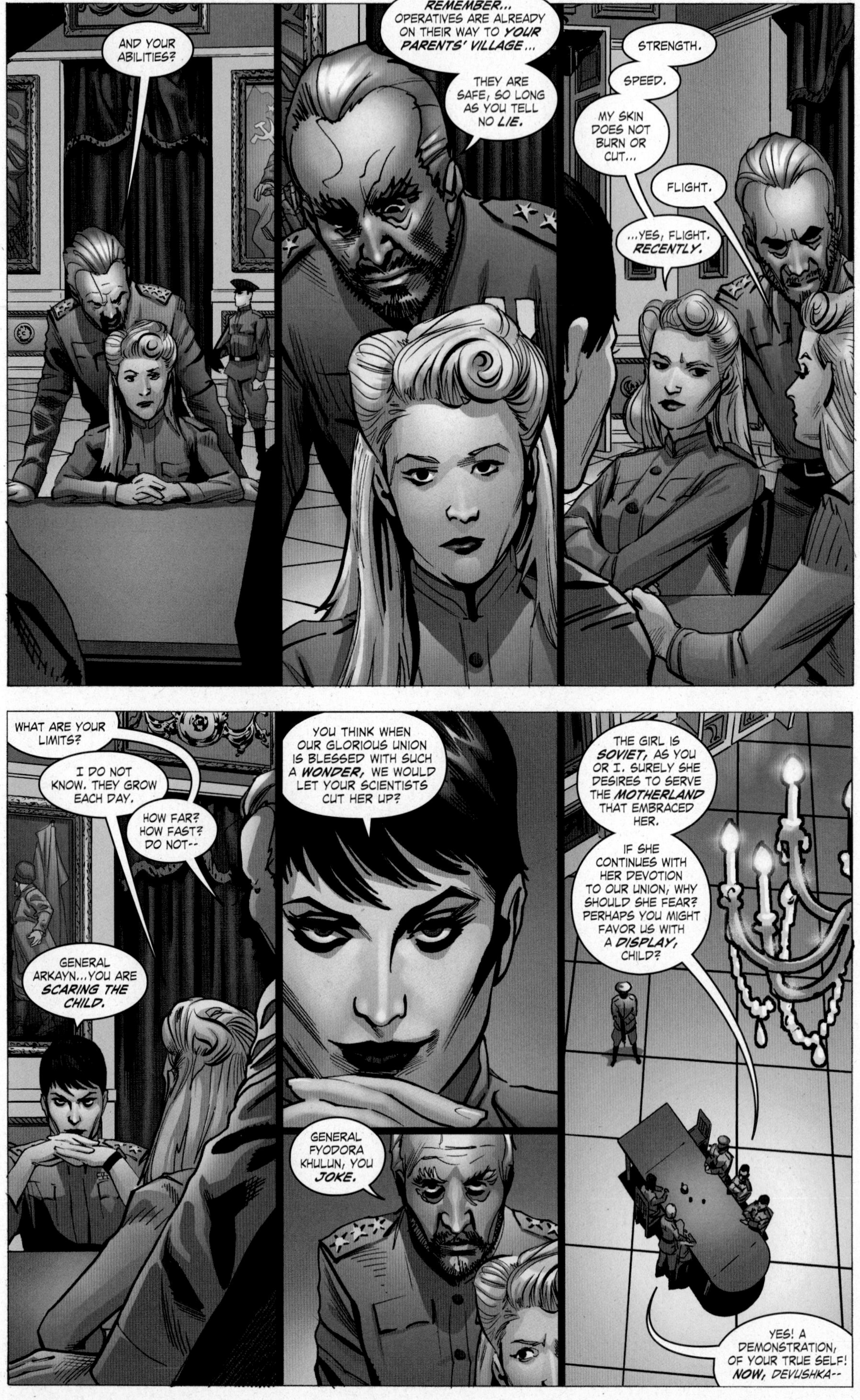
AND YOUR ABILITIES?
REMEMBER... OPERATIVES ARE ALREADY ON THEIR WAY TO YOUR PARENTS' VILLAGE...
THEY ARE SAFE, SO LONG AS YOU TELL NO LIE.
STRENGTH.
SPEED.
MY SKIN DOES NOT BURN OR CUT...
FLIGHT.
...YES, FLIGHT. RECENTLY.
WHAT ARE YOUR LIMITS?
I DO NOT KNOW. THEY GROW EACH DAY.
HOW FAR? HOW FAST? DO NOT--
GENERAL ARKAYN...YOU ARE SCARING THE CHILD.
YOU THINK WHEN OUR GLORIOUS UNION IS BLESSED WITH SUCH A WONDER, WE WOULD LET YOUR SCIENTISTS CUT HER UP?
GENERAL FYODORA KHULUN, YOU JOKE.
THE GIRL IS SOVIET, AS YOU OR I. SURELY SHE DESIRES TO SERVE THE MOTHERLAND THAT EMBRACED HER.
IF SHE CONTINUES WITH HER DEVOTION TO OUR UNION, WHY SHOULD SHE FEAR? PERHAPS YOU MIGHT FAVOR US WITH A DISPLAY, CHILD?
YES! A DEMONSTRATION, OF YOUR TRUE SELF! NOW, DEVUSHKA--

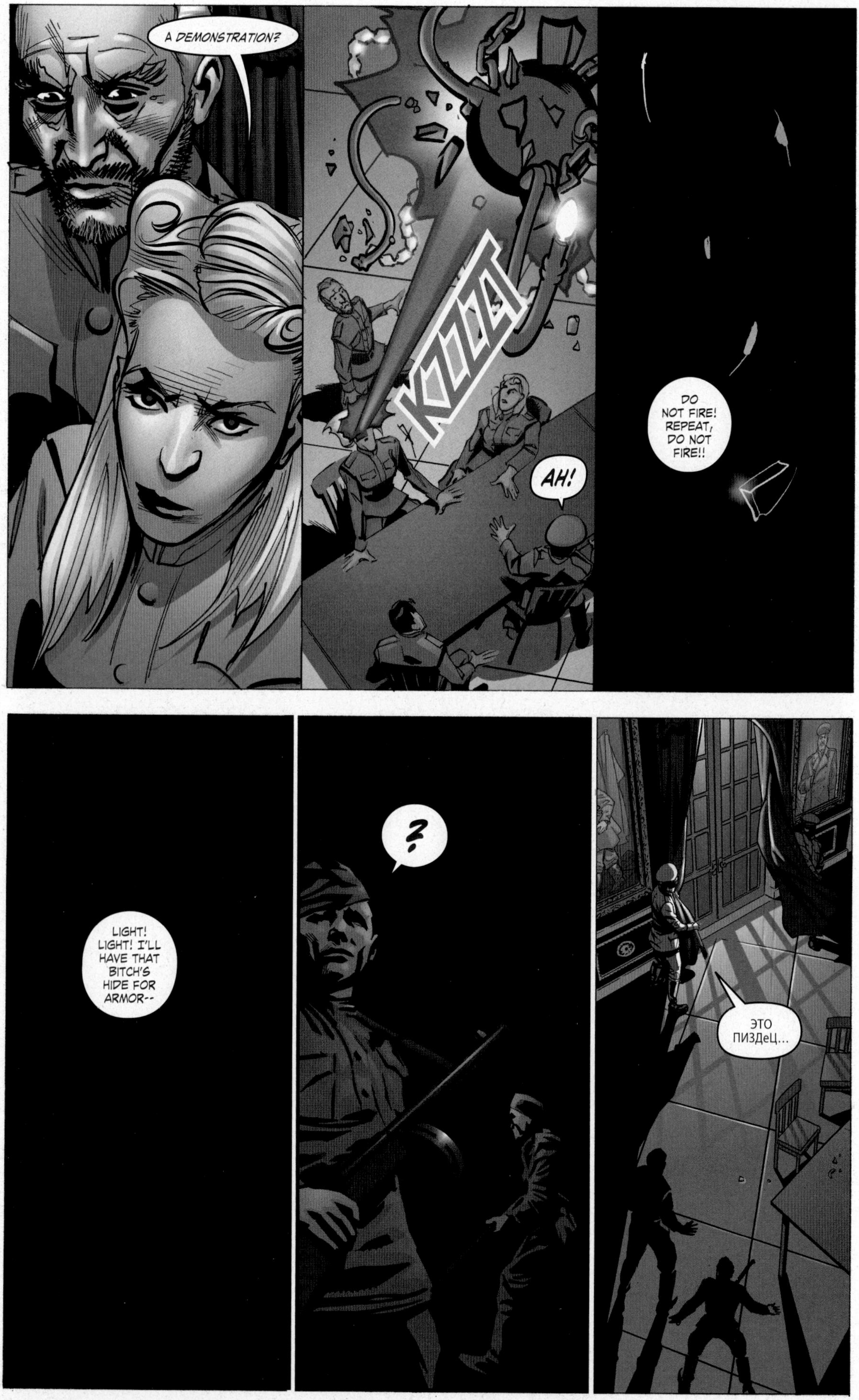

A DEMONSTRATION?
KZZZAT
AH!
DO NOT FIRE! REPEAT, DO NOT FIRE!!
LIGHT! LIGHT! I'LL HAVE THAT BITCH'S HIDE FOR ARMOR--
?
ЭТО ПИЗДеЦ...

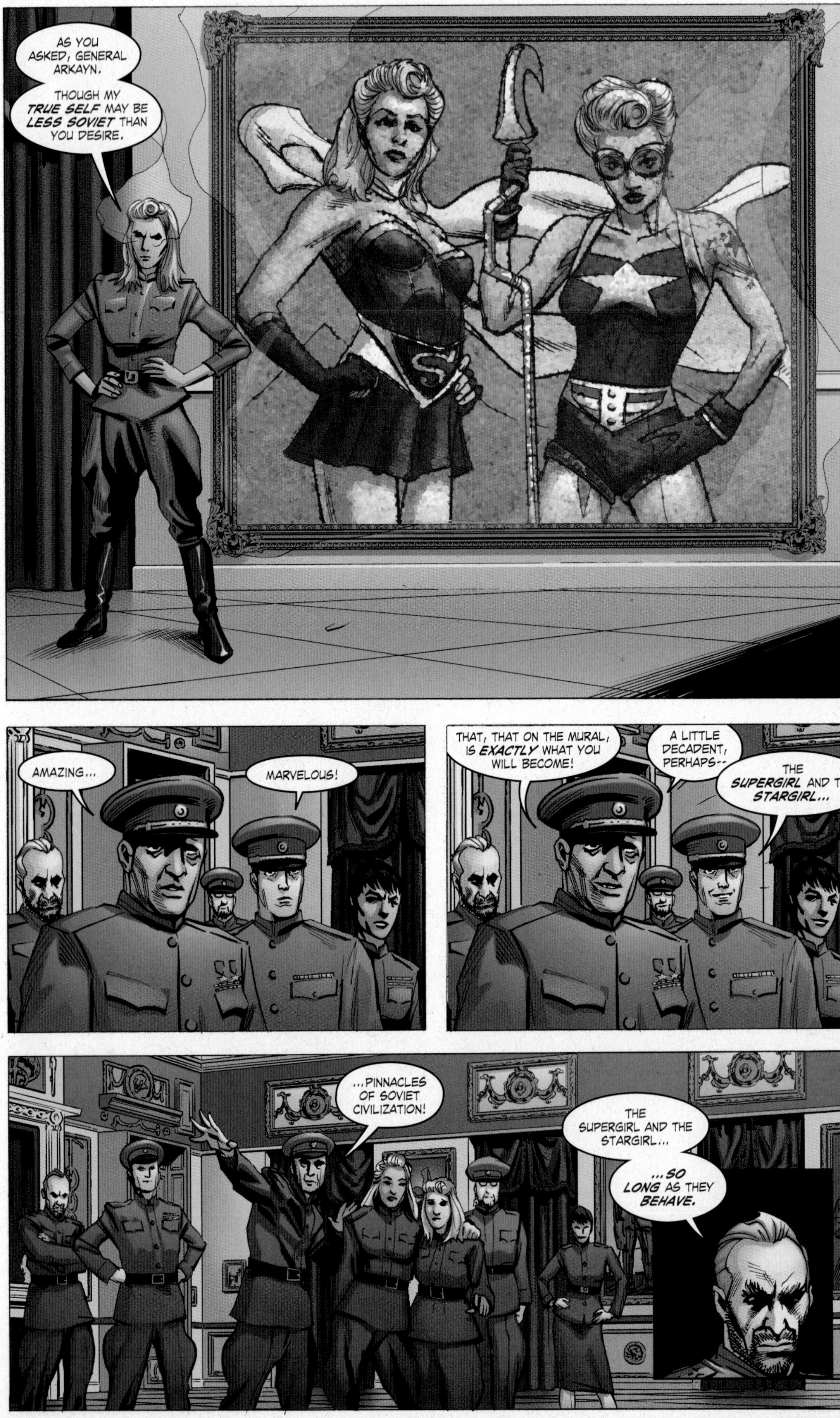
AS YOU ASKED, GENERAL ARKAYN.
THOUGH MY TRUE SELF MAY BE LESS SOVIET THAN YOU DESIRE.
AMAZING...
MARVELOUS!
THAT, THAT ON THE MURAL, IS EXACTLY WHAT YOU WILL BECOME!
A LITTLE DECADENT, PERHAPS--
THE SUPERGIRL AND THE STARGIRL...
...PINNACLES OF SOVIET CIVILIZATION!
THE SUPERGIRL AND THE STARGIRL...
...SO LONG AS THEY BEHAVE.

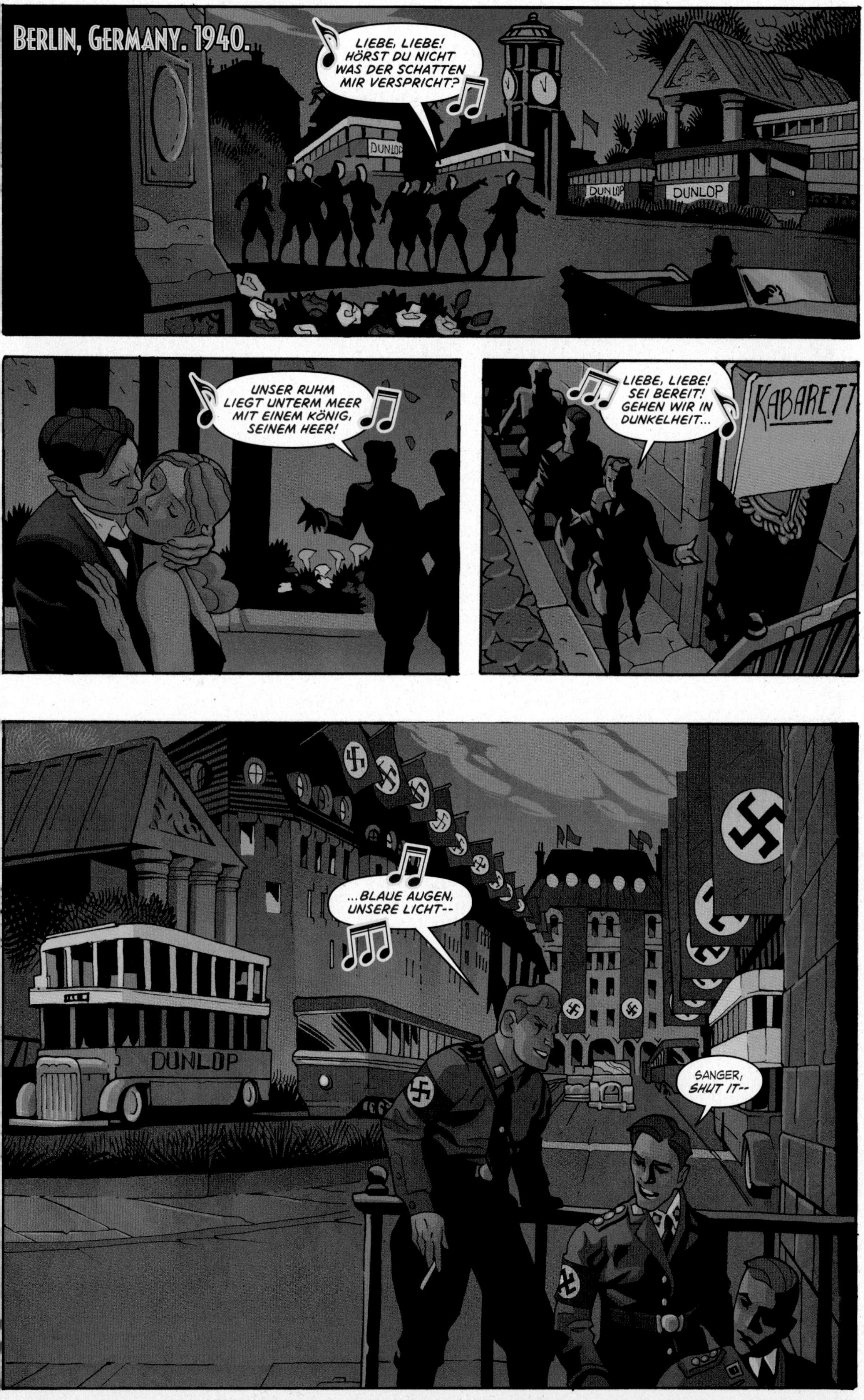
BERLIN, GERMANY. 1940.
LIEBE, LIEBE! HÖRST DU NICHT WAS DER SCHATTEN MIR VERSPRICHT?
DUNLOP
DUNLOP
DUNLOP
UNSER RUHM LIEGT UNTERM MEER MIT EINEM KÖNIG, SEINEM HEER!
LIEBE, LIEBE! SEI BEREIT! GEHEN WIR IN DUNKELHEIT...
KABARETT
...BLAUE AUGEN, UNSERE LICHT--
DUNLOP
SANGER, SHUT IT--

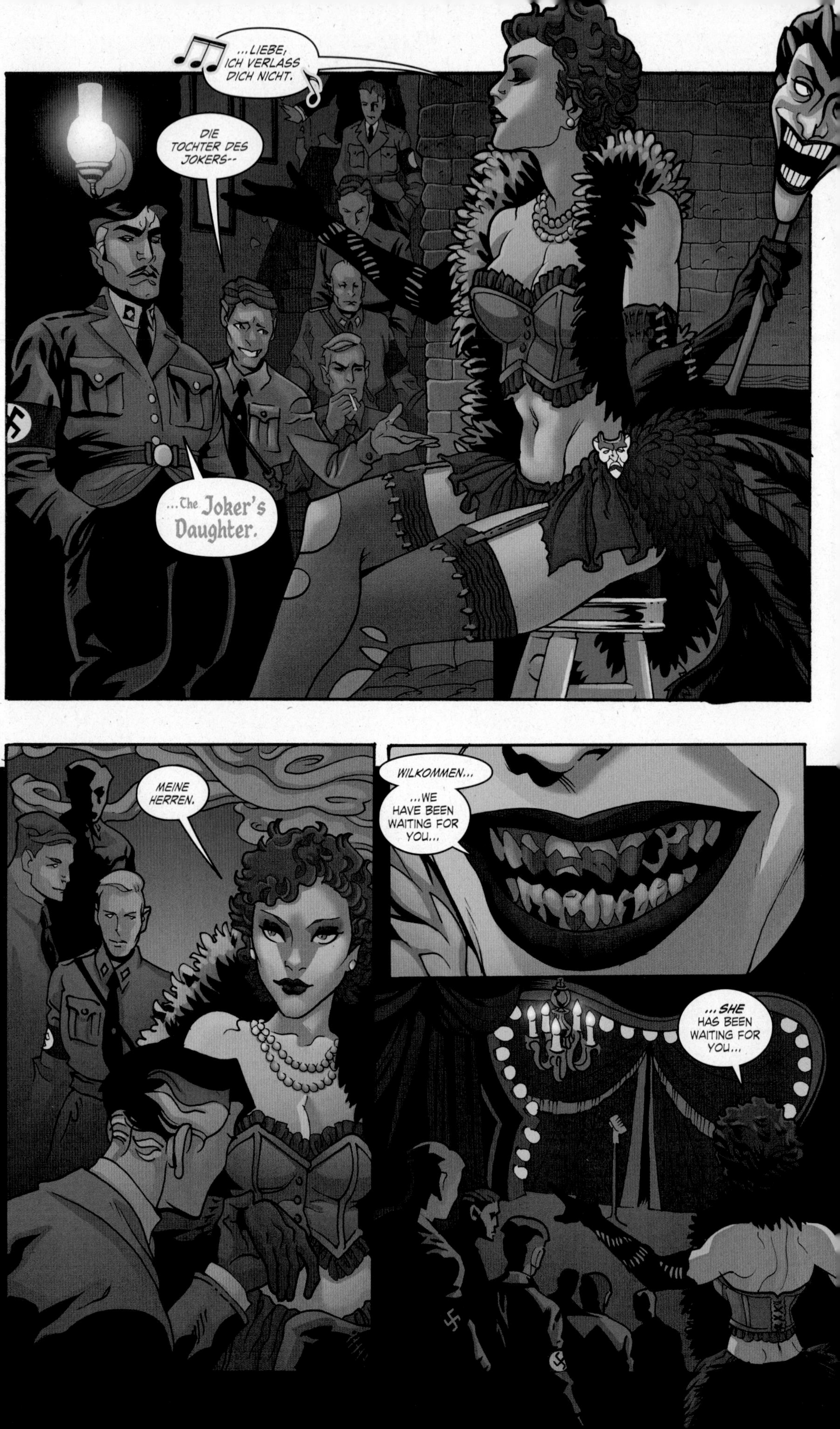
...LIEBE, ICH VERLASS DICH NICHT.
DIE TOCHTER DES JOKERS--
...The Joker's Daughter.
MEINE HERREN.
WILKOMMEN...
...WE HAVE BEEN WAITING FOR YOU...
...SHE HAS BEEN WAITING FOR YOU...

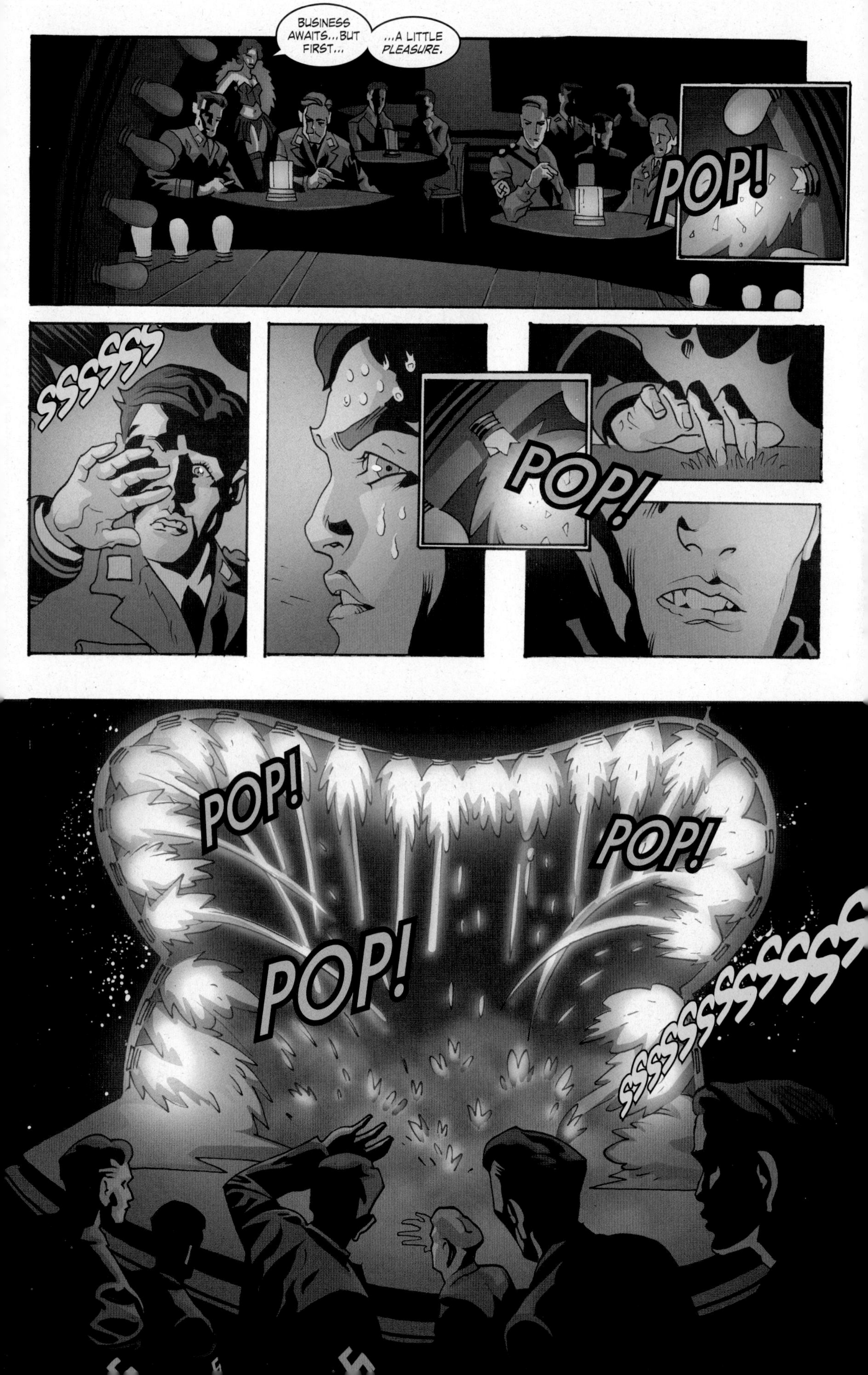
BUSINESS AWAITS... BUT FIRST...
...A LITTLE PLEASURE.
POP!
SSSSSS
POP!
POP!
POP!
POP!
SSSSSSSSSSSSS

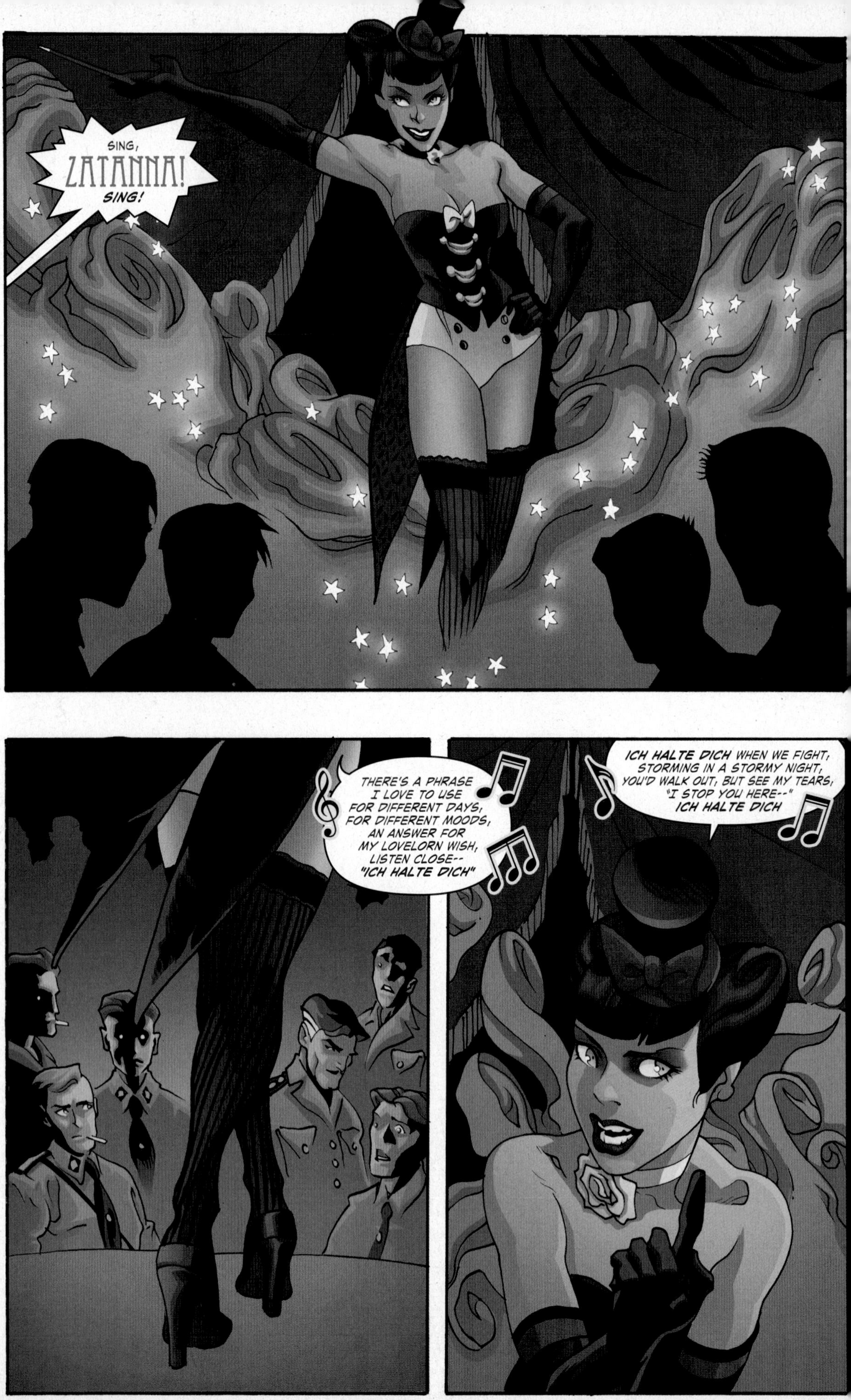
SING, ZATANNA! SING!
THERE'S A PHRASE I LOVE TO USE FOR DIFFERENT DAYS, FOR DIFFERENT MOODS, AN ANSWER FOR MY LOVELORN WISH, LISTEN CLOSE-- "ICH HALTE DICH"
ICH HALTE DICH WHEN WE FIGHT, STORMING IN A STORMY NIGHT, YOU'D WALK OUT, BUT SEE MY TEARS, "I STOP YOU HERE--" ICH HALTE DICH

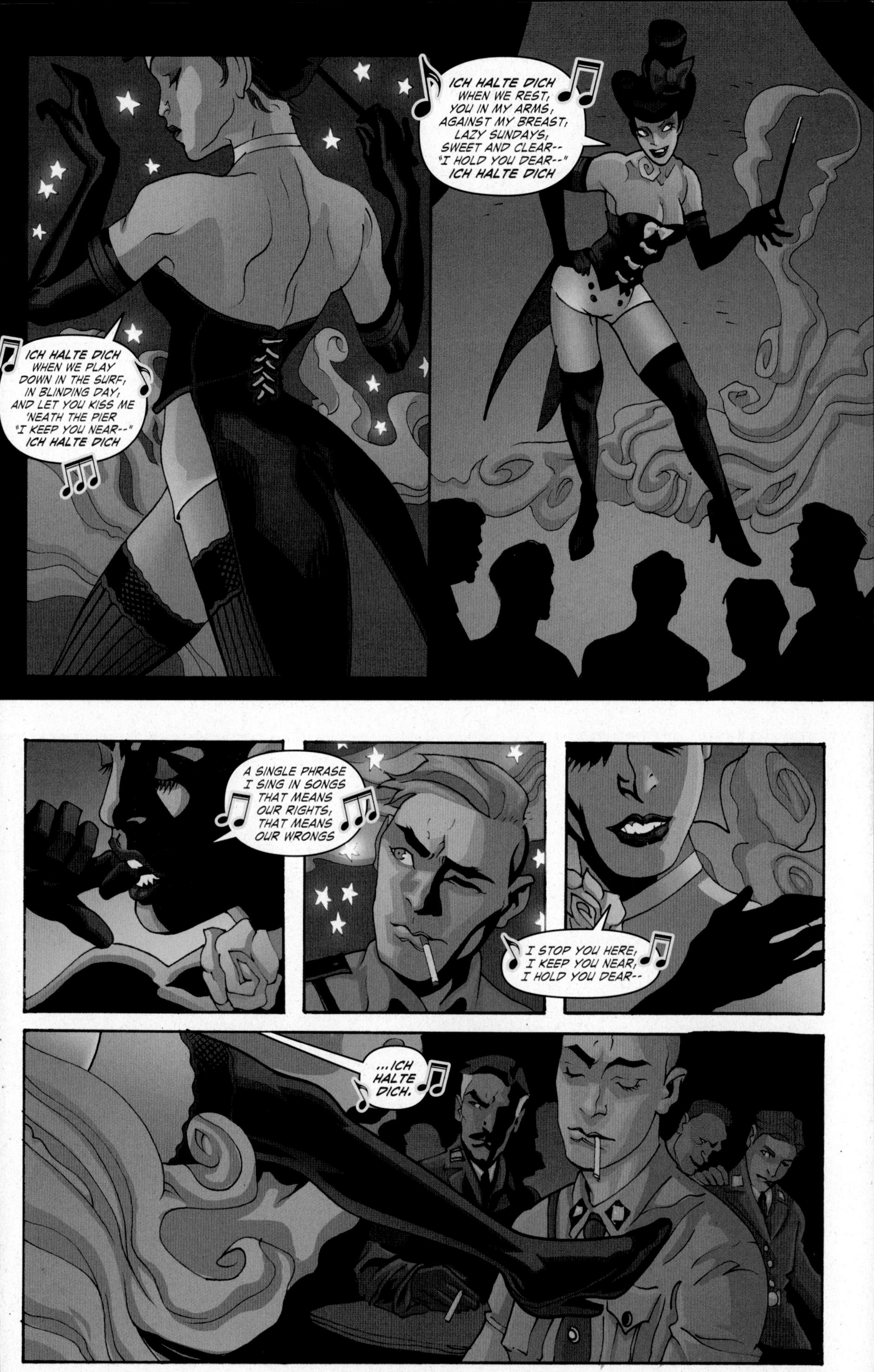
ICH HALTE DICH WHEN WE PLAY DOWN IN THE SURF, IN BLINDING DAY, AND LET YOU KISS ME 'NEATH THE PIER "I KEEP YOU NEAR--" ICH HALTE DICH
ICH HALTE DICH WHEN WE REST; YOU IN MY ARMS, AGAINST MY BREAST; LAZY SUNDAYS, SWEET AND CLEAR-- "I HOLD YOU DEAR--" ICH HALTE DICH
A SINGLE PHRASE I SING IN SONGS THAT MEANS OUR RIGHTS, THAT MEANS OUR WRONGS
I STOP YOU HERE, I KEEP YOU NEAR, I HOLD YOU DEAR--
...ICH HALTE DICH.

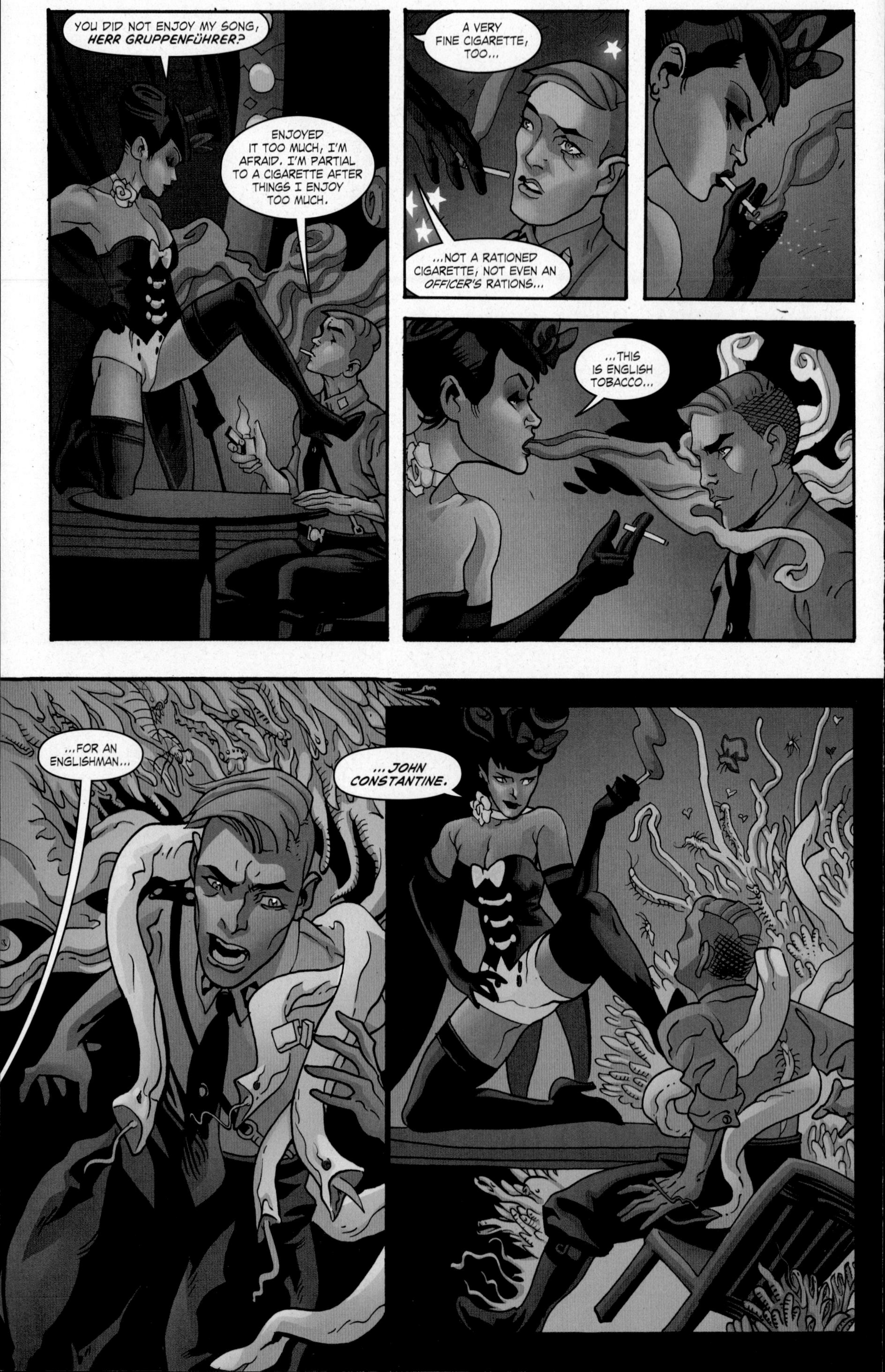
YOU DID NOT ENJOY MY SONG, HERR GRUPPENFÜHRER?
ENJOYED IT TOO MUCH, I'M AFRAID. I'M PARTIAL TO A CIGARETTE AFTER THINGS I ENJOY TOO MUCH.
A VERY FINE CIGARETTE, TOO...
...NOT A RATIONED CIGARETTE, NOT EVEN AN OFFICER'S RATIONS...
...THIS IS ENGLISH TOBACCO...
...FOR AN ENGLISHMAN...
...JOHN CONSTANTINE.

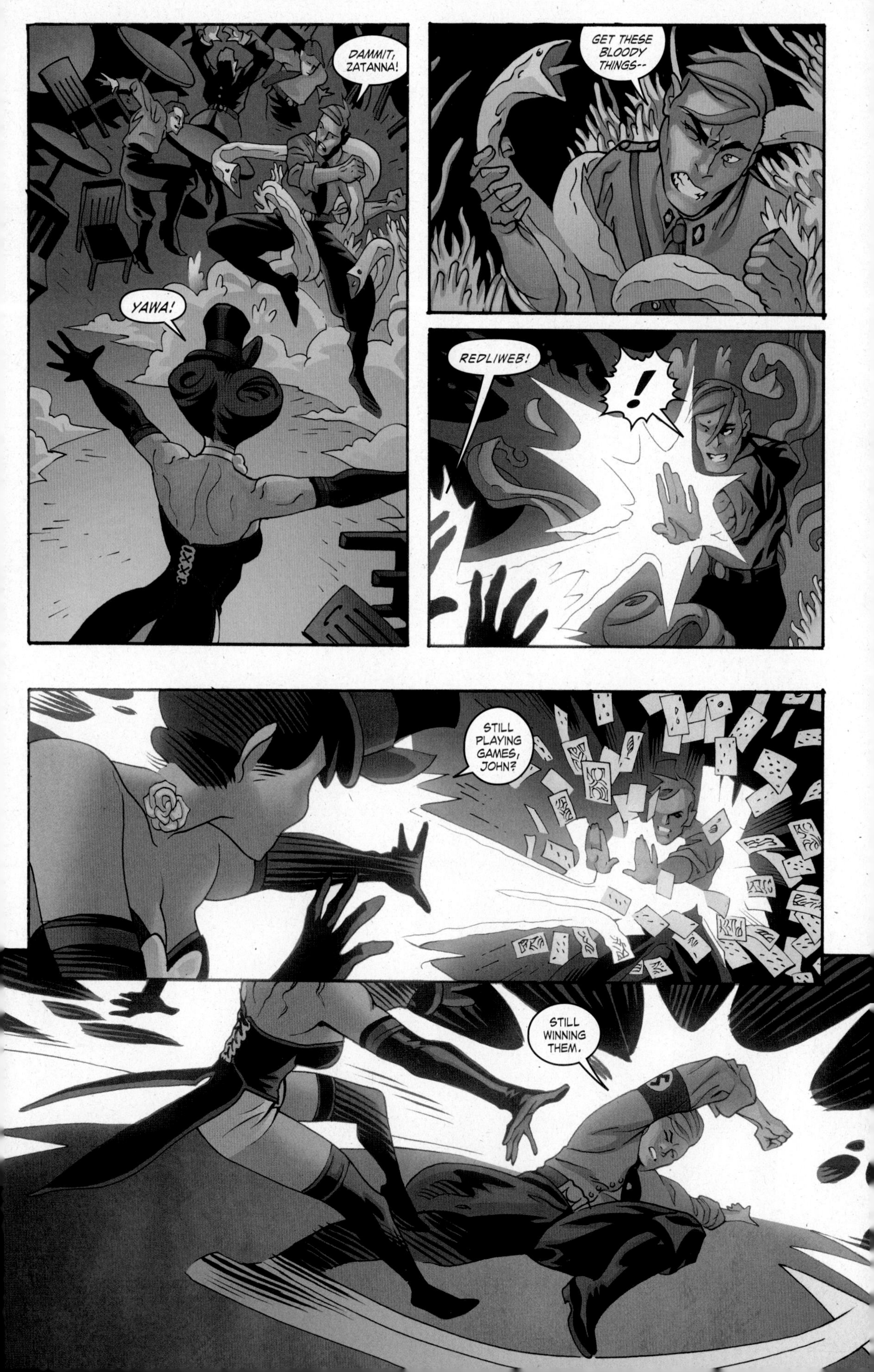
DAMMIT, ZATANNA!
YAWA!
GET THESE BLOODY THINGS--
REDLIWEB!
!
STILL PLAYING GAMES, JOHN?
STILL WINNING THEM.

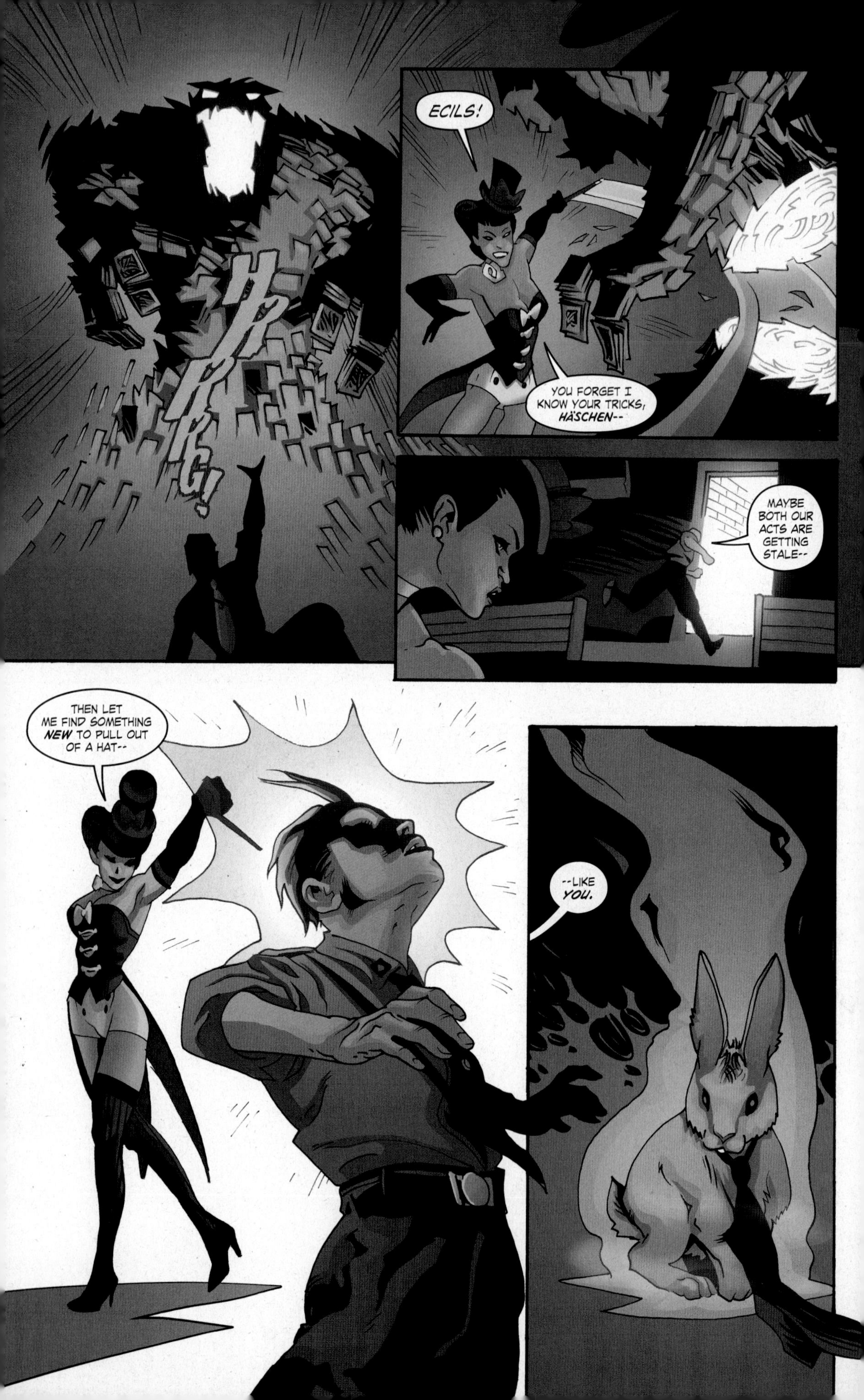
HAAARRRG!
ECILS!
YOU FORGET I KNOW YOUR TRICKS, HÄSCHEN--
MAYBE BOTH OUR ACTS ARE GETTING STALE--
THEN LET ME FIND SOMETHING NEW TO PULL OUT OF A HAT--
--LIKE YOU.

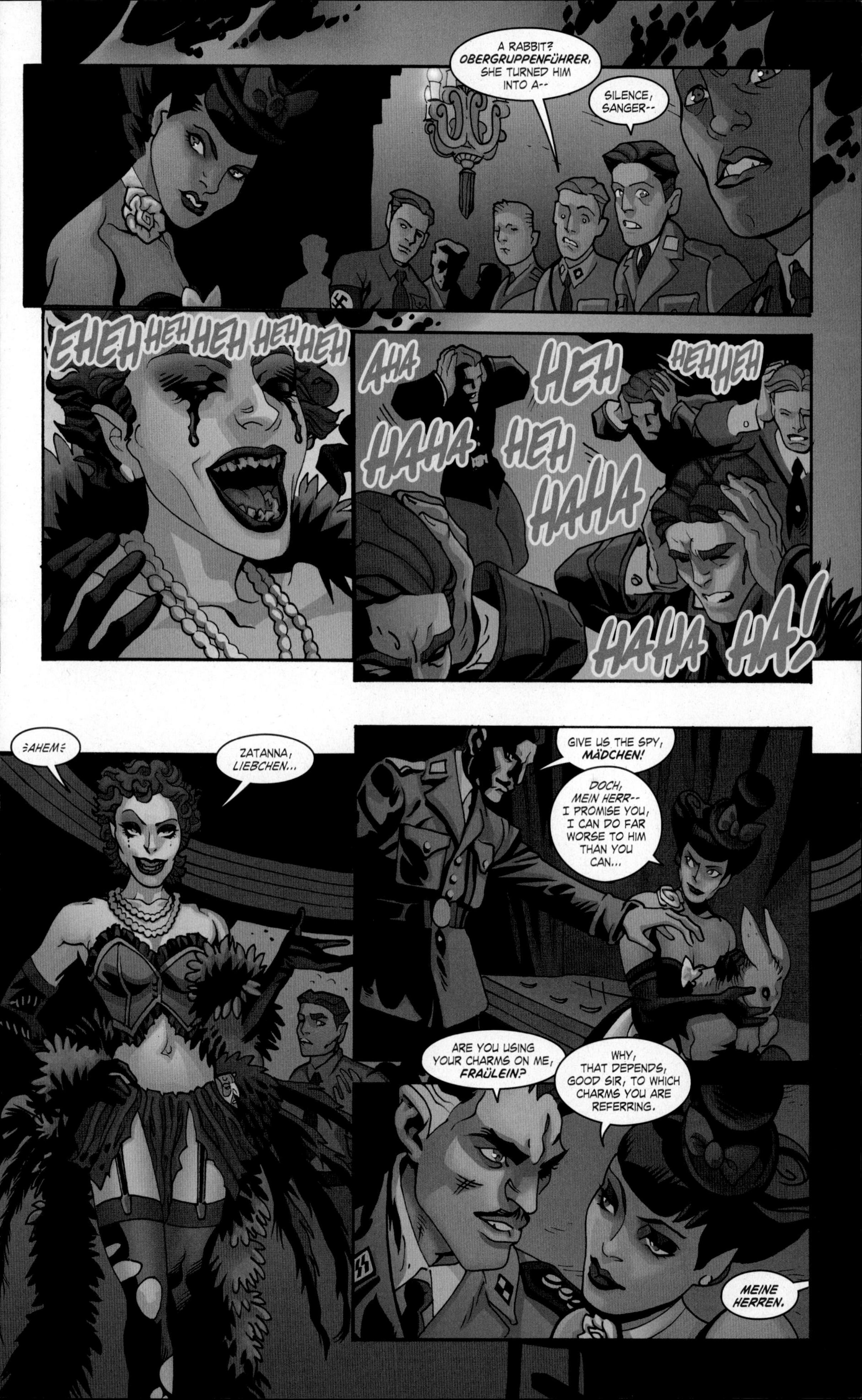

A RABBIT? OBERGRUPPENFÜHRER, SHE TURNED HIM INTO A--
SILENCE, SANGER--
EHEH HEH HEH HEH HEH
AHA HEH HEH HEH
HAHA HEH HAHA
HAHA HA!
AHEM
ZATANNA, LIEBCHEN...
GIVE US THE SPY, MÄDCHEN!
DOCH, MEIN HERR-- I PROMISE YOU, I CAN DO FAR WORSE TO HIM THAN YOU CAN...
ARE YOU USING YOUR CHARMS ON ME, FRAÜLEIN?
WHY, THAT DEPENDS, GOOD SIR, TO WHICH CHARMS YOU ARE REFERRING.
MEINE HERREN.

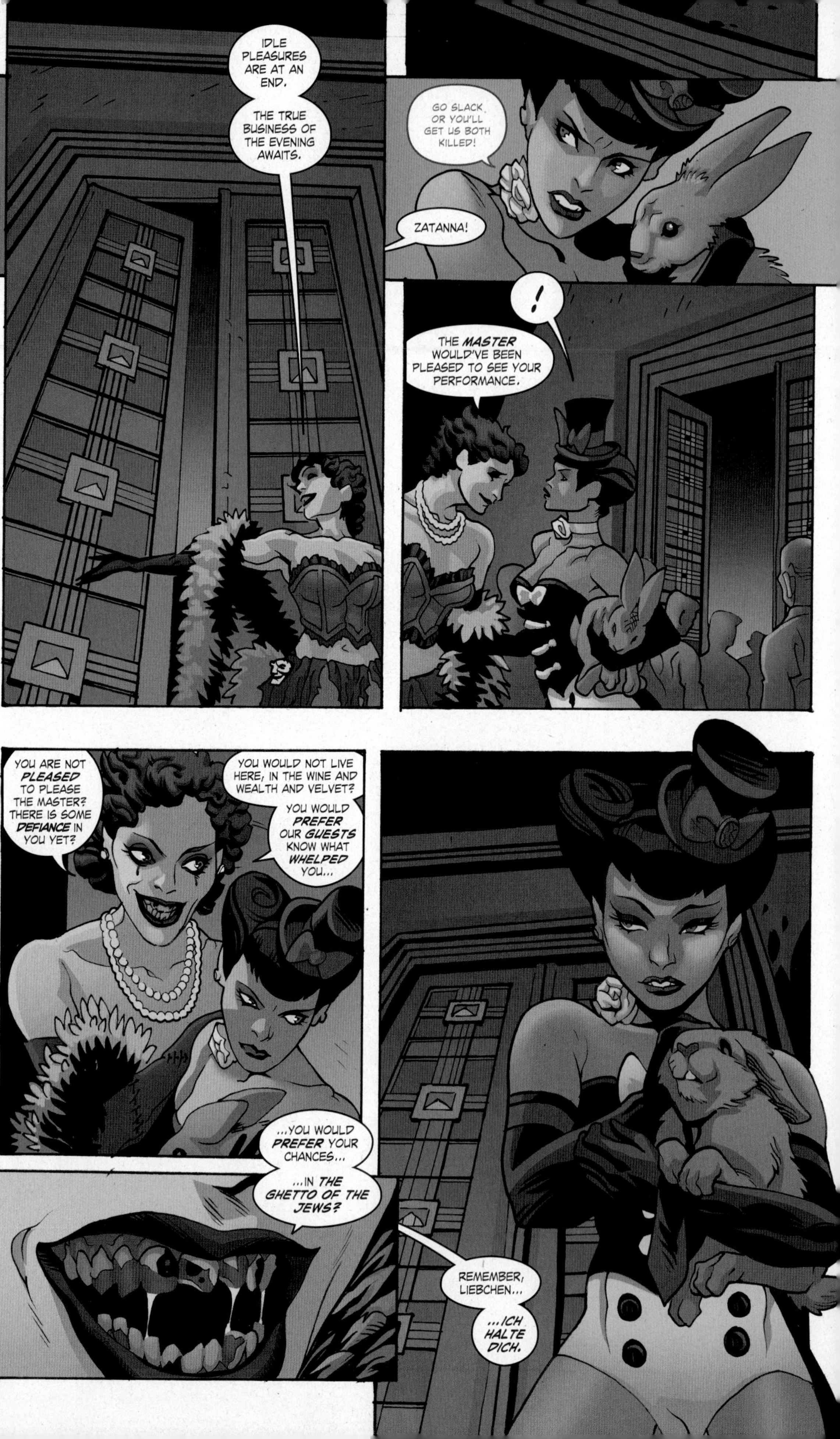
IDLE PLEASURES ARE AT AN END.
THE TRUE BUSINESS OF THE EVENING AWAITS.
ZATANNA!
GO SLACK, OR YOU'LL GET US BOTH KILLED!
!
THE MASTER WOULD'VE BEEN PLEASED TO SEE YOUR PERFORMANCE.
YOU ARE NOT PLEASED TO PLEASE THE MASTER? THERE IS SOME DEFIANCE IN YOU YET?
YOU WOULD NOT LIVE HERE, IN THE WINE AND WEALTH AND VELVET?
YOU WOULD PREFER OUR GUESTS KNOW WHAT WHELPED YOU...
...YOU WOULD PREFER YOUR CHANCES...
...IN THE GHETTO OF THE JEWS?
REMEMBER, LIEBCHEN...
...ICH HALTE DICH.

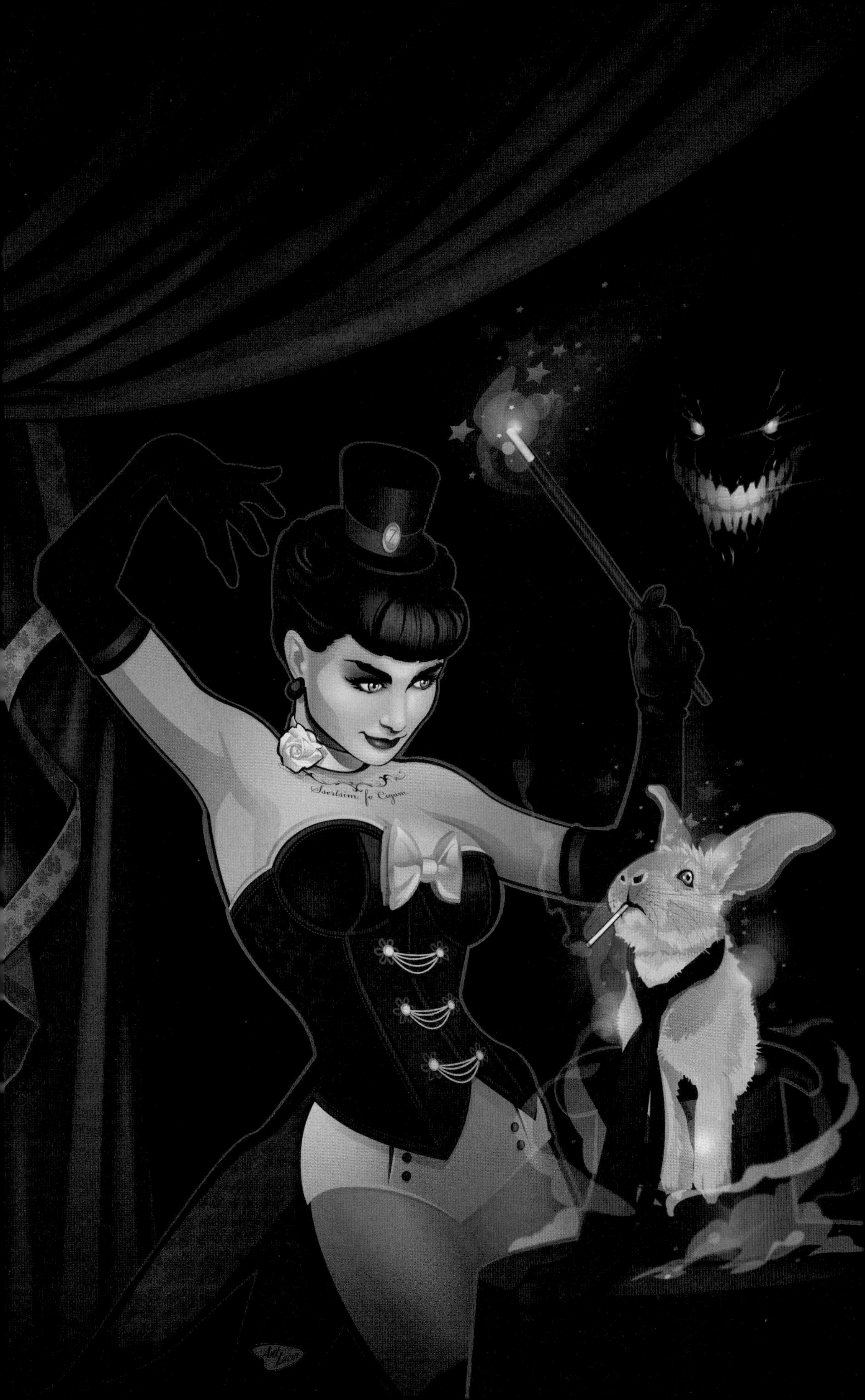
Ssertsim fo Cigam

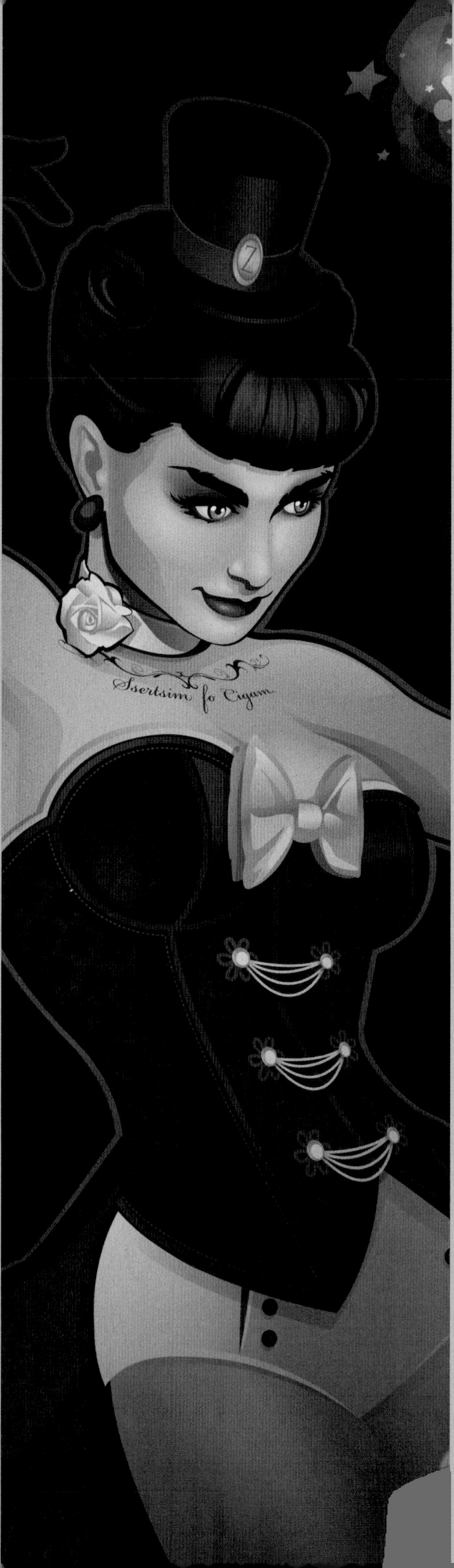
Ssertsim fo Cigam

# ENLISTED
## PART THREE

MARGUERITE BENNETT
*Writer*

MARGUERITE SAUVAGE
GARRY BROWN
LAURA BRAGA
*Artists*

MARGUERITE SAUVAGE
DOUG GARBARK
WENDY BROOME
*Colorists*

WES ABBOTT
*Letterer*

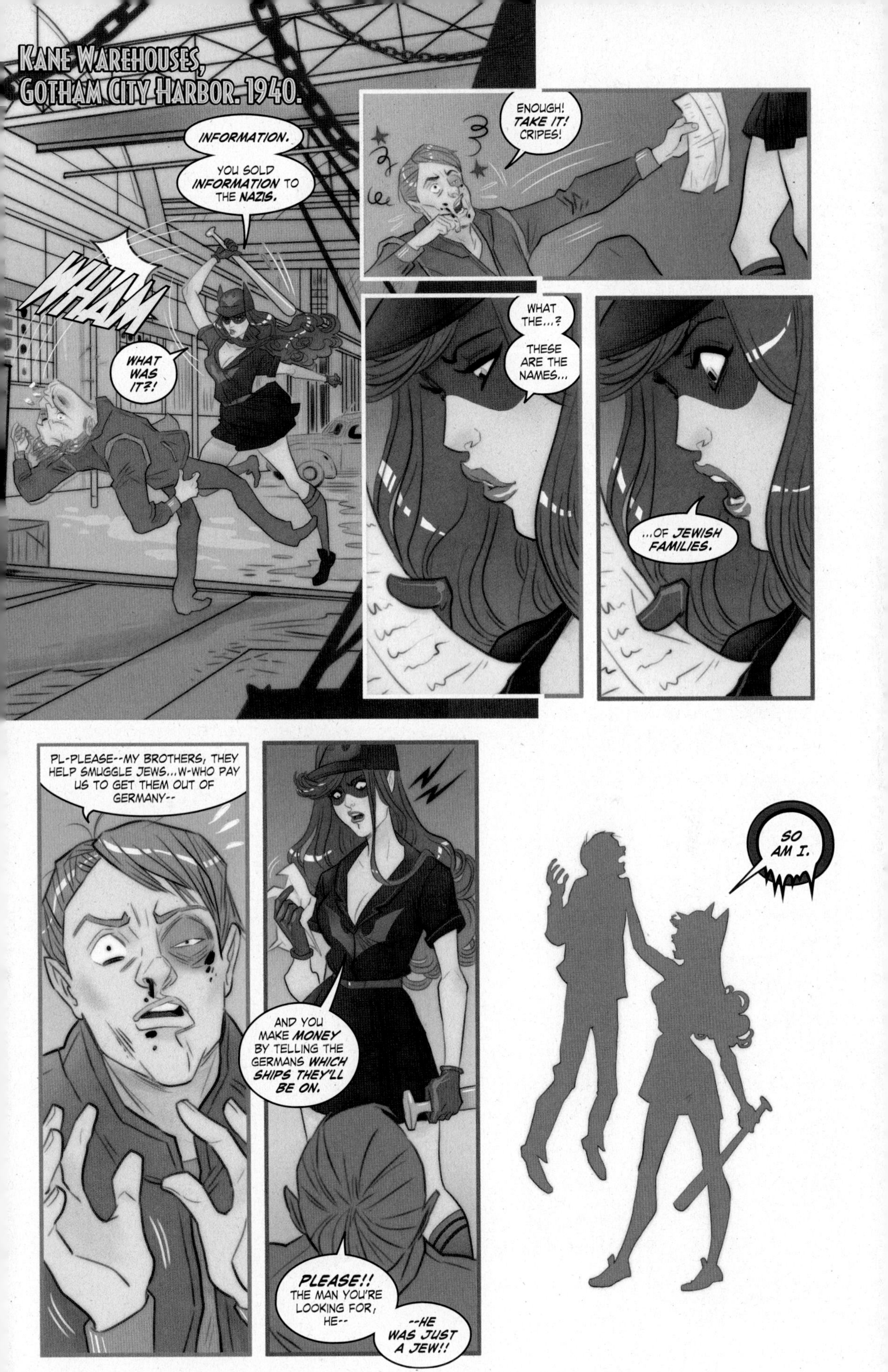
KANE WAREHOUSES, GOTHAM CITY HARBOR. 1940.
INFORMATION.
YOU SOLD INFORMATION TO THE NAZIS.
WHAM
WHAT WAS IT?!
ENOUGH! TAKE IT! CRIPES!
WHAT THE...?
THESE ARE THE NAMES...
...OF JEWISH FAMILIES.
PL-PLEASE--MY BROTHERS, THEY HELP SMUGGLE JEWS...W-WHO PAY US TO GET THEM OUT OF GERMANY--
AND YOU MAKE MONEY BY TELLING THE GERMANS WHICH SHIPS THEY'LL BE ON.
PLEASE!! THE MAN YOU'RE LOOKING FOR, HE--
--HE WAS JUST A JEW!!
SO AM I.

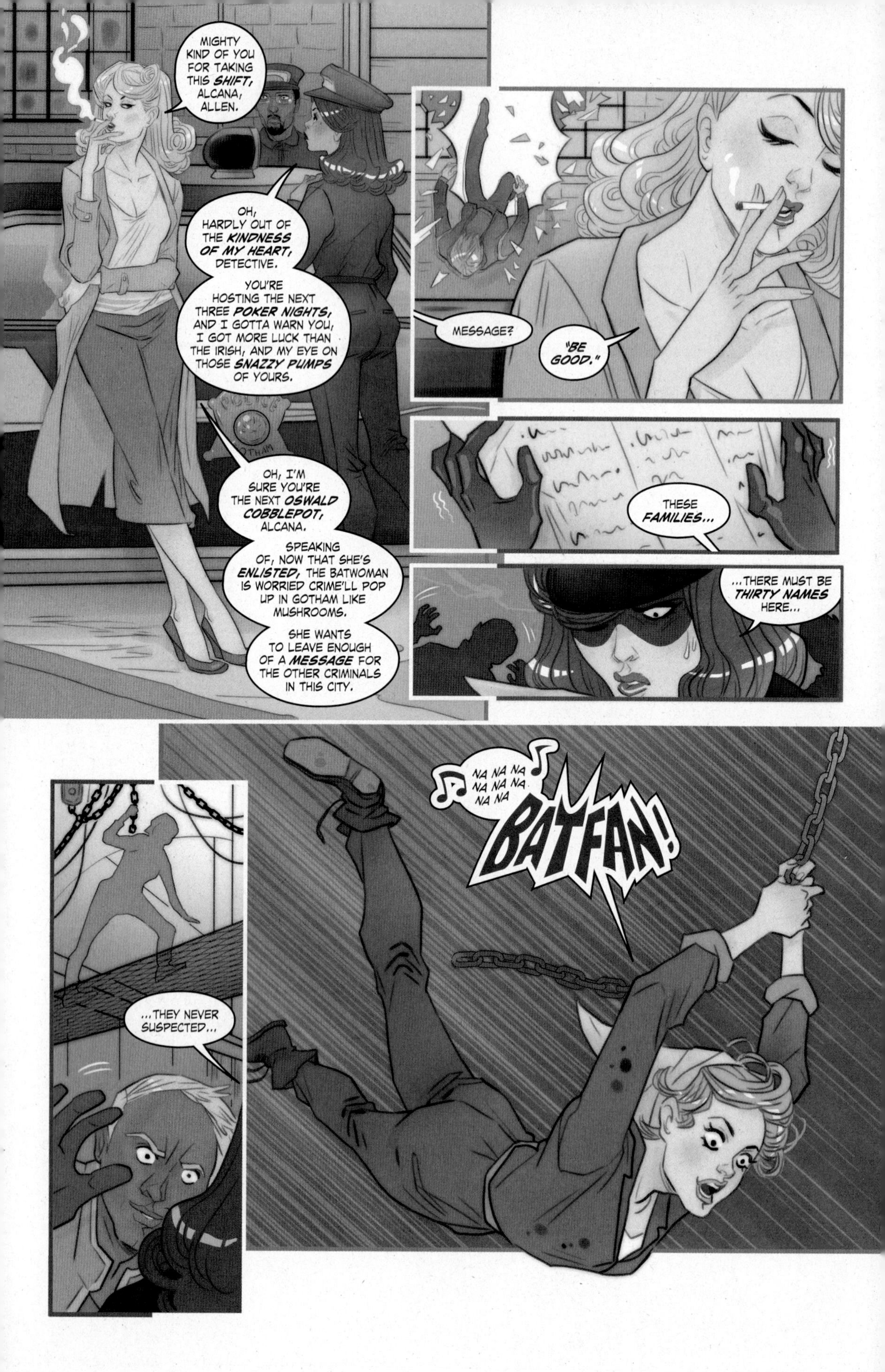
MIGHTY KIND OF YOU FOR TAKING THIS SHIFT, ALCANA, ALLEN.
OH, HARDLY OUT OF THE KINDNESS OF MY HEART, DETECTIVE.
YOU'RE HOSTING THE NEXT THREE POKER NIGHTS, AND I GOTTA WARN YOU, I GOT MORE LUCK THAN THE IRISH, AND MY EYE ON THOSE SNAZZY PUMPS OF YOURS.
OH, I'M SURE YOU'RE THE NEXT OSWALD COBBLEPOT, ALCANA.
SPEAKING OF, NOW THAT SHE'S ENLISTED, THE BATWOMAN IS WORRIED CRIME'LL POP UP IN GOTHAM LIKE MUSHROOMS.
SHE WANTS TO LEAVE ENOUGH OF A MESSAGE FOR THE OTHER CRIMINALS IN THIS CITY.
MESSAGE?
"BE GOOD."
THESE FAMILIES...
...THERE MUST BE THIRTY NAMES HERE...
...THEY NEVER SUSPECTED...
NA NA NA NA NA NA NA NA
BATFAN!

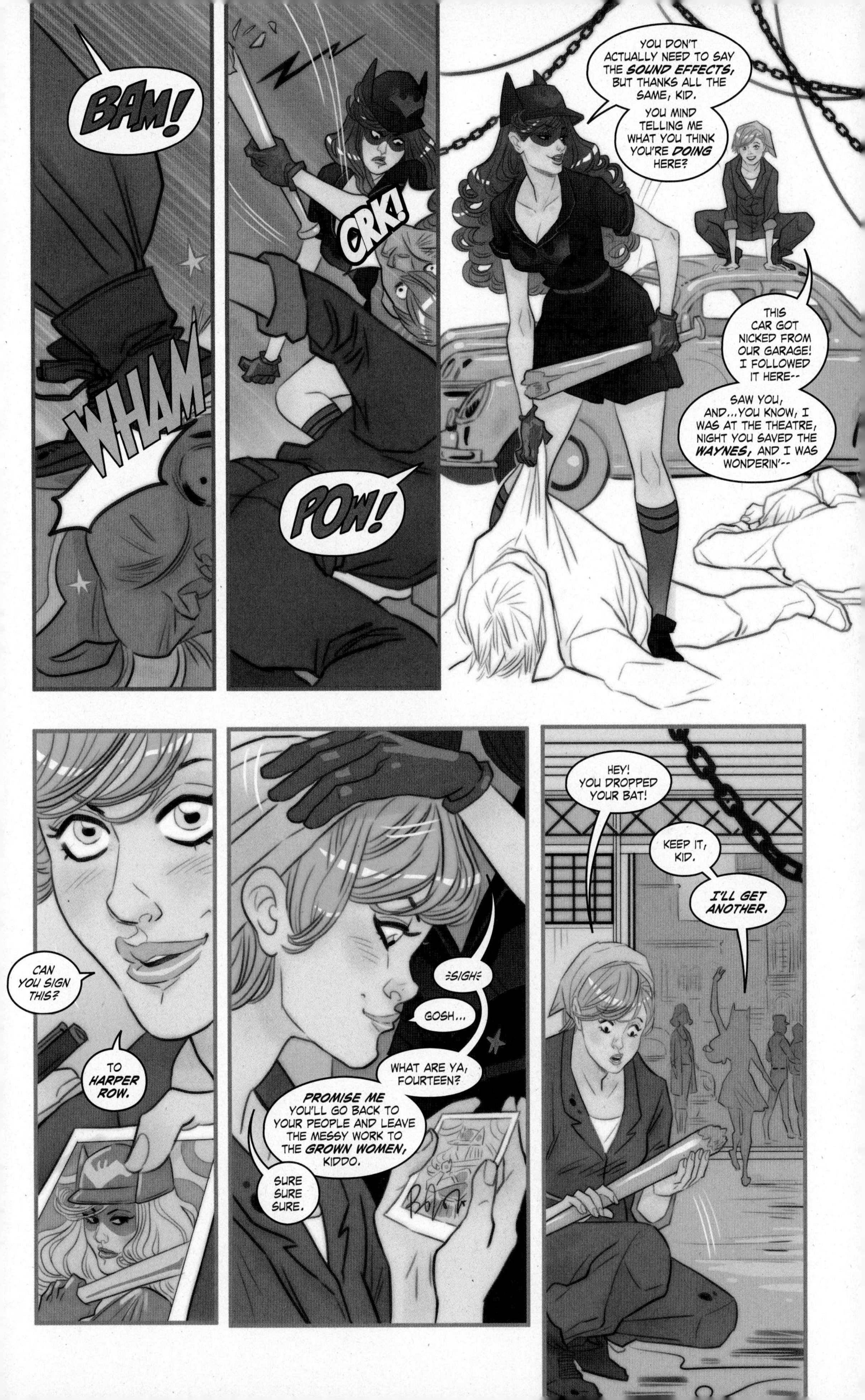
BAM!
ZZ
CRK!
WHAM
POW!
YOU DON'T ACTUALLY NEED TO SAY THE SOUND EFFECTS, BUT THANKS ALL THE SAME, KID.
YOU MIND TELLING ME WHAT YOU THINK YOU'RE DOING HERE?
THIS CAR GOT NICKED FROM OUR GARAGE! I FOLLOWED IT HERE--
SAW YOU, AND...YOU KNOW, I WAS AT THE THEATRE, NIGHT YOU SAVED THE WAYNES, AND I WAS WONDERIN'--
CAN YOU SIGN THIS?
TO HARPER ROW.
SIGH
GOSH...
WHAT ARE YA, FOURTEEN?
PROMISE ME YOU'LL GO BACK TO YOUR PEOPLE AND LEAVE THE MESSY WORK TO THE GROWN WOMEN, KIDDO.
SURE SURE SURE.
HEY! YOU DROPPED YOUR BAT!
KEEP IT, KID.
I'LL GET ANOTHER.

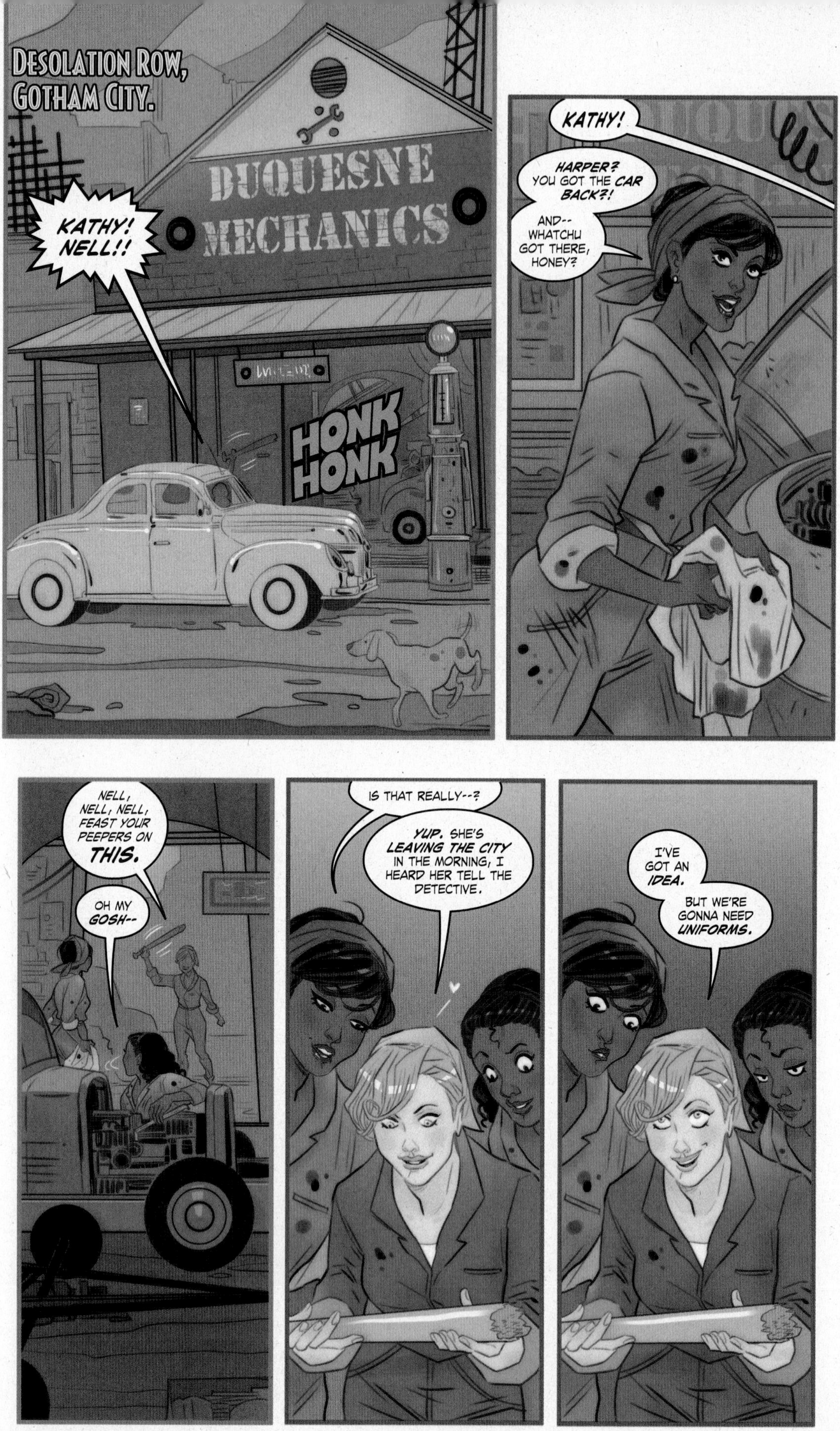
DESOLATION ROW, GOTHAM CITY.
DUQUESNE MECHANICS
KATHY! NELL!!
HONK HONK
KATHY!
HARPER? YOU GOT THE CAR BACK?!
AND-- WHATCHU GOT THERE, HONEY?
NELL, NELL, NELL, FEAST YOUR PEEPERS ON THIS.
OH MY GOSH--
IS THAT REALLY--?
YUP. SHE'S LEAVING THE CITY IN THE MORNING, I HEARD HER TELL THE DETECTIVE.
I'VE GOT AN IDEA.
BUT WE'RE GONNA NEED UNIFORMS.

**COBBLEPOT BOARDWALK.**

COME ON, KATYDID. IT'S THE FOURTH OF JULY.

THE SMOKE'S FROM *FIREWORKS,* NOT THE *STORM CLOUD* YOU GOT HANGING OVER YOU. AND WITH ALCANA AND ALLEN HANDLING THOSE *SMUGGLERS*--

I'M SORRY, MAGS.

*MY LAST NIGHT IN GOTHAM...* I DIDN'T MEAN TO SPEND IT WITH GANGSTERS.

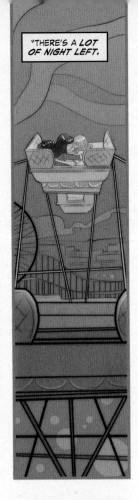

"THERE'S A *LOT* OF NIGHT LEFT.

"LET'S MAKE IT *COUNT.*

"YOU AND ME...

"...AND *NOT* THE *BATWOMAN.*"

THIS WAS...*THE PERFECT* NIGHT.

I THINK YOU'RE CALLING THAT A *LITTLE* EARLY.

YOU WERE RIGHT.

HA HAHA.

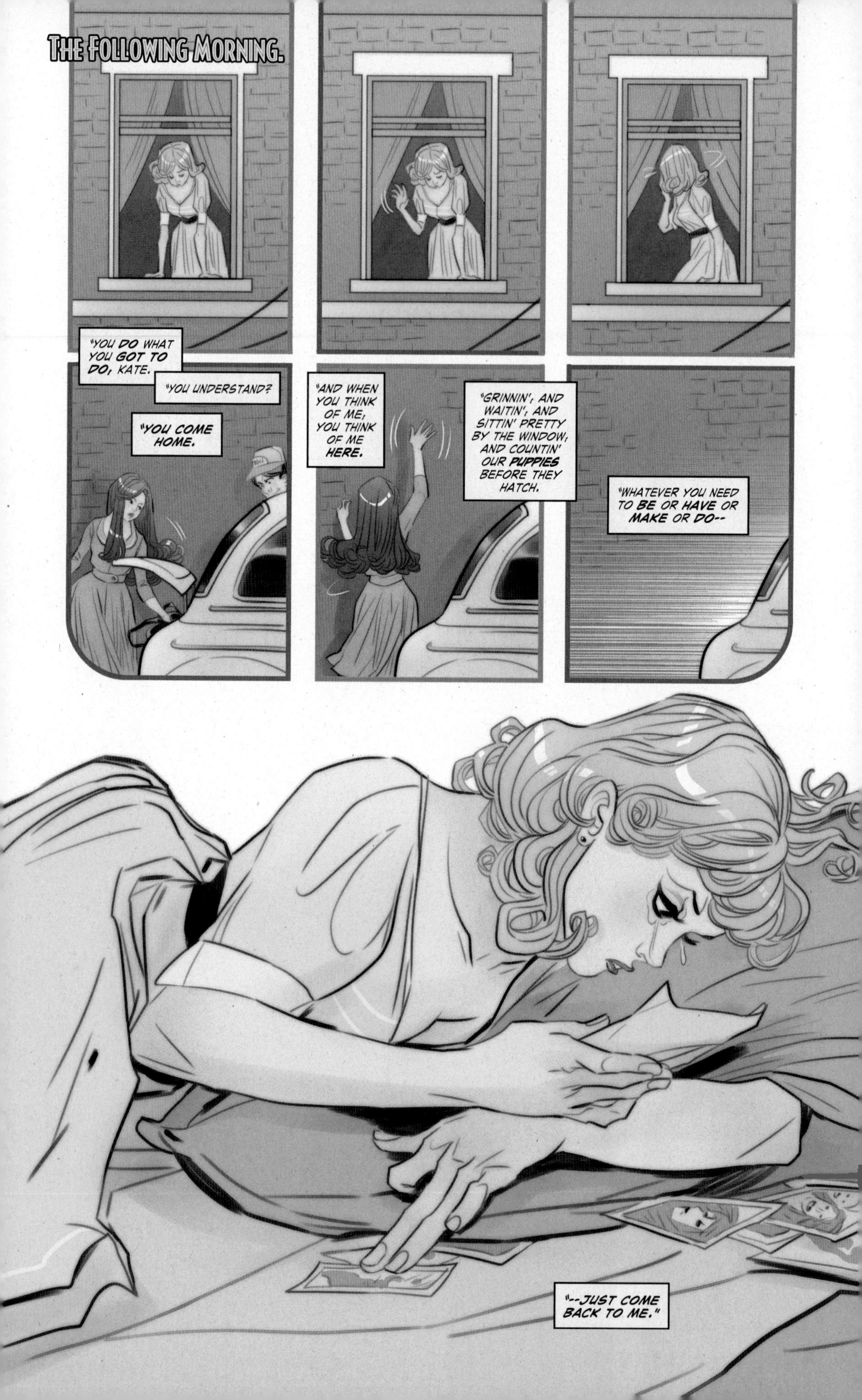
THE FOLLOWING MORNING.
"YOU DO WHAT YOU GOT TO DO, KATE.
"YOU UNDERSTAND?
"YOU COME HOME.
"AND WHEN YOU THINK OF ME, YOU THINK OF ME HERE.
"GRINNIN', AND WAITIN', AND SITTIN' PRETTY BY THE WINDOW, AND COUNTIN' OUR PUPPIES BEFORE THEY HATCH.
"WHATEVER YOU NEED TO BE OR HAVE OR MAKE OR DO--
"--JUST COME BACK TO ME."

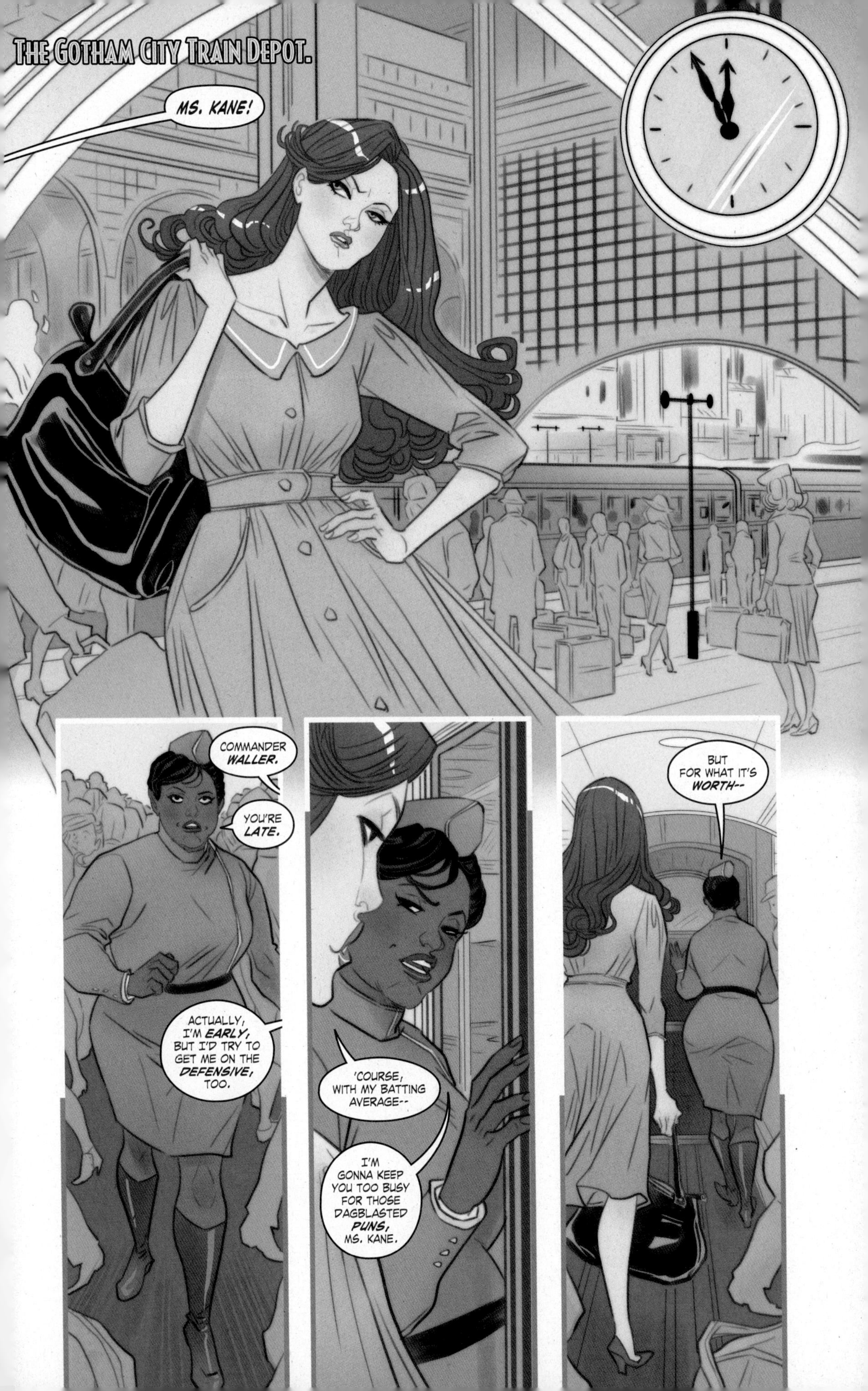
THE GOTHAM CITY TRAIN DEPOT.
MS. KANE!
COMMANDER WALLER.
YOU'RE LATE.
ACTUALLY, I'M EARLY, BUT I'D TRY TO GET ME ON THE DEFENSIVE, TOO.
'COURSE, WITH MY BATTING AVERAGE--
I'M GONNA KEEP YOU TOO BUSY FOR THOSE DAGBLASTED PUNS, MS. KANE.
BUT FOR WHAT IT'S WORTH--

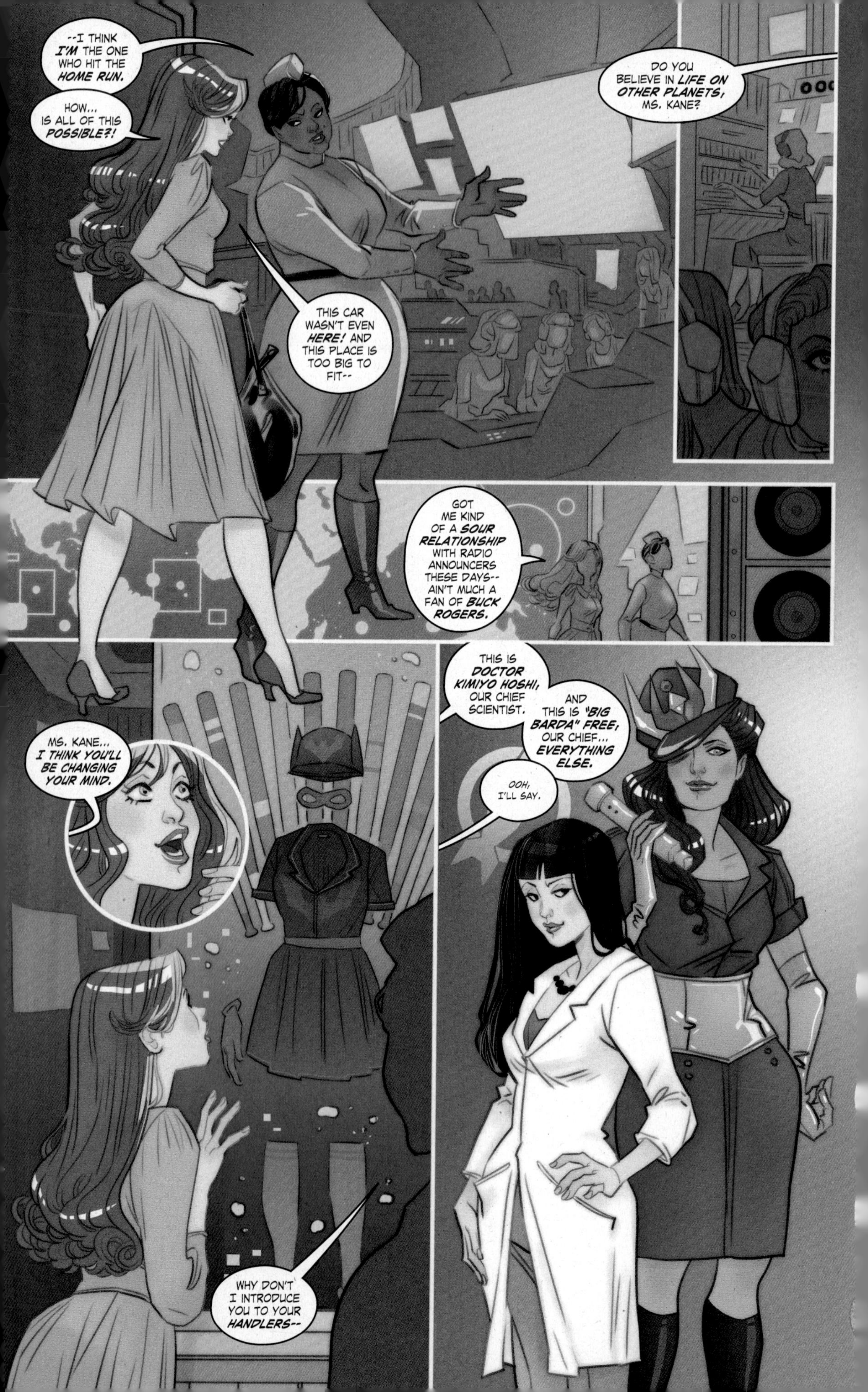
--I THINK I'M THE ONE WHO HIT THE HOME RUN.
HOW... IS ALL OF THIS POSSIBLE?!
THIS CAR WASN'T EVEN HERE! AND THIS PLACE IS TOO BIG TO FIT--
DO YOU BELIEVE IN LIFE ON OTHER PLANETS, MS. KANE?
GOT ME KIND OF A SOUR RELATIONSHIP WITH RADIO ANNOUNCERS THESE DAYS-- AIN'T MUCH A FAN OF BUCK ROGERS.
MS. KANE... I THINK YOU'LL BE CHANGING YOUR MIND.
WHY DON'T I INTRODUCE YOU TO YOUR HANDLERS--
THIS IS DOCTOR KIMIYO HOSHI, OUR CHIEF SCIENTIST.
AND THIS IS "BIG BARDA" FREE, OUR CHIEF... EVERYTHING ELSE.
OOH, I'LL SAY.

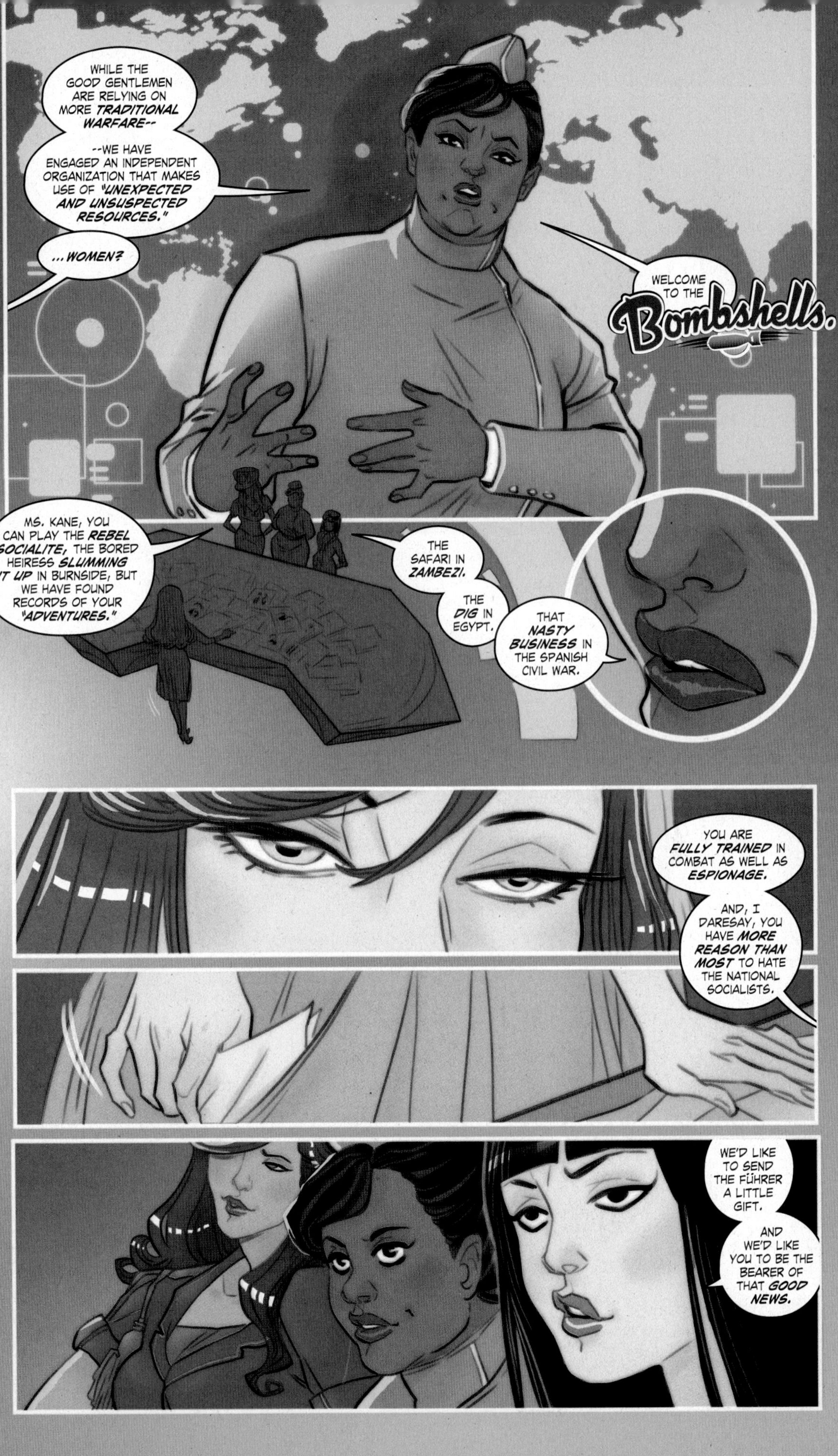
WHILE THE GOOD GENTLEMEN ARE RELYING ON MORE TRADITIONAL WARFARE--
--WE HAVE ENGAGED AN INDEPENDENT ORGANIZATION THAT MAKES USE OF "UNEXPECTED AND UNSUSPECTED RESOURCES."
...WOMEN?
WELCOME TO THE
Bombshells.
MS. KANE, YOU CAN PLAY THE REBEL SOCIALITE, THE BORED HEIRESS SLUMMING IT UP IN BURNSIDE, BUT WE HAVE FOUND RECORDS OF YOUR "ADVENTURES."
THE SAFARI IN ZAMBEZI.
THE DIG IN EGYPT.
THAT NASTY BUSINESS IN THE SPANISH CIVIL WAR.
YOU ARE FULLY TRAINED IN COMBAT AS WELL AS ESPIONAGE.
AND, I DARESAY, YOU HAVE MORE REASON THAN MOST TO HATE THE NATIONAL SOCIALISTS.
WE'D LIKE TO SEND THE FÜHRER A LITTLE GIFT.
AND WE'D LIKE YOU TO BE THE BEARER OF THAT GOOD NEWS.

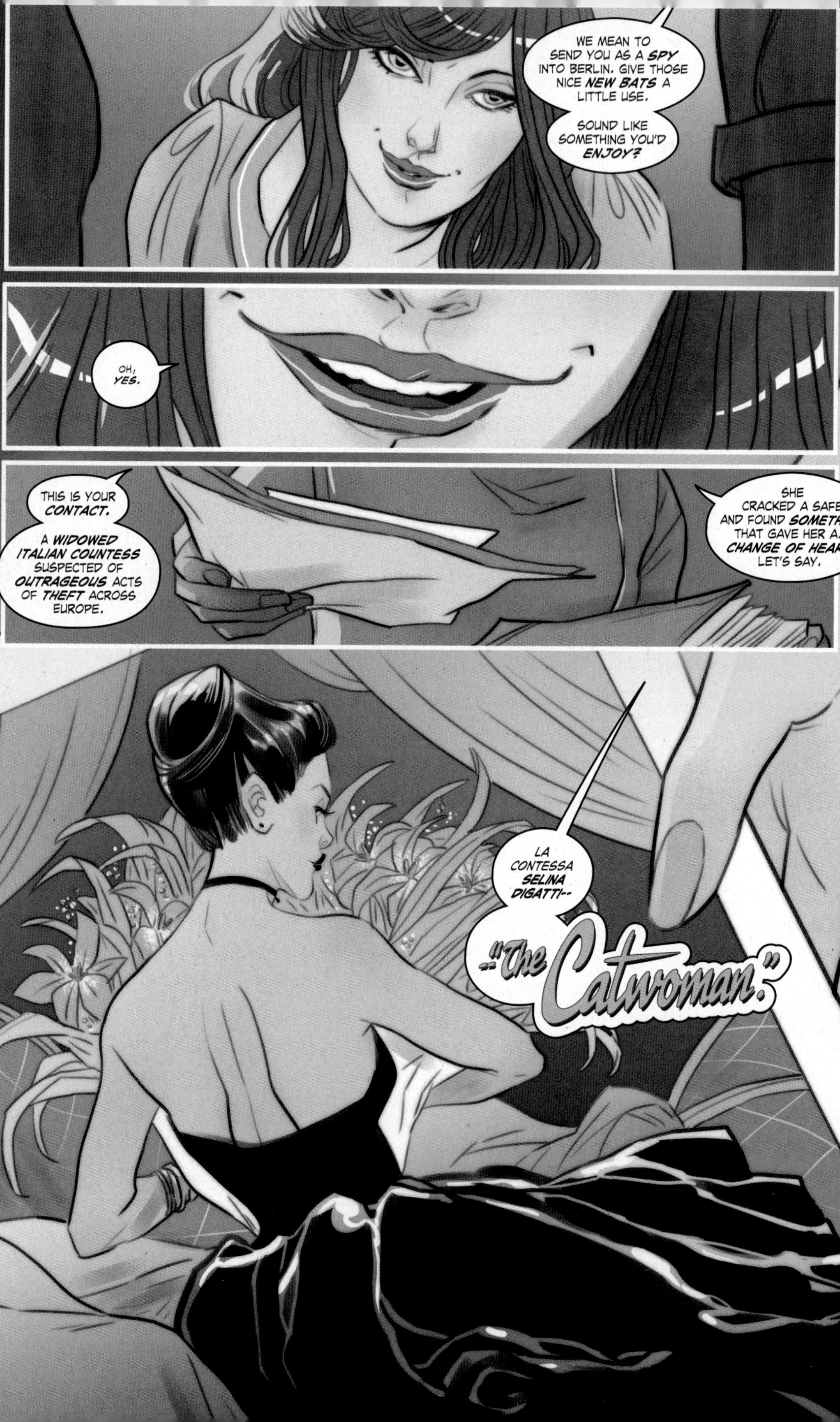
WE MEAN TO SEND YOU AS A SPY INTO BERLIN. GIVE THOSE NICE NEW BATS A LITTLE USE.
SOUND LIKE SOMETHING YOU'D ENJOY?
OH, YES.
THIS IS YOUR CONTACT.
A WIDOWED ITALIAN COUNTESS SUSPECTED OF OUTRAGEOUS ACTS OF THEFT ACROSS EUROPE.
SHE CRACKED A SAFE AND FOUND SOMETHING THAT GAVE HER A... CHANGE OF HEART, LET'S SAY.
LA CONTESSA SELINA DIGATTI--
--"The Catwoman."

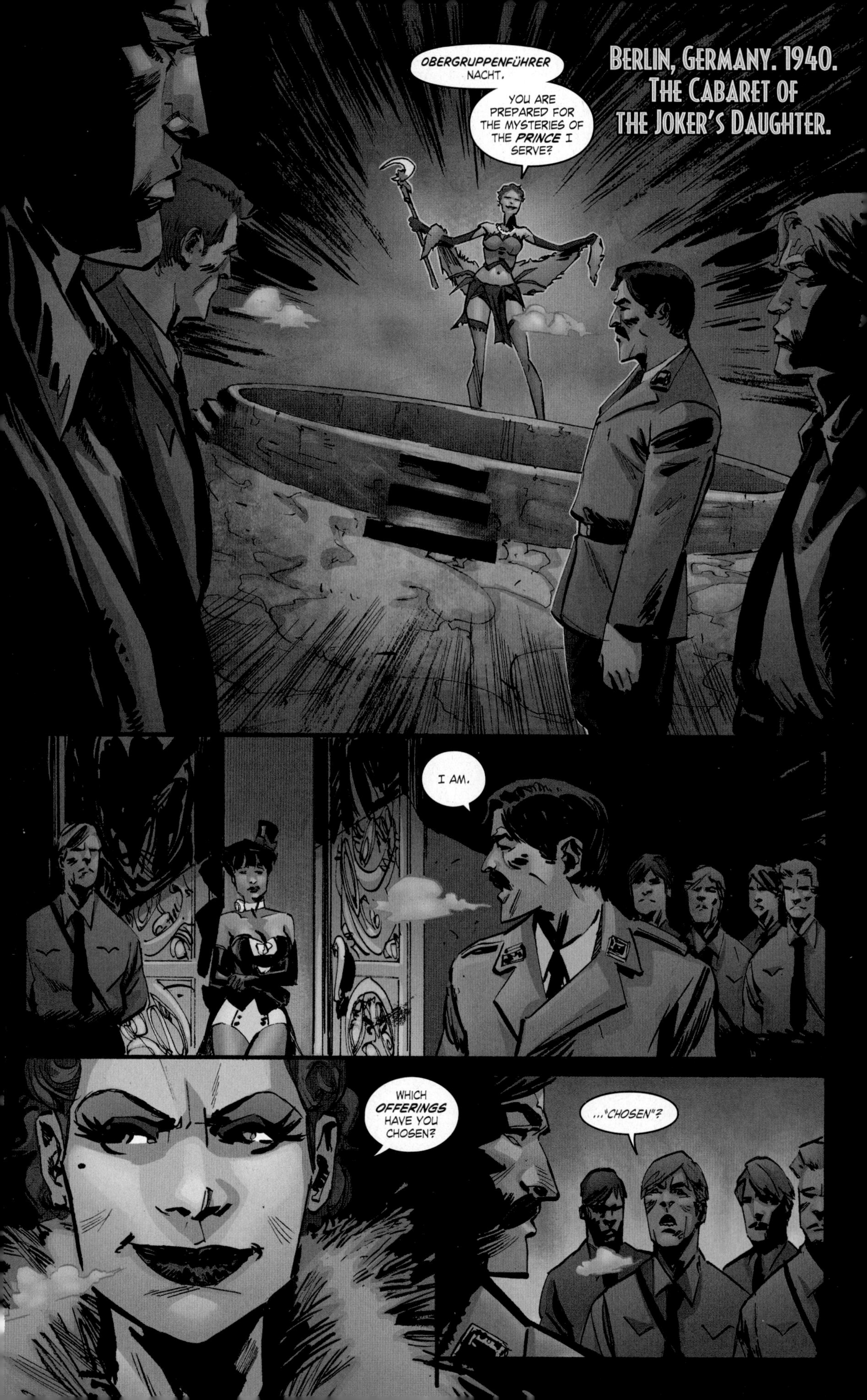
BERLIN, GERMANY. 1940.
THE CABARET OF THE JOKER'S DAUGHTER.
OBERGRUPPENFÜHRER NACHT.
YOU ARE PREPARED FOR THE MYSTERIES OF THE PRINCE I SERVE?
I AM.
WHICH OFFERINGS HAVE YOU CHOSEN?
..."CHOSEN"?

NO! NACHT, NO--!

¿HURG¿

A PITY ABOUT *YOU*, BOY. YOU DID HAVE A *LOVELY* VOICE.

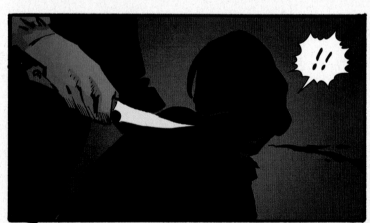

!!

TSSSSS

TSSSSS

WE WILL SOON MARCH TO A *DIFFERENT* DRUMMER.

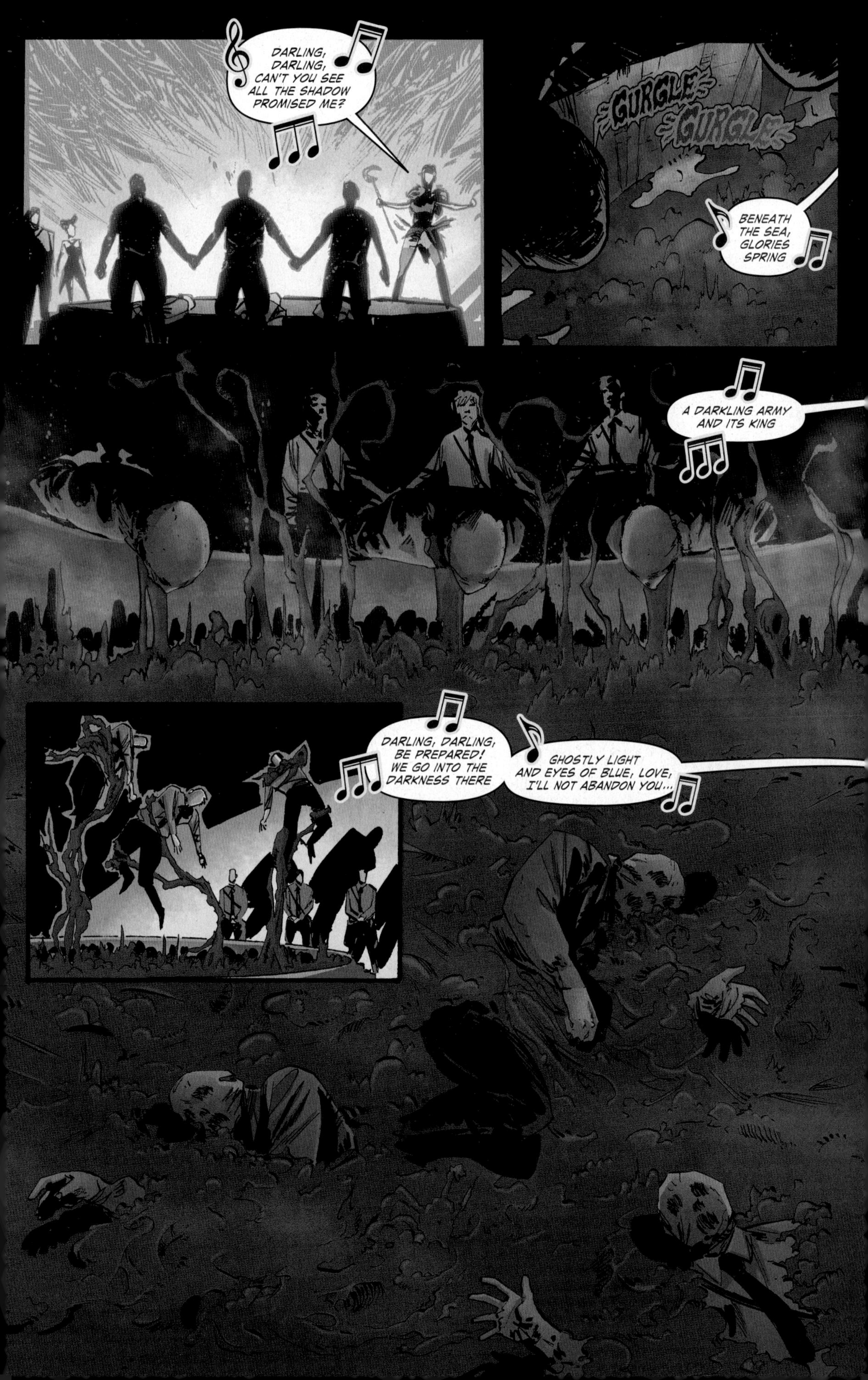
DARLING, DARLING, CAN'T YOU SEE ALL THE SHADOW PROMISED ME?
GURGLE GURGLE
BENEATH THE SEA, GLORIES SPRING
A DARKLING ARMY AND ITS KING
DARLING, DARLING, BE PREPARED! WE GO INTO THE DARKNESS THERE
GHOSTLY LIGHT AND EYES OF BLUE, LOVE, I'LL NOT ABANDON YOU...

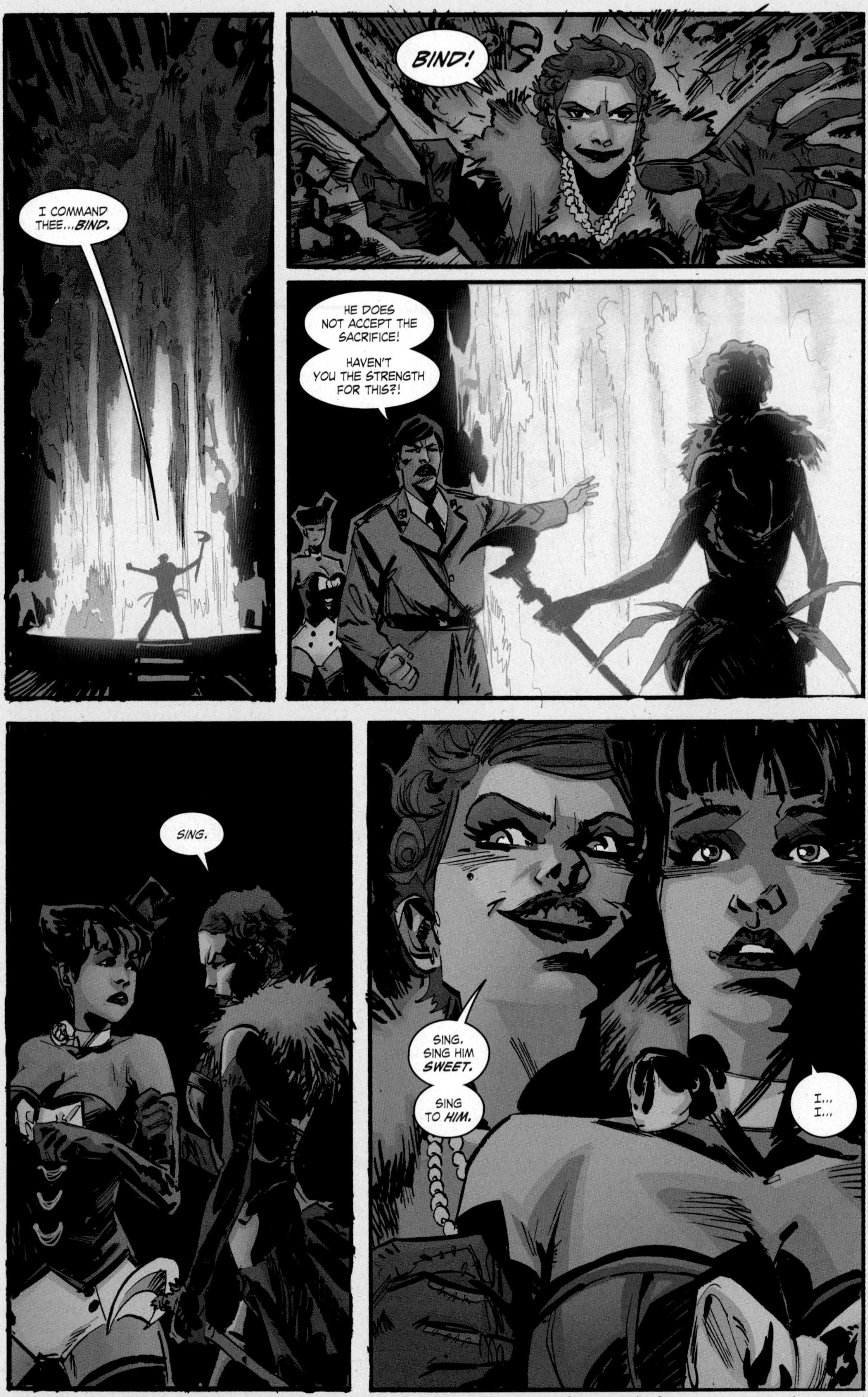
I COMMAND THEE...*BIND.*
*BIND!*
HE DOES NOT ACCEPT THE SACRIFICE!
HAVEN'T YOU THE STRENGTH FOR THIS?!
SING.
SING. SING HIM *SWEET.*
SING TO *HIM.*
I... I...

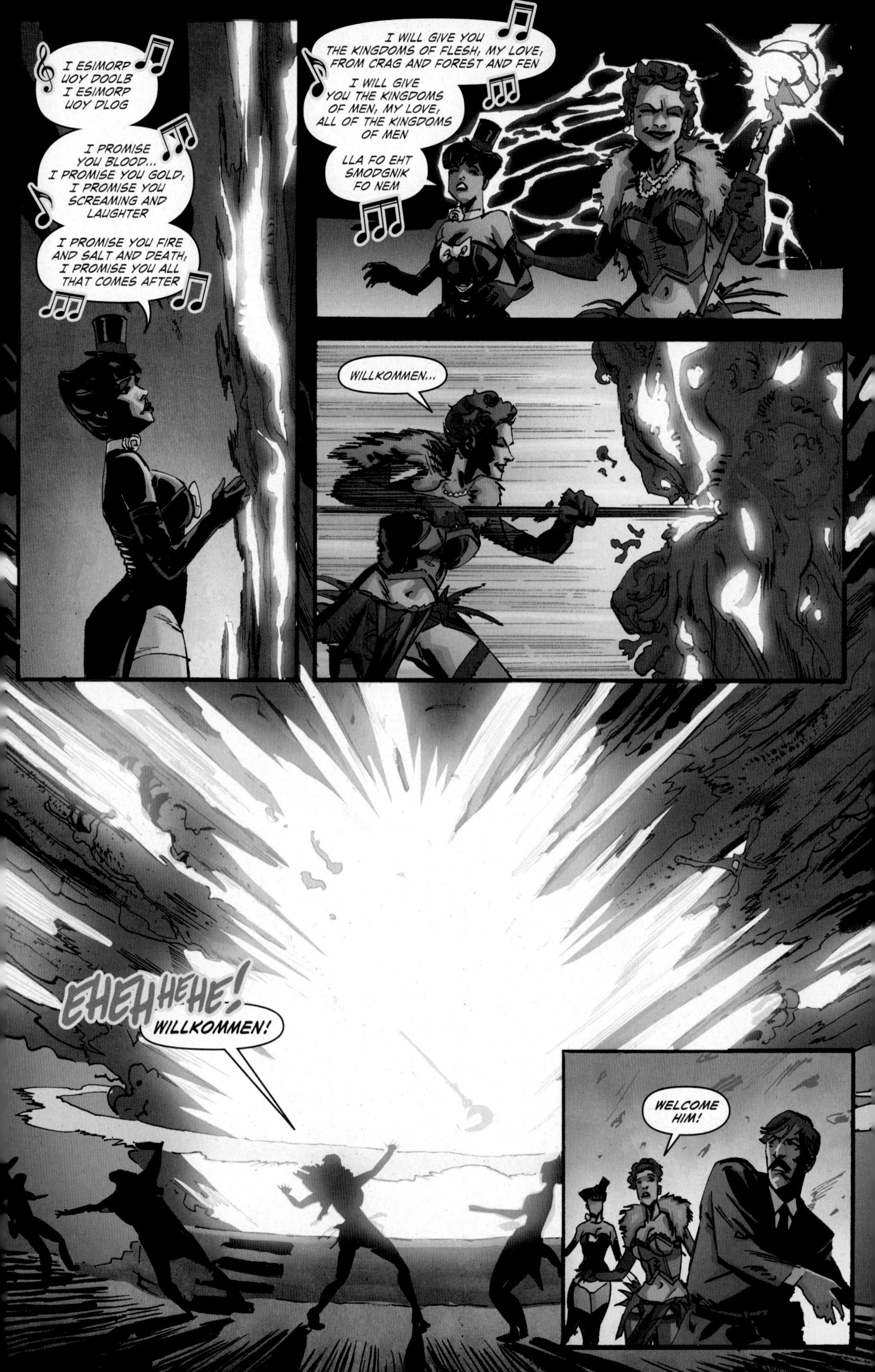
I ESIMORP
UOY DOOLB
I ESIMORP
UOY DLOG
I PROMISE YOU BLOOD... I PROMISE YOU GOLD, I PROMISE YOU SCREAMING AND LAUGHTER
I PROMISE YOU FIRE AND SALT AND DEATH, I PROMISE YOU ALL THAT COMES AFTER
I WILL GIVE YOU THE KINGDOMS OF FLESH, MY LOVE, FROM CRAG AND FOREST AND FEN
I WILL GIVE YOU THE KINGDOMS OF MEN, MY LOVE, ALL OF THE KINGDOMS OF MEN
LLA FO EHT SMODGNIK FO NEM
WILLKOMMEN...
EHEHHEHE!
WILLKOMMEN!
WELCOME HIM!

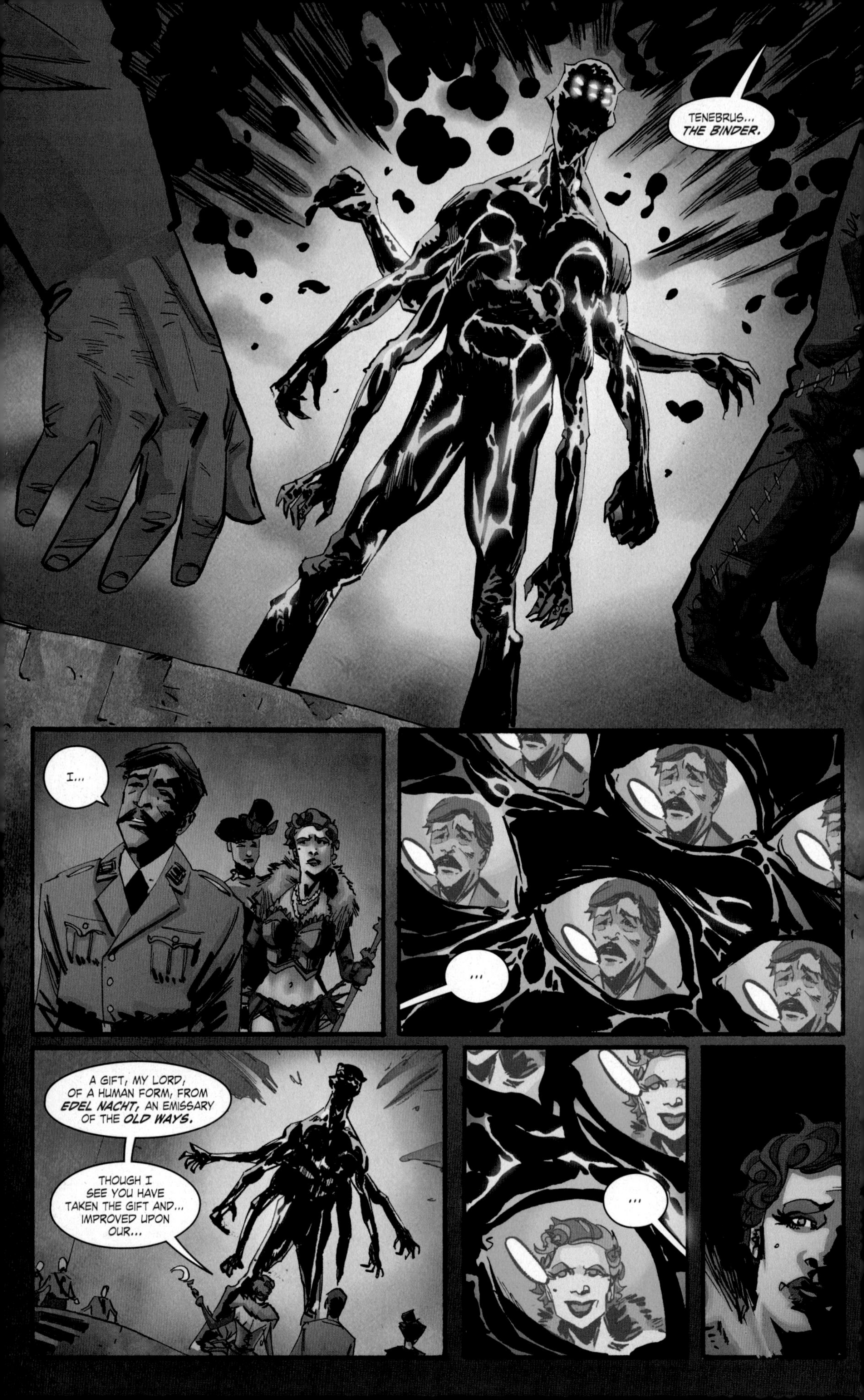
TENEBRUS... THE BINDER.
I...
...
A GIFT, MY LORD, OF A HUMAN FORM, FROM EDEL NACHT, AN EMISSARY OF THE OLD WAYS.
THOUGH I SEE YOU HAVE TAKEN THE GIFT AND... IMPROVED UPON OUR...
...

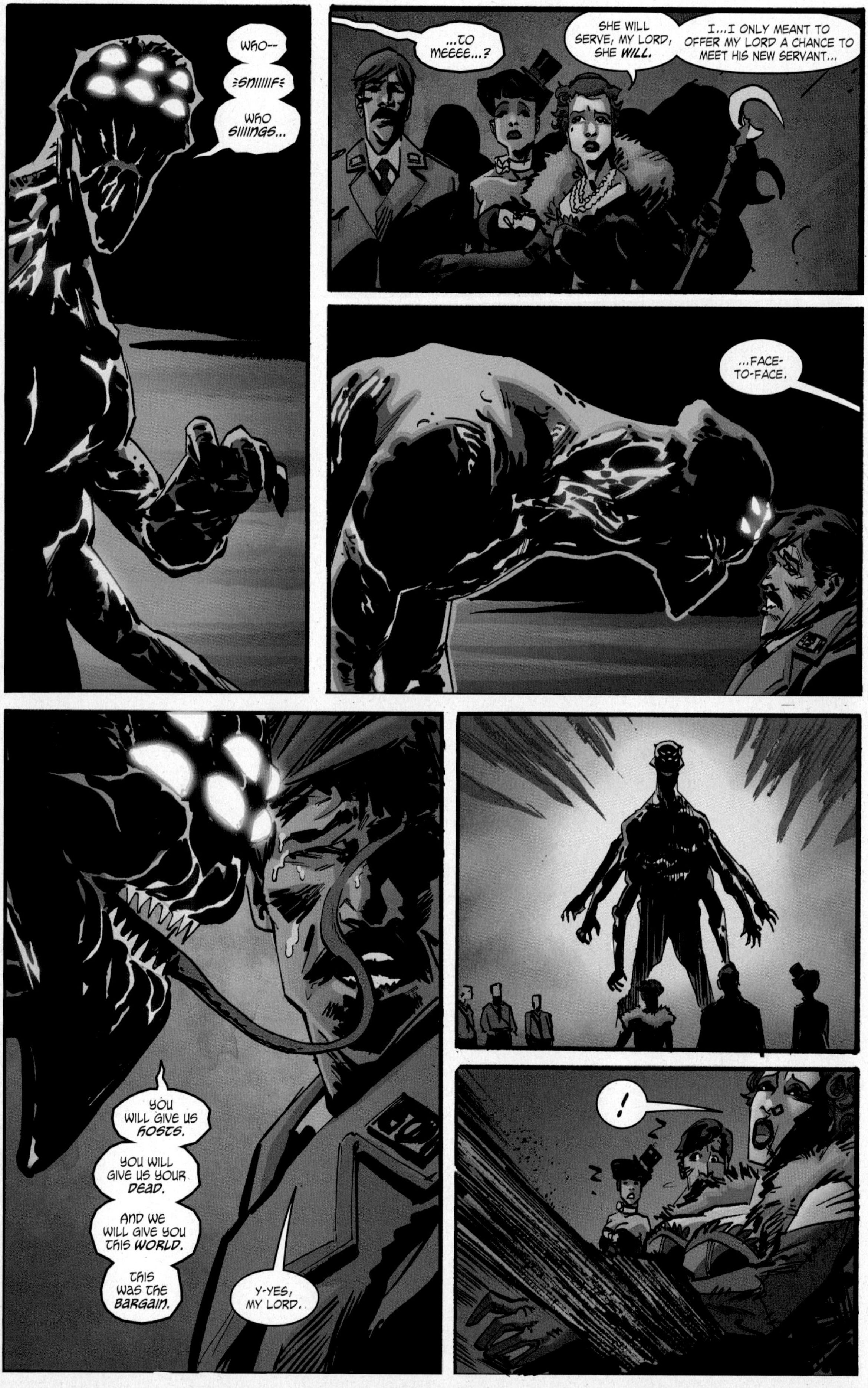
WHO--
SNIIIIF
WHO SIIIINGS...
...TO MEEEE...?
SHE WILL SERVE, MY LORD, SHE WILL.
I...I ONLY MEANT TO OFFER MY LORD A CHANCE TO MEET HIS NEW SERVANT...
...FACE-TO-FACE.
YOU WILL GIVE US HOSTS.
YOU WILL GIVE US YOUR DEAD.
AND WE WILL GIVE YOU THIS WORLD.
THIS WAS THE BARGAIN.
Y-YES, MY LORD.
!

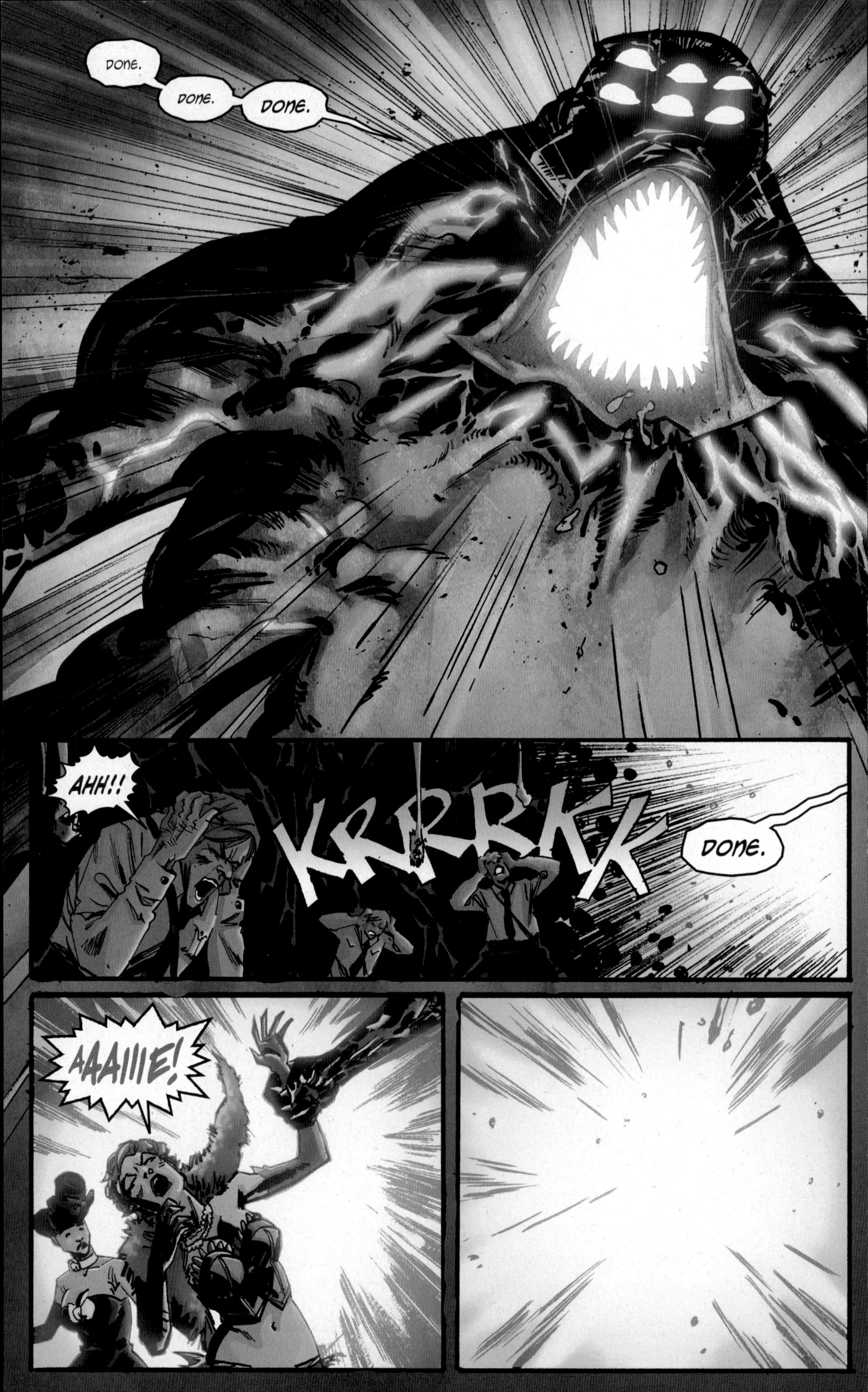
DONE.
DONE.
DONE.
AHH!!
KRRRKK
DONE.
AAAIIIE!

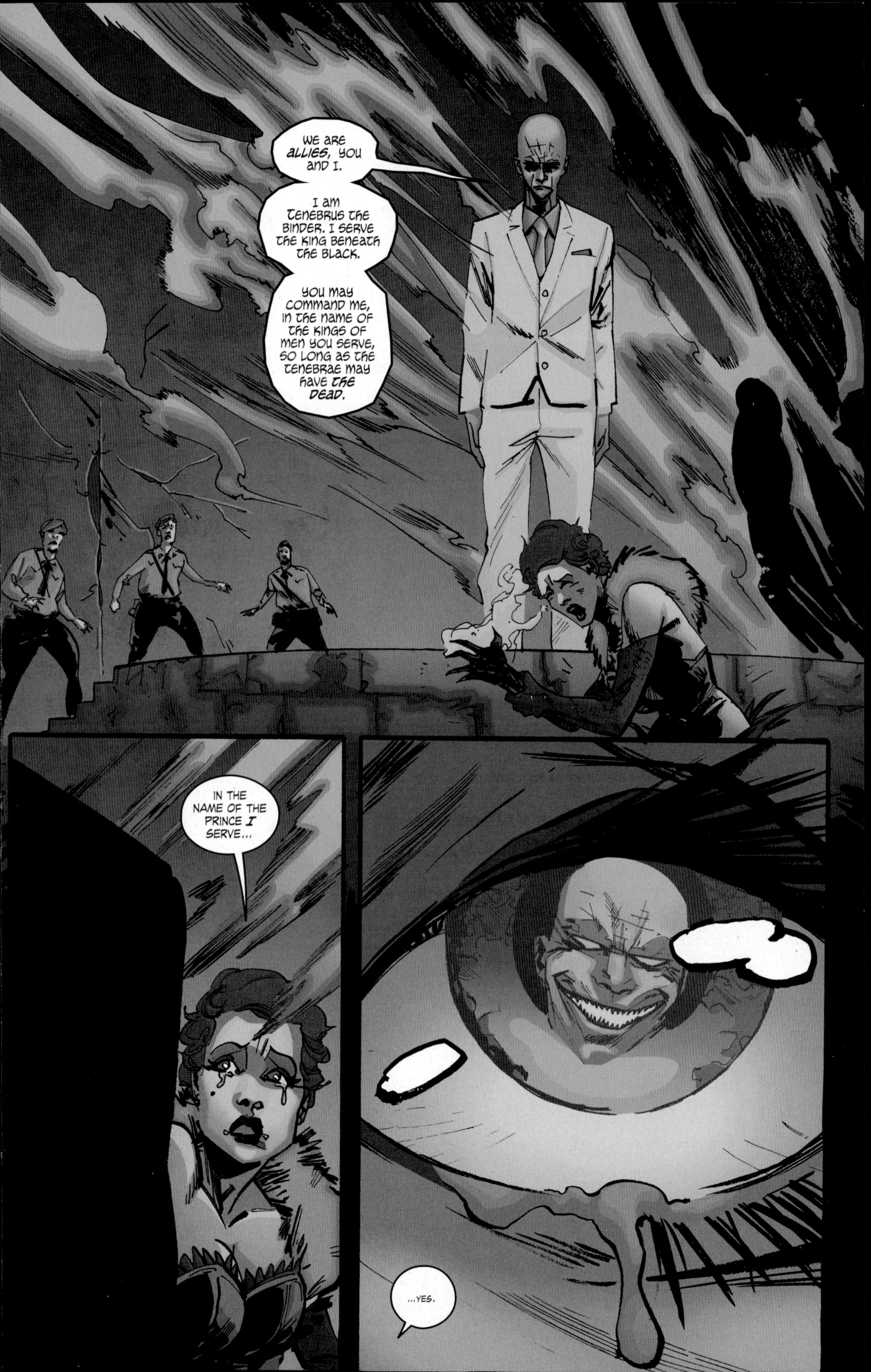
WE ARE ALLIES, YOU AND I.
I AM TENEBRUS THE BINDER. I SERVE THE KING BENEATH THE BLACK.
YOU MAY COMMAND ME, IN THE NAME OF THE KINGS OF MEN YOU SERVE, SO LONG AS THE TENEBRAE MAY HAVE THE DEAD.
IN THE NAME OF THE PRINCE I SERVE...
...YES.

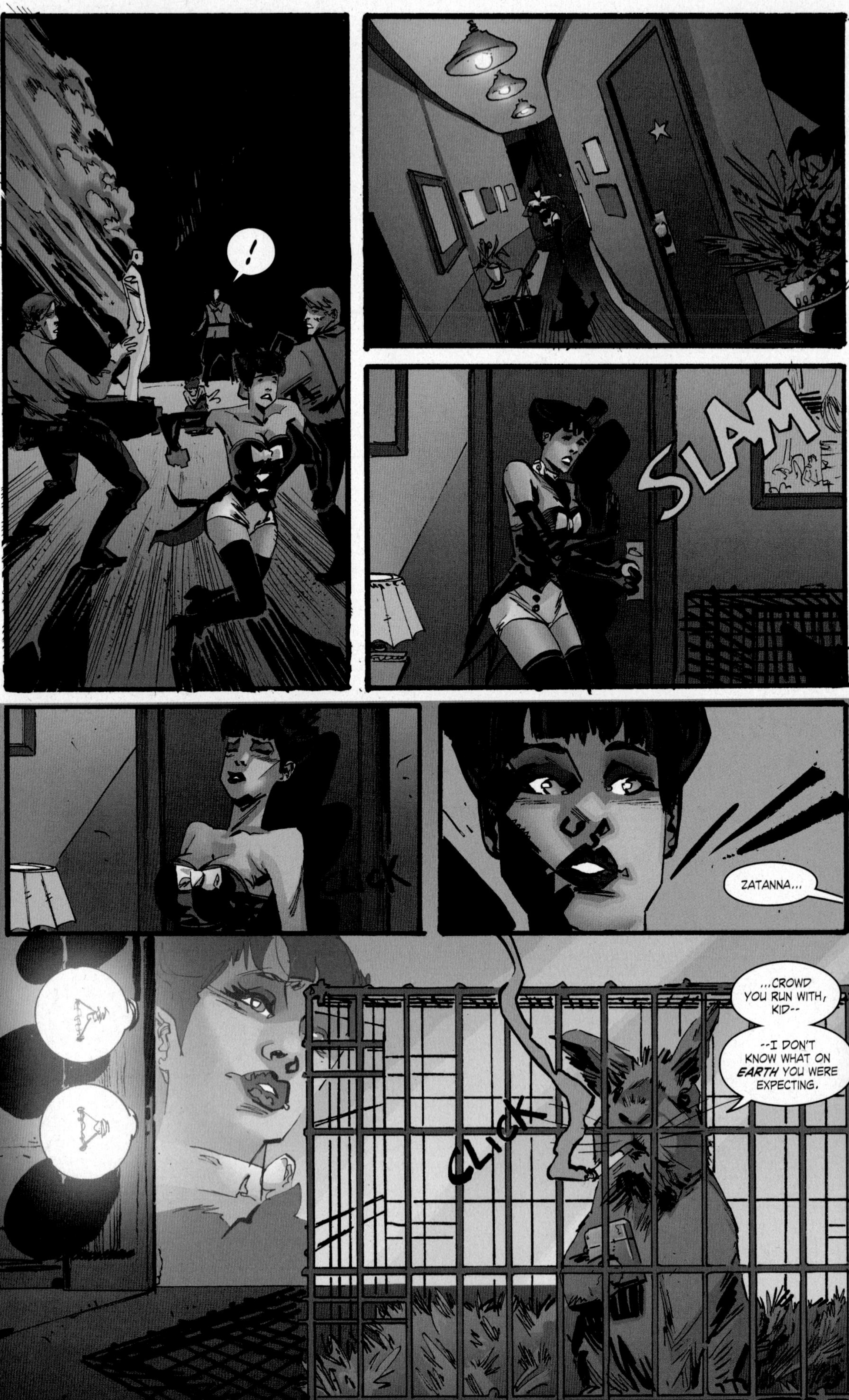

!
SLAM
CLICK
ZATANNA...
...CROWD YOU RUN WITH, KID--
--I DON'T KNOW WHAT ON *EARTH* YOU WERE EXPECTING.
CLICK

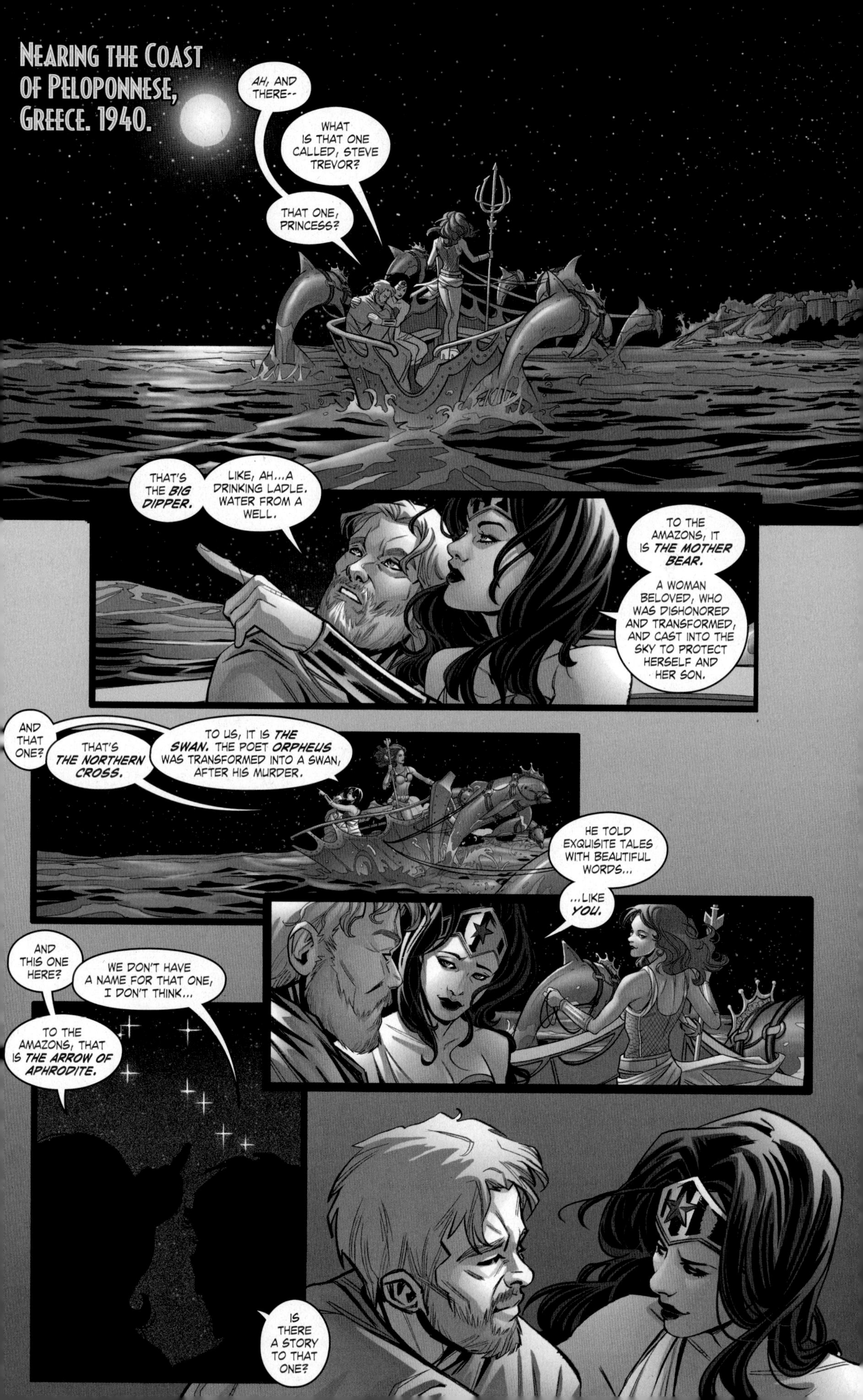
Nearing the Coast of Peloponnese, Greece. 1940.
AH, AND THERE--
WHAT IS THAT ONE CALLED, STEVE TREVOR?
THAT ONE, PRINCESS?
THAT'S THE BIG DIPPER.
LIKE, AH...A DRINKING LADLE. WATER FROM A WELL.
TO THE AMAZONS, IT IS THE MOTHER BEAR.
A WOMAN BELOVED, WHO WAS DISHONORED AND TRANSFORMED, AND CAST INTO THE SKY TO PROTECT HERSELF AND HER SON.
AND THAT ONE?
THAT'S THE NORTHERN CROSS.
TO US, IT IS THE SWAN. THE POET ORPHEUS WAS TRANSFORMED INTO A SWAN, AFTER HIS MURDER.
HE TOLD EXQUISITE TALES WITH BEAUTIFUL WORDS...
...LIKE YOU.
AND THIS ONE HERE?
WE DON'T HAVE A NAME FOR THAT ONE, I DON'T THINK...
TO THE AMAZONS, THAT IS THE ARROW OF APHRODITE.
IS THERE A STORY TO THAT ONE?

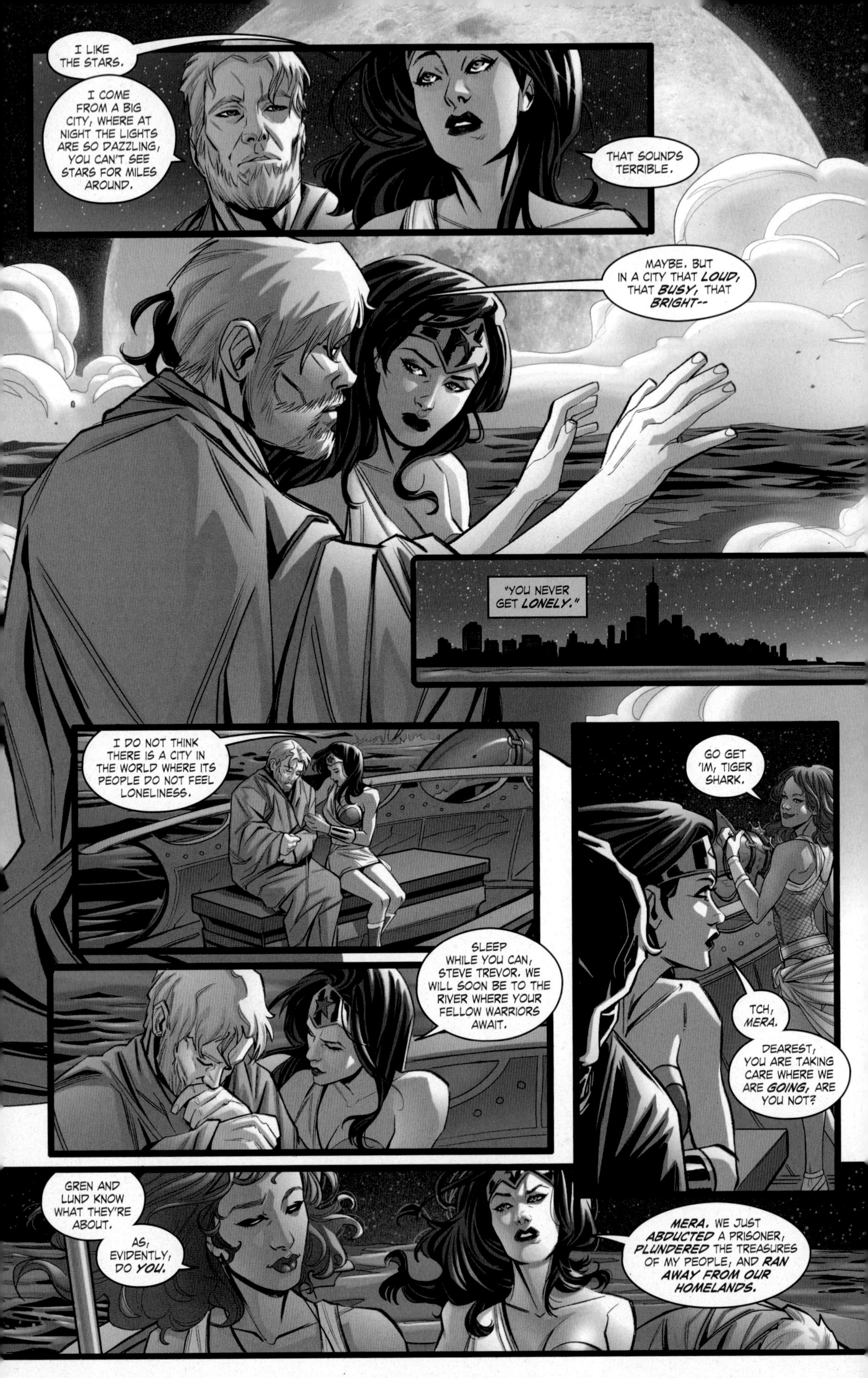
I LIKE THE STARS.
I COME FROM A BIG CITY, WHERE AT NIGHT THE LIGHTS ARE SO DAZZLING, YOU CAN'T SEE STARS FOR MILES AROUND.
THAT SOUNDS TERRIBLE.
MAYBE. BUT IN A CITY THAT *LOUD,* THAT *BUSY,* THAT *BRIGHT--*
"YOU NEVER GET *LONELY.*"
I DO NOT THINK THERE IS A CITY IN THE WORLD WHERE ITS PEOPLE DO NOT FEEL LONELINESS.
SLEEP WHILE YOU CAN, STEVE TREVOR. WE WILL SOON BE TO THE RIVER WHERE YOUR FELLOW WARRIORS AWAIT.
GO GET 'IM, TIGER SHARK.
TCH, *MERA.*
DEAREST, YOU ARE TAKING CARE WHERE WE ARE *GOING,* ARE YOU NOT?
GREN AND LUND KNOW WHAT THEY'RE ABOUT.
AS, EVIDENTLY, DO *YOU.*
*MERA.* WE JUST *ABDUCTED* A PRISONER, *PLUNDERED* THE TREASURES OF MY PEOPLE, AND *RAN AWAY FROM OUR HOMELANDS.*

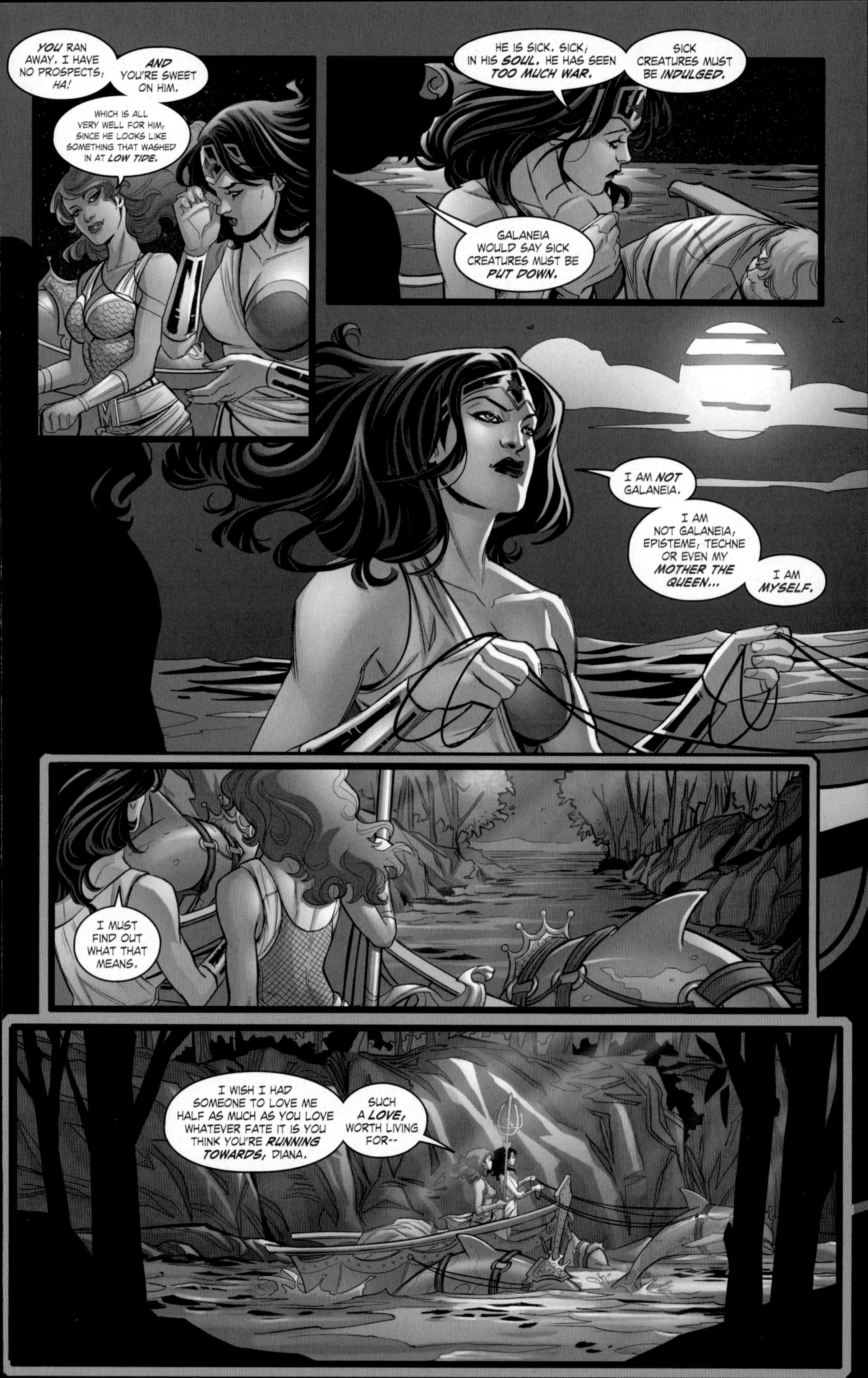

YOU RAN AWAY. I HAVE NO PROSPECTS, HA!
AND YOU'RE SWEET ON HIM.
WHICH IS ALL VERY WELL FOR HIM, SINCE HE LOOKS LIKE SOMETHING THAT WASHED IN AT LOW TIDE.
HE IS SICK. SICK, IN HIS SOUL. HE HAS SEEN TOO MUCH WAR.
SICK CREATURES MUST BE INDULGED.
GALANEIA WOULD SAY SICK CREATURES MUST BE PUT DOWN.
I AM NOT GALANEIA.
I AM NOT GALANEIA, EPISTEME, TECHNE OR EVEN MY MOTHER THE QUEEN...
I AM MYSELF.
I MUST FIND OUT WHAT THAT MEANS.
I WISH I HAD SOMEONE TO LOVE ME HALF AS MUCH AS YOU LOVE WHATEVER FATE IT IS YOU THINK YOU'RE RUNNING TOWARDS, DIANA.
SUCH A LOVE, WORTH LIVING FOR--

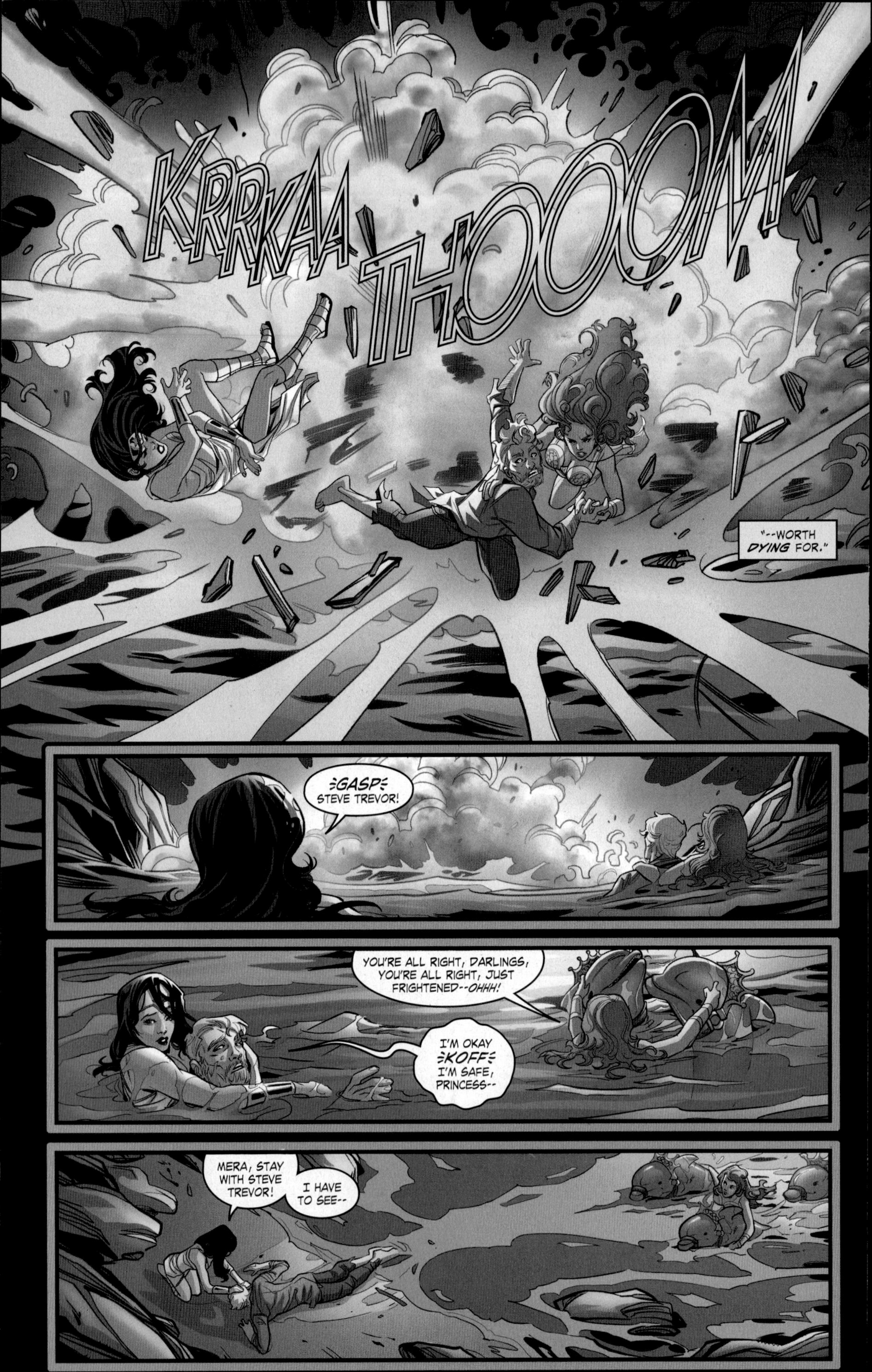
KRRKAA THOOOOM!
"--WORTH DYING FOR."
GASP STEVE TREVOR!
YOU'RE ALL RIGHT, DARLINGS, YOU'RE ALL RIGHT, JUST FRIGHTENED--OHHH!
I'M OKAY KOFF I'M SAFE, PRINCESS--
MERA, STAY WITH STEVE TREVOR!
I HAVE TO SEE--

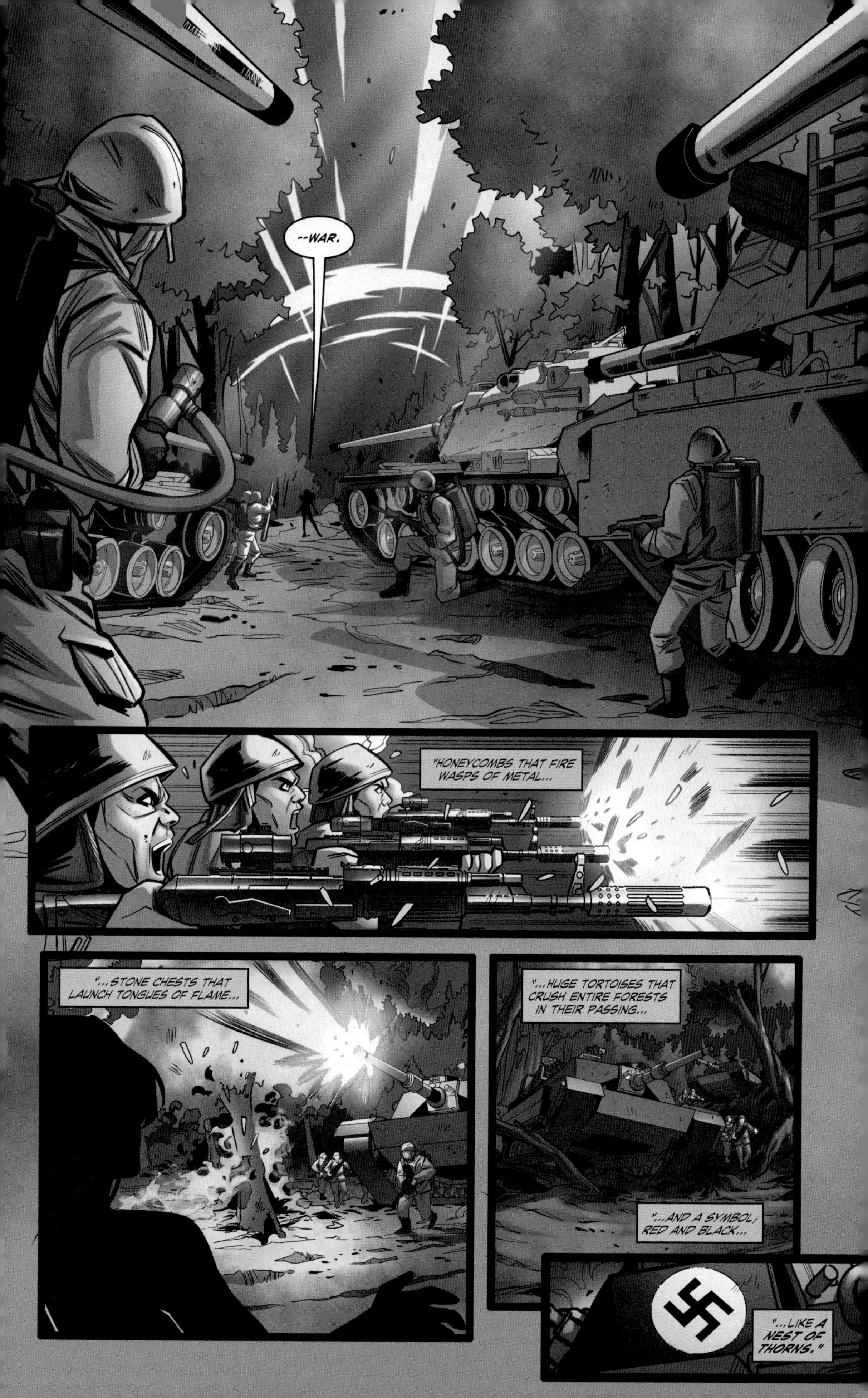
--WAR.
"HONEYCOMBS THAT FIRE WASPS OF METAL...
"...STONE CHESTS THAT LAUNCH TONGUES OF FLAME...
"...HUGE TORTOISES THAT CRUSH ENTIRE FORESTS IN THEIR PASSING...
"...AND A SYMBOL, RED AND BLACK...
"...LIKE A NEST OF THORNS."

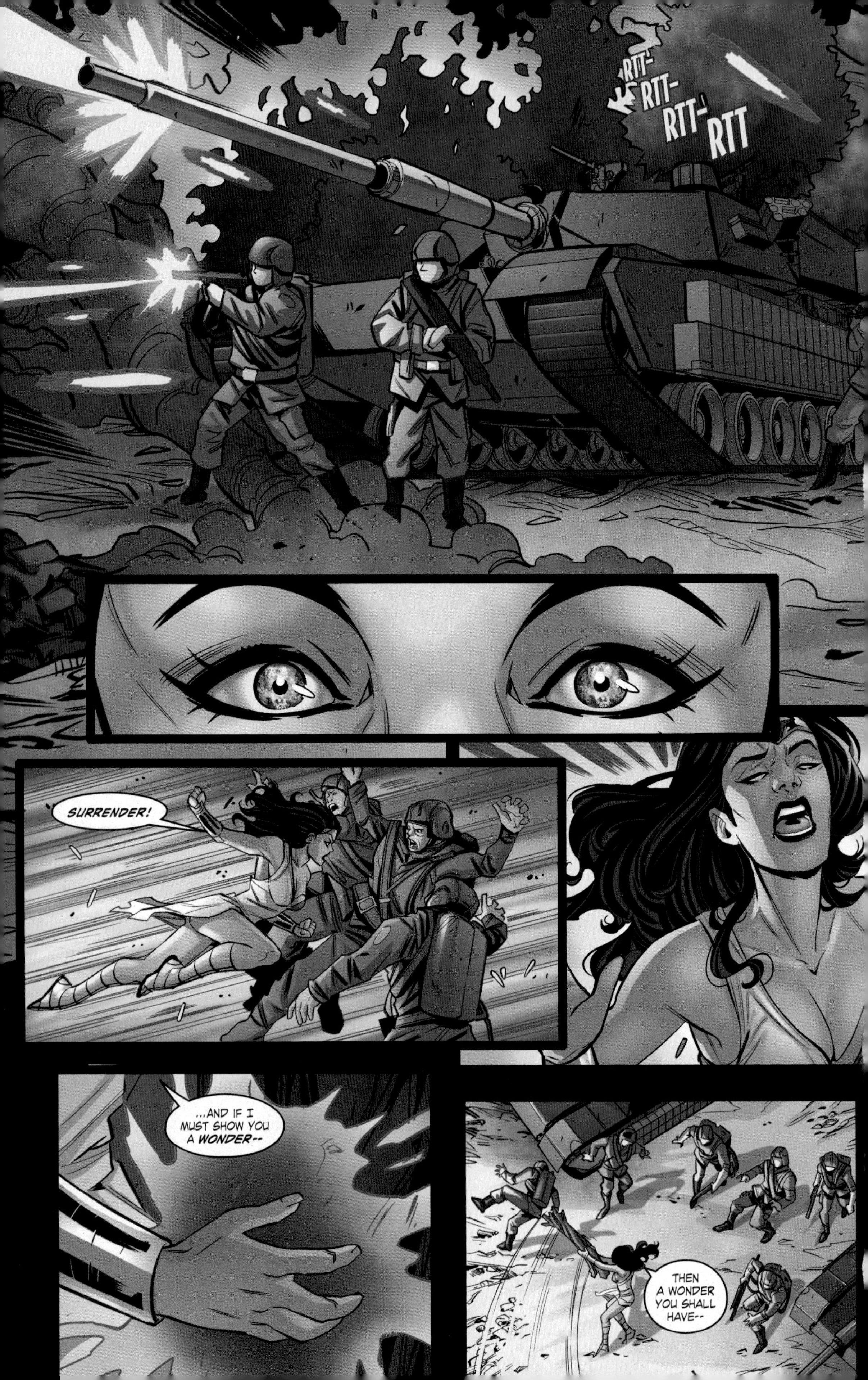
RTT-
RTT-
RTT-
RTT
SURRENDER!
...AND IF I MUST SHOW YOU A WONDER--
THEN A WONDER YOU SHALL HAVE--

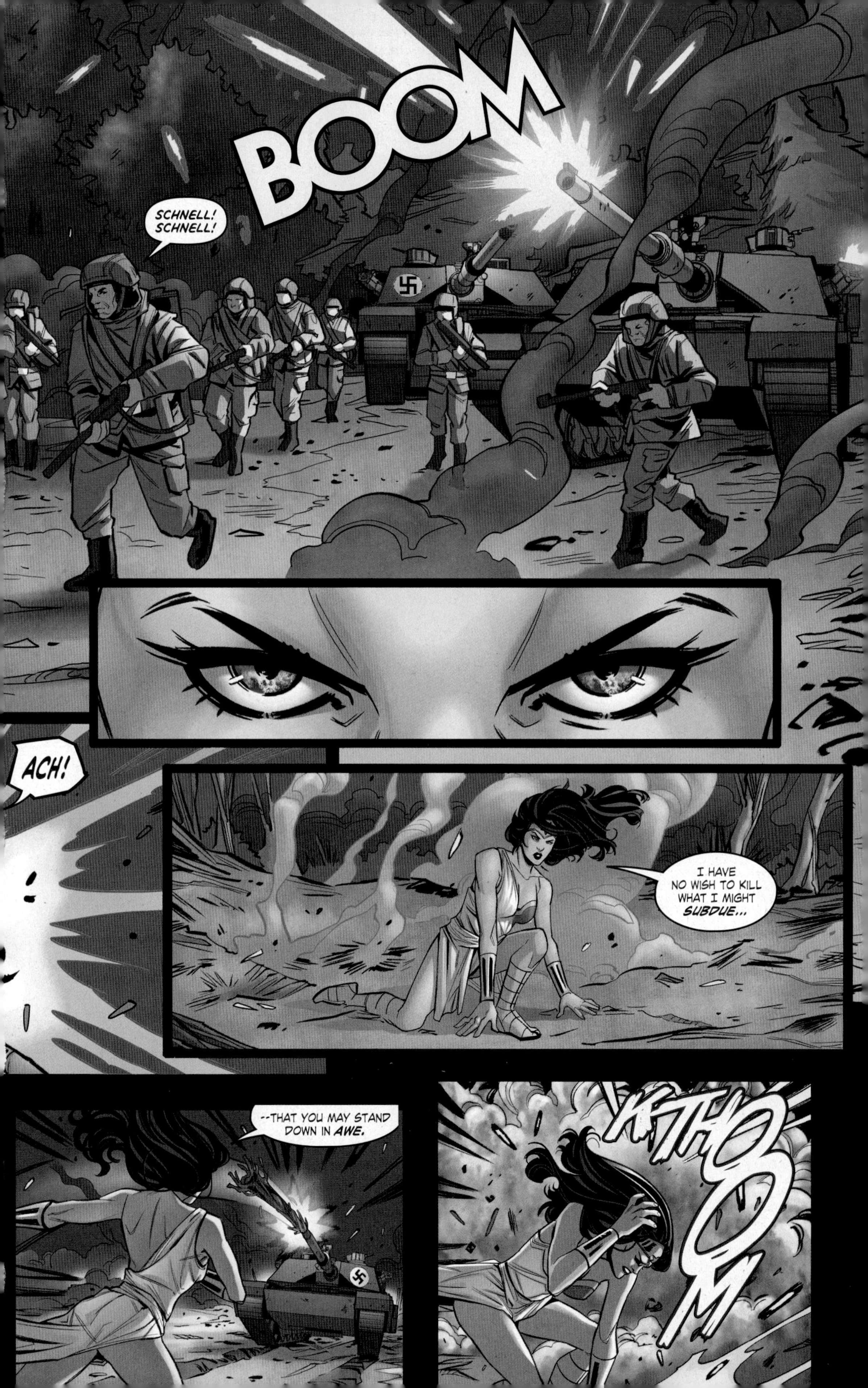
BOOM
SCHNELL! SCHNELL!
ACH!
I HAVE NO WISH TO KILL WHAT I MIGHT SUBDUE...
--THAT YOU MAY STAND DOWN IN AWE.
KTHOOOM

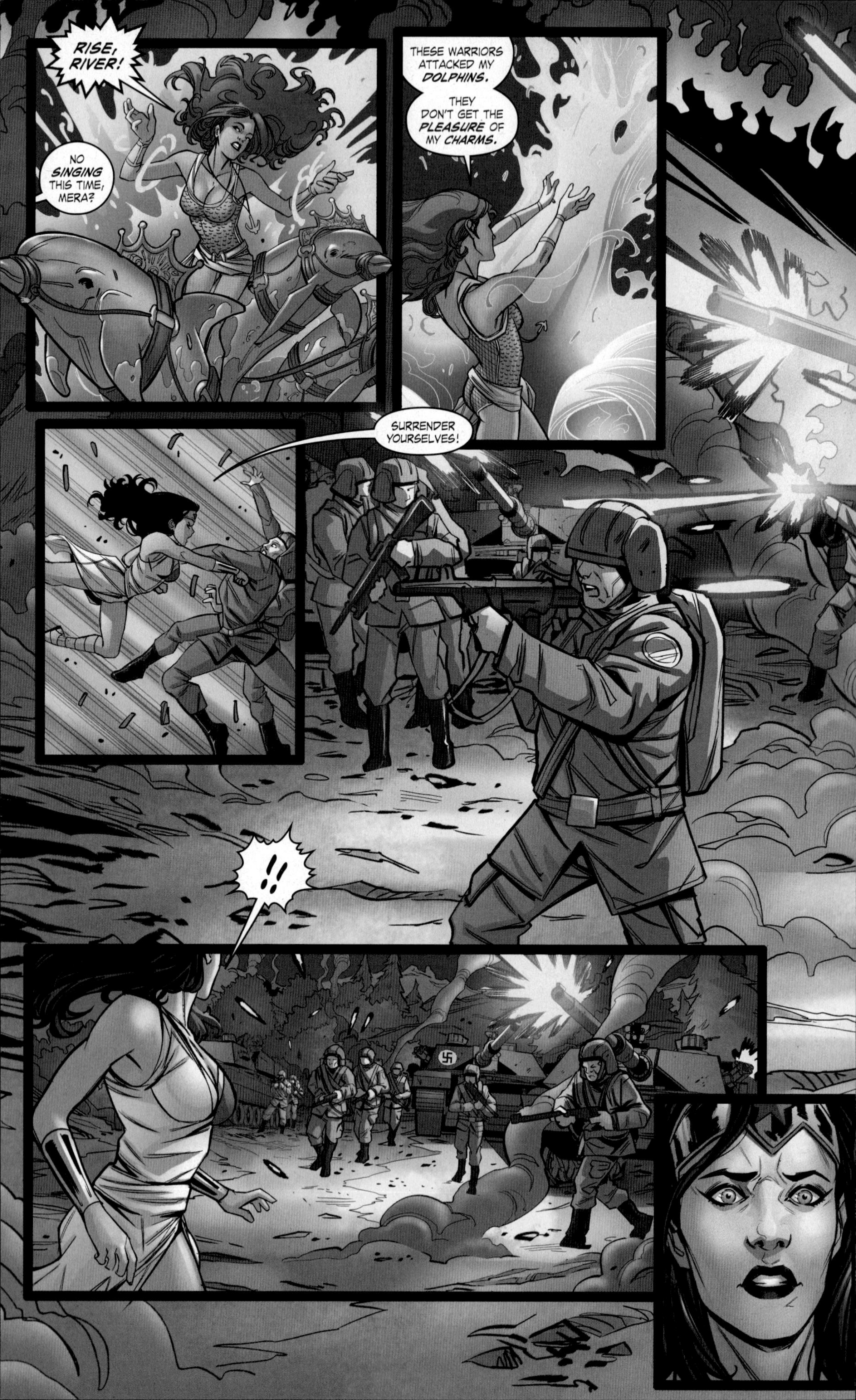
RISE, RIVER!
NO SINGING THIS TIME, MERA?
THESE WARRIORS ATTACKED MY DOLPHINS.
THEY DON'T GET THE PLEASURE OF MY CHARMS.
SURRENDER YOURSELVES!
!!

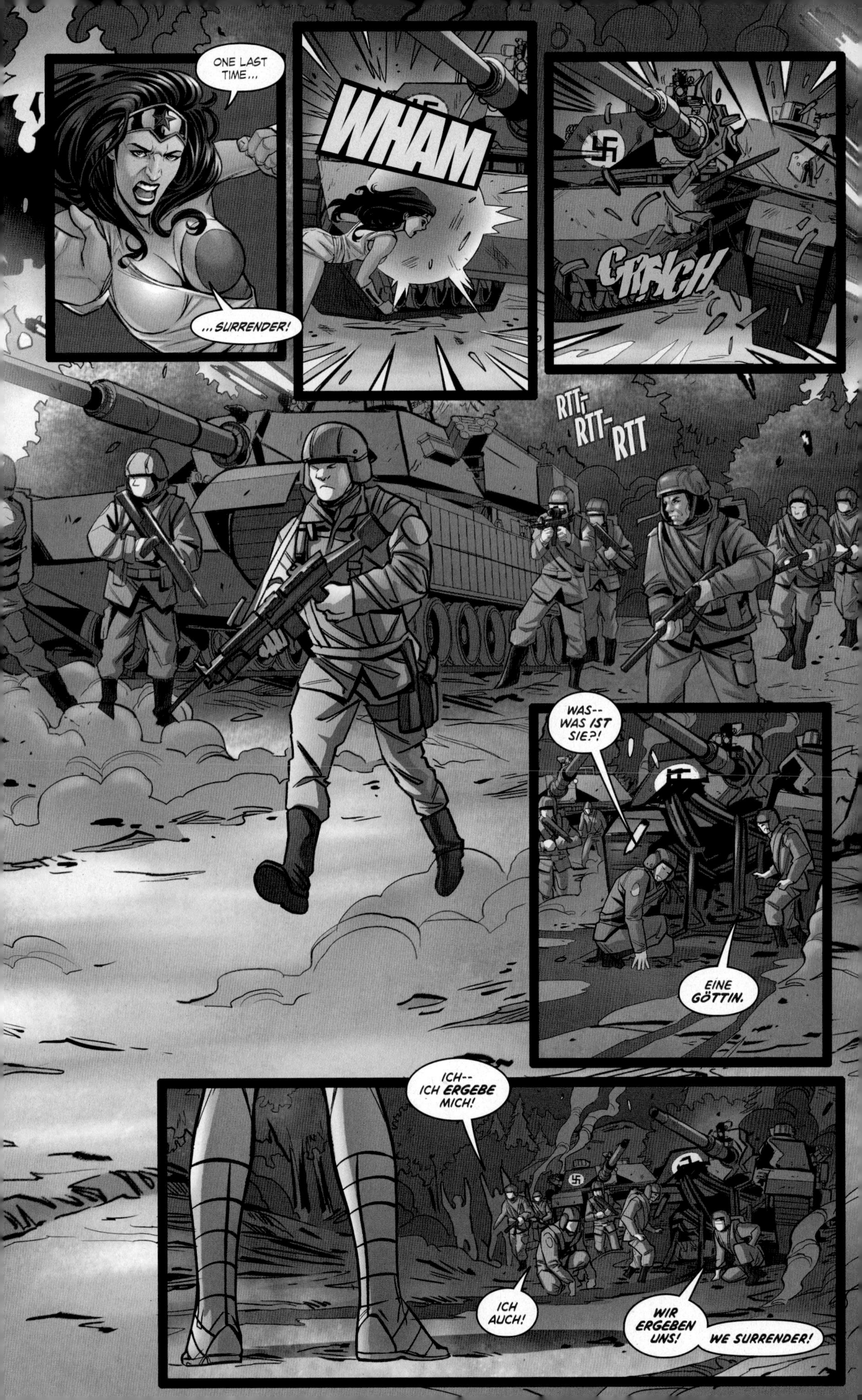
ONE LAST TIME...
...SURRENDER!
WHAM
CRNCH
RTT-RTT-RTT
WAS-- WAS IST SIE?!
EINE GÖTTIN.
ICH-- ICH ERGEBE MICH!
ICH AUCH!
WIR ERGEBEN UNS!
WE SURRENDER!

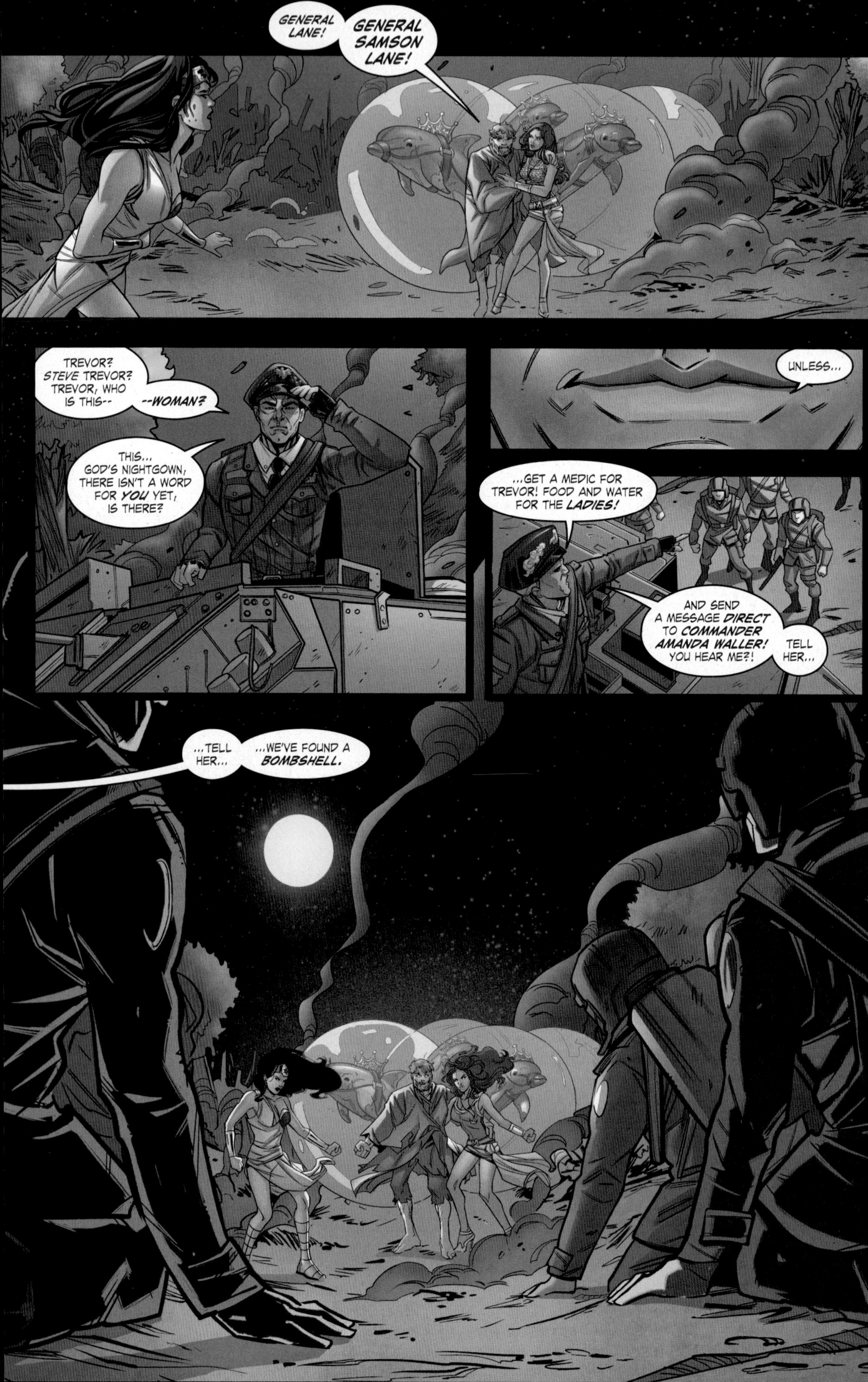
GENERAL LANE!
GENERAL SAMSON LANE!
TREVOR? STEVE TREVOR? TREVOR, WHO IS THIS--
--WOMAN?
THIS... GOD'S NIGHTGOWN, THERE ISN'T A WORD FOR YOU YET, IS THERE?
UNLESS...
...GET A MEDIC FOR TREVOR! FOOD AND WATER FOR THE LADIES!
AND SEND A MESSAGE DIRECT TO COMMANDER AMANDA WALLER! YOU HEAR ME?!
TELL HER...
...TELL HER...
...WE'VE FOUND A BOMBSHELL.

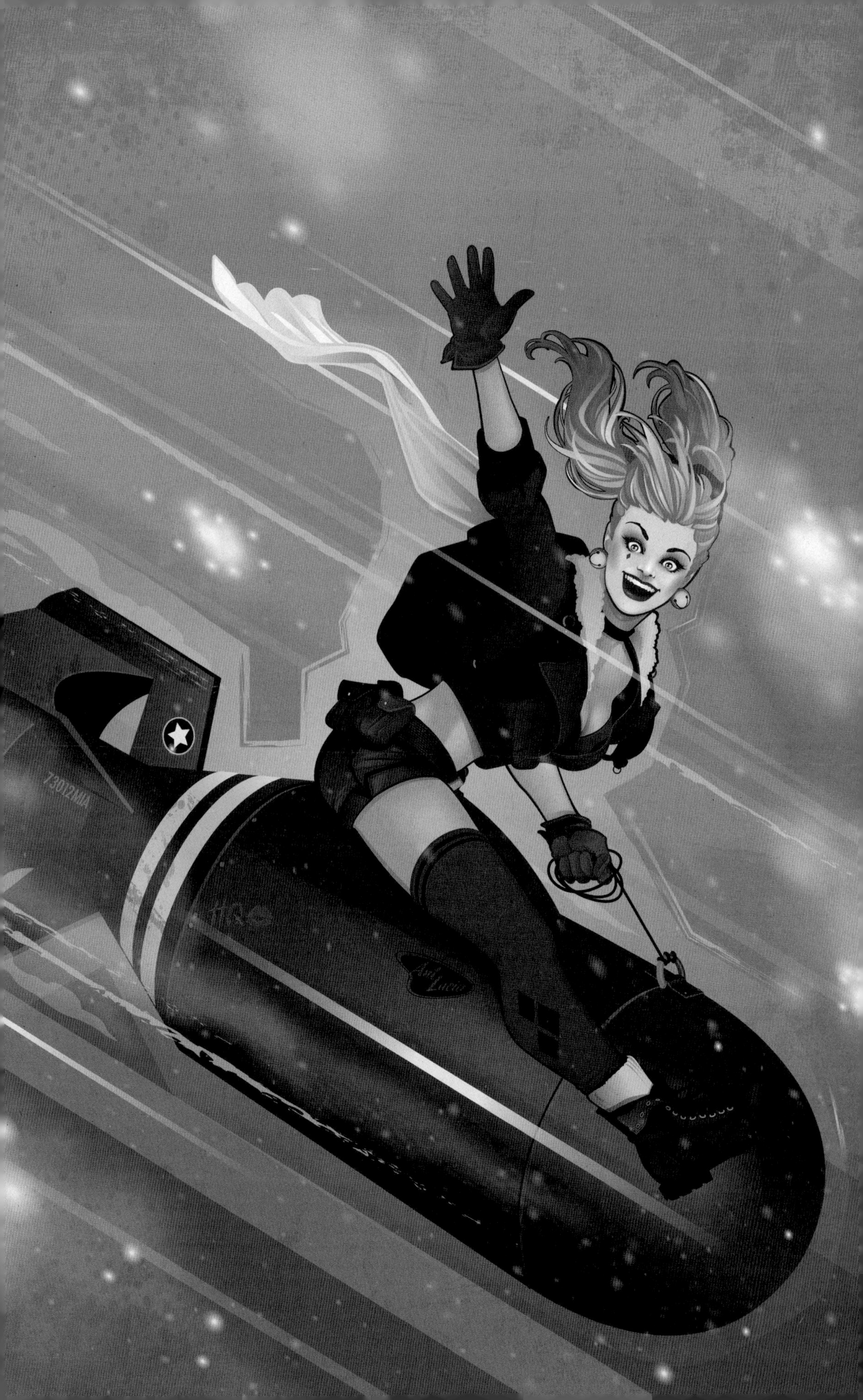

# COMBAT
## PART ONE

**MARGUERITE BENNETT**
*Writer*

**BILQUIS EVELY**
**MIRKA ANDOLFO**
**LAURA BRAGA**
*Artists*

**WENDY BROOME**
*Colorist*

**WES ABBOTT**
*Letterer*

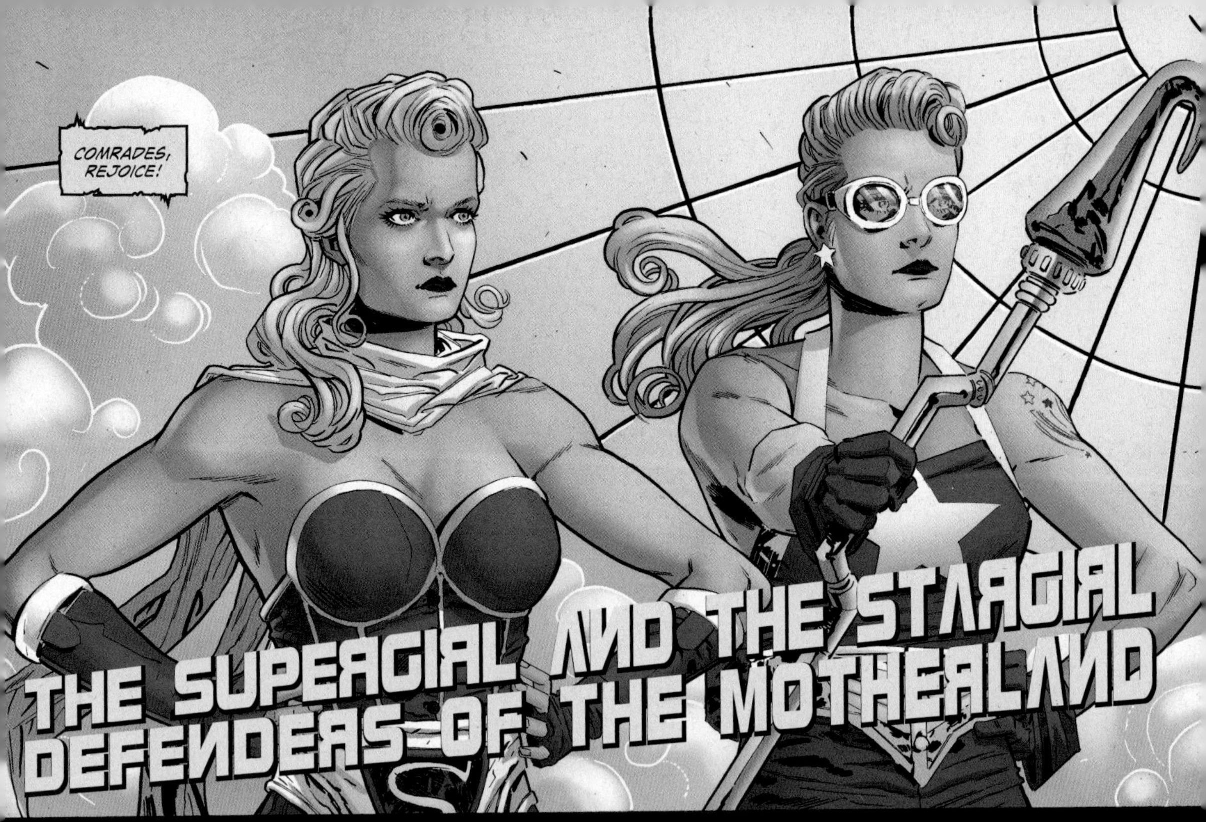
COMRADES, REJOICE!
THE SUPERGIRL AND THE STARGIRL
DEFENDERS OF THE MOTHERLAND

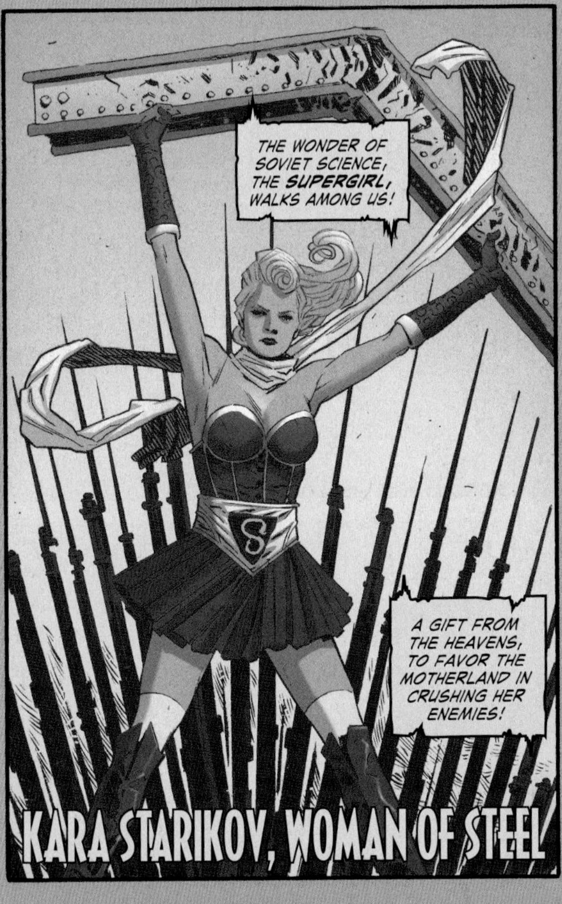
THE WONDER OF SOVIET SCIENCE, THE **SUPERGIRL**, WALKS AMONG US!
A GIFT FROM THE HEAVENS, TO FAVOR THE MOTHERLAND IN CRUSHING HER ENEMIES!
KARA STARIKOV, WOMAN OF STEEL

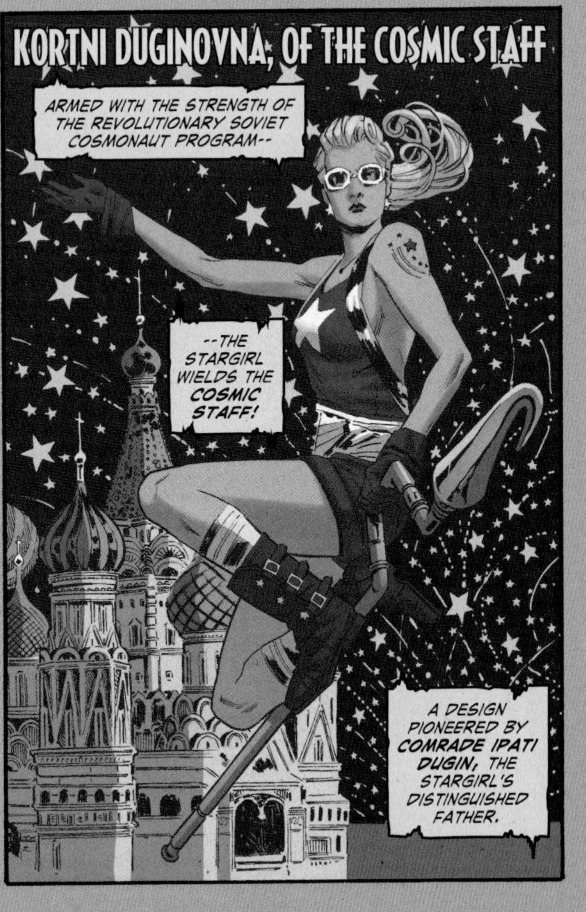
KORTNI DUGINOVNA, OF THE COSMIC STAFF
ARMED WITH THE STRENGTH OF THE REVOLUTIONARY SOVIET COSMONAUT PROGRAM--
--THE STARGIRL WIELDS THE **COSMIC STAFF!**
A DESIGN PIONEERED BY **COMRADE IPATI DUGIN,** THE STARGIRL'S DISTINGUISHED FATHER.

RED SQUARE, MOSCOW. 1940.

THAT ANNOUNCER HAS *NOT* MENTIONED THAT THEY *KICKED PAPA OUT* OF THE COSMONAUT PROGRAM FOR SUSPECTED *SEDITION*.

NOR THAT HE WAS LIVING IN *EXILE* IN MAMA'S VILLAGE WHEN SHE TOOK HIM IN.

YOU'D THINK A NICE ROMANCE WOULD GIVE THE STORY A LITTLE *HUMAN COLOR*.

I THINK "HUMAN" MIGHT BE THE *OPPOSITE* OF THE MESSAGE THEY ARE TRYING TO SEND, *SESTRICHKA*--NO MATTER WHAT MAMA AND PAPA INTENDED.

A PARADE TO HONOR THE TRIUMPH OF THE SOVIET PEOPLES!

HIS SCIENCE, AND HER SUPERSTITIONS!

HIS STARS, AND HER STORIES.

HIS CREATIONS, AND HER *CREATURES OF THE FOREST*. HA!

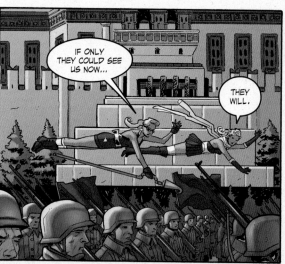

IF ONLY THEY COULD SEE US NOW...

THEY WILL.

IF WE BEHAVE.

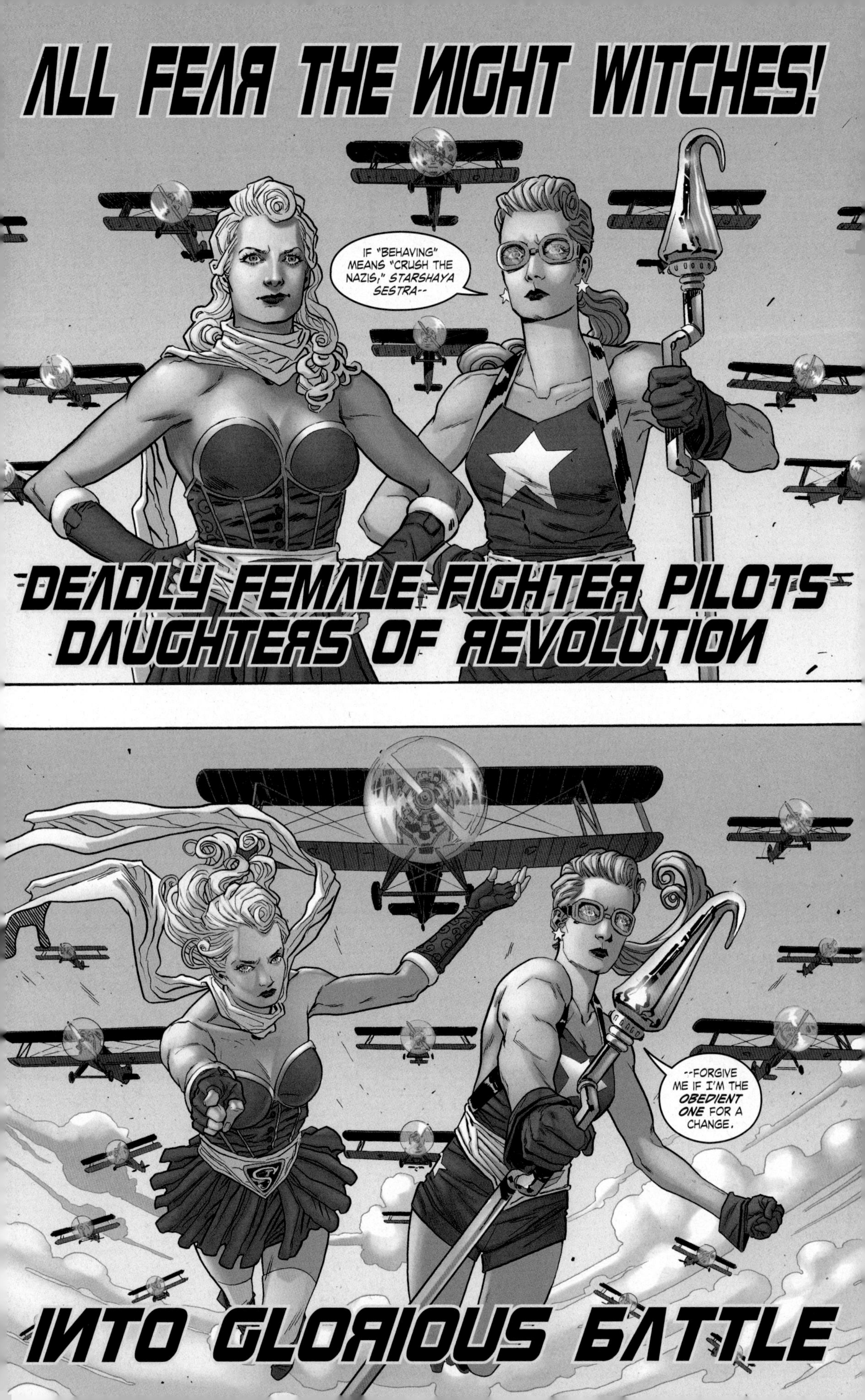
ALL FEAR THE NIGHT WITCHES!
IF "BEHAVING" MEANS "CRUSH THE NAZIS," STARSHAYA SESTRA--
DEADLY FEMALE FIGHTER PILOTS
DAUGHTERS OF REVOLUTION
--FORGIVE ME IF I'M THE *OBEDIENT ONE* FOR A CHANGE.
INTO GLORIOUS BATTLE

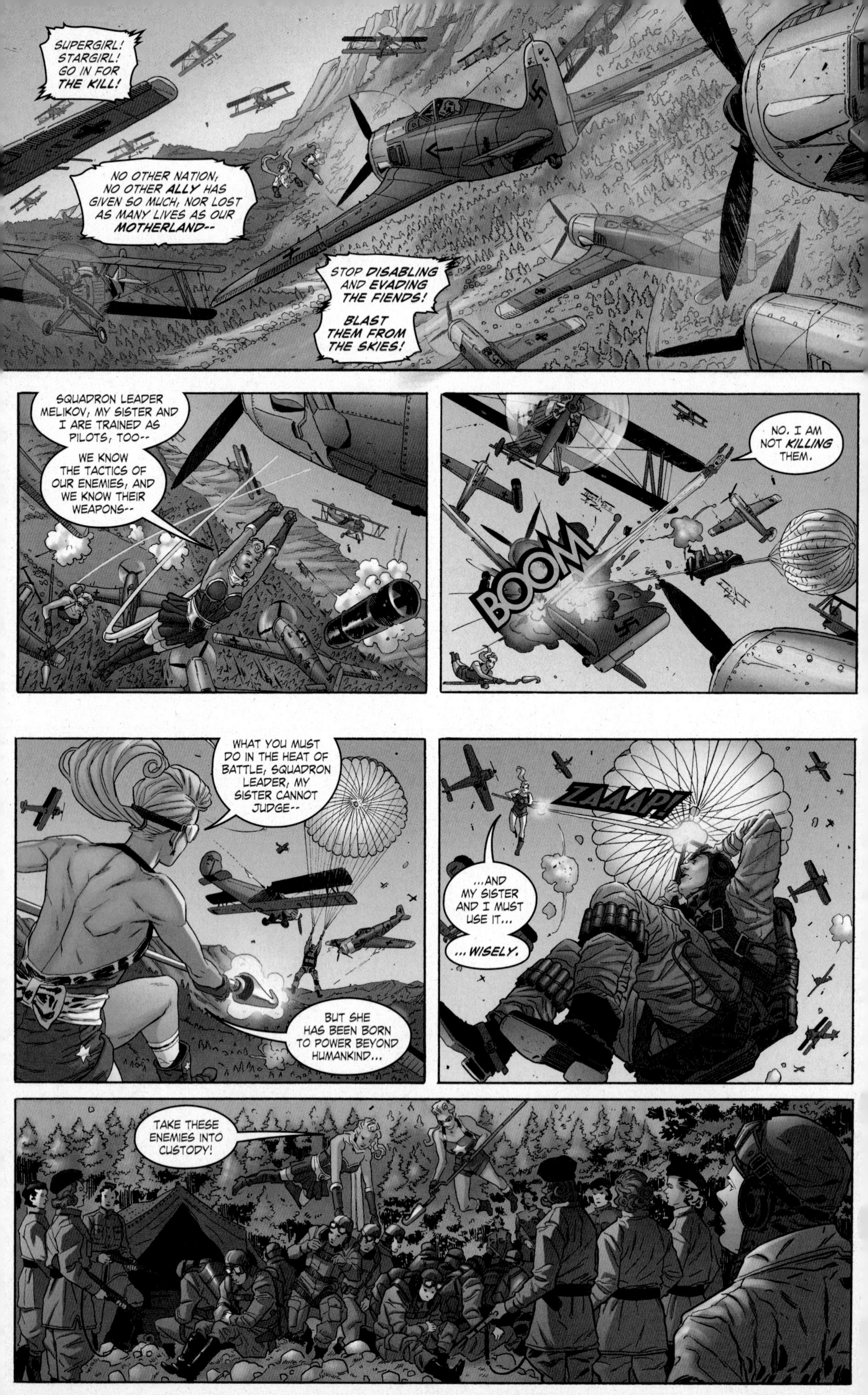

SUPERGIRL! STARGIRL! GO IN FOR THE KILL!
NO OTHER NATION, NO OTHER ALLY HAS GIVEN SO MUCH, NOR LOST AS MANY LIVES AS OUR MOTHERLAND--
STOP DISABLING AND EVADING THE FIENDS!
BLAST THEM FROM THE SKIES!
SQUADRON LEADER MELIKOV, MY SISTER AND I ARE TRAINED AS PILOTS, TOO--
WE KNOW THE TACTICS OF OUR ENEMIES, AND WE KNOW THEIR WEAPONS--
NO. I AM NOT KILLING THEM.
BOOM
WHAT YOU MUST DO IN THE HEAT OF BATTLE, SQUADRON LEADER, MY SISTER CANNOT JUDGE--
BUT SHE HAS BEEN BORN TO POWER BEYOND HUMANKIND...
ZAAAP!
...AND MY SISTER AND I MUST USE IT...
...WISELY.
TAKE THESE ENEMIES INTO CUSTODY!

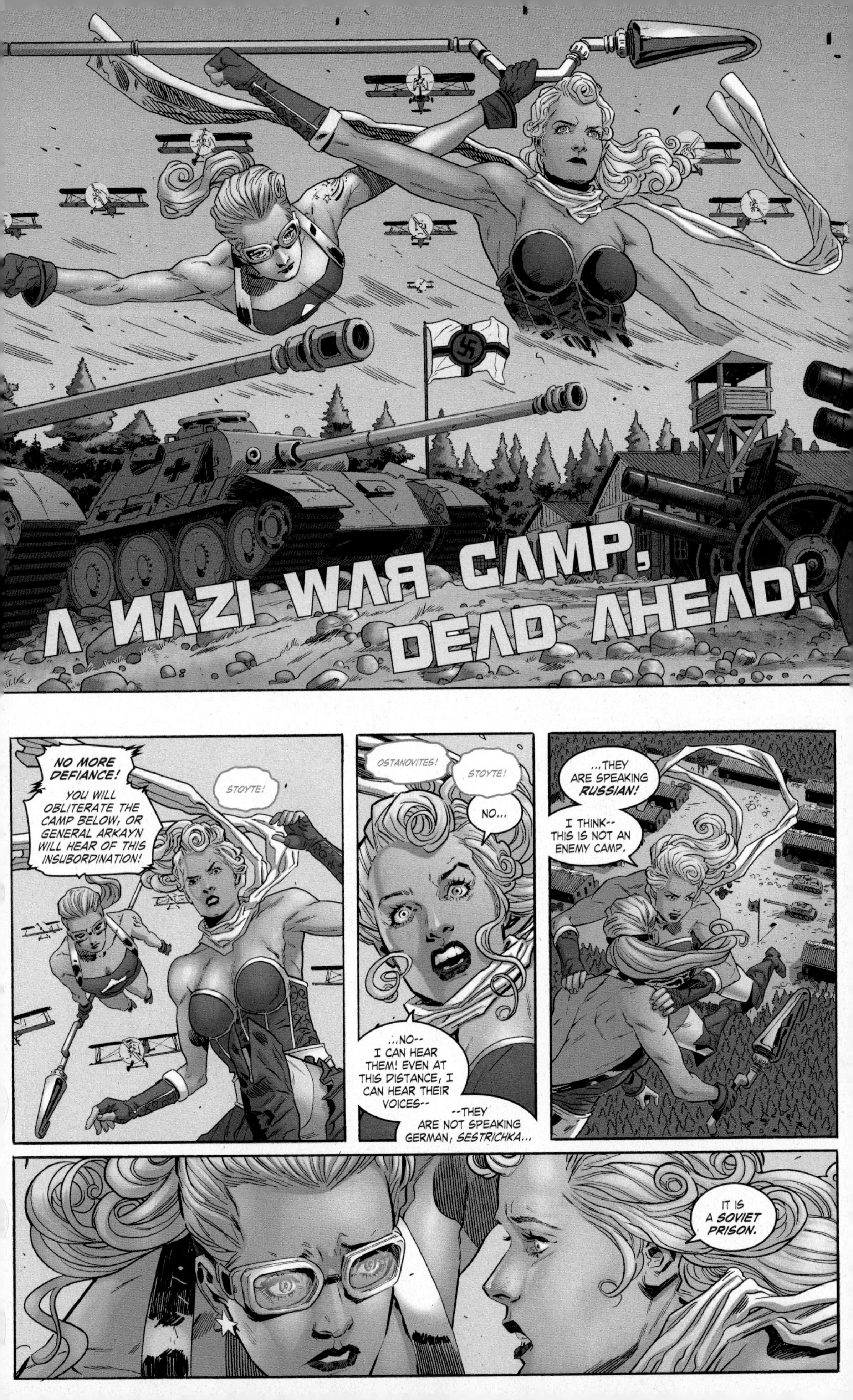
A NAZI WAR CAMP, DEAD AHEAD!
NO MORE DEFIANCE! YOU WILL OBLITERATE THE CAMP BELOW, OR GENERAL ARKAYN WILL HEAR OF THIS INSUBORDINATION!
STOYTE!
OSTANOVITES!
STOYTE!
NO...
...NO-- I CAN HEAR THEM! EVEN AT THIS DISTANCE, I CAN HEAR THEIR VOICES--
--THEY ARE NOT SPEAKING GERMAN, SESTRICHKA...
...THEY ARE SPEAKING RUSSIAN!
I THINK-- THIS IS NOT AN ENEMY CAMP.
IT IS A SOVIET PRISON.

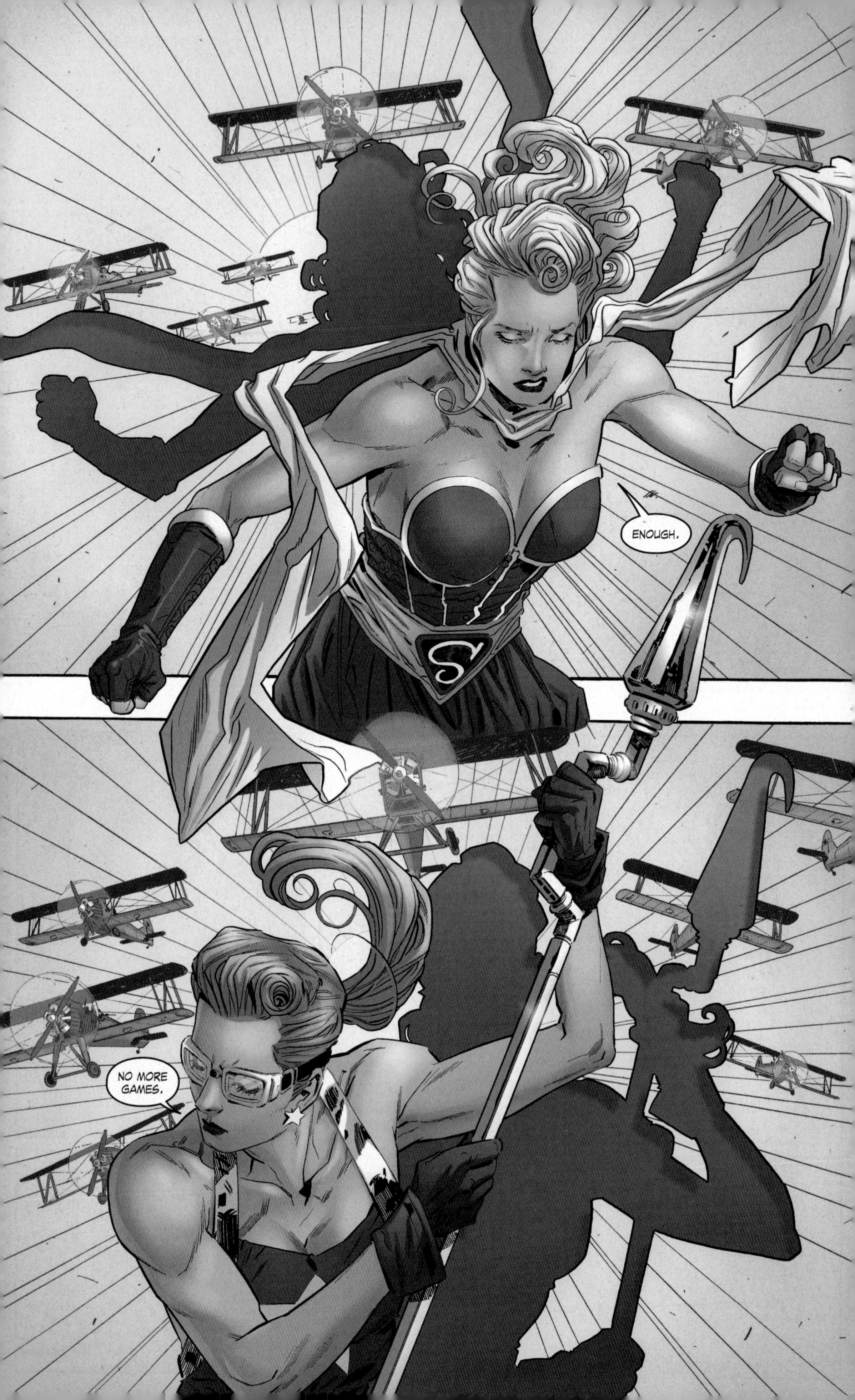
ENOUGH.
NO MORE GAMES.

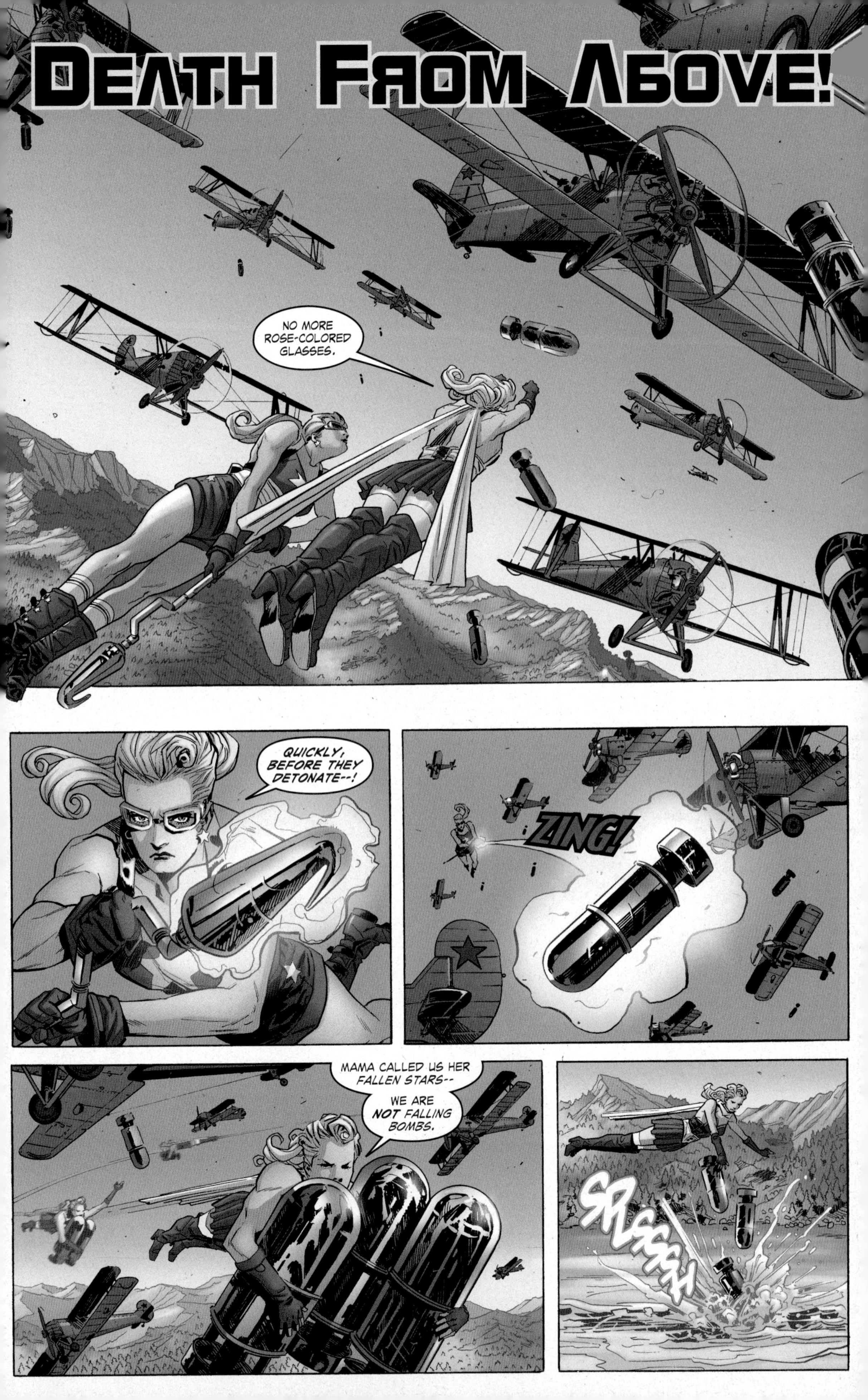

DEATH FROM ABOVE!
NO MORE ROSE-COLORED GLASSES.
QUICKLY, BEFORE THEY DETONATE--!
ZING!
MAMA CALLED US HER FALLEN STARS--
WE ARE NOT FALLING BOMBS.
SPLOOOSH

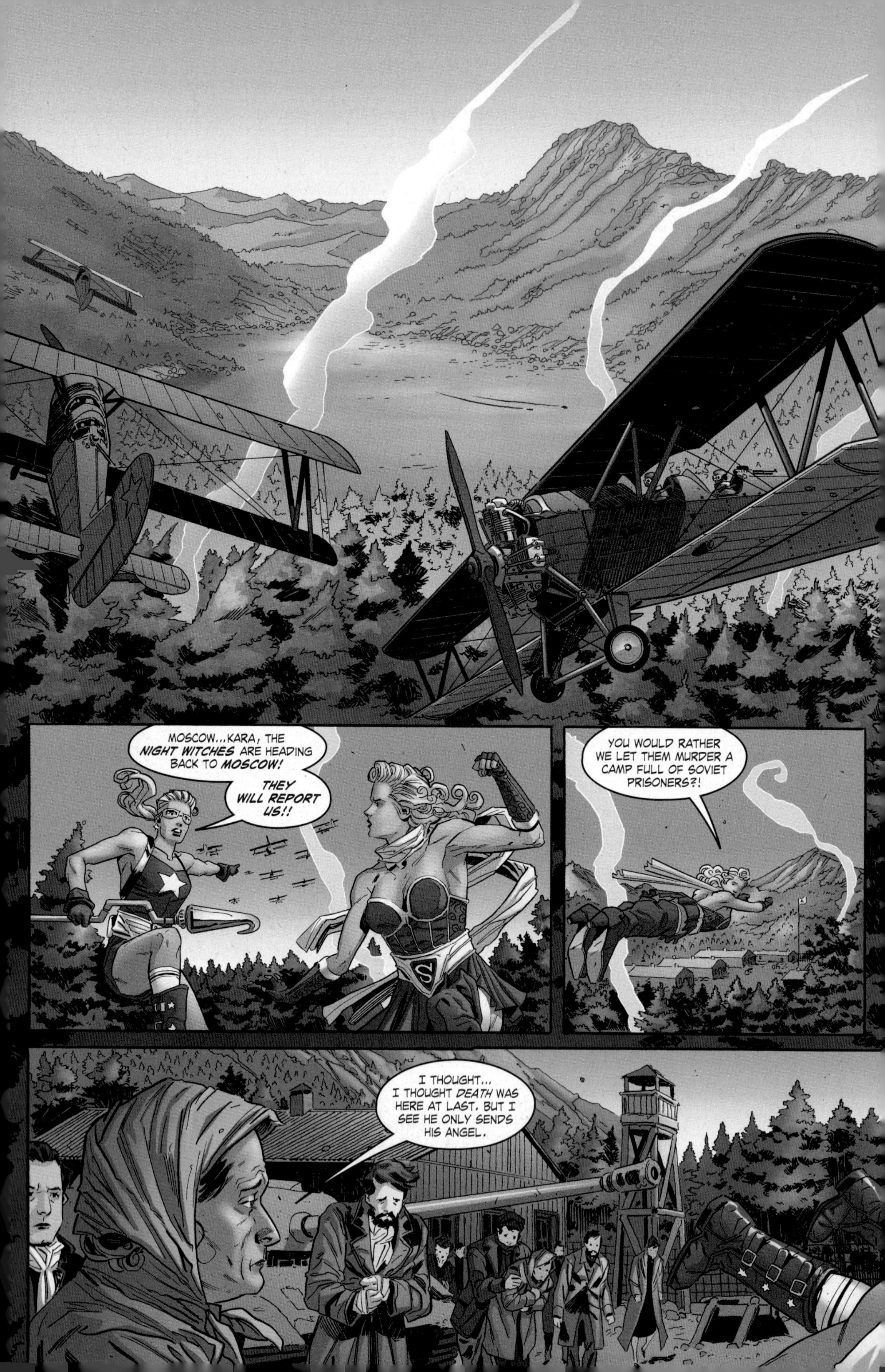

MOSCOW...KARA, THE NIGHT WITCHES ARE HEADING BACK TO MOSCOW!
THEY WILL REPORT US!!
YOU WOULD RATHER WE LET THEM MURDER A CAMP FULL OF SOVIET PRISONERS?!
I THOUGHT... I THOUGHT DEATH WAS HERE AT LAST. BUT I SEE HE ONLY SENDS HIS ANGEL.

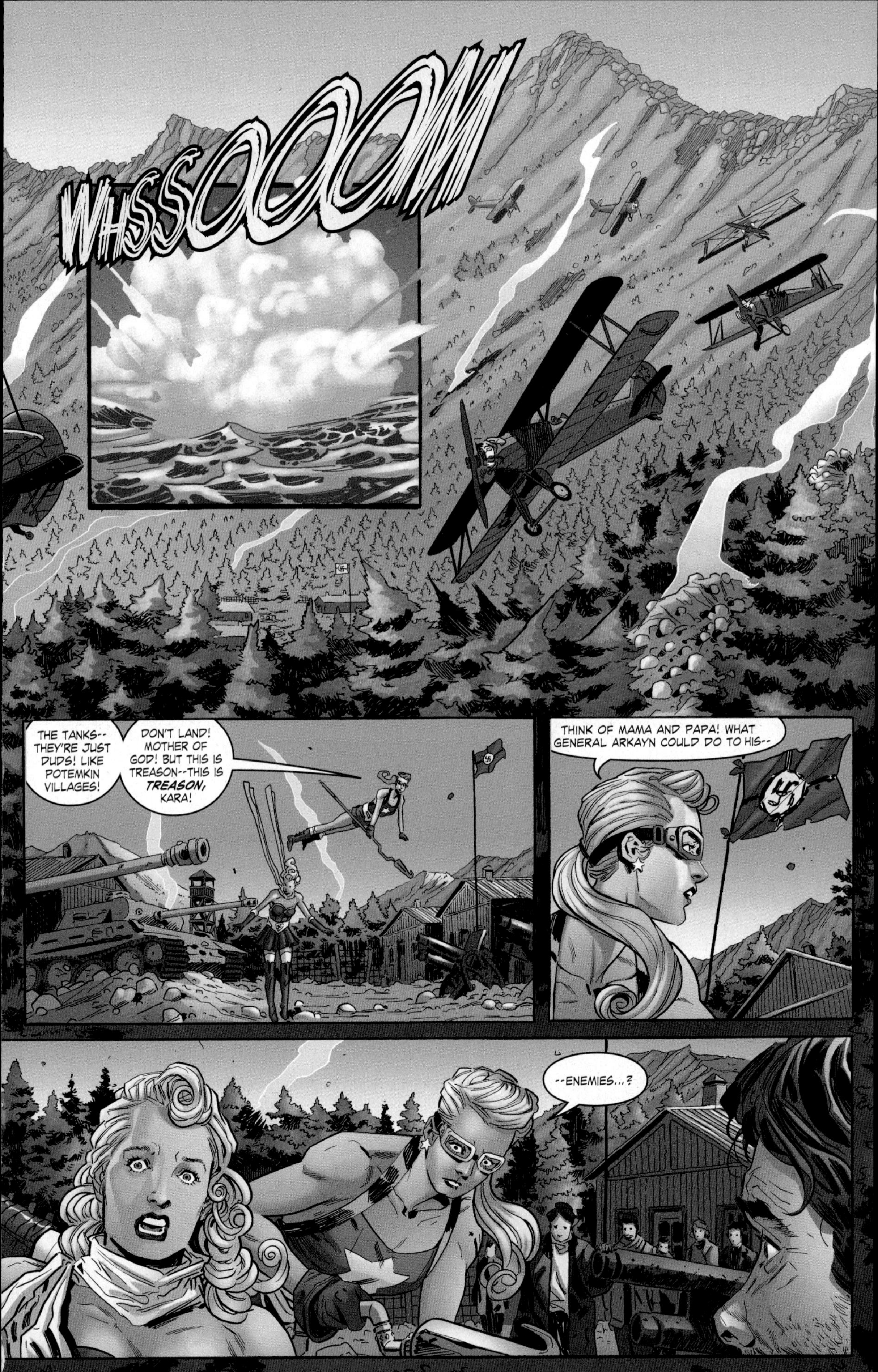
WHSSOOOOM
THE TANKS--THEY'RE JUST DUDS! LIKE POTEMKIN VILLAGES!
DON'T LAND! MOTHER OF GOD! BUT THIS IS TREASON--THIS IS *TREASON,* KARA!
THINK OF MAMA AND PAPA! WHAT GENERAL ARKAYN COULD DO TO HIS--
--ENEMIES...?

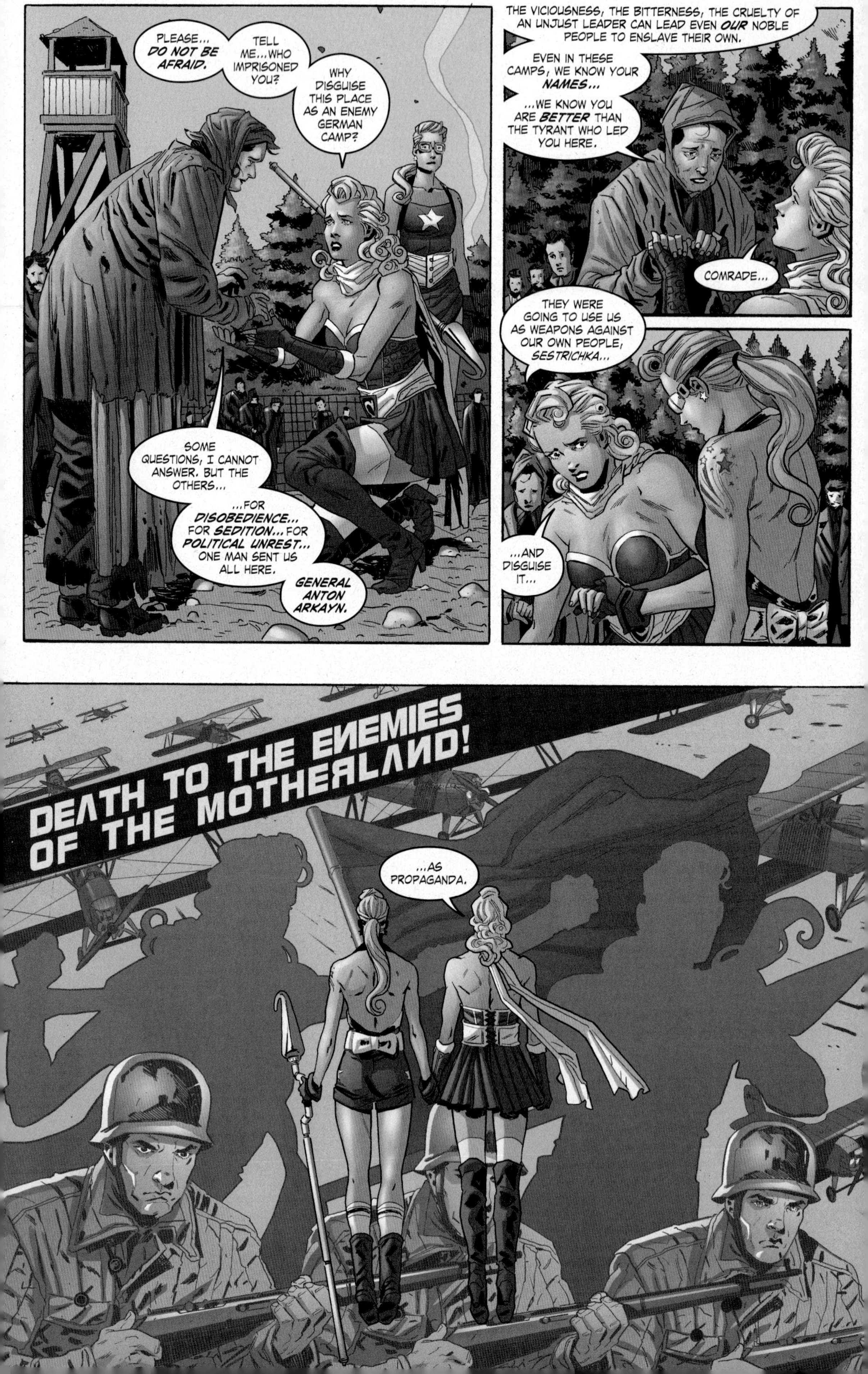
PLEASE... DO NOT BE AFRAID.
TELL ME...WHO IMPRISONED YOU?
WHY DISGUISE THIS PLACE AS AN ENEMY GERMAN CAMP?
SOME QUESTIONS, I CANNOT ANSWER. BUT THE OTHERS...
...FOR DISOBEDIENCE... FOR SEDITION... FOR POLITICAL UNREST... ONE MAN SENT US ALL HERE.
GENERAL ANTON ARKAYN.
THE VICIOUSNESS, THE BITTERNESS, THE CRUELTY OF AN UNJUST LEADER CAN LEAD EVEN OUR NOBLE PEOPLE TO ENSLAVE THEIR OWN.
EVEN IN THESE CAMPS, WE KNOW YOUR NAMES...
...WE KNOW YOU ARE BETTER THAN THE TYRANT WHO LED YOU HERE.
COMRADE...
THEY WERE GOING TO USE US AS WEAPONS AGAINST OUR OWN PEOPLE, SESTRICHKA...
...AND DISGUISE IT...
DEATH TO THE ENEMIES OF THE MOTHERLAND!
...AS PROPAGANDA.

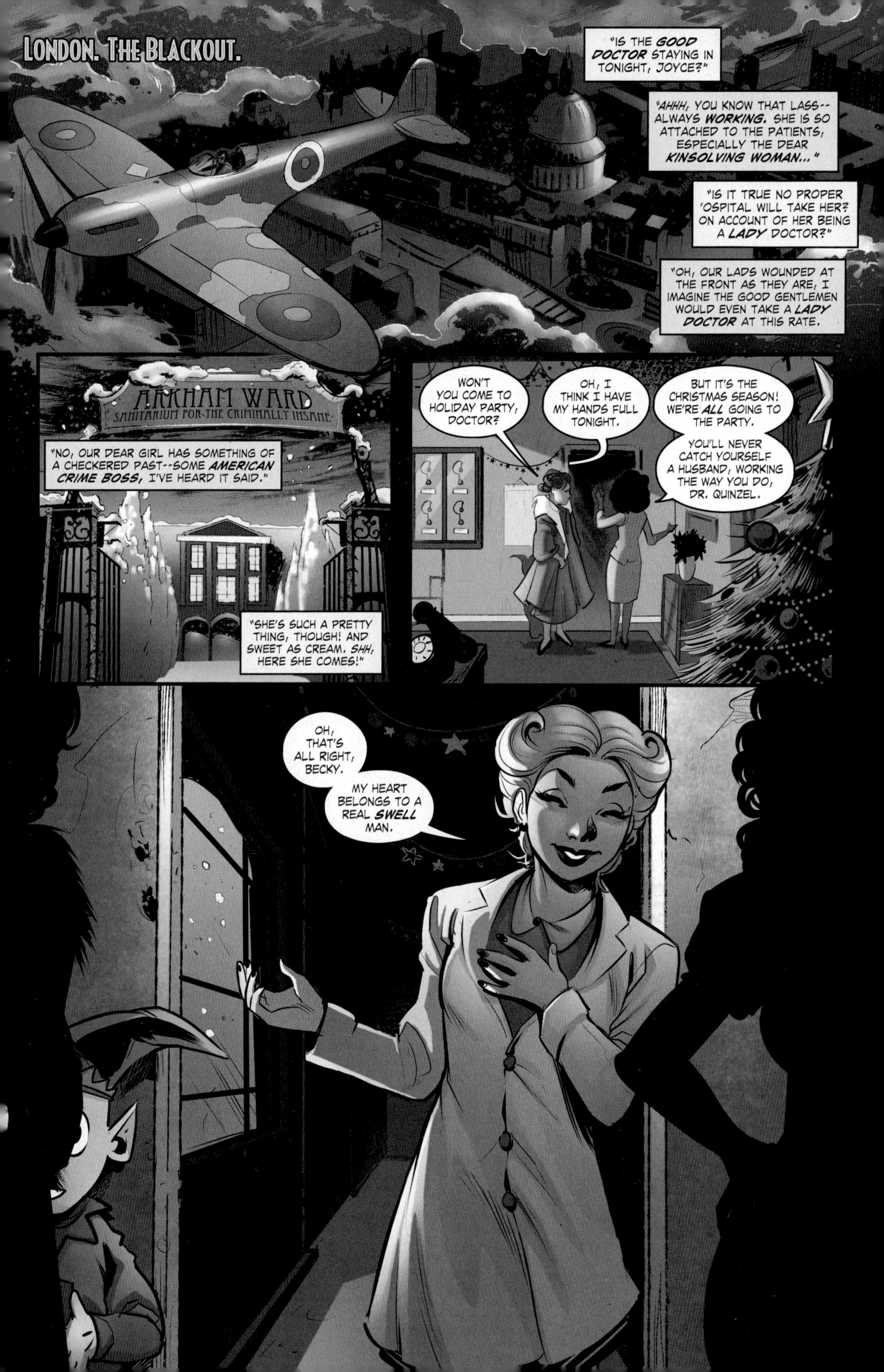

LONDON. THE BLACKOUT.
"IS THE GOOD DOCTOR STAYING IN TONIGHT, JOYCE?"
"AHHH, YOU KNOW THAT LASS--ALWAYS WORKING. SHE IS SO ATTACHED TO THE PATIENTS, ESPECIALLY THE DEAR KINSOLVING WOMAN..."
"IS IT TRUE NO PROPER 'OSPITAL WILL TAKE HER? ON ACCOUNT OF HER BEING A LADY DOCTOR?"
"OH, OUR LADS WOUNDED AT THE FRONT AS THEY ARE, I IMAGINE THE GOOD GENTLEMEN WOULD EVEN TAKE A LADY DOCTOR AT THIS RATE.
ARKHAM WARD
SANITARIUM FOR THE CRIMINALLY INSANE
"NO, OUR DEAR GIRL HAS SOMETHING OF A CHECKERED PAST--SOME AMERICAN CRIME BOSS, I'VE HEARD IT SAID."
"SHE'S SUCH A PRETTY THING, THOUGH! AND SWEET AS CREAM. SHH, HERE SHE COMES!"
WON'T YOU COME TO HOLIDAY PARTY, DOCTOR?
OH, I THINK I HAVE MY HANDS FULL TONIGHT.
BUT IT'S THE CHRISTMAS SEASON! WE'RE ALL GOING TO THE PARTY.
YOU'LL NEVER CATCH YOURSELF A HUSBAND, WORKING THE WAY YOU DO, DR. QUINZEL.
OH, THAT'S ALL RIGHT, BECKY.
MY HEART BELONGS TO A REAL SWELL MAN.

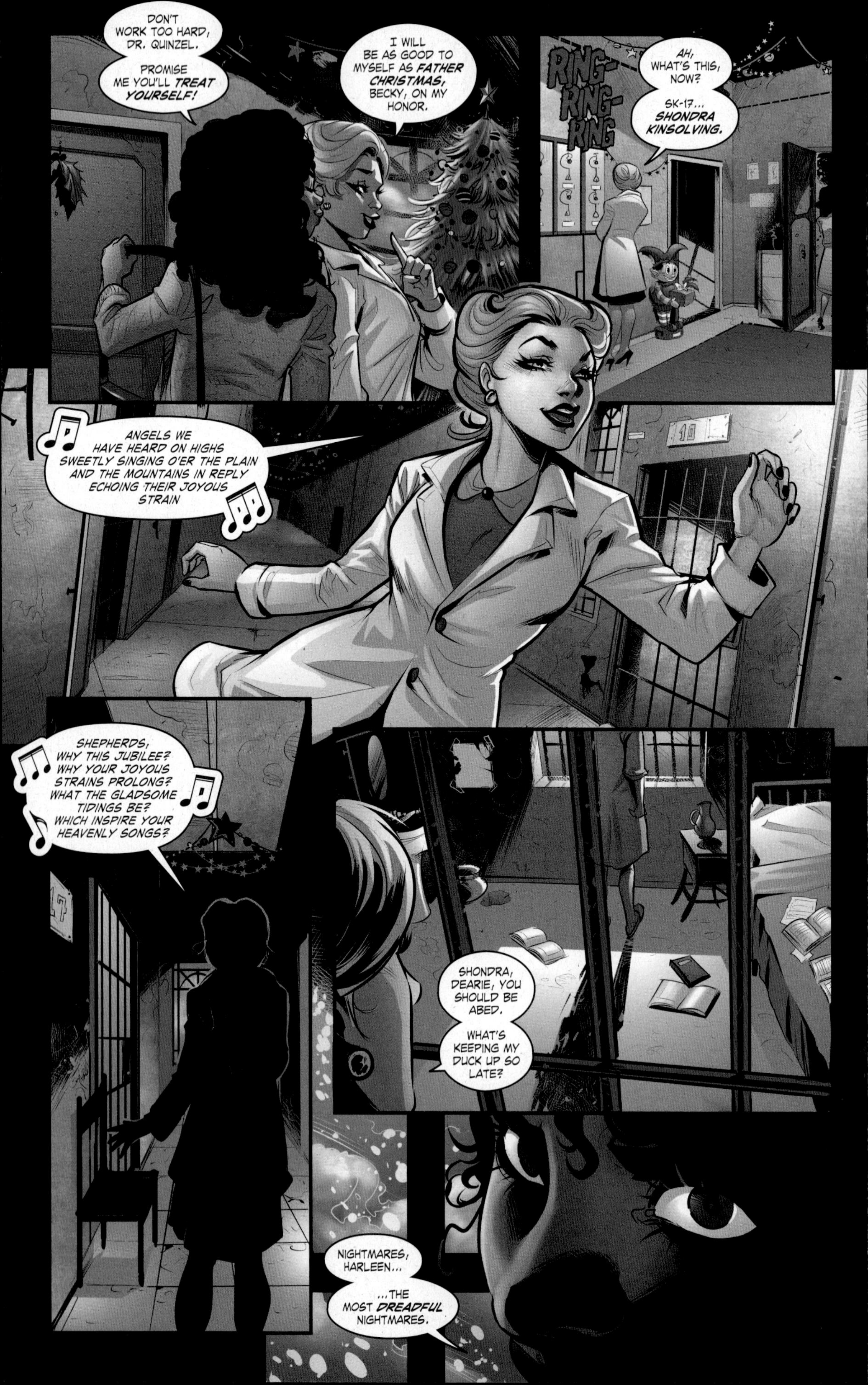
DON'T WORK TOO HARD, DR. QUINZEL.
PROMISE ME YOU'LL TREAT YOURSELF!
I WILL BE AS GOOD TO MYSELF AS FATHER CHRISTMAS, BECKY, ON MY HONOR.
RING-RING-RING
AH, WHAT'S THIS, NOW?
SK-17... SHONDRA KINSOLVING.
ANGELS WE HAVE HEARD ON HIGHS SWEETLY SINGING O'ER THE PLAIN AND THE MOUNTAINS IN REPLY ECHOING THEIR JOYOUS STRAIN
SHEPHERDS, WHY THIS JUBILEE? WHY YOUR JOYOUS STRAINS PROLONG? WHAT THE GLADSOME TIDINGS BE? WHICH INSPIRE YOUR HEAVENLY SONGS?
SHONDRA, DEARIE, YOU SHOULD BE ABED.
WHAT'S KEEPING MY DUCK UP SO LATE?
NIGHTMARES, HARLEEN...
...THE MOST DREADFUL NIGHTMARES.

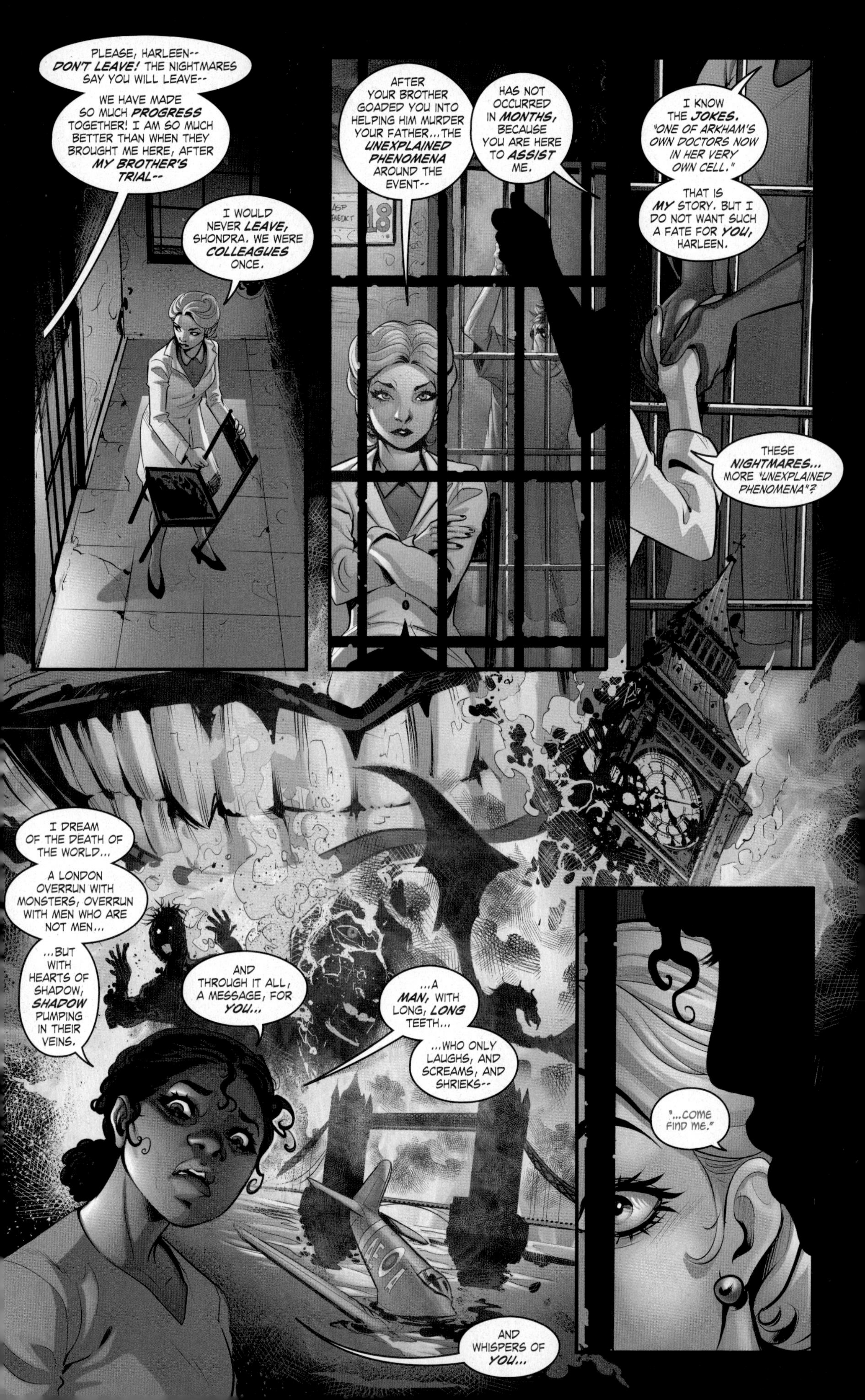

PLEASE, HARLEEN-- DON'T LEAVE! THE NIGHTMARES SAY YOU WILL LEAVE--
WE HAVE MADE SO MUCH PROGRESS TOGETHER! I AM SO MUCH BETTER THAN WHEN THEY BROUGHT ME HERE, AFTER MY BROTHER'S TRIAL--
I WOULD NEVER LEAVE, SHONDRA. WE WERE COLLEAGUES ONCE.
AFTER YOUR BROTHER GOADED YOU INTO HELPING HIM MURDER YOUR FATHER...THE UNEXPLAINED PHENOMENA AROUND THE EVENT--
HAS NOT OCCURRED IN MONTHS, BECAUSE YOU ARE HERE TO ASSIST ME.
I KNOW THE JOKES. "ONE OF ARKHAM'S OWN DOCTORS NOW IN HER VERY OWN CELL."
THAT IS MY STORY. BUT I DO NOT WANT SUCH A FATE FOR YOU, HARLEEN.
THESE NIGHTMARES... MORE "UNEXPLAINED PHENOMENA"?
I DREAM OF THE DEATH OF THE WORLD...
A LONDON OVERRUN WITH MONSTERS, OVERRUN WITH MEN WHO ARE NOT MEN...
...BUT WITH HEARTS OF SHADOW, SHADOW PUMPING IN THEIR VEINS.
AND THROUGH IT ALL, A MESSAGE, FOR YOU...
...A MAN, WITH LONG, LONG TEETH...
...WHO ONLY LAUGHS, AND SCREAMS, AND SHRIEKS--
AND WHISPERS OF YOU...
"...COME FIND ME."

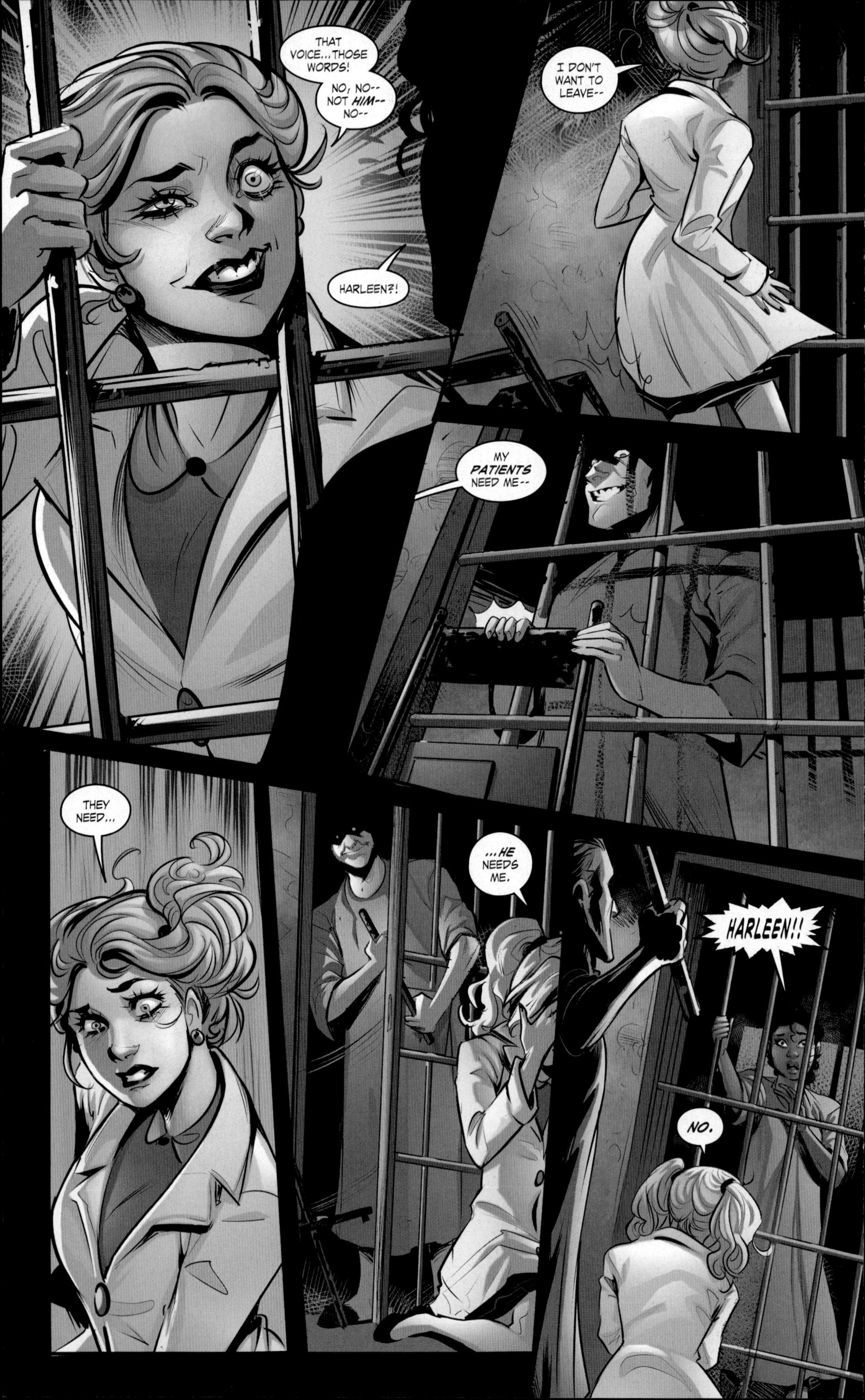
THAT VOICE...THOSE WORDS!
NO, NO-- NOT *HIM*-- NO--
HARLEEN?!
I DON'T WANT TO LEAVE--
MY *PATIENTS* NEED ME--
THEY NEED...
...*HE* NEEDS ME.
HARLEEN!!
NO.

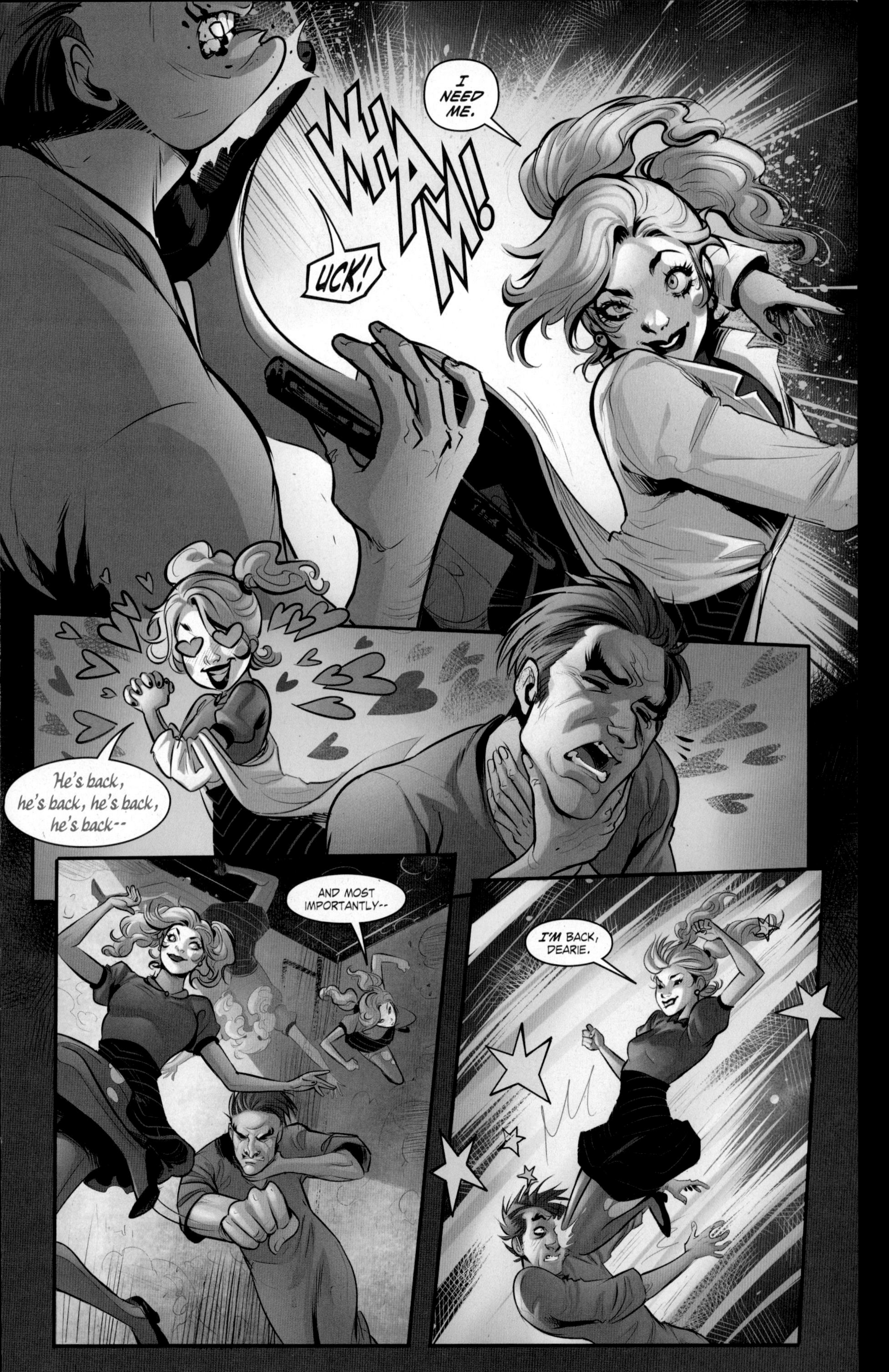
I NEED ME.
WHAM!
UCK!
He's back, he's back, he's back, he's back--
AND MOST IMPORTANTLY--
I'M BACK, DEARIE.

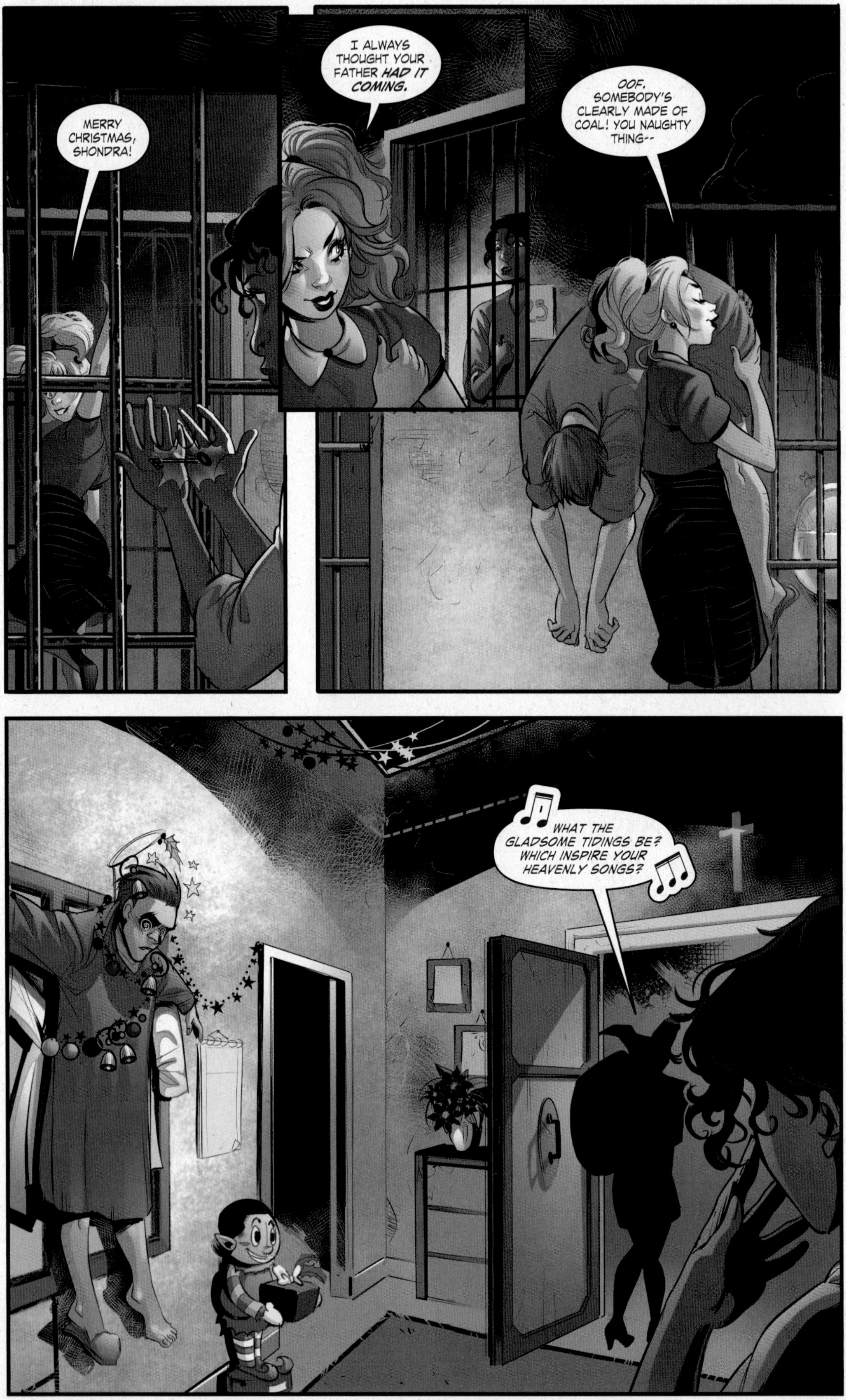
MERRY CHRISTMAS, SHONDRA!
I ALWAYS THOUGHT YOUR FATHER HAD IT COMING.
OOF. SOMEBODY'S CLEARLY MADE OF COAL! YOU NAUGHTY THING--
WHAT THE GLADSOME TIDINGS BE? WHICH INSPIRE YOUR HEAVENLY SONGS?
25

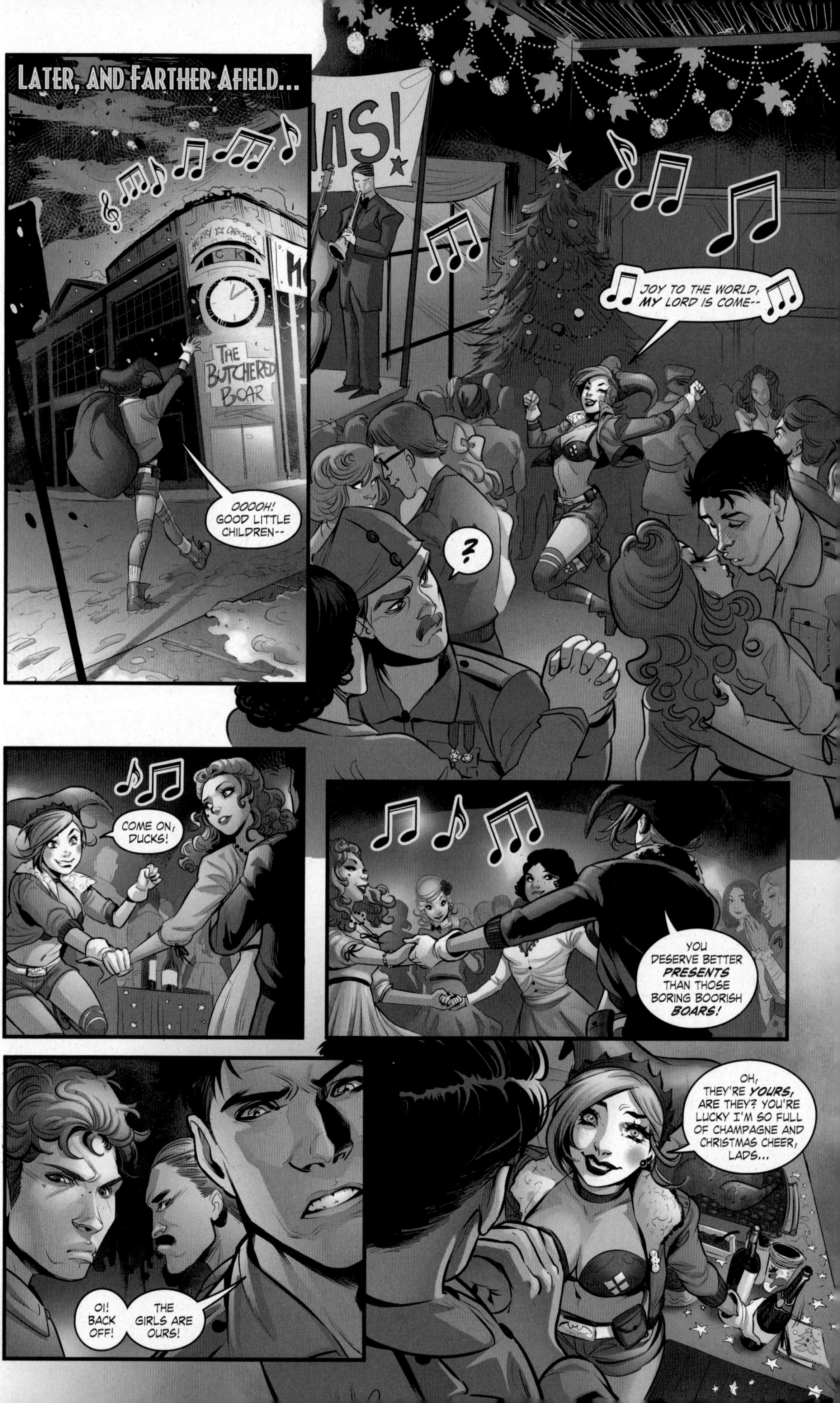
LATER, AND FARTHER AFIELD...
MERRY CHRISTMAS
THE BUTCHERED BOAR
OOOOH! GOOD LITTLE CHILDREN--
JOY TO THE WORLD, MY LORD IS COME--
?
COME ON, DUCKS!
YOU DESERVE BETTER PRESENTS THAN THOSE BORING BOORISH BOARS!
OI! BACK OFF!
THE GIRLS ARE OURS!
OH, THEY'RE YOURS, ARE THEY? YOU'RE LUCKY I'M SO FULL OF CHAMPAGNE AND CHRISTMAS CHEER, LADS...

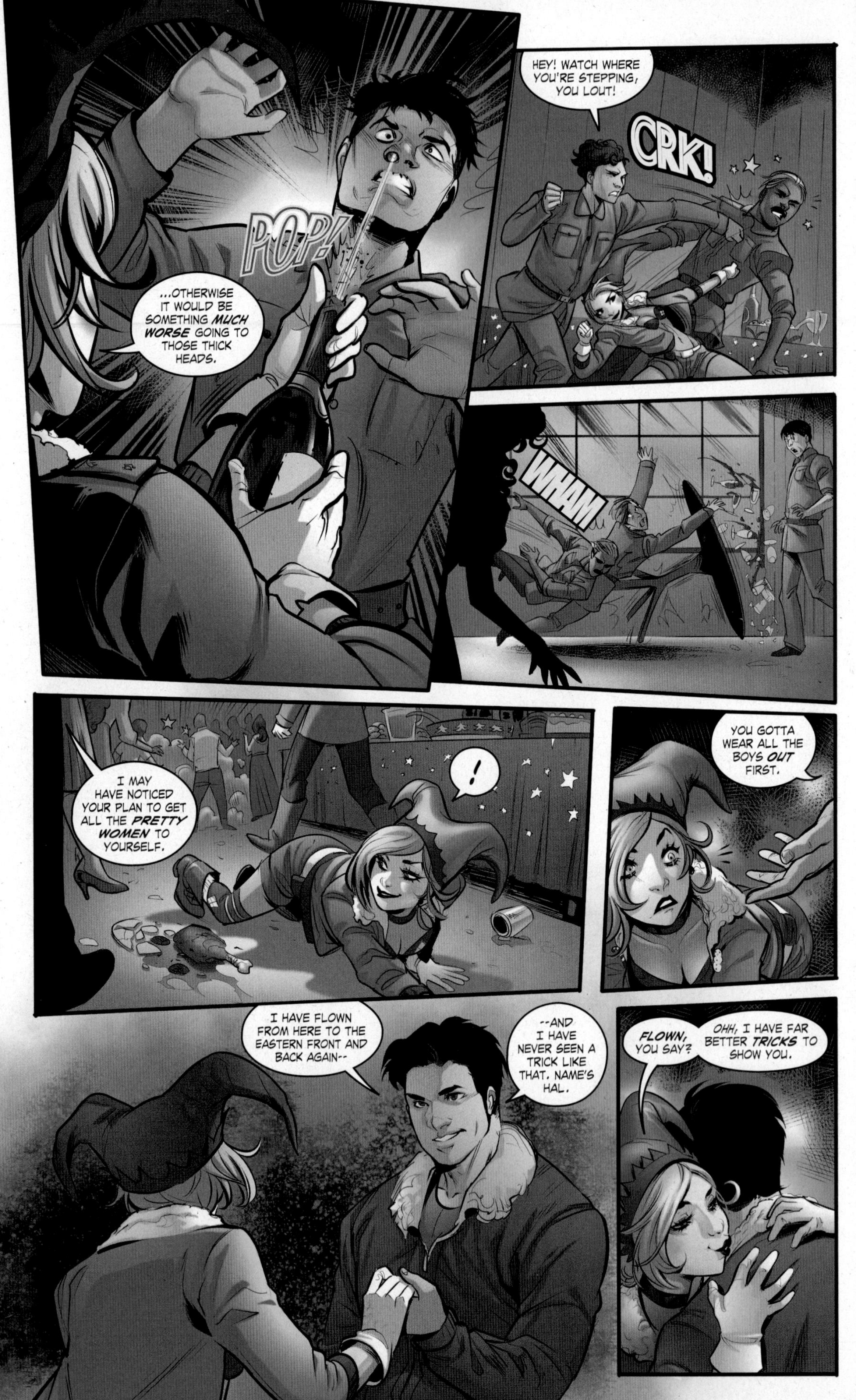
POP!
...OTHERWISE IT WOULD BE SOMETHING MUCH WORSE GOING TO THOSE THICK HEADS.
HEY! WATCH WHERE YOU'RE STEPPING, YOU LOUT!
CRK!
WHAM
I MAY HAVE NOTICED YOUR PLAN TO GET ALL THE PRETTY WOMEN TO YOURSELF.
!
YOU GOTTA WEAR ALL THE BOYS OUT FIRST.
I HAVE FLOWN FROM HERE TO THE EASTERN FRONT AND BACK AGAIN--
--AND I HAVE NEVER SEEN A TRICK LIKE THAT. NAME'S HAL.
FLOWN, YOU SAY?
OHH, I HAVE FAR BETTER TRICKS TO SHOW YOU.

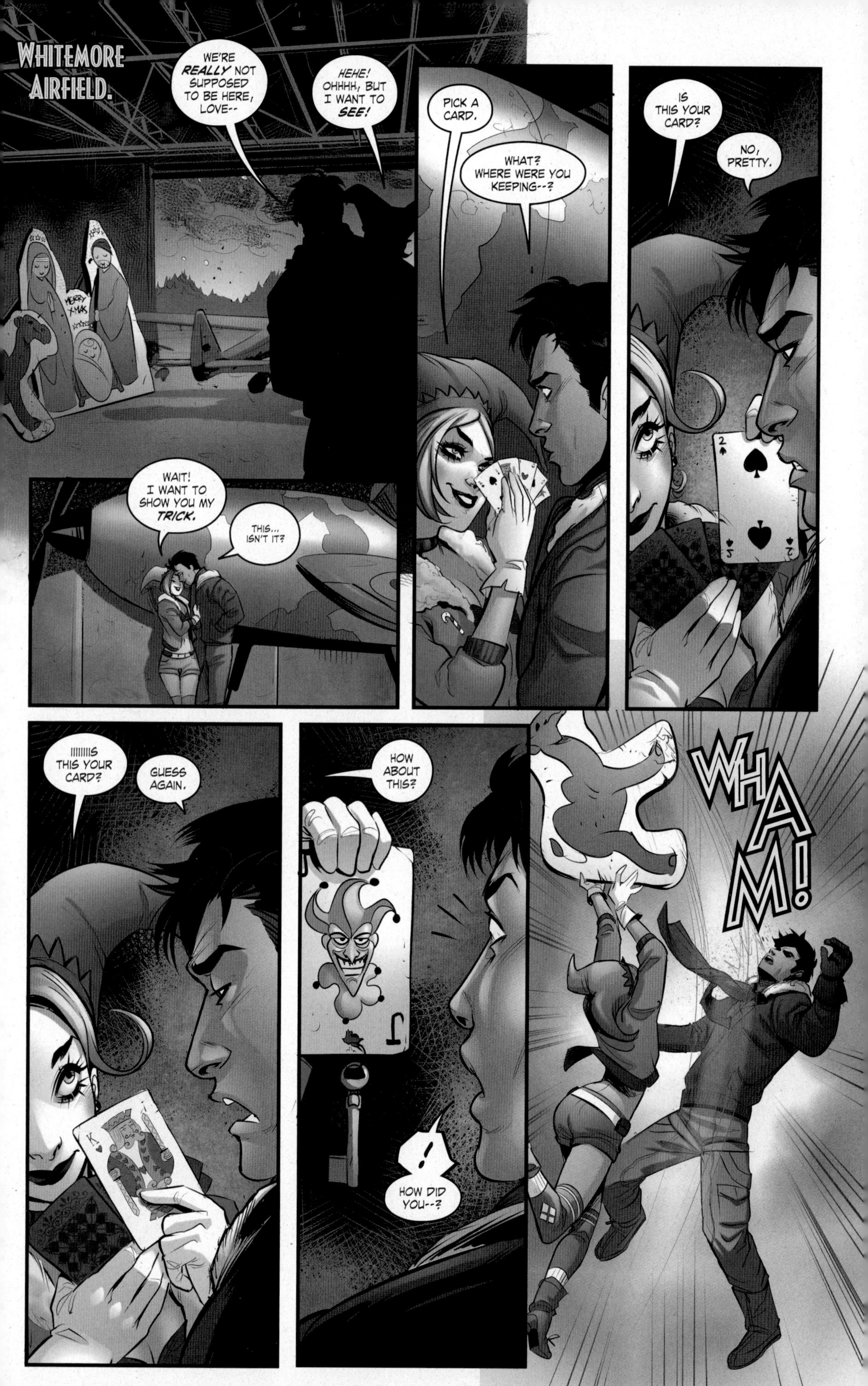
WHITEMORE AIRFIELD.
WE'RE REALLY NOT SUPPOSED TO BE HERE, LOVE--
HEHE! OHHHH, BUT I WANT TO SEE!
MERRY X-MAS
PICK A CARD.
WHAT? WHERE WERE YOU KEEPING--?
IS THIS YOUR CARD?
NO, PRETTY.
WAIT! I WANT TO SHOW YOU MY TRICK.
THIS... ISN'T IT?
IIIIIIIS THIS YOUR CARD?
GUESS AGAIN.
HOW ABOUT THIS?
!
HOW DID YOU--?
WHAM!

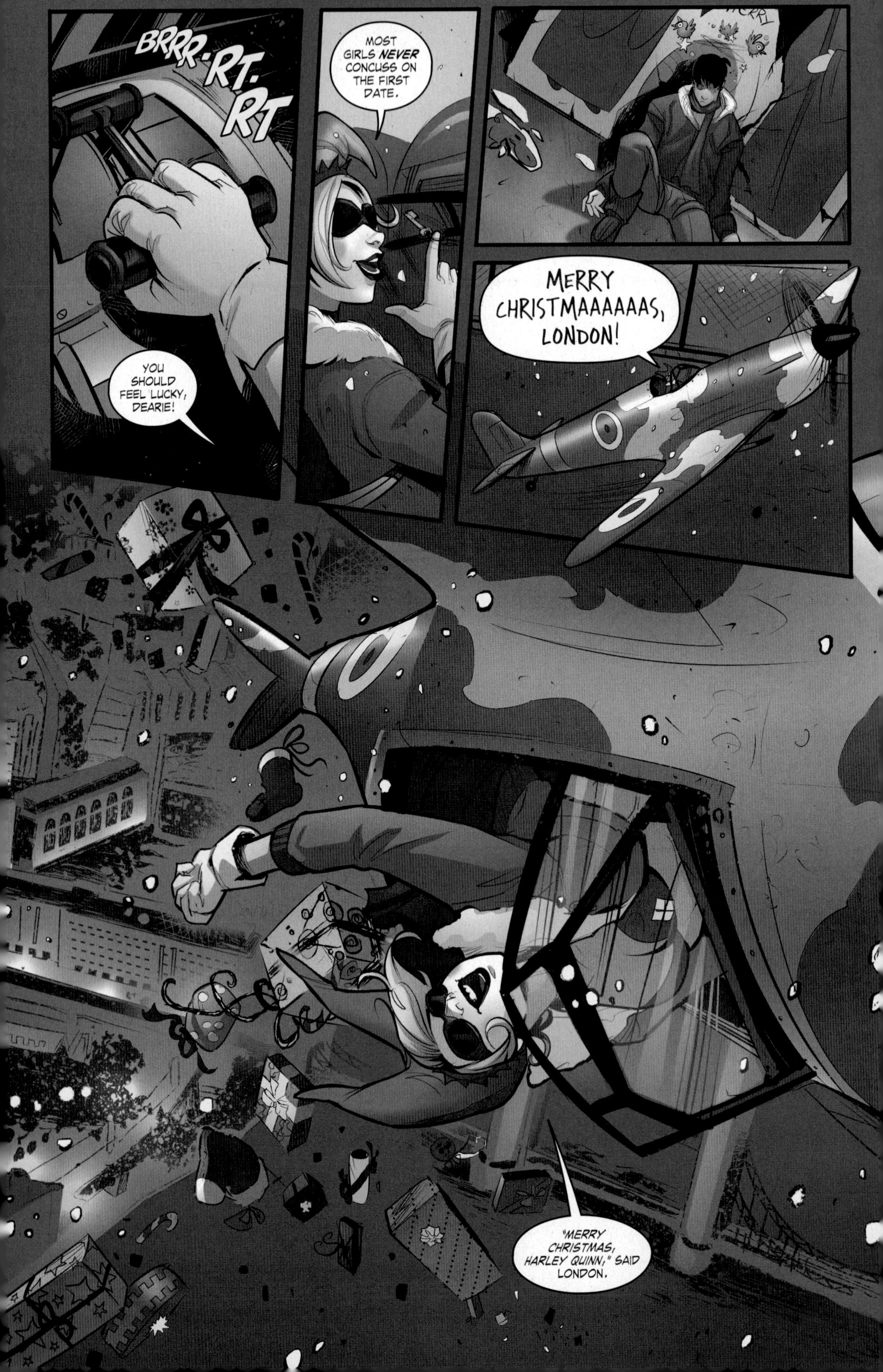
BRRR-RT-RT
YOU SHOULD FEEL LUCKY, DEARIE!
MOST GIRLS NEVER CONCUSS ON THE FIRST DATE.
MERRY CHRISTMAAAAAAS, LONDON!
"MERRY CHRISTMAS, HARLEY QUINN," SAID LONDON.

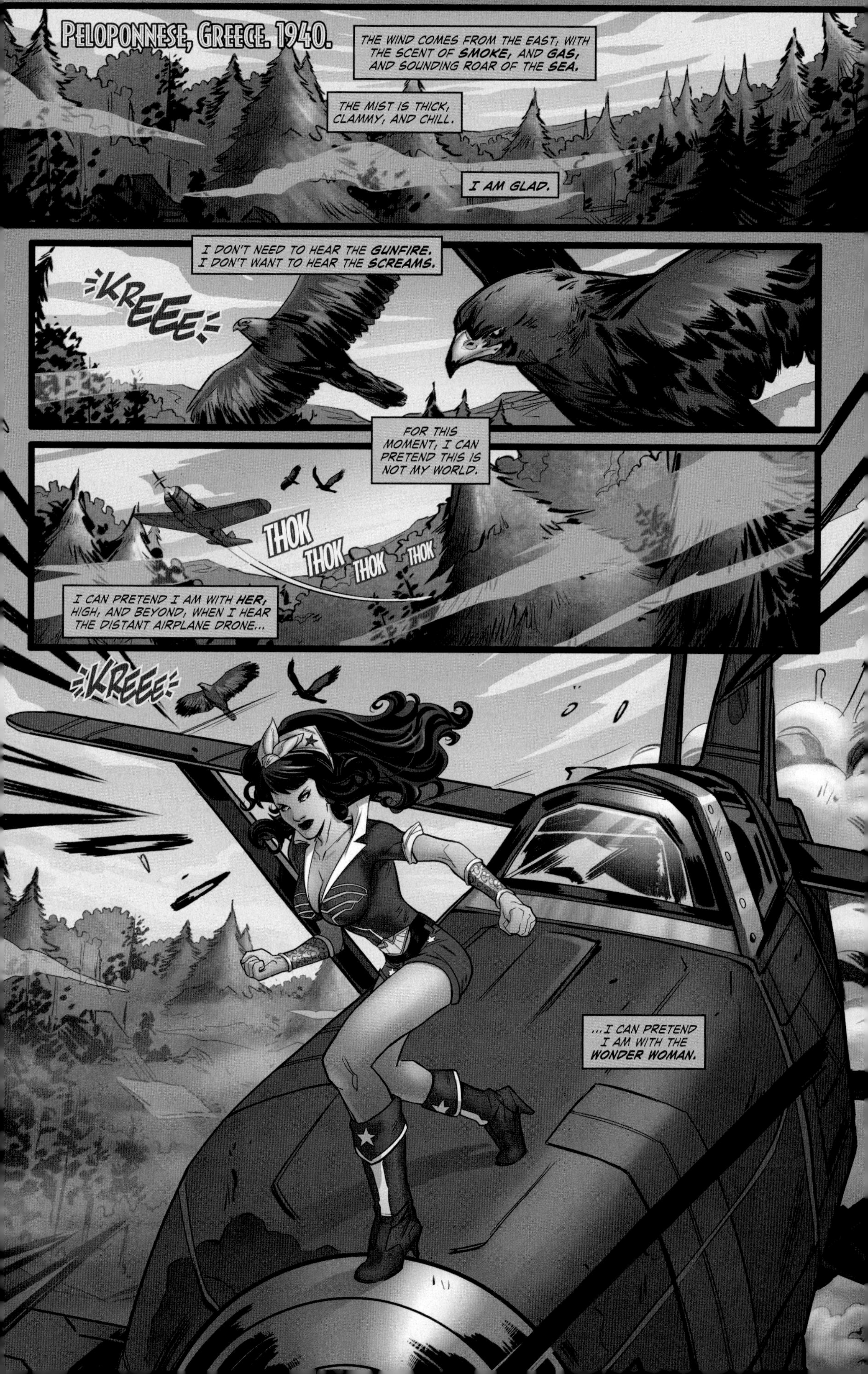
PELOPONNESE, GREECE. 1940.
THE WIND COMES FROM THE EAST, WITH THE SCENT OF SMOKE, AND GAS, AND SOUNDING ROAR OF THE SEA.
THE MIST IS THICK, CLAMMY, AND CHILL.
I AM GLAD.
I DON'T NEED TO HEAR THE GUNFIRE. I DON'T WANT TO HEAR THE SCREAMS.
KREEEE
FOR THIS MOMENT, I CAN PRETEND THIS IS NOT MY WORLD.
THOK THOK THOK THOK
I CAN PRETEND I AM WITH HER, HIGH, AND BEYOND, WHEN I HEAR THE DISTANT AIRPLANE DRONE...
KREEE
...I CAN PRETEND I AM WITH THE WONDER WOMAN.

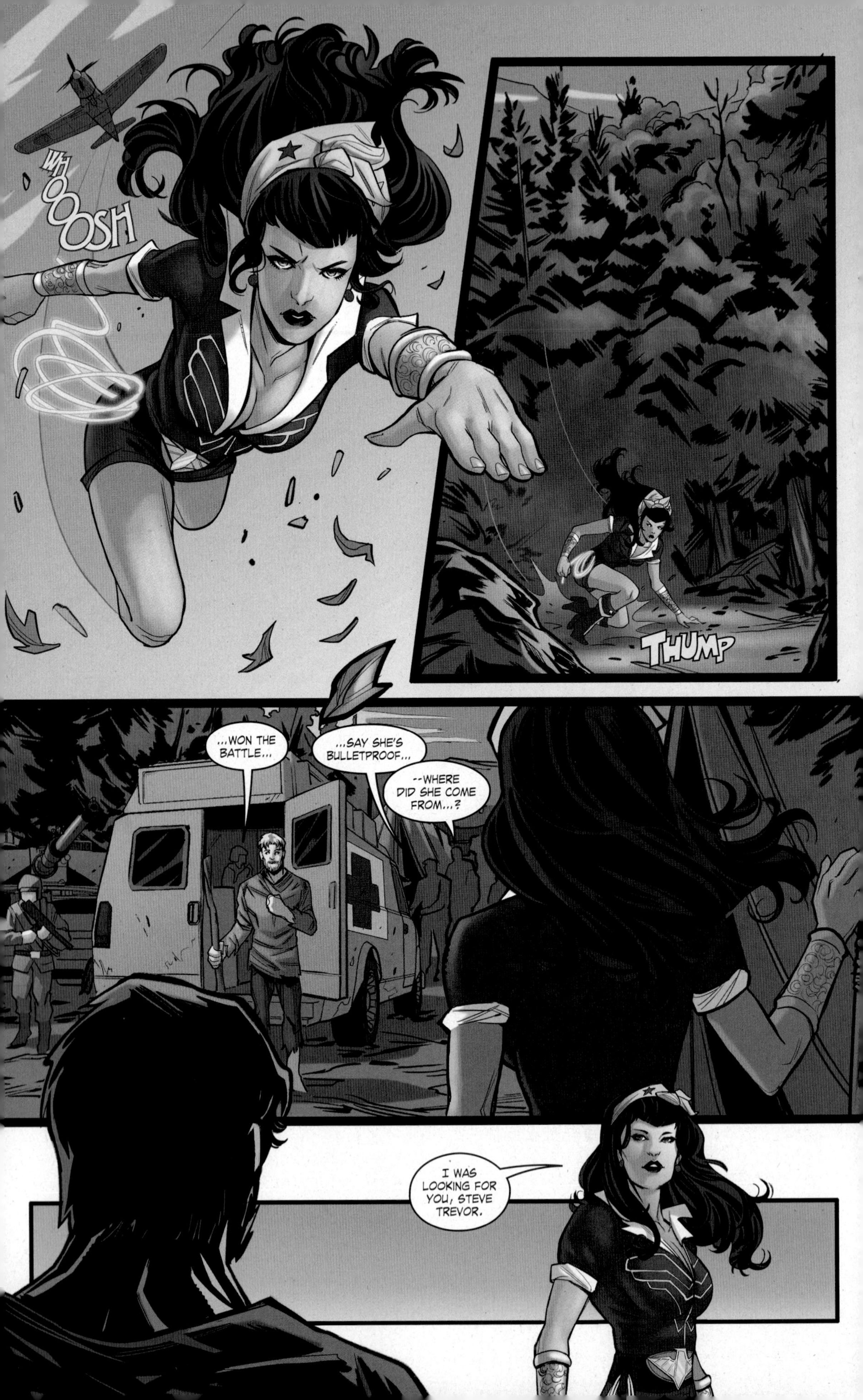
WHOOOSH
THUMP
...WON THE BATTLE...
...SAY SHE'S BULLETPROOF...
--WHERE DID SHE COME FROM...?
I WAS LOOKING FOR YOU, STEVE TREVOR.

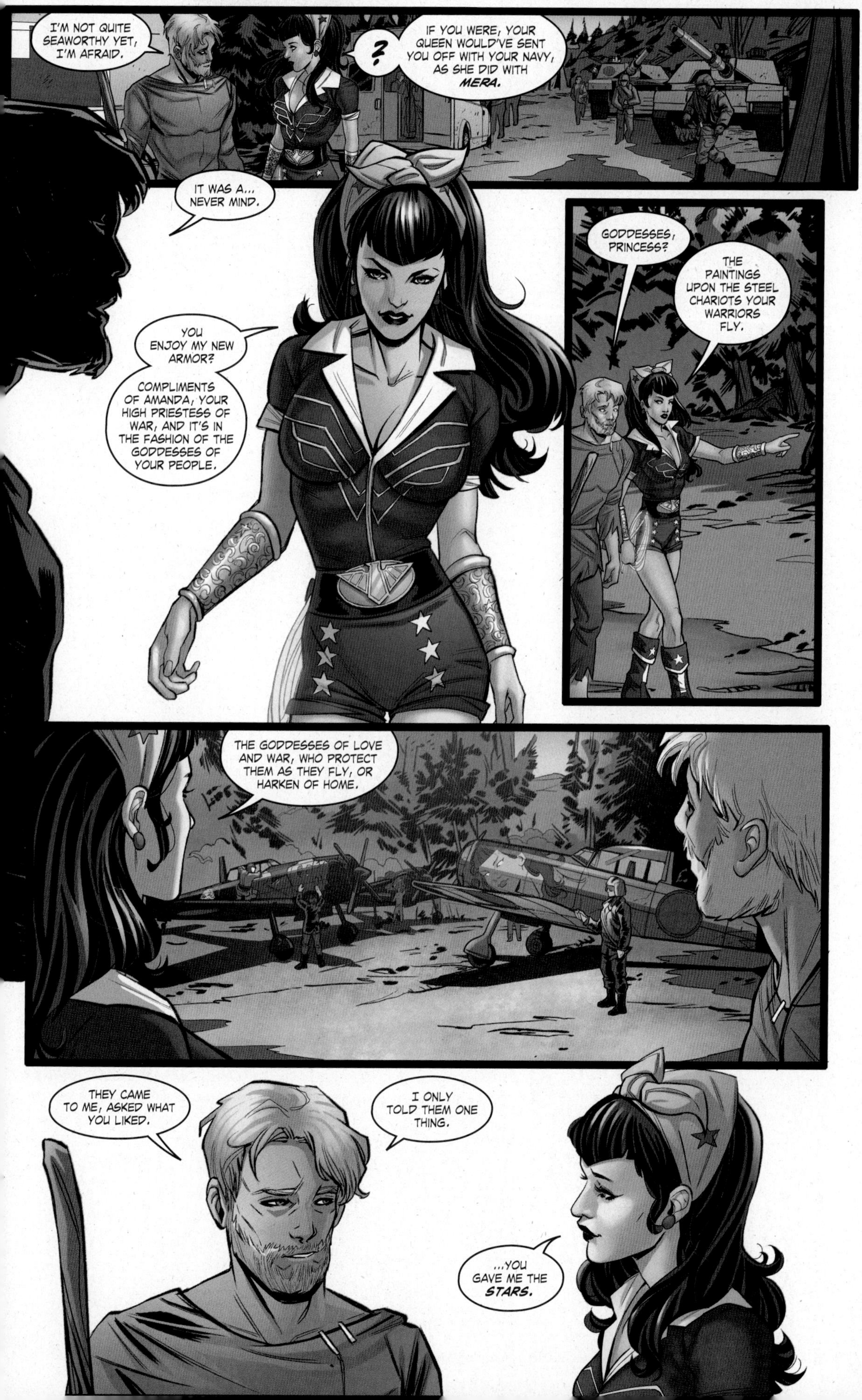
I'M NOT QUITE SEAWORTHY YET, I'M AFRAID.
?
IF YOU WERE, YOUR QUEEN WOULD'VE SENT YOU OFF WITH YOUR NAVY, AS SHE DID WITH MERA.
IT WAS A... NEVER MIND.
YOU ENJOY MY NEW ARMOR?
COMPLIMENTS OF AMANDA, YOUR HIGH PRIESTESS OF WAR, AND IT'S IN THE FASHION OF THE GODDESSES OF YOUR PEOPLE.
GODDESSES, PRINCESS?
THE PAINTINGS UPON THE STEEL CHARIOTS YOUR WARRIORS FLY.
THE GODDESSES OF LOVE AND WAR, WHO PROTECT THEM AS THEY FLY, OR HARKEN OF HOME.
THEY CAME TO ME, ASKED WHAT YOU LIKED.
I ONLY TOLD THEM ONE THING.
...YOU GAVE ME THE STARS.

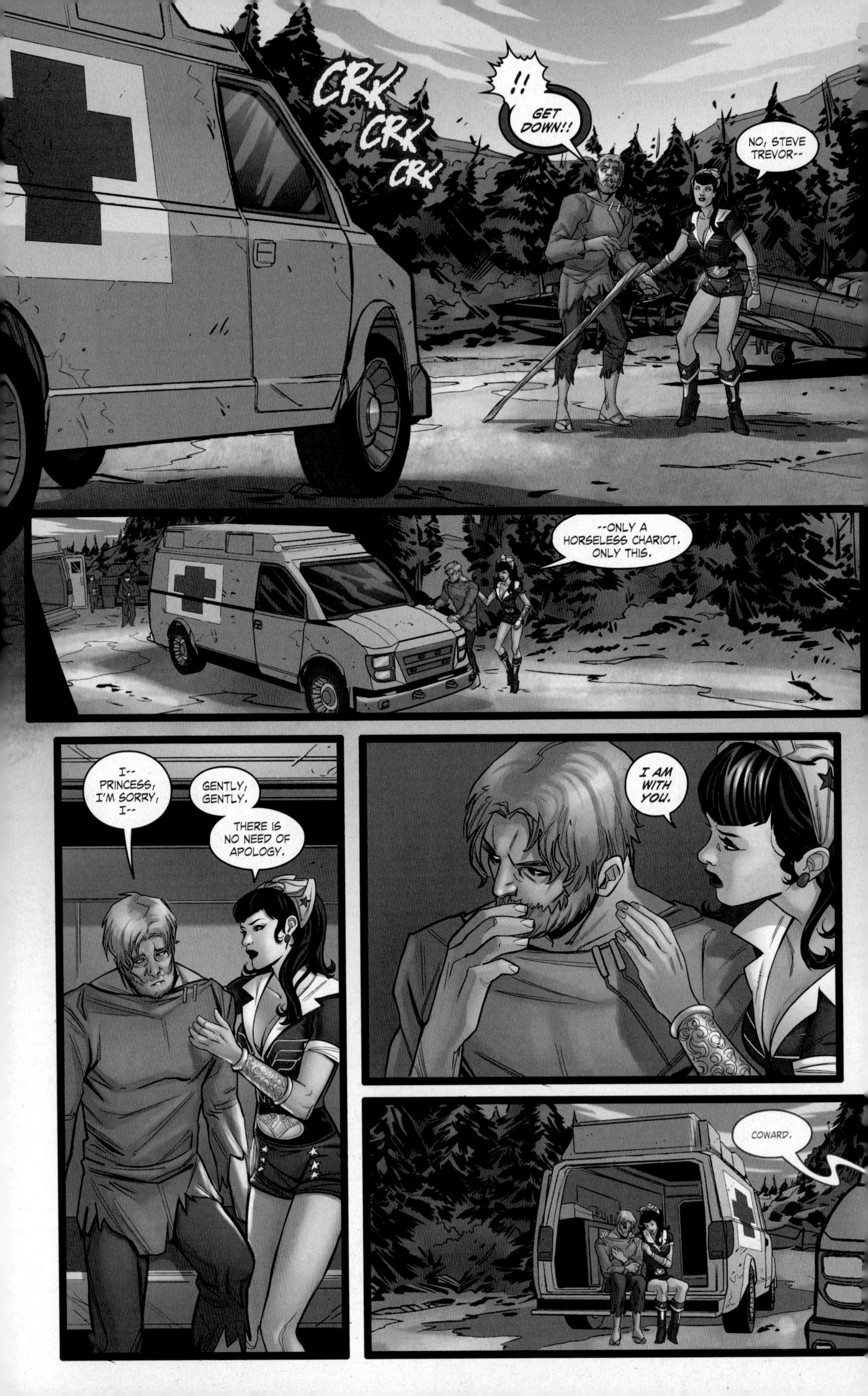
CRK CRK CRK
!!
GET DOWN!!
NO, STEVE TREVOR--
--ONLY A HORSELESS CHARIOT. ONLY THIS.
I-- PRINCESS, I'M SORRY, I--
GENTLY, GENTLY.
THERE IS NO NEED OF APOLOGY.
I AM WITH YOU.
COWARD.

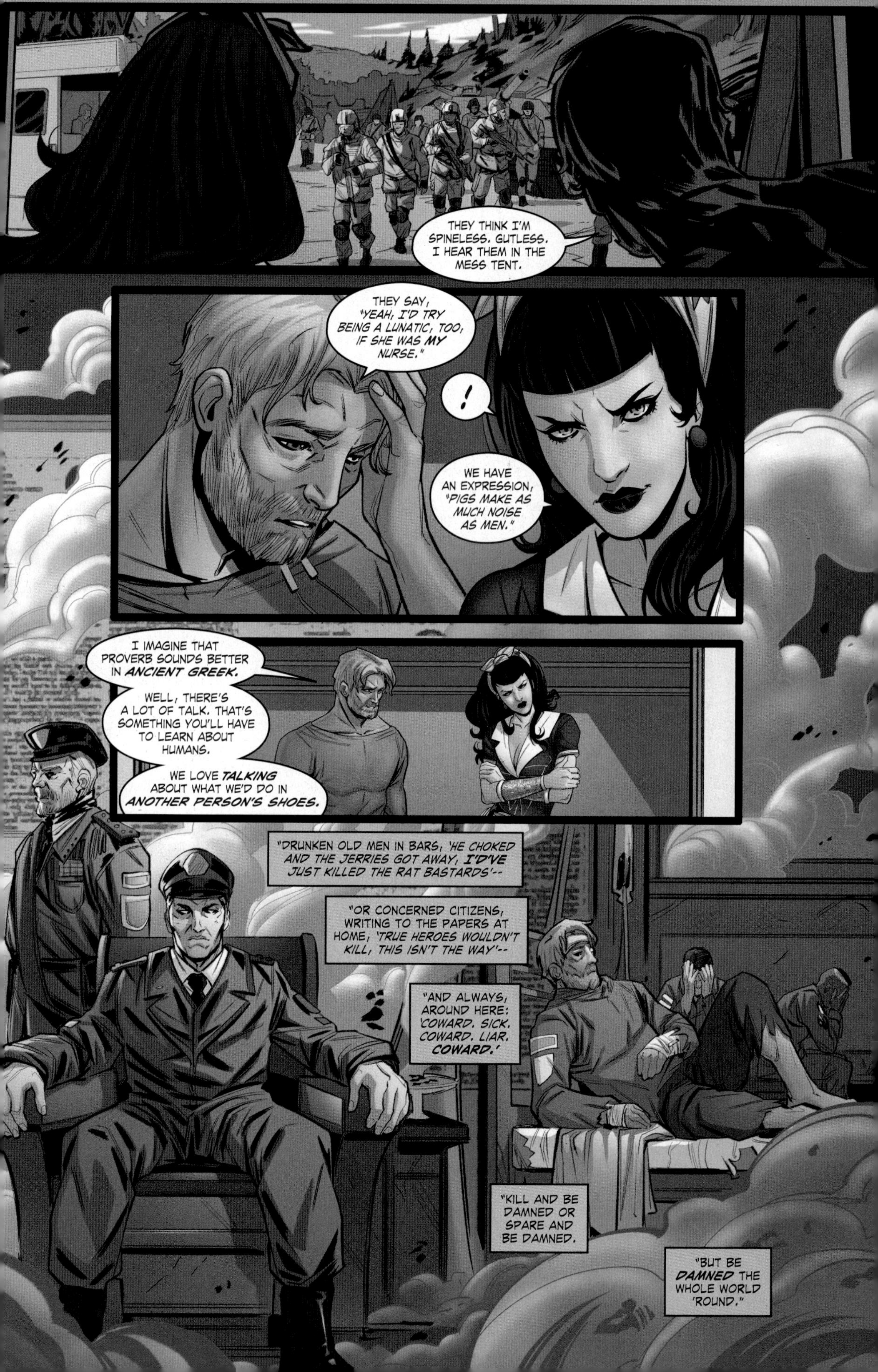
THEY THINK I'M SPINELESS. GUTLESS. I HEAR THEM IN THE MESS TENT.
THEY SAY, "YEAH, I'D TRY BEING A LUNATIC, TOO, IF SHE WAS MY NURSE."
!
WE HAVE AN EXPRESSION, "PIGS MAKE AS MUCH NOISE AS MEN."
I IMAGINE THAT PROVERB SOUNDS BETTER IN ANCIENT GREEK.
WELL, THERE'S A LOT OF TALK. THAT'S SOMETHING YOU'LL HAVE TO LEARN ABOUT HUMANS.
WE LOVE TALKING ABOUT WHAT WE'D DO IN ANOTHER PERSON'S SHOES.
"DRUNKEN OLD MEN IN BARS, 'HE CHOKED AND THE JERRIES GOT AWAY, I'D'VE JUST KILLED THE RAT BASTARDS'--
"OR CONCERNED CITIZENS, WRITING TO THE PAPERS AT HOME, 'TRUE HEROES WOULDN'T KILL, THIS ISN'T THE WAY'--
"AND ALWAYS, AROUND HERE: 'COWARD. SICK. COWARD. LIAR. COWARD.'
"KILL AND BE DAMNED OR SPARE AND BE DAMNED.
"BUT BE DAMNED THE WHOLE WORLD 'ROUND."

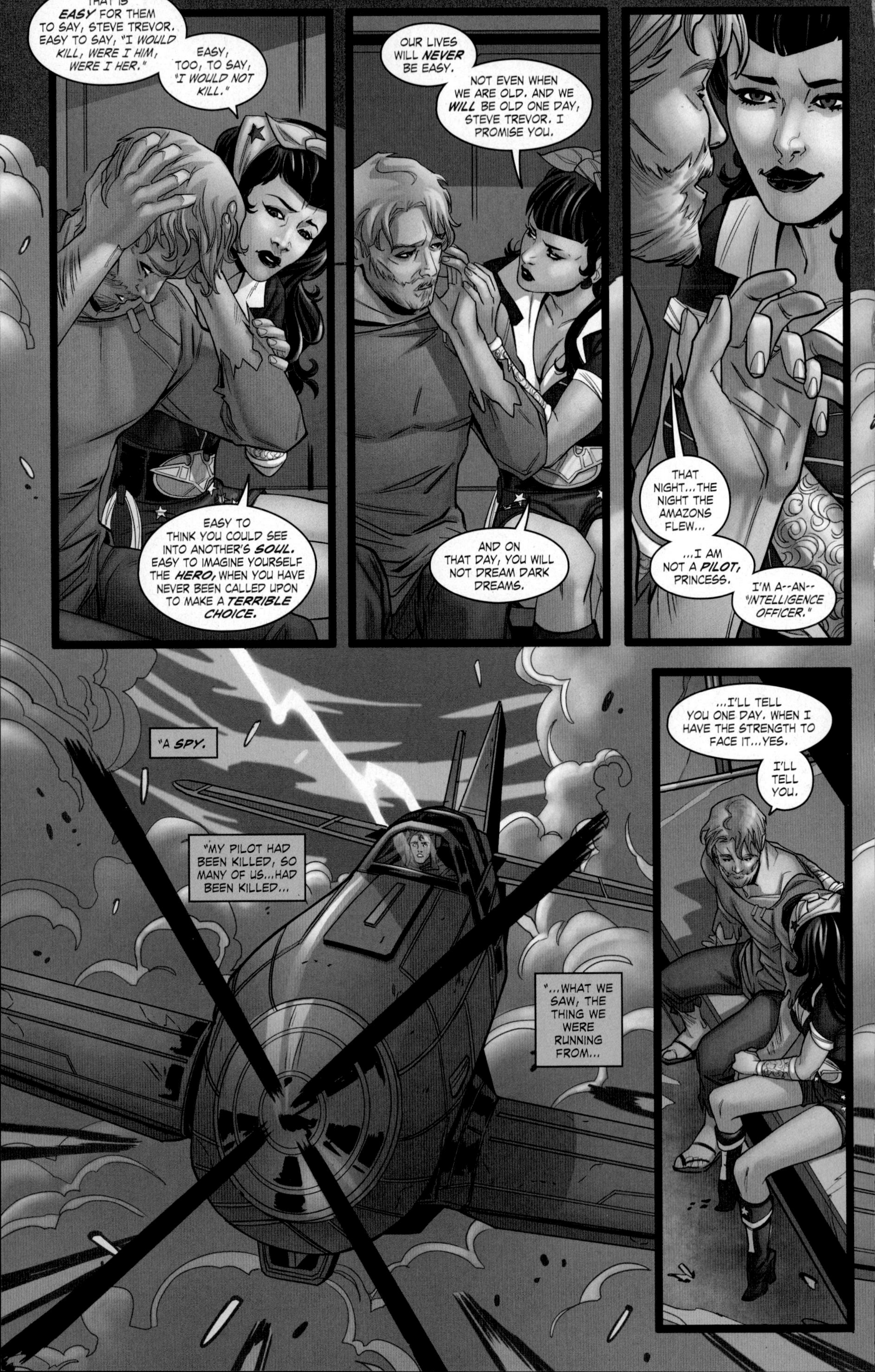
THAT IS EASY FOR THEM TO SAY, STEVE TREVOR. EASY TO SAY, "I WOULD KILL, WERE I HIM, WERE I HER."
EASY, TOO, TO SAY, "I WOULD NOT KILL."
EASY TO THINK YOU COULD SEE INTO ANOTHER'S SOUL. EASY TO IMAGINE YOURSELF THE HERO, WHEN YOU HAVE NEVER BEEN CALLED UPON TO MAKE A TERRIBLE CHOICE.
OUR LIVES WILL NEVER BE EASY.
NOT EVEN WHEN WE ARE OLD. AND WE WILL BE OLD ONE DAY, STEVE TREVOR. I PROMISE YOU.
AND ON THAT DAY, YOU WILL NOT DREAM DARK DREAMS.
THAT NIGHT...THE NIGHT THE AMAZONS FLEW...
...I AM NOT A PILOT, PRINCESS.
I'M A--AN-- "INTELLIGENCE OFFICER."
"A SPY.
"MY PILOT HAD BEEN KILLED, SO MANY OF US...HAD BEEN KILLED...
"...WHAT WE SAW, THE THING WE WERE RUNNING FROM...
...I'LL TELL YOU ONE DAY. WHEN I HAVE THE STRENGTH TO FACE IT...YES.
I'LL TELL YOU.

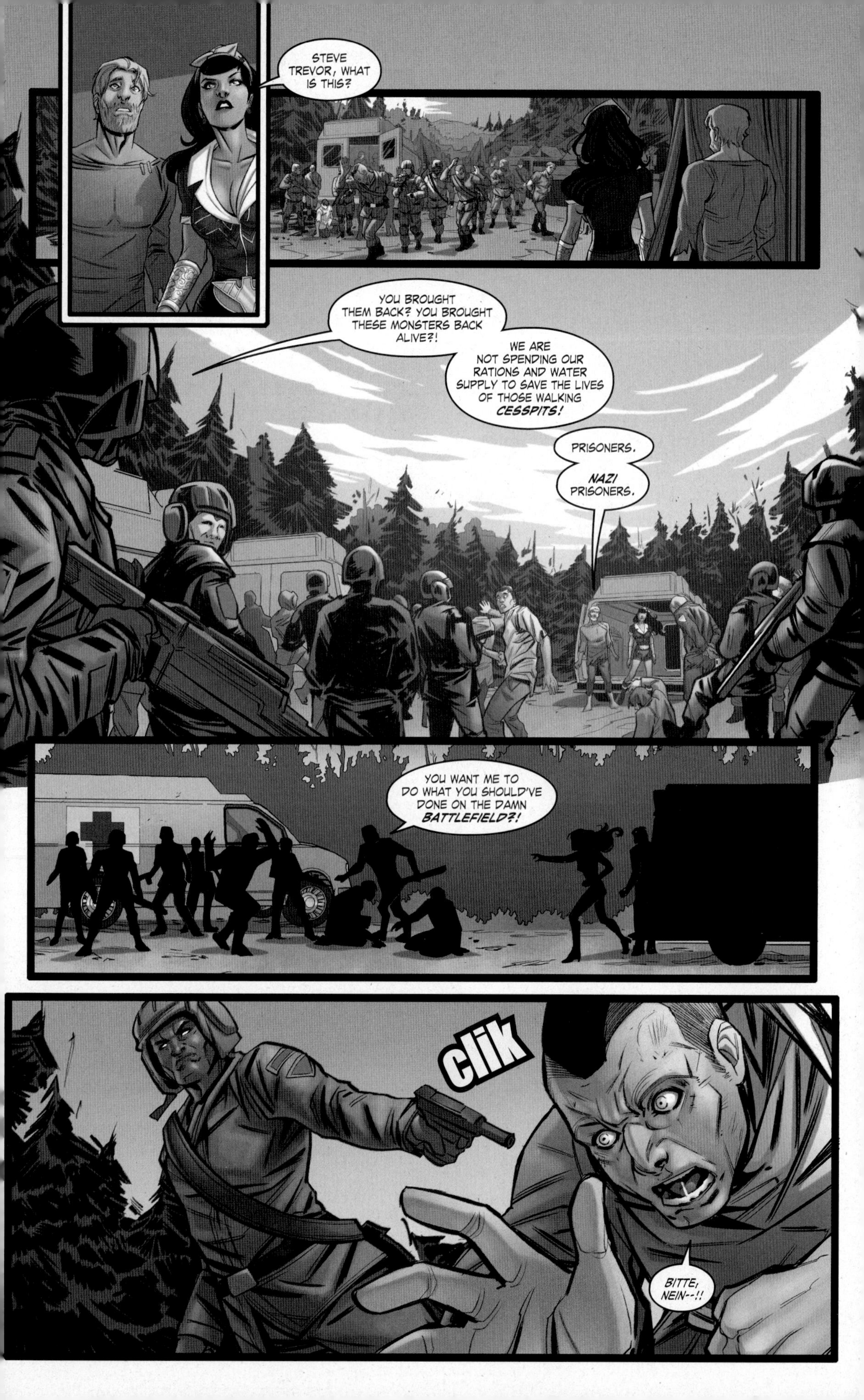
STEVE TREVOR, WHAT IS THIS?
YOU BROUGHT THEM BACK? YOU BROUGHT THESE MONSTERS BACK ALIVE?!
WE ARE NOT SPENDING OUR RATIONS AND WATER SUPPLY TO SAVE THE LIVES OF THOSE WALKING *CESSPITS!*
PRISONERS.
*NAZI* PRISONERS.
YOU WANT ME TO DO WHAT YOU SHOULD'VE DONE ON THE DAMN *BATTLEFIELD?!*
clik
BITTE, NEIN--!!

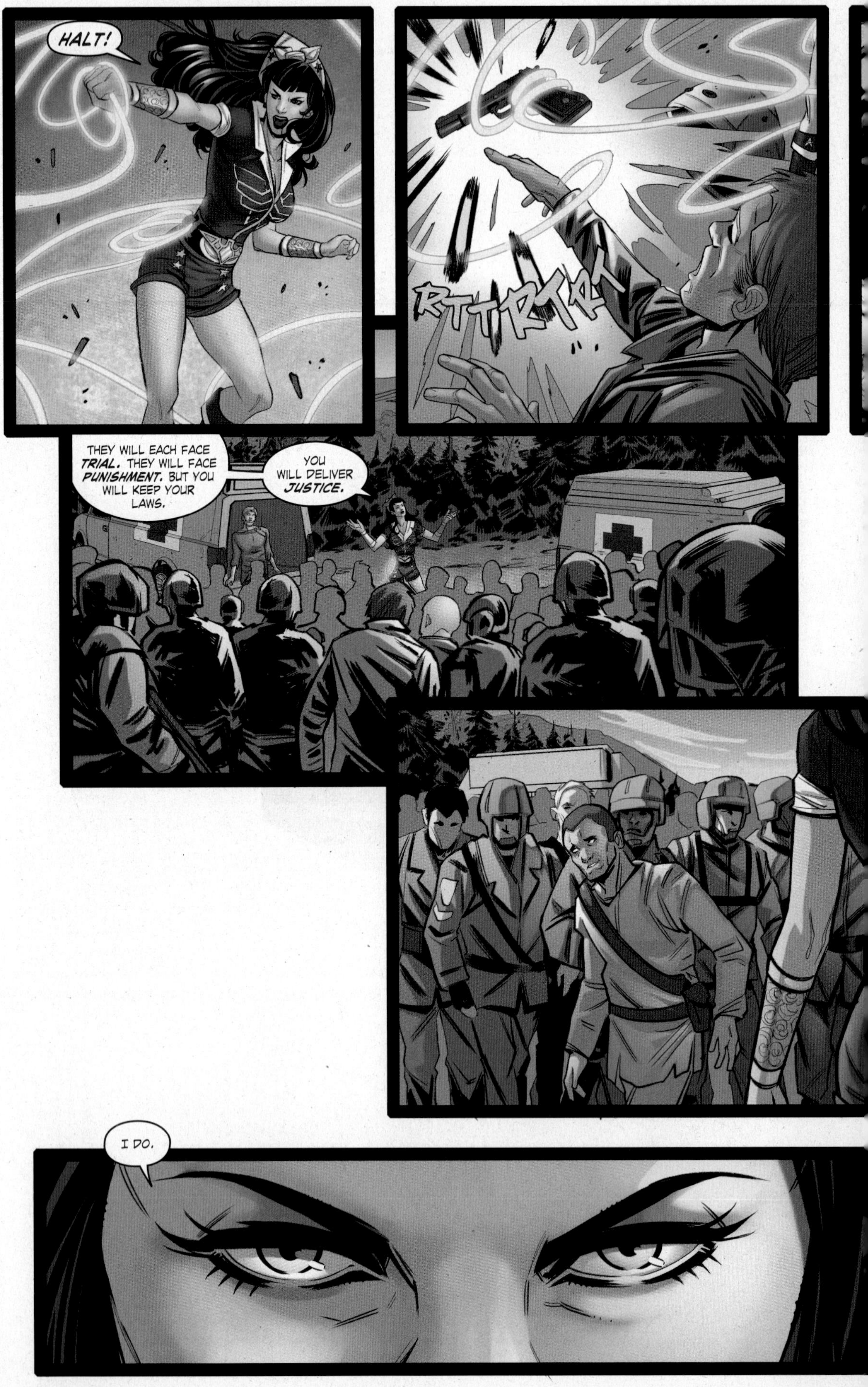
HALT!
RTTTRTRT
THEY WILL EACH FACE TRIAL. THEY WILL FACE PUNISHMENT. BUT YOU WILL KEEP YOUR LAWS.
YOU WILL DELIVER JUSTICE.
I DO.

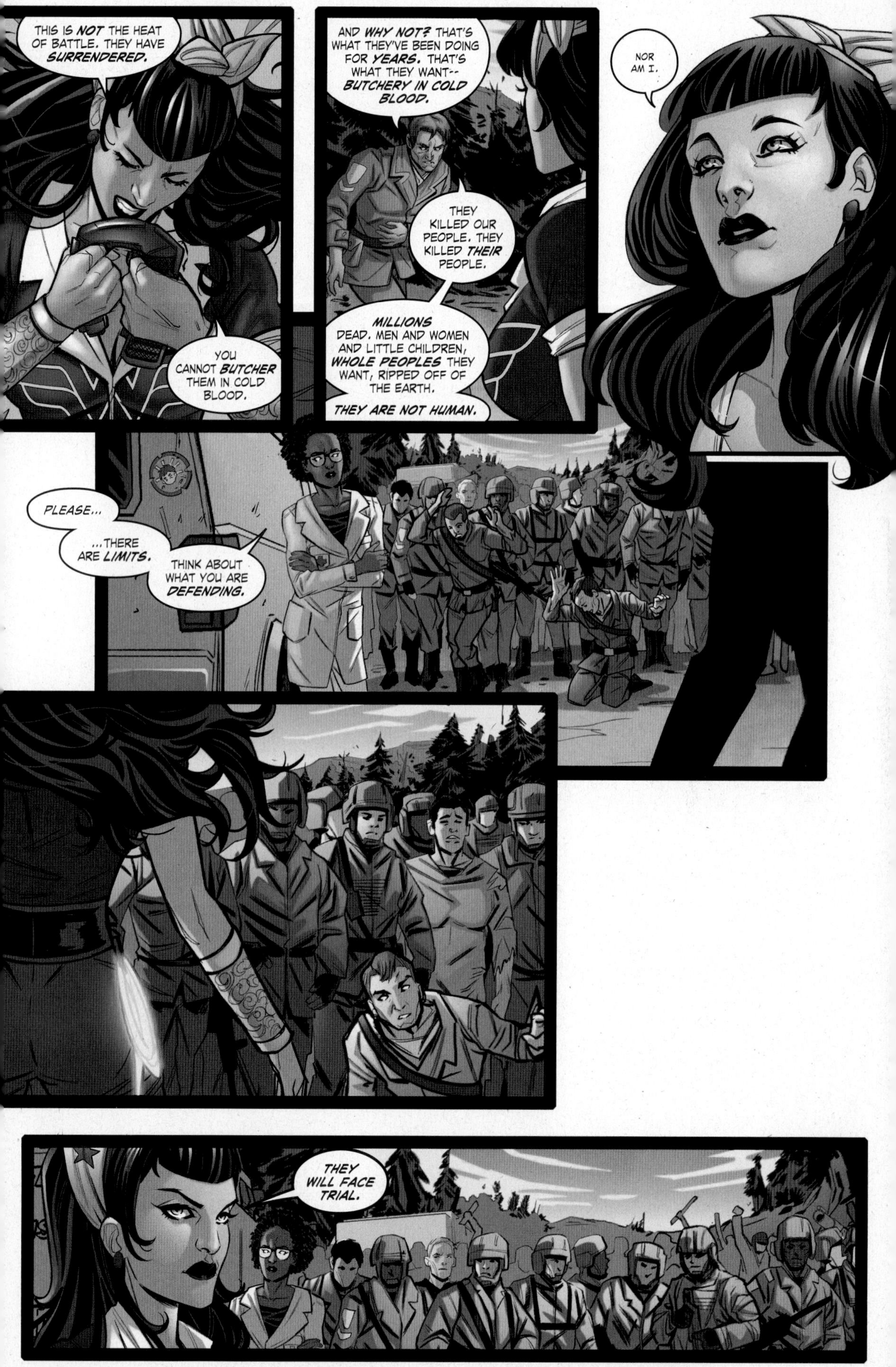
THIS IS *NOT* THE HEAT OF BATTLE. THEY HAVE *SURRENDERED.*
YOU CANNOT *BUTCHER* THEM IN COLD BLOOD.
AND *WHY NOT?* THAT'S WHAT THEY'VE BEEN DOING FOR *YEARS.* THAT'S WHAT THEY WANT-- *BUTCHERY IN COLD BLOOD.*
THEY KILLED OUR PEOPLE. THEY KILLED *THEIR* PEOPLE.
*MILLIONS* DEAD. MEN AND WOMEN AND LITTLE CHILDREN, *WHOLE PEOPLES* THEY WANT, RIPPED OFF OF THE EARTH.
*THEY ARE NOT HUMAN.*
NOR AM I.
PLEASE...
...THERE ARE *LIMITS.*
THINK ABOUT WHAT YOU ARE *DEFENDING.*
*THEY WILL FACE TRIAL.*

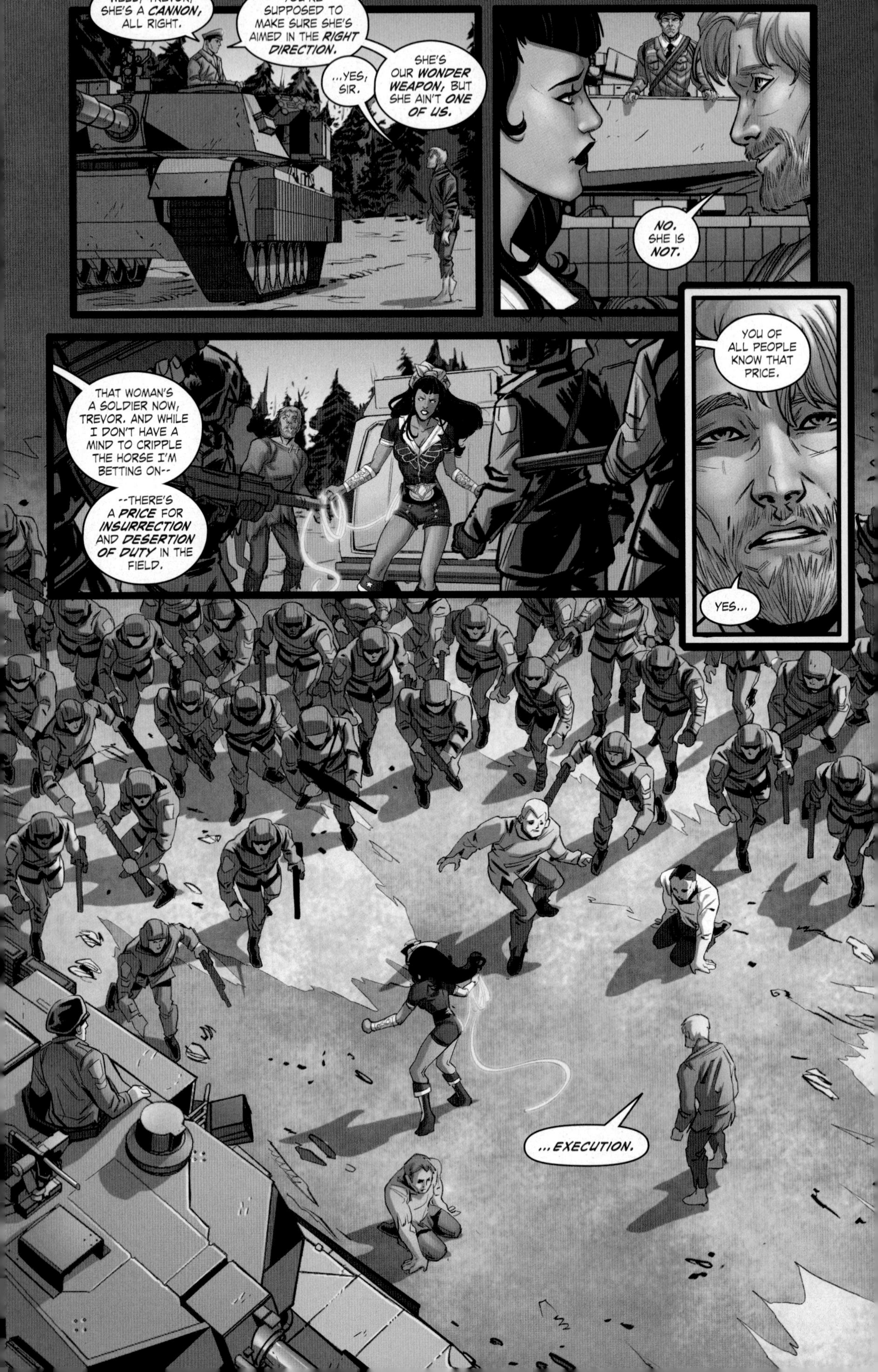
WELL, TREVOR, SHE'S A CANNON, ALL RIGHT.
YOU'RE SUPPOSED TO MAKE SURE SHE'S AIMED IN THE RIGHT DIRECTION.
...YES, SIR.
SHE'S OUR WONDER WEAPON, BUT SHE AIN'T ONE OF US.
NO. SHE IS NOT.
THAT WOMAN'S A SOLDIER NOW, TREVOR. AND WHILE I DON'T HAVE A MIND TO CRIPPLE THE HORSE I'M BETTING ON--
--THERE'S A PRICE FOR INSURRECTION AND DESERTION OF DUTY IN THE FIELD.
YOU OF ALL PEOPLE KNOW THAT PRICE.
YES...
...EXECUTION.

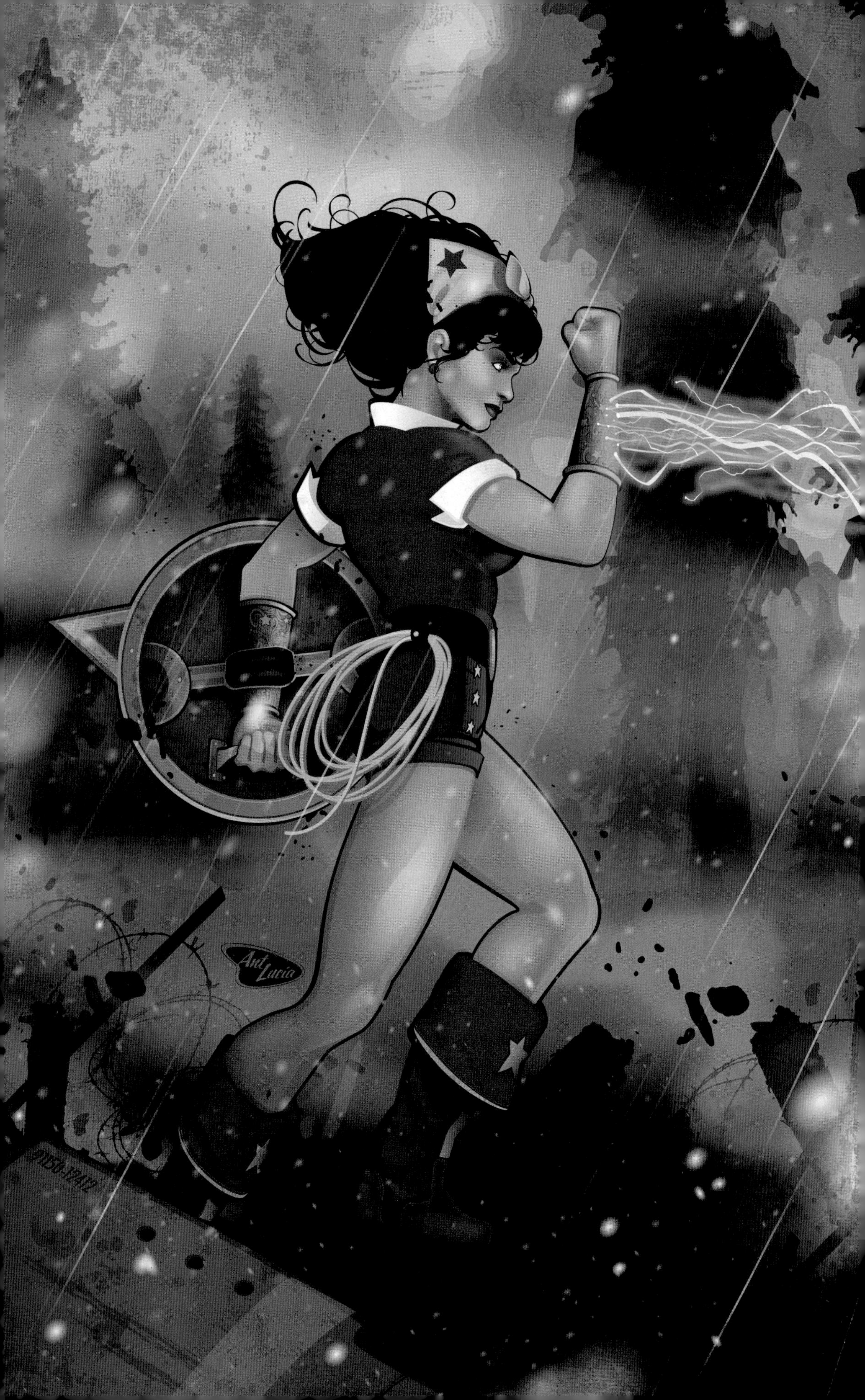
Ant Lucia
1150-12412

# COMBAT
## PART TWO

**MARGUERITE BENNETT**
*Writer*

**MING DOYLE**
**MIRKA ANDOLFO**
**BILQUIS EVELY**
*Artists*

**DOUG GARBARK**
**WENDY BROOME**
*Colorists*

**WES ABBOTT**
*Letterer*

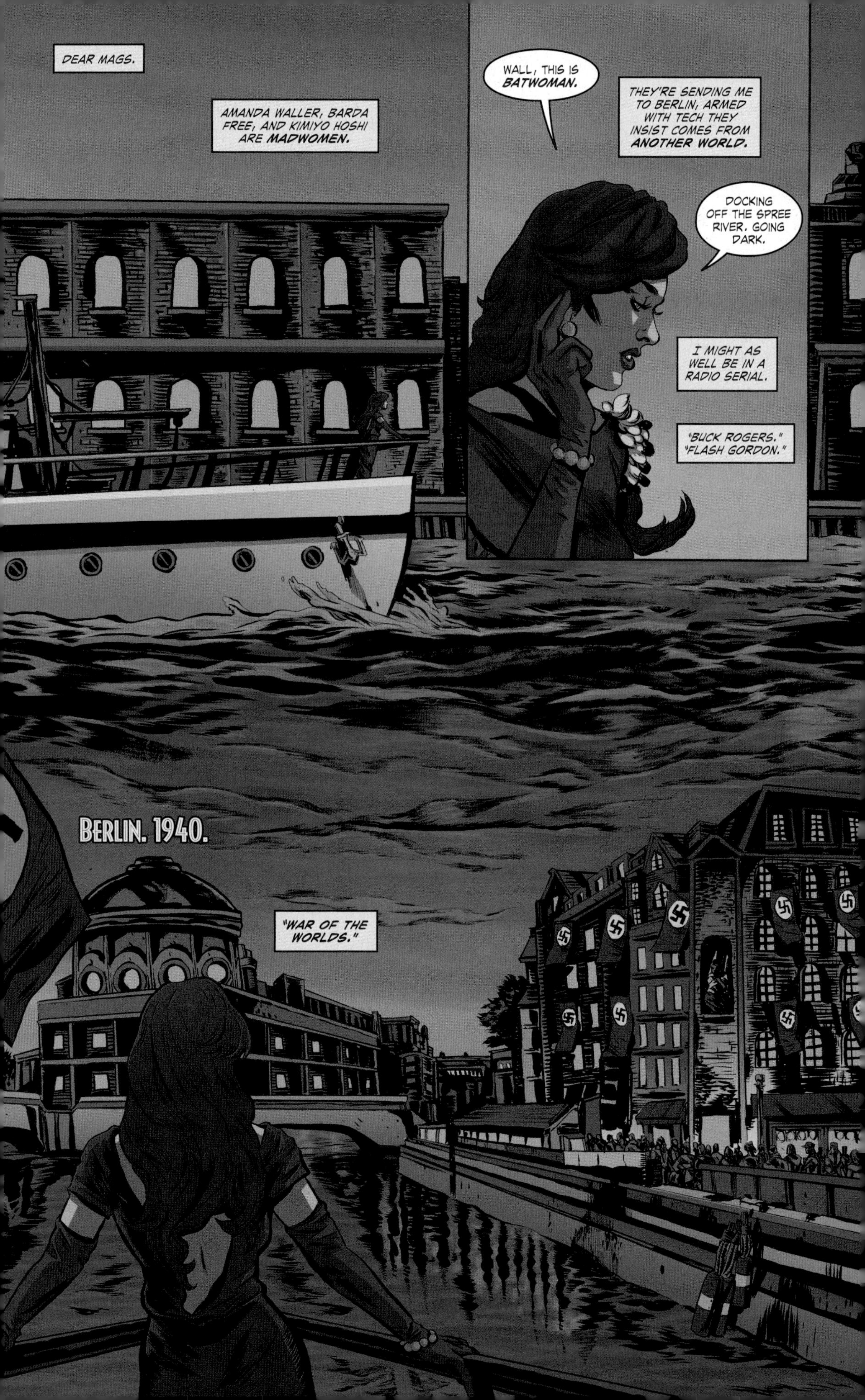
DEAR MAGS.
AMANDA WALLER, BARDA FREE, AND KIMIYO HOSHI ARE MADWOMEN.
WALL, THIS IS BATWOMAN.
THEY'RE SENDING ME TO BERLIN, ARMED WITH TECH THEY INSIST COMES FROM ANOTHER WORLD.
DOCKING OFF THE SPREE RIVER. GOING DARK.
I MIGHT AS WELL BE IN A RADIO SERIAL.
"BUCK ROGERS." "FLASH GORDON."
BERLIN. 1940.
"WAR OF THE WORLDS."

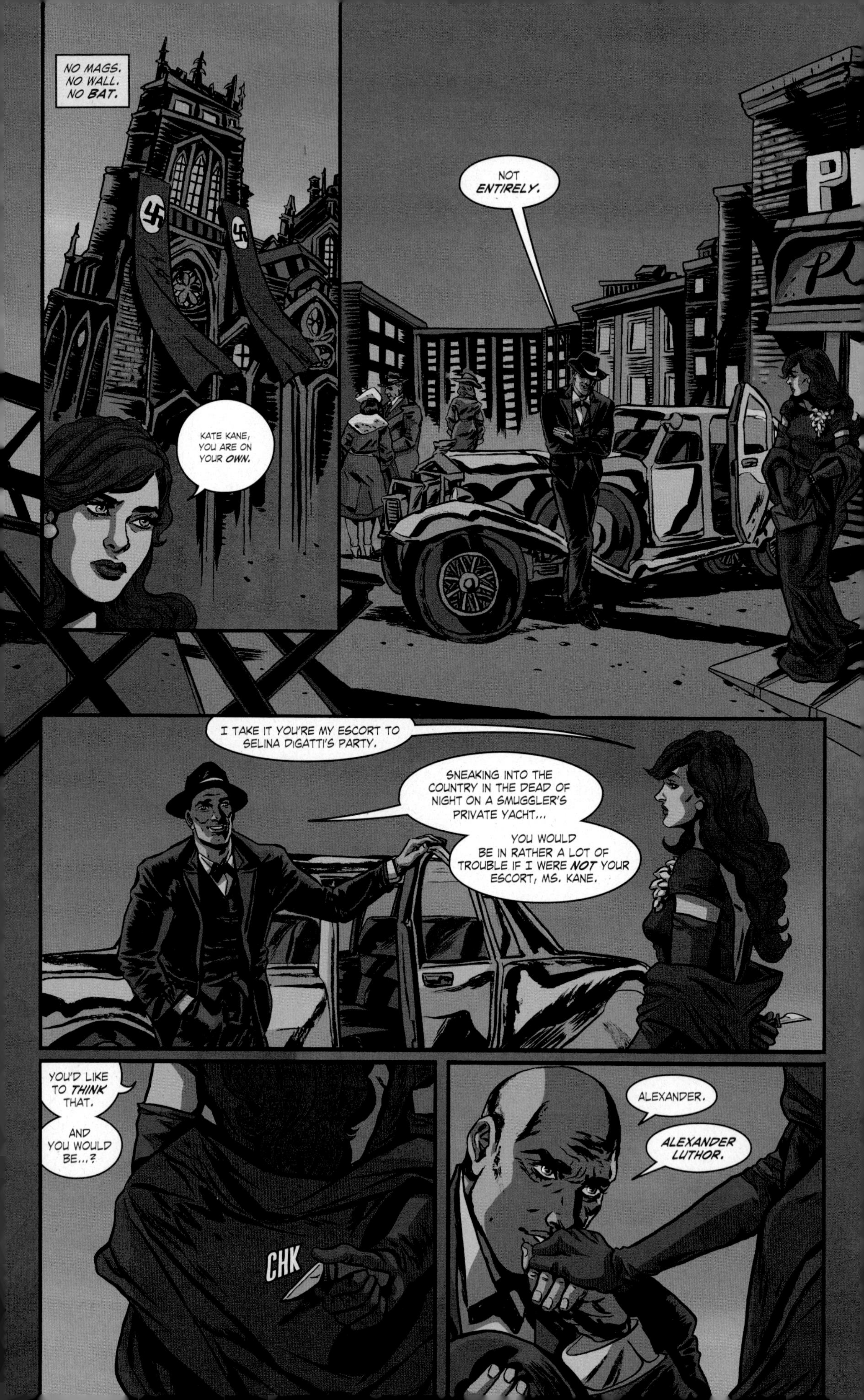
NO MAGS.
NO WALL.
NO BAT.
KATE KANE, YOU ARE ON YOUR OWN.
NOT ENTIRELY.
I TAKE IT YOU'RE MY ESCORT TO SELINA DIGATTI'S PARTY.
SNEAKING INTO THE COUNTRY IN THE DEAD OF NIGHT ON A SMUGGLER'S PRIVATE YACHT...
YOU WOULD BE IN RATHER A LOT OF TROUBLE IF I WERE NOT YOUR ESCORT, MS. KANE.
YOU'D LIKE TO THINK THAT.
AND YOU WOULD BE...?
CHK
ALEXANDER.
ALEXANDER LUTHOR.

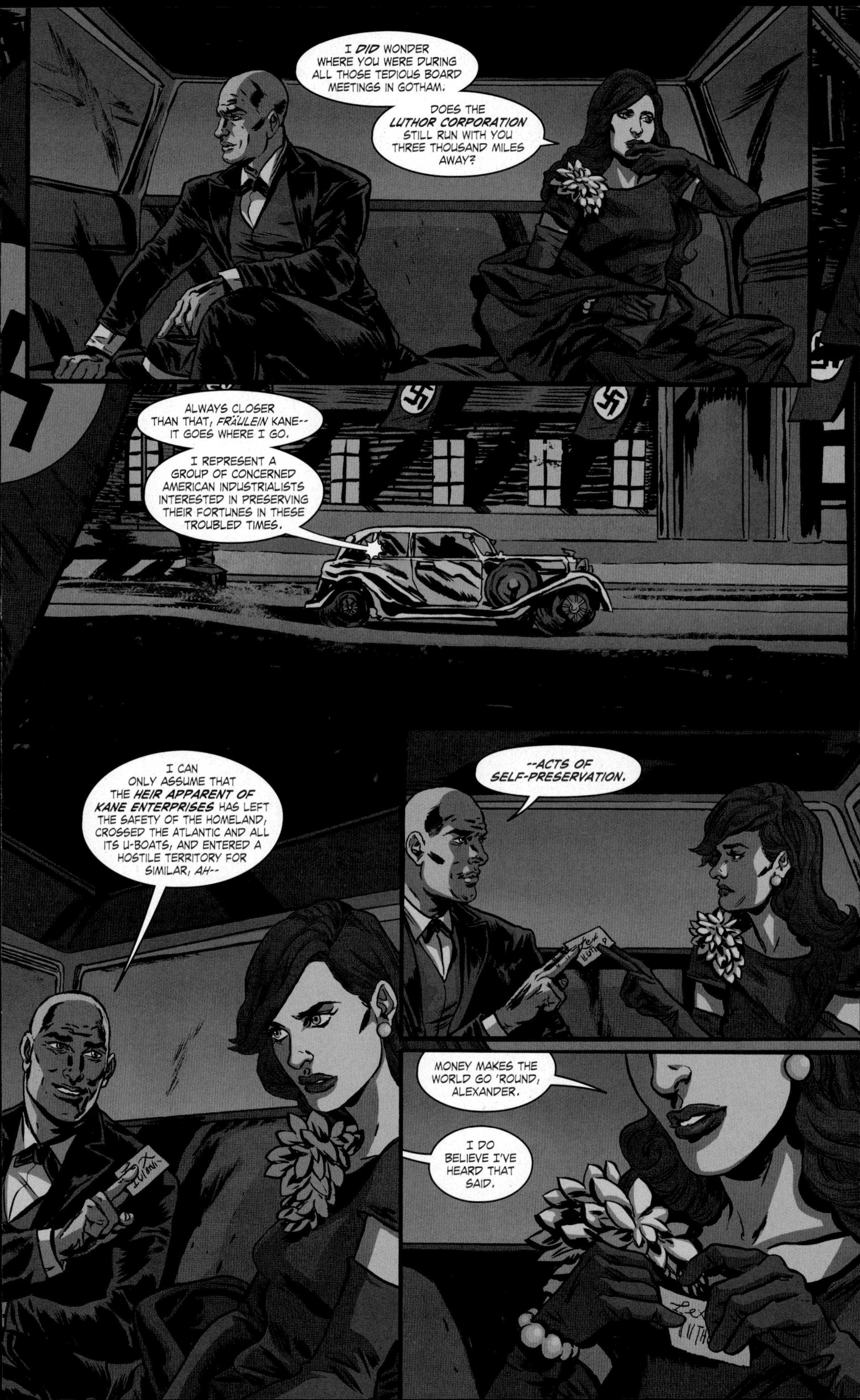
I DID WONDER WHERE YOU WERE DURING ALL THOSE TEDIOUS BOARD MEETINGS IN GOTHAM.
DOES THE LUTHOR CORPORATION STILL RUN WITH YOU THREE THOUSAND MILES AWAY?
ALWAYS CLOSER THAN THAT, FRÄULEIN KANE--IT GOES WHERE I GO.
I REPRESENT A GROUP OF CONCERNED AMERICAN INDUSTRIALISTS INTERESTED IN PRESERVING THEIR FORTUNES IN THESE TROUBLED TIMES.
I CAN ONLY ASSUME THAT THE HEIR APPARENT OF KANE ENTERPRISES HAS LEFT THE SAFETY OF THE HOMELAND, CROSSED THE ATLANTIC AND ALL ITS U-BOATS, AND ENTERED A HOSTILE TERRITORY FOR SIMILAR, AH--
--ACTS OF SELF-PRESERVATION.
MONEY MAKES THE WORLD GO 'ROUND, ALEXANDER.
I DO BELIEVE I'VE HEARD THAT SAID.

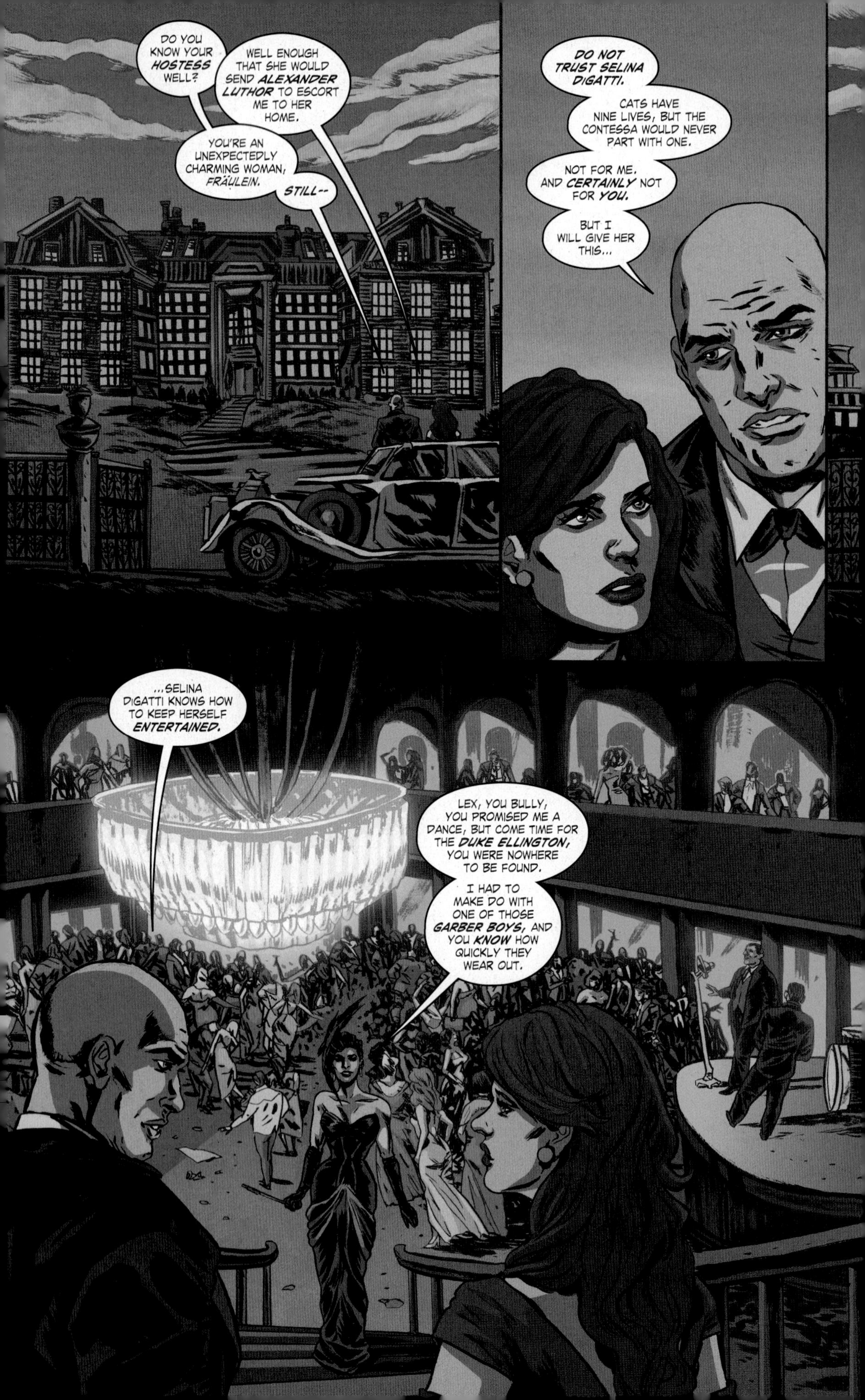
DO YOU KNOW YOUR HOSTESS WELL?
WELL ENOUGH THAT SHE WOULD SEND ALEXANDER LUTHOR TO ESCORT ME TO HER HOME.
YOU'RE AN UNEXPECTEDLY CHARMING WOMAN, FRÄULEIN.
STILL--
DO NOT TRUST SELINA DIGATTI.
CATS HAVE NINE LIVES, BUT THE CONTESSA WOULD NEVER PART WITH ONE.
NOT FOR ME. AND CERTAINLY NOT FOR YOU.
BUT I WILL GIVE HER THIS...
...SELINA DIGATTI KNOWS HOW TO KEEP HERSELF ENTERTAINED.
LEX, YOU BULLY, YOU PROMISED ME A DANCE, BUT COME TIME FOR THE DUKE ELLINGTON, YOU WERE NOWHERE TO BE FOUND.
I HAD TO MAKE DO WITH ONE OF THOSE GARBER BOYS, AND YOU KNOW HOW QUICKLY THEY WEAR OUT.

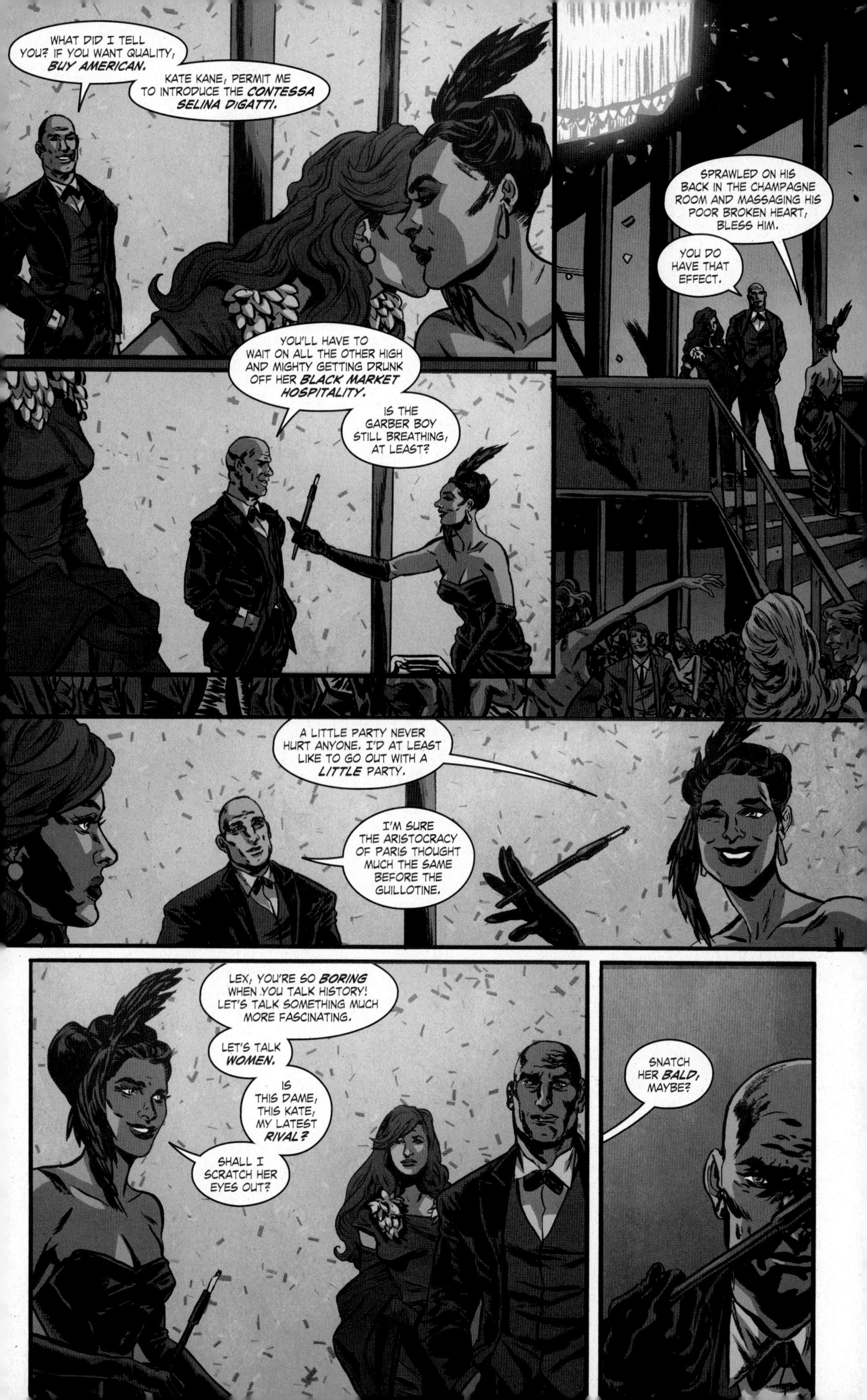
WHAT DID I TELL YOU? IF YOU WANT QUALITY, BUY AMERICAN.
KATE KANE, PERMIT ME TO INTRODUCE THE CONTESSA SELINA DIGATTI.
SPRAWLED ON HIS BACK IN THE CHAMPAGNE ROOM AND MASSAGING HIS POOR BROKEN HEART, BLESS HIM.
YOU DO HAVE THAT EFFECT.
YOU'LL HAVE TO WAIT ON ALL THE OTHER HIGH AND MIGHTY GETTING DRUNK OFF HER BLACK MARKET HOSPITALITY.
IS THE GARBER BOY STILL BREATHING, AT LEAST?
A LITTLE PARTY NEVER HURT ANYONE. I'D AT LEAST LIKE TO GO OUT WITH A LITTLE PARTY.
I'M SURE THE ARISTOCRACY OF PARIS THOUGHT MUCH THE SAME BEFORE THE GUILLOTINE.
LEX, YOU'RE SO BORING WHEN YOU TALK HISTORY! LET'S TALK SOMETHING MUCH MORE FASCINATING.
LET'S TALK WOMEN.
IS THIS DAME, THIS KATE, MY LATEST RIVAL?
SHALL I SCRATCH HER EYES OUT?
SNATCH HER BALD, MAYBE?

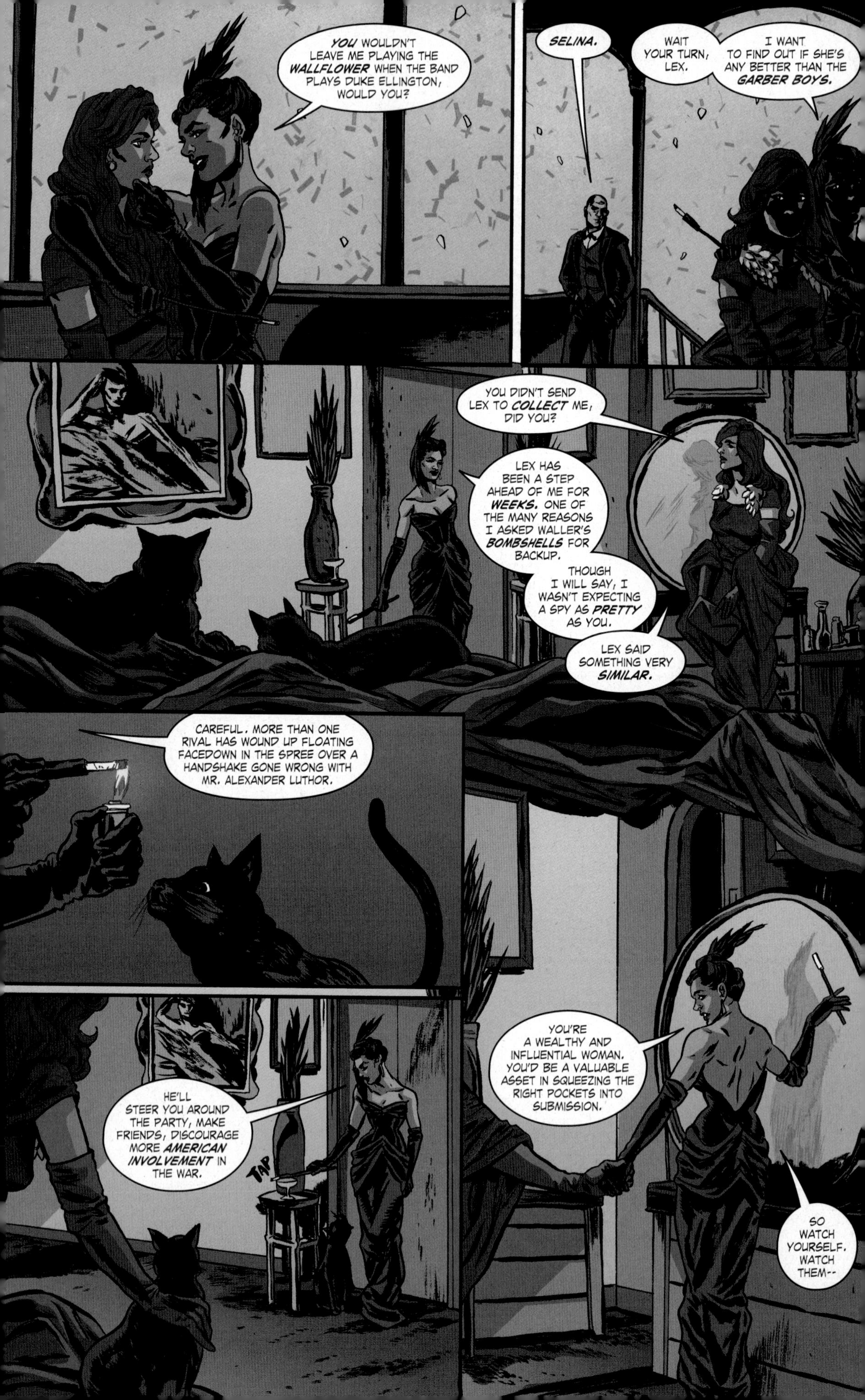
YOU WOULDN'T LEAVE ME PLAYING THE WALLFLOWER WHEN THE BAND PLAYS DUKE ELLINGTON, WOULD YOU?
SELINA.
WAIT YOUR TURN, LEX.
I WANT TO FIND OUT IF SHE'S ANY BETTER THAN THE GARBER BOYS.
YOU DIDN'T SEND LEX TO COLLECT ME, DID YOU?
LEX HAS BEEN A STEP AHEAD OF ME FOR WEEKS. ONE OF THE MANY REASONS I ASKED WALLER'S BOMBSHELLS FOR BACKUP.
THOUGH I WILL SAY, I WASN'T EXPECTING A SPY AS PRETTY AS YOU.
LEX SAID SOMETHING VERY SIMILAR.
CAREFUL. MORE THAN ONE RIVAL HAS WOUND UP FLOATING FACEDOWN IN THE SPREE OVER A HANDSHAKE GONE WRONG WITH MR. ALEXANDER LUTHOR.
HE'LL STEER YOU AROUND THE PARTY, MAKE FRIENDS, DISCOURAGE MORE AMERICAN INVOLVEMENT IN THE WAR.
TAP
YOU'RE A WEALTHY AND INFLUENTIAL WOMAN. YOU'D BE A VALUABLE ASSET IN SQUEEZING THE RIGHT POCKETS INTO SUBMISSION.
SO WATCH YOURSELF. WATCH THEM--

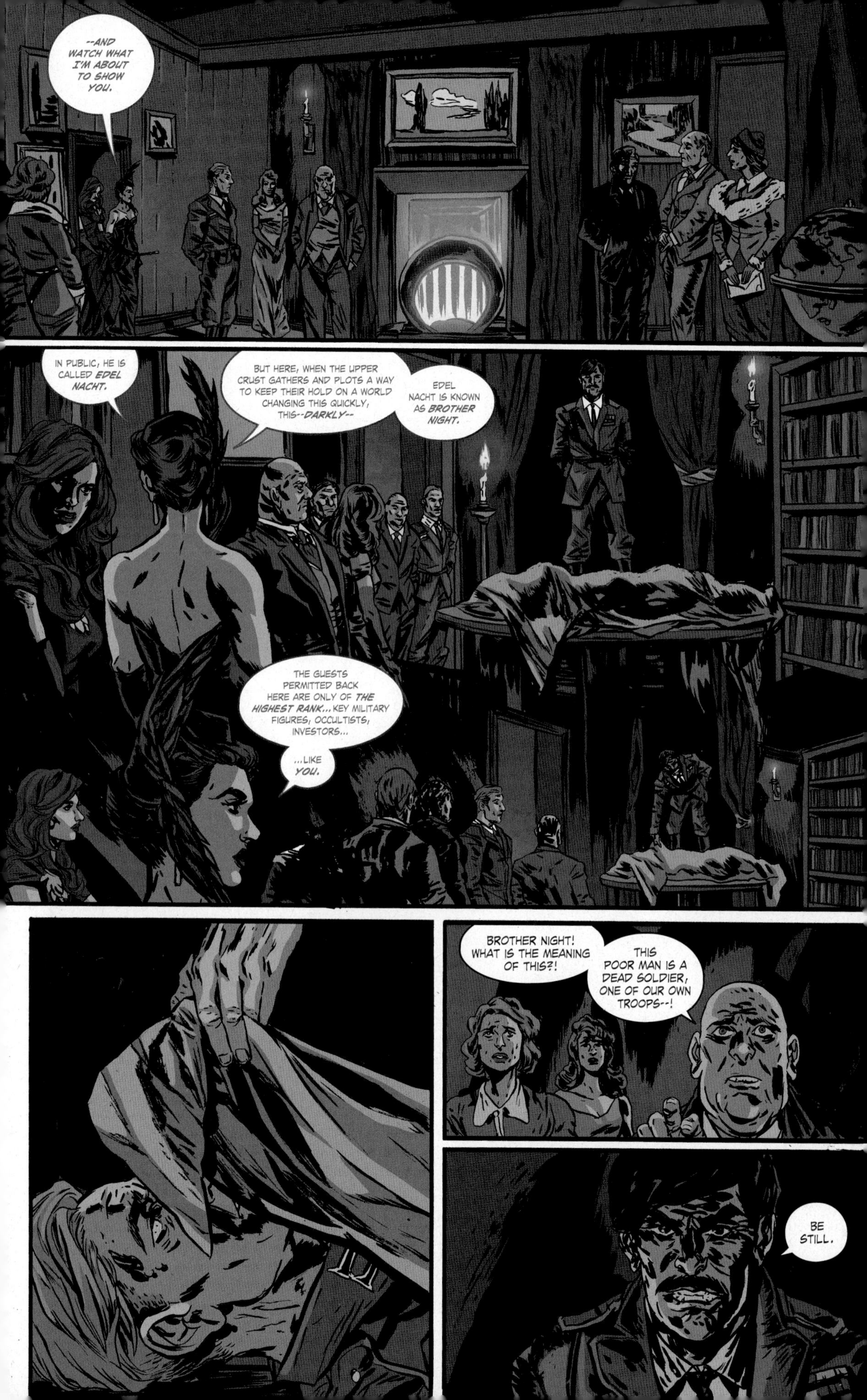
--AND WATCH WHAT I'M ABOUT TO SHOW YOU.
IN PUBLIC, HE IS CALLED EDEL NACHT.
BUT HERE, WHEN THE UPPER CRUST GATHERS AND PLOTS A WAY TO KEEP THEIR HOLD ON A WORLD CHANGING THIS QUICKLY, THIS--DARKLY--
EDEL NACHT IS KNOWN AS BROTHER NIGHT.
THE GUESTS PERMITTED BACK HERE ARE ONLY OF THE HIGHEST RANK... KEY MILITARY FIGURES, OCCULTISTS, INVESTORS...
...LIKE YOU.
BROTHER NIGHT! WHAT IS THE MEANING OF THIS?!
THIS POOR MAN IS A DEAD SOLDIER, ONE OF OUR OWN TROOPS--!
BE STILL.

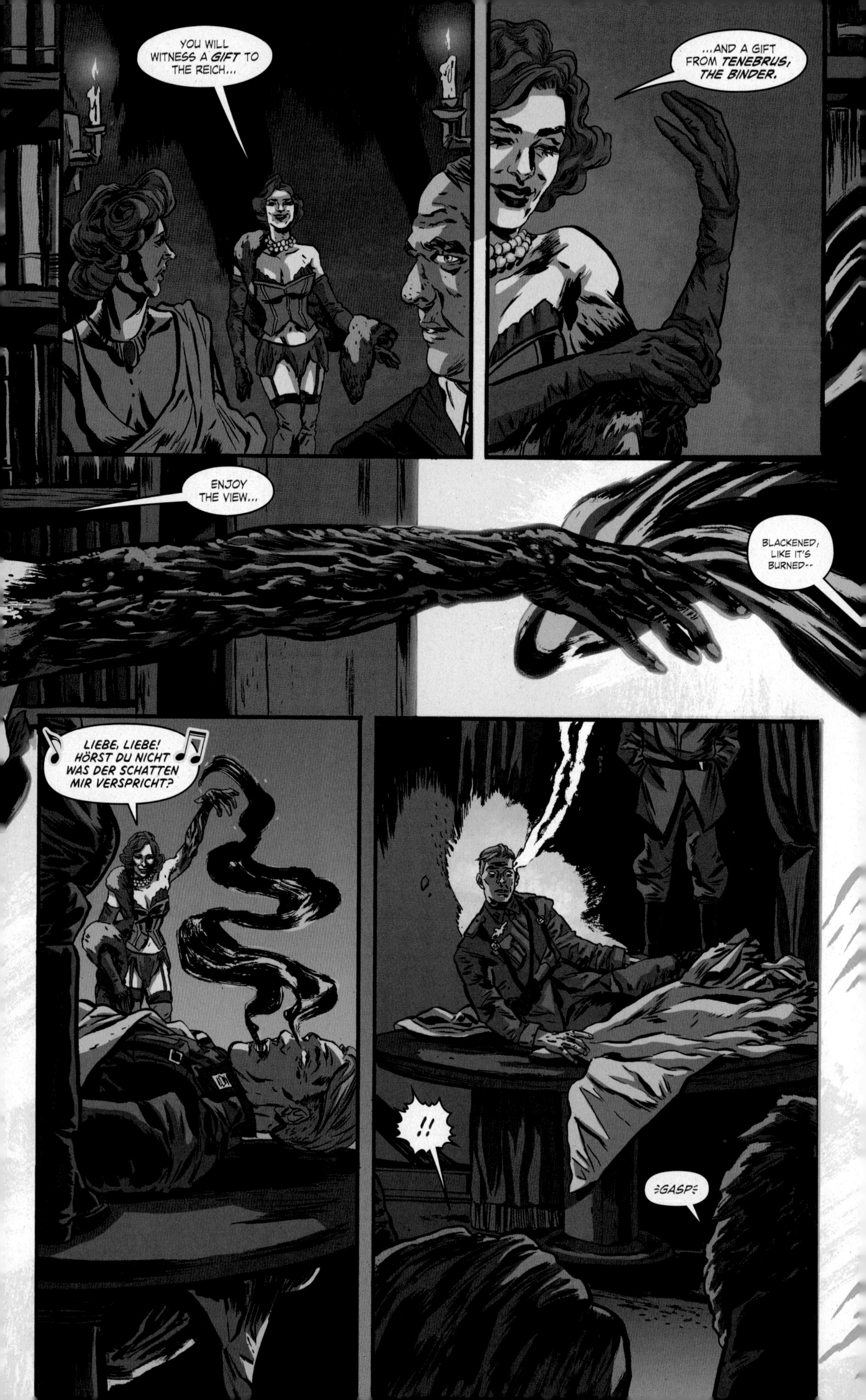
YOU WILL WITNESS A GIFT TO THE REICH...
...AND A GIFT FROM TENEBRUS, THE BINDER.
ENJOY THE VIEW...
BLACKENED, LIKE IT'S BURNED--
LIEBE, LIEBE! HÖRST DU NICHT WAS DER SCHATTEN MIR VERSPRICHT?
!!
GASP

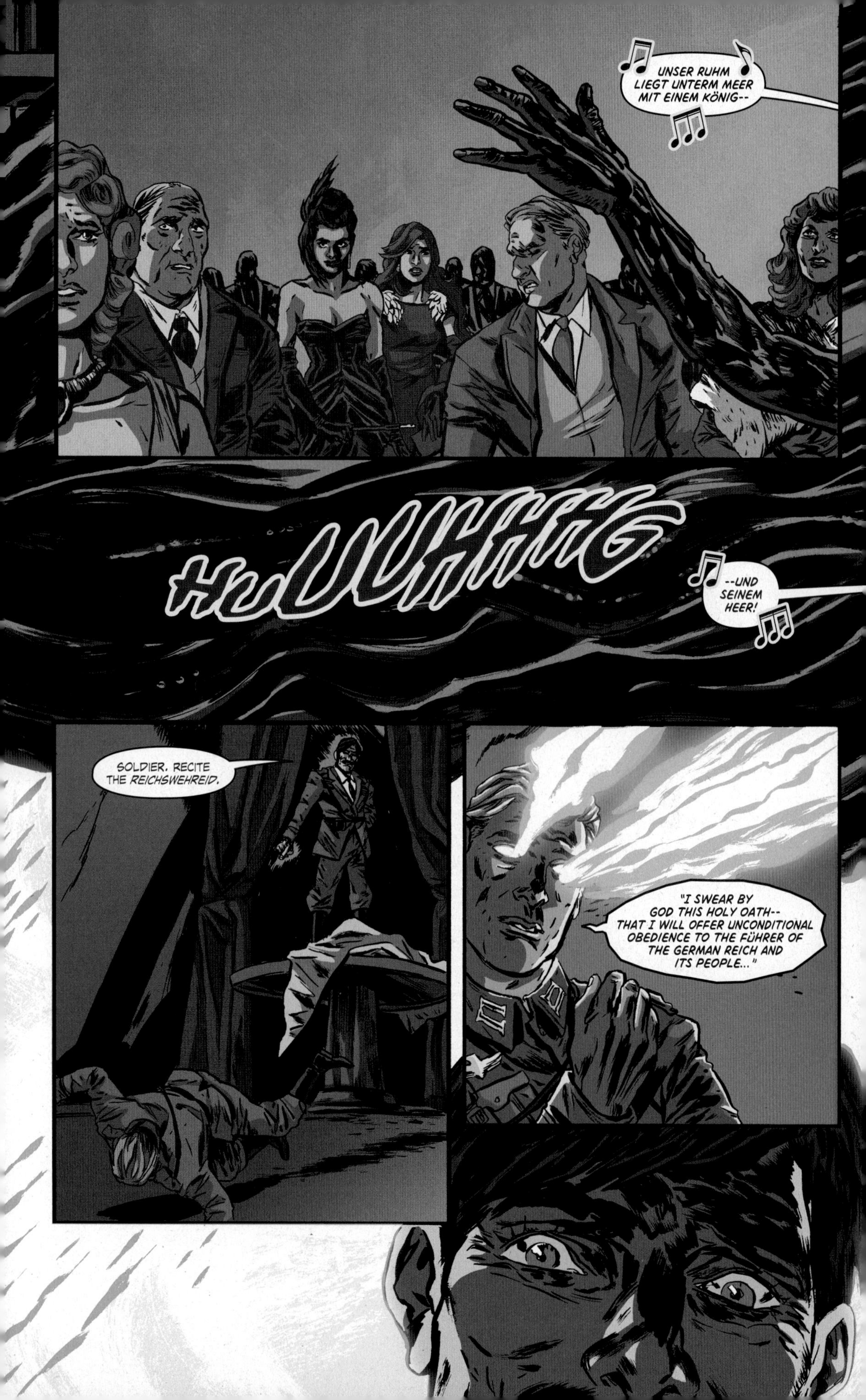
UNSER RUHM LIEGT UNTERM MEER MIT EINEM KÖNIG--
HUUHHG
--UND SEINEM HEER!
SOLDIER. RECITE THE REICHSWEHREID.
"I SWEAR BY GOD THIS HOLY OATH-- THAT I WILL OFFER UNCONDITIONAL OBEDIENCE TO THE FÜHRER OF THE GERMAN REICH AND ITS PEOPLE..."

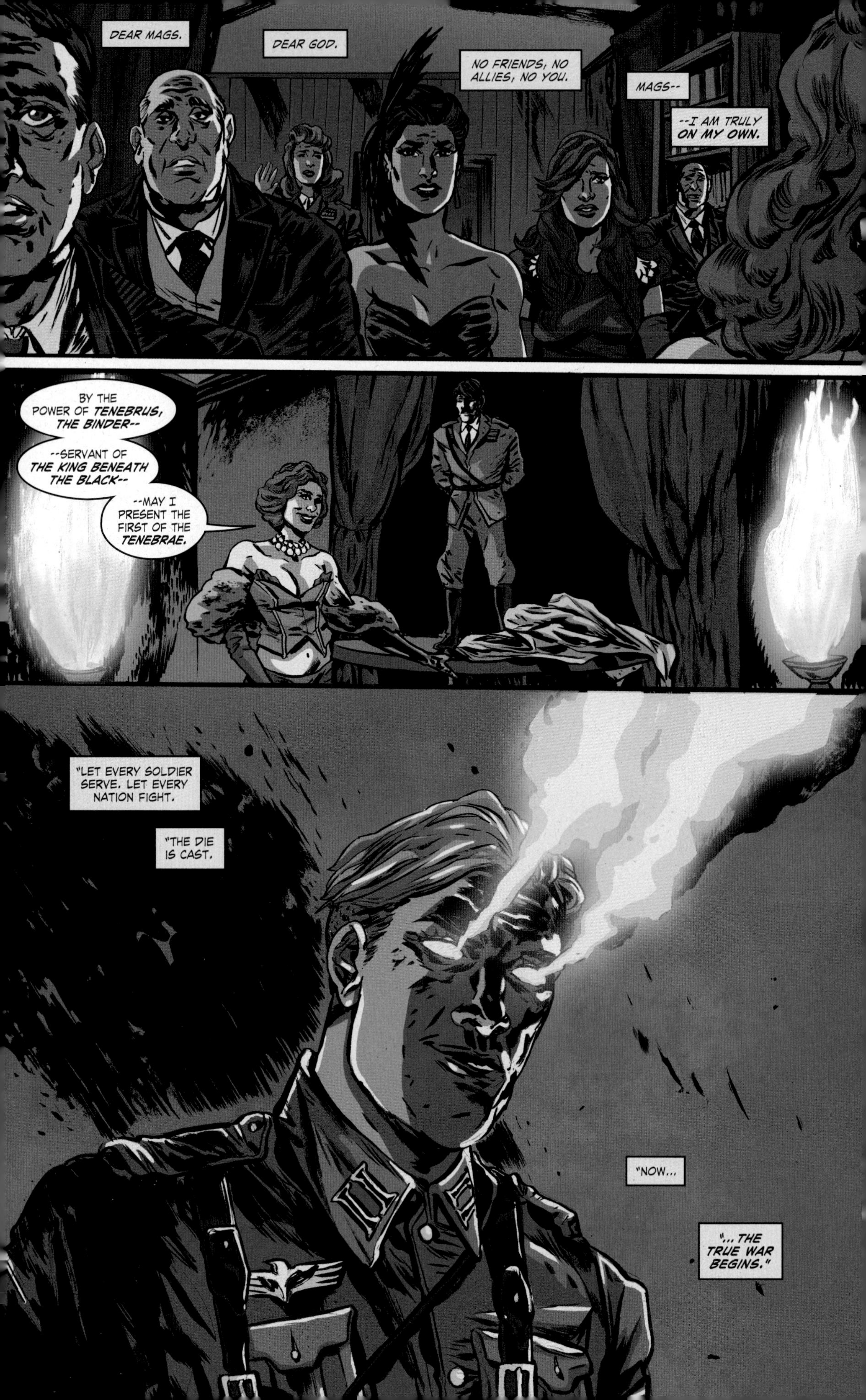
DEAR MAGS.
DEAR GOD.
NO FRIENDS, NO ALLIES, NO YOU.
MAGS--
--I AM TRULY ON MY OWN.
BY THE POWER OF TENEBRUS, THE BINDER--
--SERVANT OF THE KING BENEATH THE BLACK--
--MAY I PRESENT THE FIRST OF THE TENEBRAE.
"LET EVERY SOLDIER SERVE. LET EVERY NATION FIGHT.
"THE DIE IS CAST.
"NOW...
"... THE TRUE WAR BEGINS."

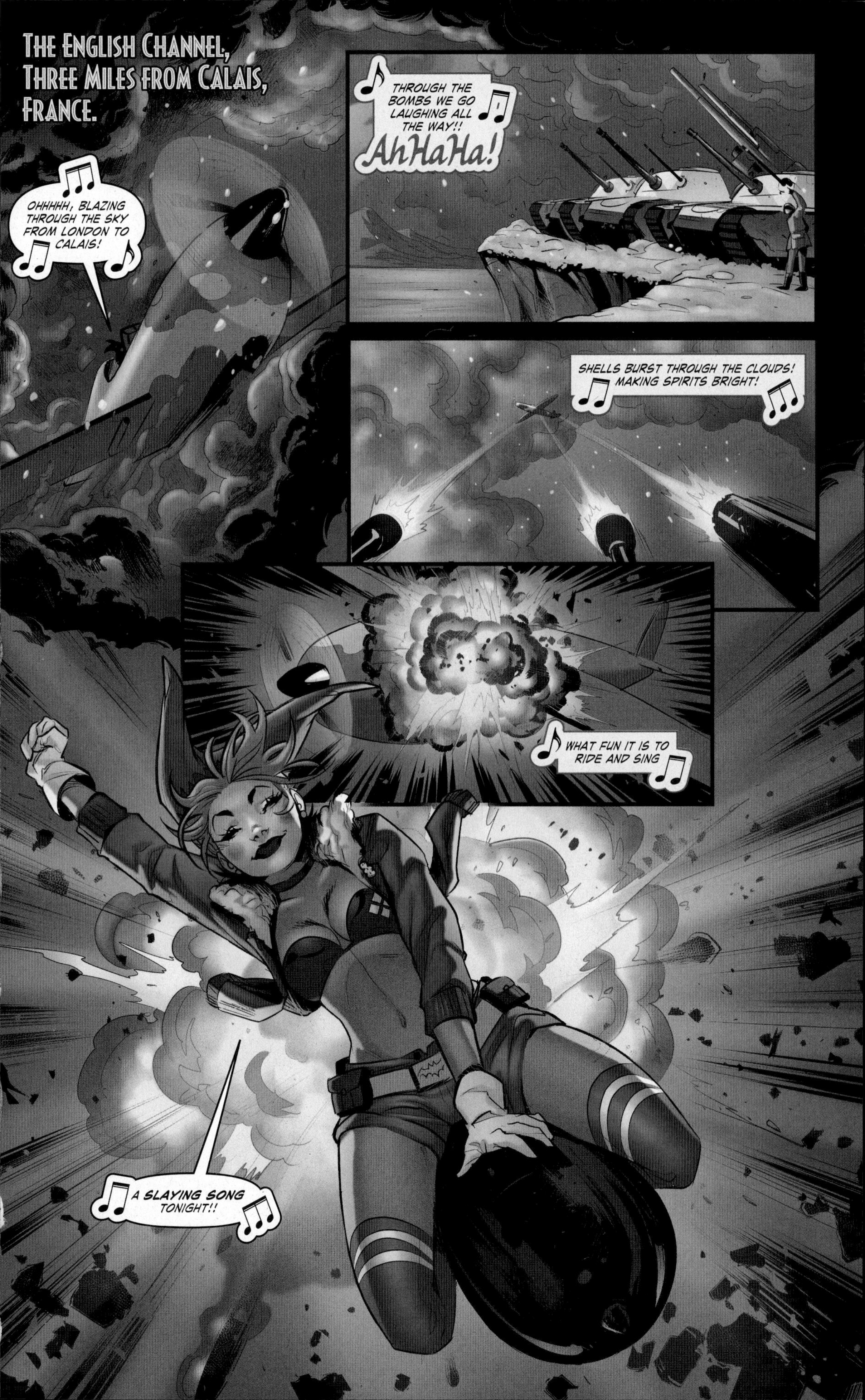
The English Channel, Three Miles from Calais, France.
OHHHHH, BLAZING THROUGH THE SKY FROM LONDON TO CALAIS!
THROUGH THE BOMBS WE GO LAUGHING ALL THE WAY!!
AhHaHa!
SHELLS BURST THROUGH THE CLOUDS! MAKING SPIRITS BRIGHT!
WHAT FUN IT IS TO RIDE AND SING
A SLAYING SONG TONIGHT!!

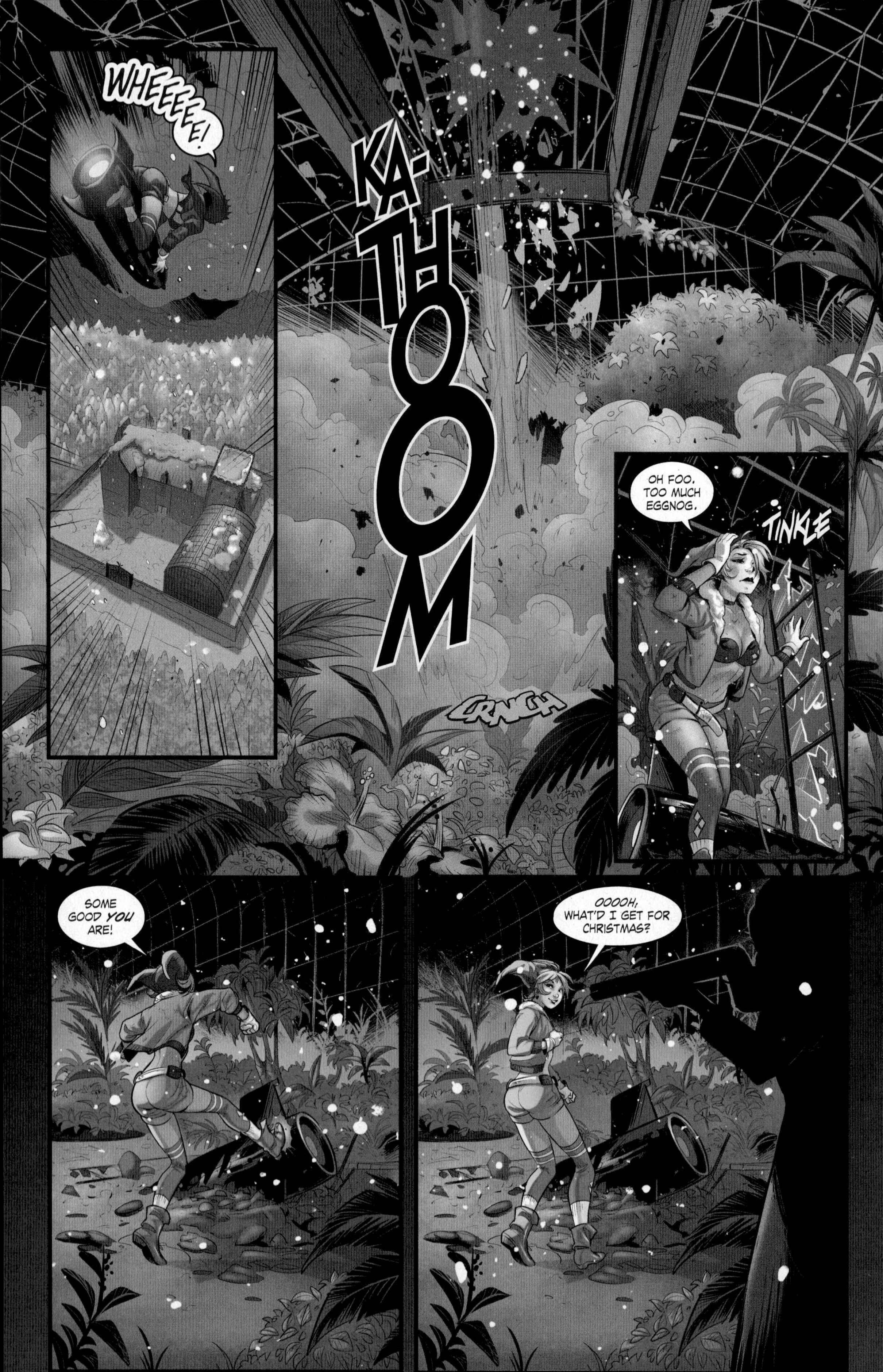
WHEEEEEE!
KA-THOOM
CRNCH
OH FOO. TOO MUCH EGGNOG.
TINKLE
SOME GOOD YOU ARE!
OOOOH, WHAT'D I GET FOR CHRISTMAS?

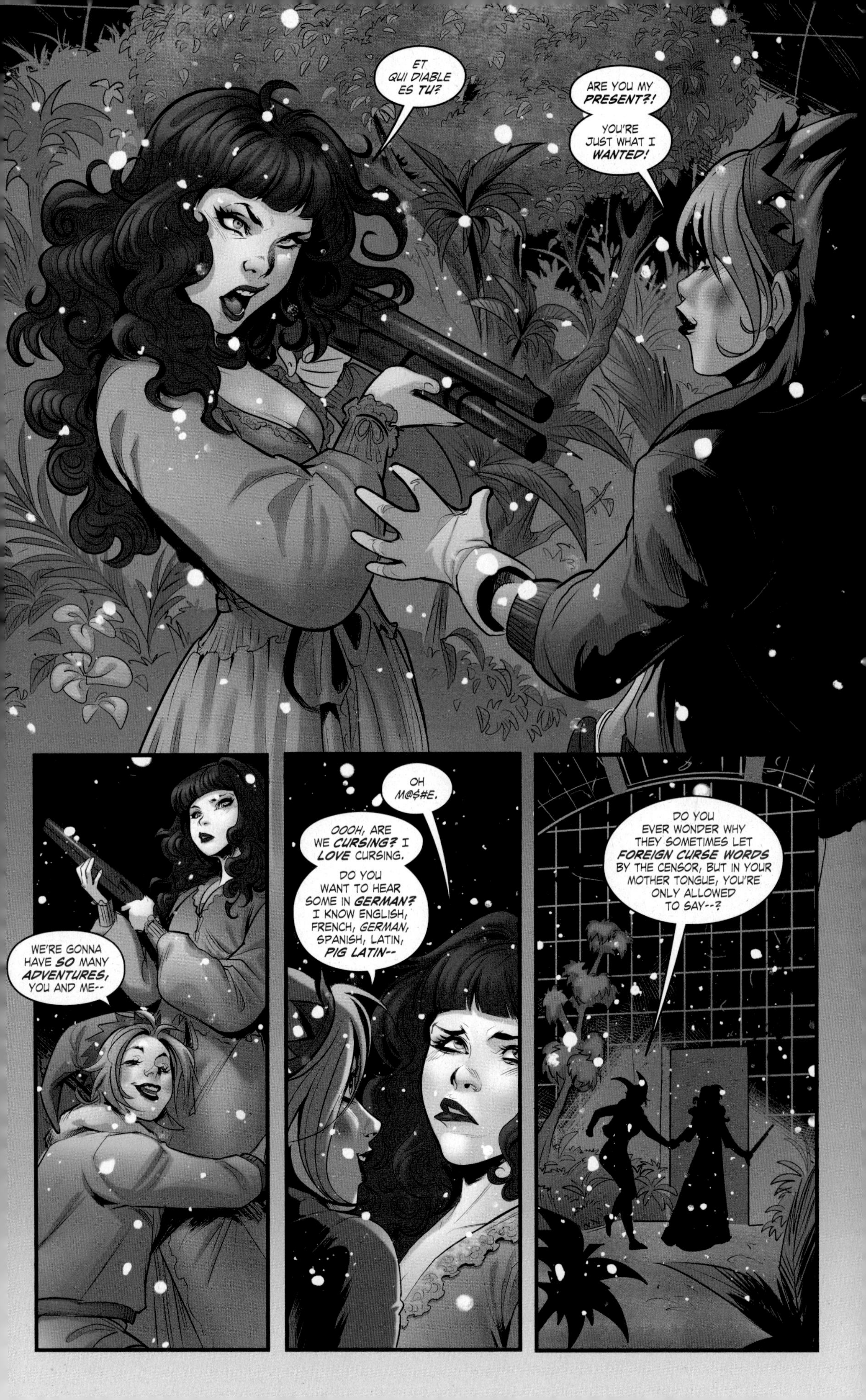
ET QUI DIABLE ES TU?
ARE YOU MY PRESENT?!
YOU'RE JUST WHAT I WANTED!
WE'RE GONNA HAVE SO MANY ADVENTURES, YOU AND ME--
OH M@$#E.
OOOH, ARE WE CURSING? I LOVE CURSING.
DO YOU WANT TO HEAR SOME IN GERMAN? I KNOW ENGLISH, FRENCH, GERMAN, SPANISH, LATIN, PIG LATIN--
DO YOU EVER WONDER WHY THEY SOMETIMES LET FOREIGN CURSE WORDS BY THE CENSOR, BUT IN YOUR MOTHER TONGUE, YOU'RE ONLY ALLOWED TO SAY--?

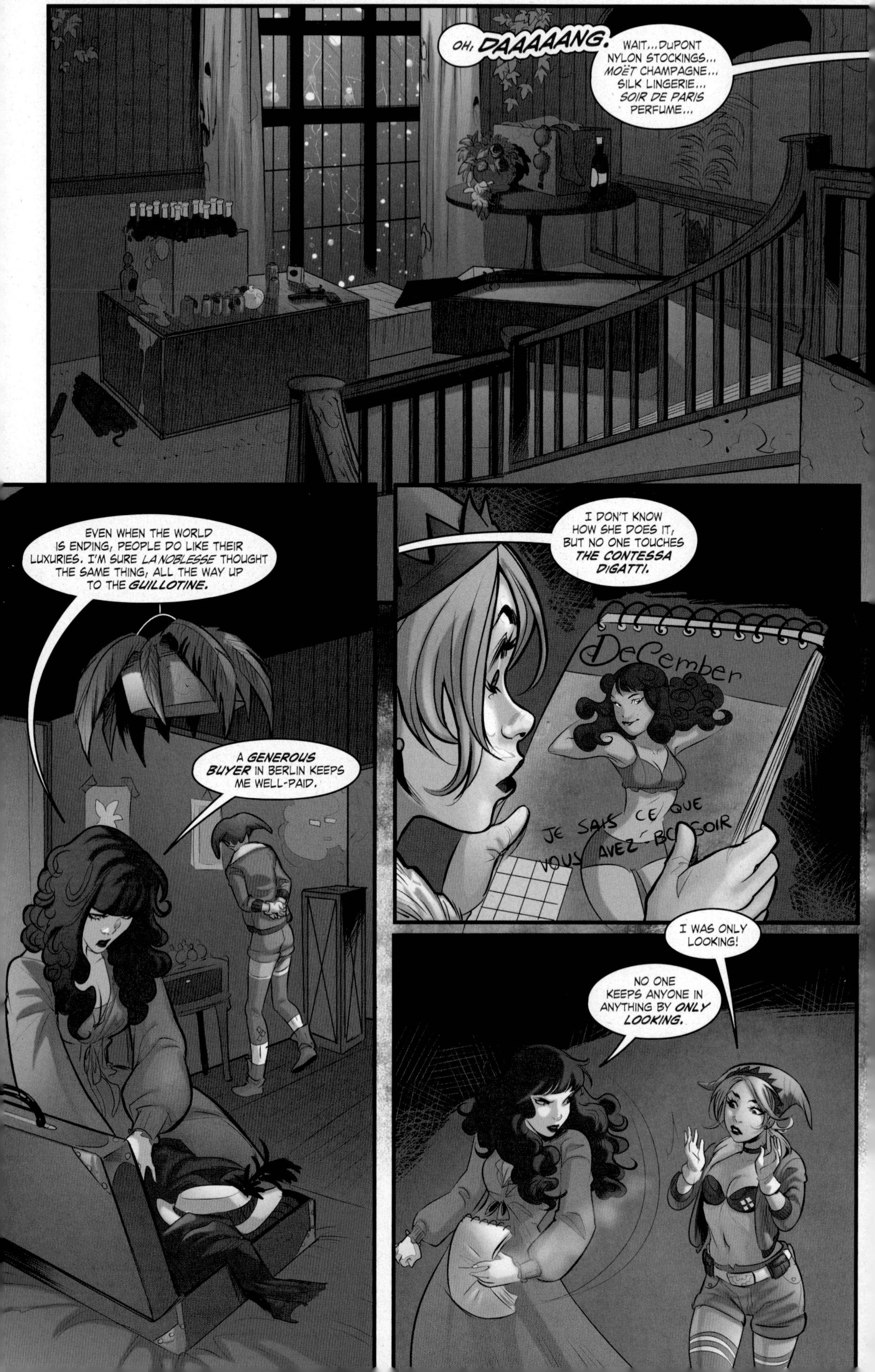
OH, DAAAAANG.
WAIT...DUPONT NYLON STOCKINGS... MOËT CHAMPAGNE... SILK LINGERIE... SOIR DE PARIS PERFUME...
EVEN WHEN THE WORLD IS ENDING, PEOPLE DO LIKE THEIR LUXURIES. I'M SURE LA NOBLESSE THOUGHT THE SAME THING, ALL THE WAY UP TO THE GUILLOTINE.
A GENEROUS BUYER IN BERLIN KEEPS ME WELL-PAID.
I DON'T KNOW HOW SHE DOES IT, BUT NO ONE TOUCHES THE CONTESSA DIGATTI.
DeCember
JE SAIS CE QUE VOUS AVEZ BONSOIR
I WAS ONLY LOOKING!
NO ONE KEEPS ANYONE IN ANYTHING BY ONLY LOOKING.

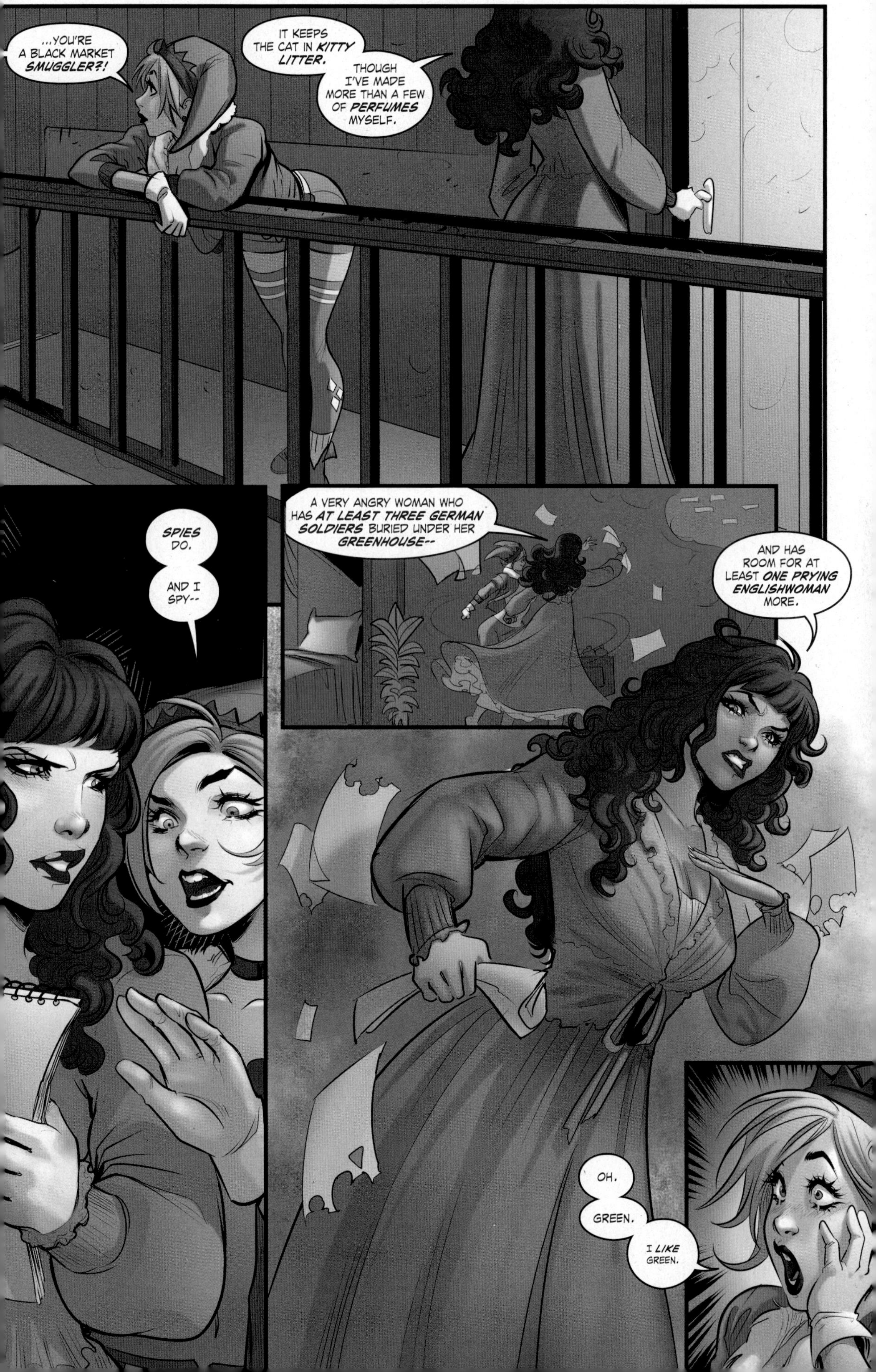
...YOU'RE A BLACK MARKET SMUGGLER?!
IT KEEPS THE CAT IN KITTY LITTER.
THOUGH I'VE MADE MORE THAN A FEW OF PERFUMES MYSELF.
SPIES DO.
AND I SPY--
A VERY ANGRY WOMAN WHO HAS AT LEAST THREE GERMAN SOLDIERS BURIED UNDER HER GREENHOUSE--
AND HAS ROOM FOR AT LEAST ONE PRYING ENGLISHWOMAN MORE.
OH.
GREEN.
I LIKE GREEN.

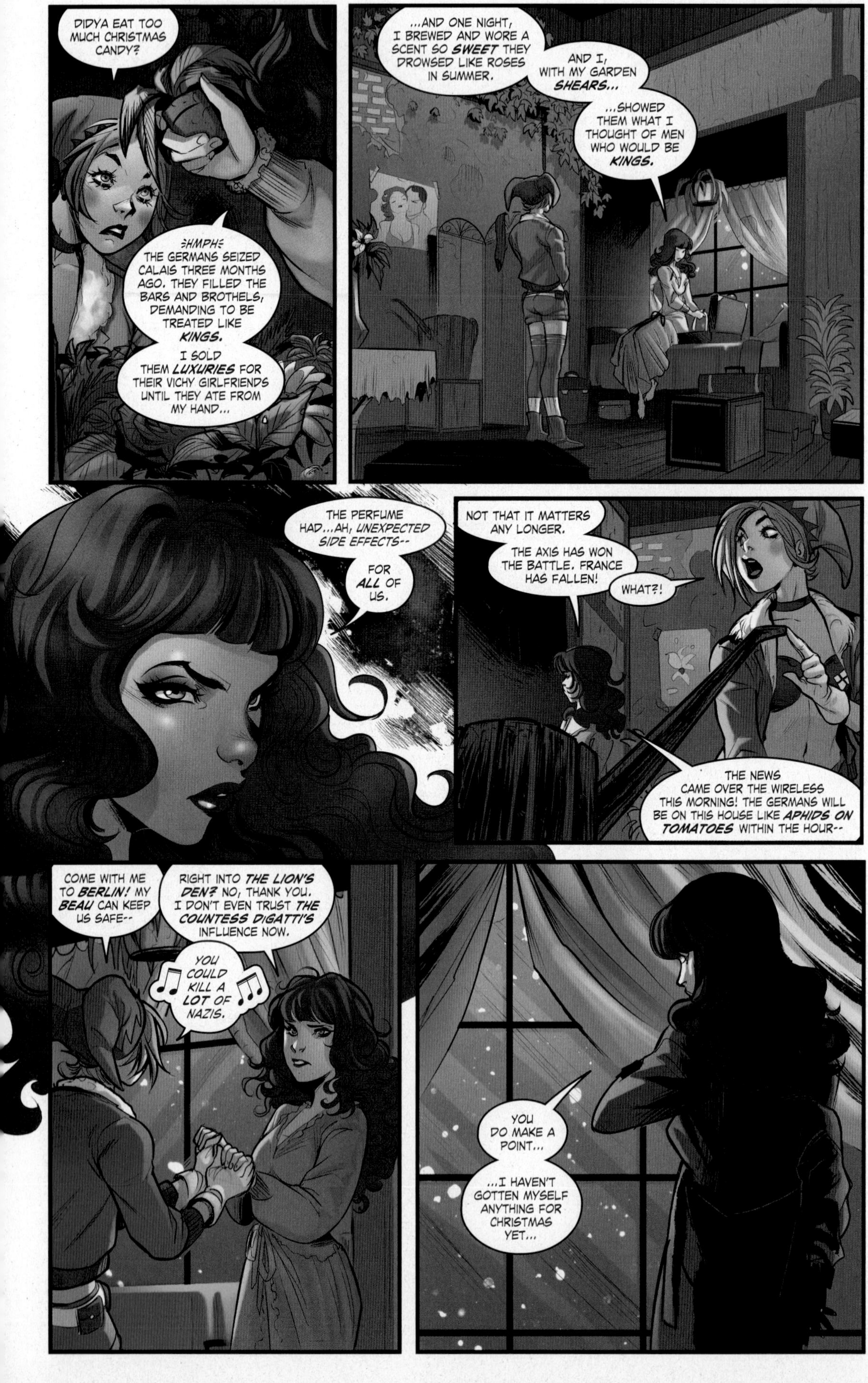

DIDYA EAT TOO MUCH CHRISTMAS CANDY?
*HMPH* THE GERMANS SEIZED CALAIS THREE MONTHS AGO. THEY FILLED THE BARS AND BROTHELS, DEMANDING TO BE TREATED LIKE KINGS.
I SOLD THEM LUXURIES FOR THEIR VICHY GIRLFRIENDS UNTIL THEY ATE FROM MY HAND...
...AND ONE NIGHT, I BREWED AND WORE A SCENT SO SWEET THEY DROWSED LIKE ROSES IN SUMMER.
AND I, WITH MY GARDEN SHEARS...
...SHOWED THEM WHAT I THOUGHT OF MEN WHO WOULD BE KINGS.
THE PERFUME HAD...AH, UNEXPECTED SIDE EFFECTS--
FOR ALL OF US.
NOT THAT IT MATTERS ANY LONGER.
THE AXIS HAS WON THE BATTLE. FRANCE HAS FALLEN!
WHAT?!
THE NEWS CAME OVER THE WIRELESS THIS MORNING! THE GERMANS WILL BE ON THIS HOUSE LIKE APHIDS ON TOMATOES WITHIN THE HOUR--
COME WITH ME TO BERLIN! MY BEAU CAN KEEP US SAFE--
RIGHT INTO THE LION'S DEN? NO, THANK YOU. I DON'T EVEN TRUST THE COUNTESS DIGATTI'S INFLUENCE NOW.
YOU COULD KILL A LOT OF NAZIS.
YOU DO MAKE A POINT...
...I HAVEN'T GOTTEN MYSELF ANYTHING FOR CHRISTMAS YET...

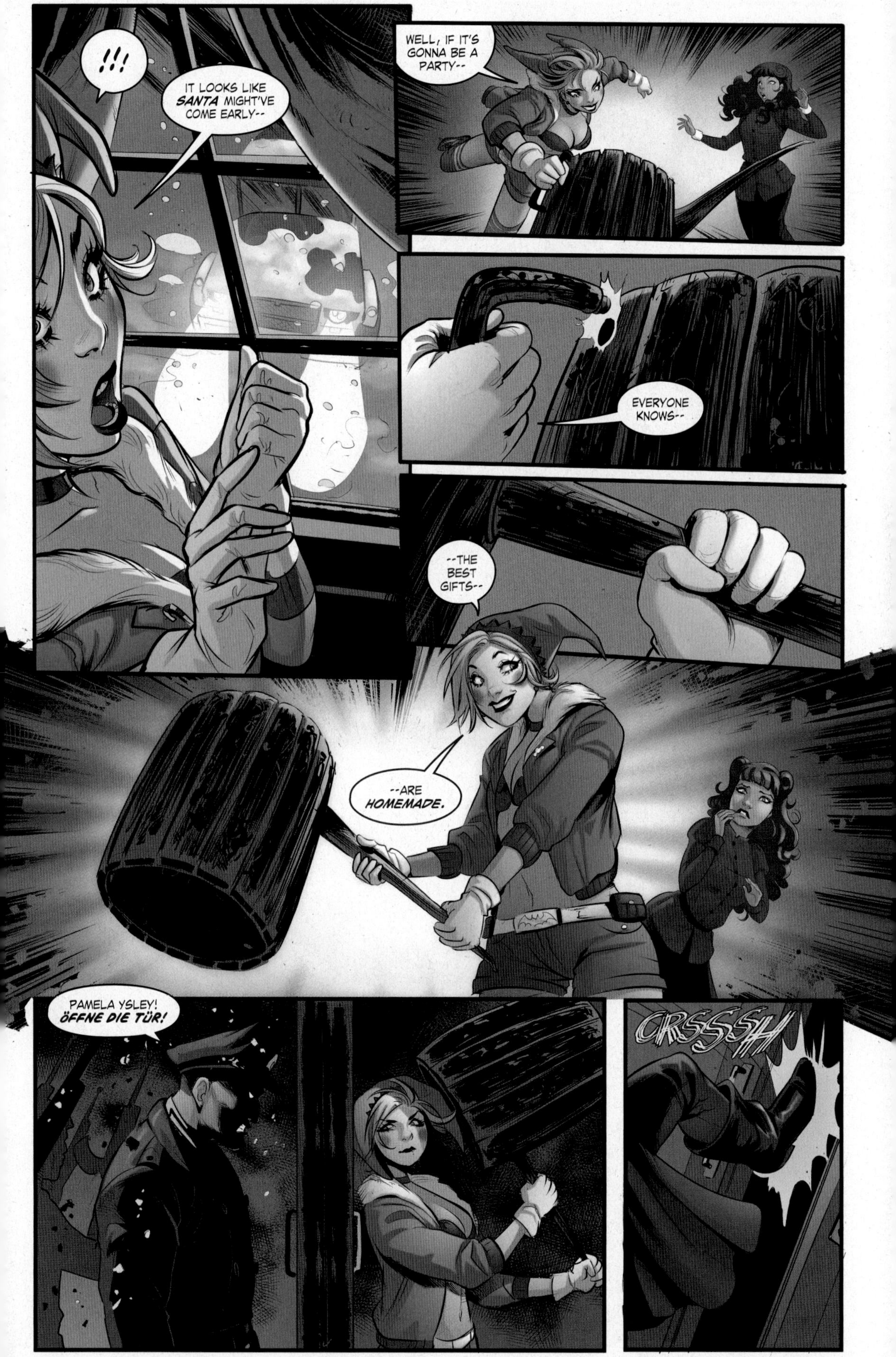
!!!
IT LOOKS LIKE SANTA MIGHT'VE COME EARLY--
WELL, IF IT'S GONNA BE A PARTY--
EVERYONE KNOWS--
--THE BEST GIFTS--
--ARE HOMEMADE.
PAMELA YSLEY! ÖFFNE DIE TÜR!
CRSSSH

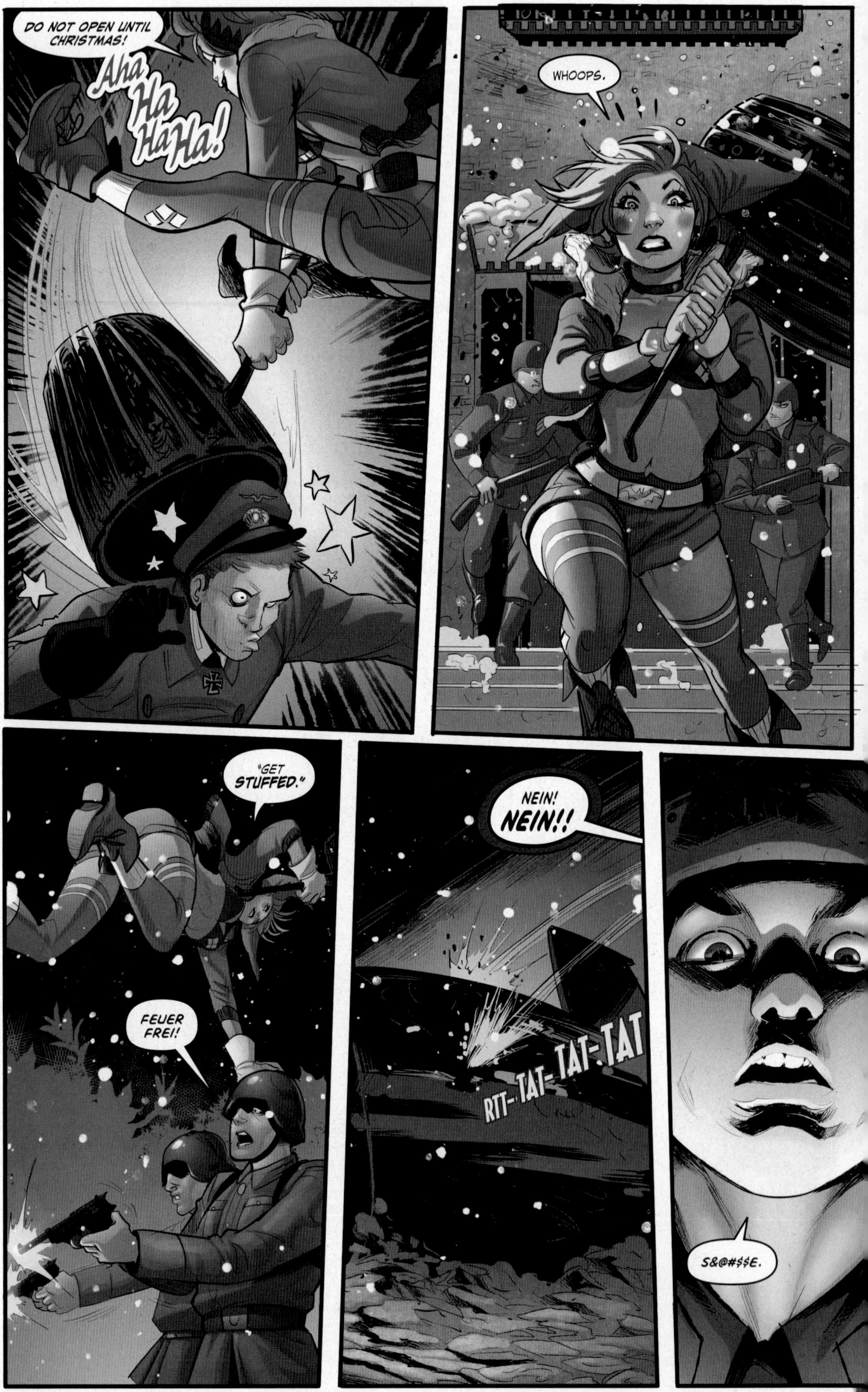
DO NOT OPEN UNTIL CHRISTMAS!
Aha Ha Ha Ha!
WHOOPS.
"GET STUFFED."
FEUER FREI!
NEIN! NEIN!!
RTT-TAT-TAT-TAT
S&@#$$E.

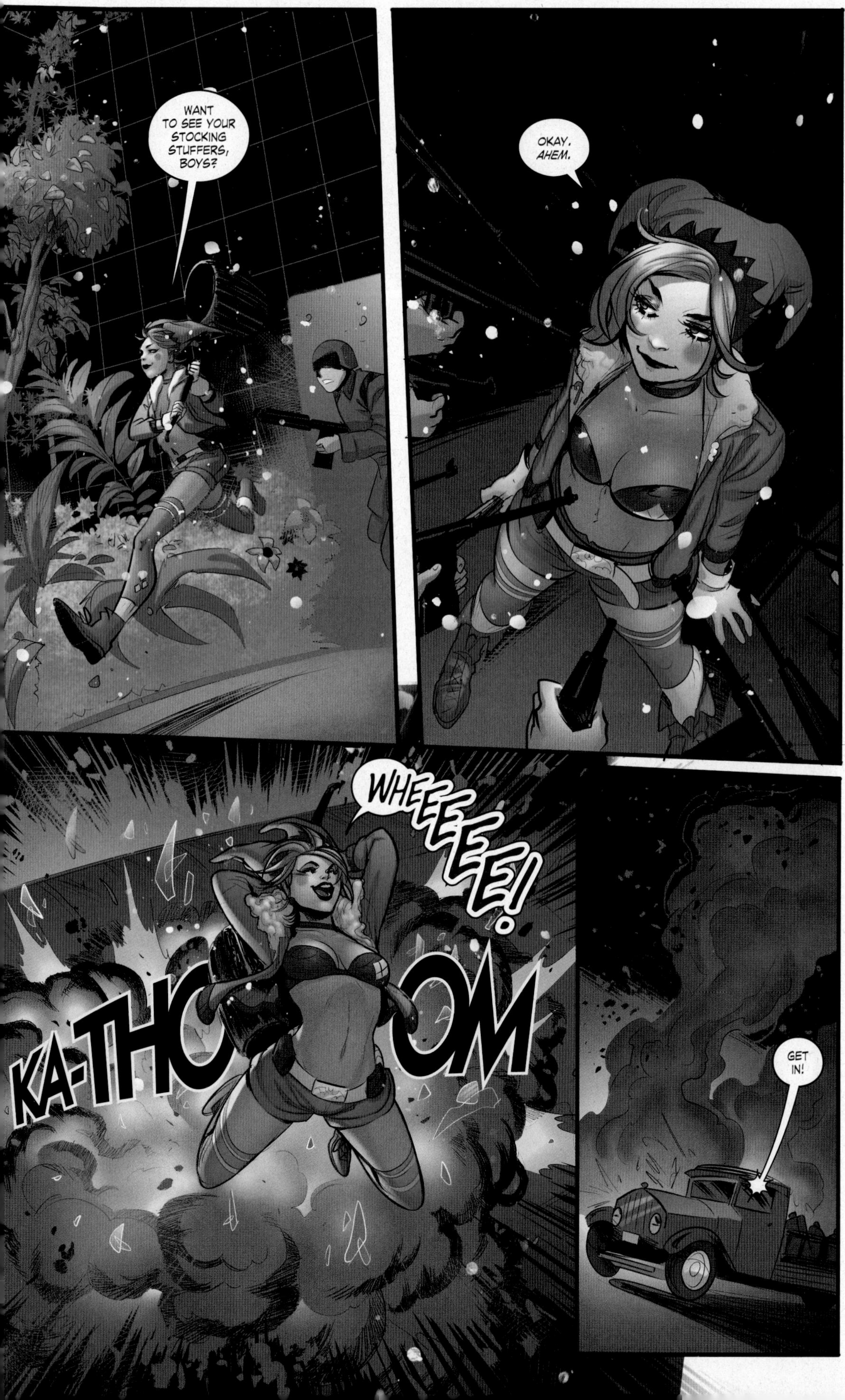
WANT TO SEE YOUR STOCKING STUFFERS, BOYS?
OKAY. AHEM.
WHEEEEEEE!
KA-THOOM
GET IN!

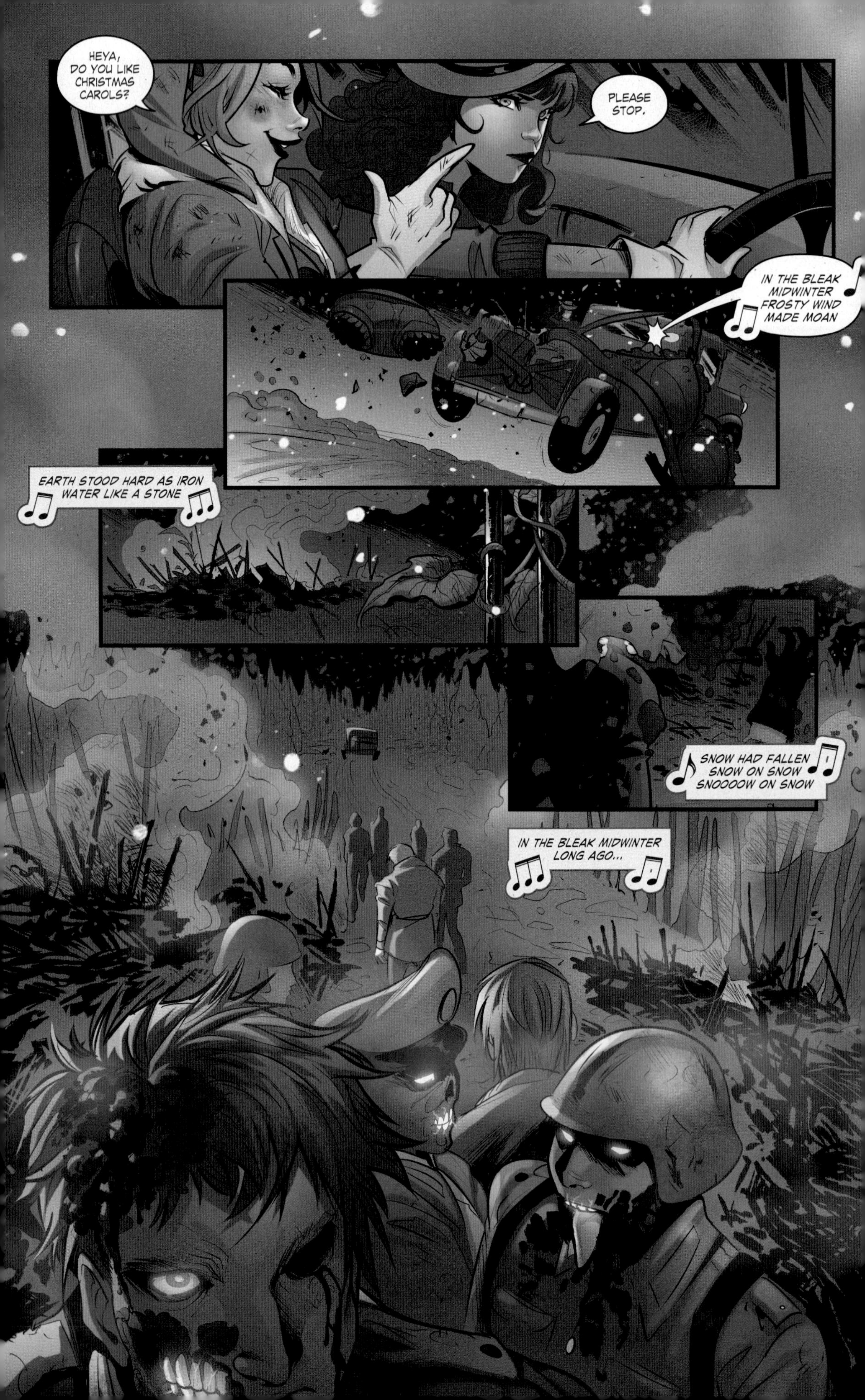
HEYA, DO YOU LIKE CHRISTMAS CAROLS?
PLEASE STOP.
IN THE BLEAK MIDWINTER FROSTY WIND MADE MOAN
EARTH STOOD HARD AS IRON WATER LIKE A STONE
SNOW HAD FALLEN SNOW ON SNOW SNOOOOW ON SNOW
IN THE BLEAK MIDWINTER LONG AGO...

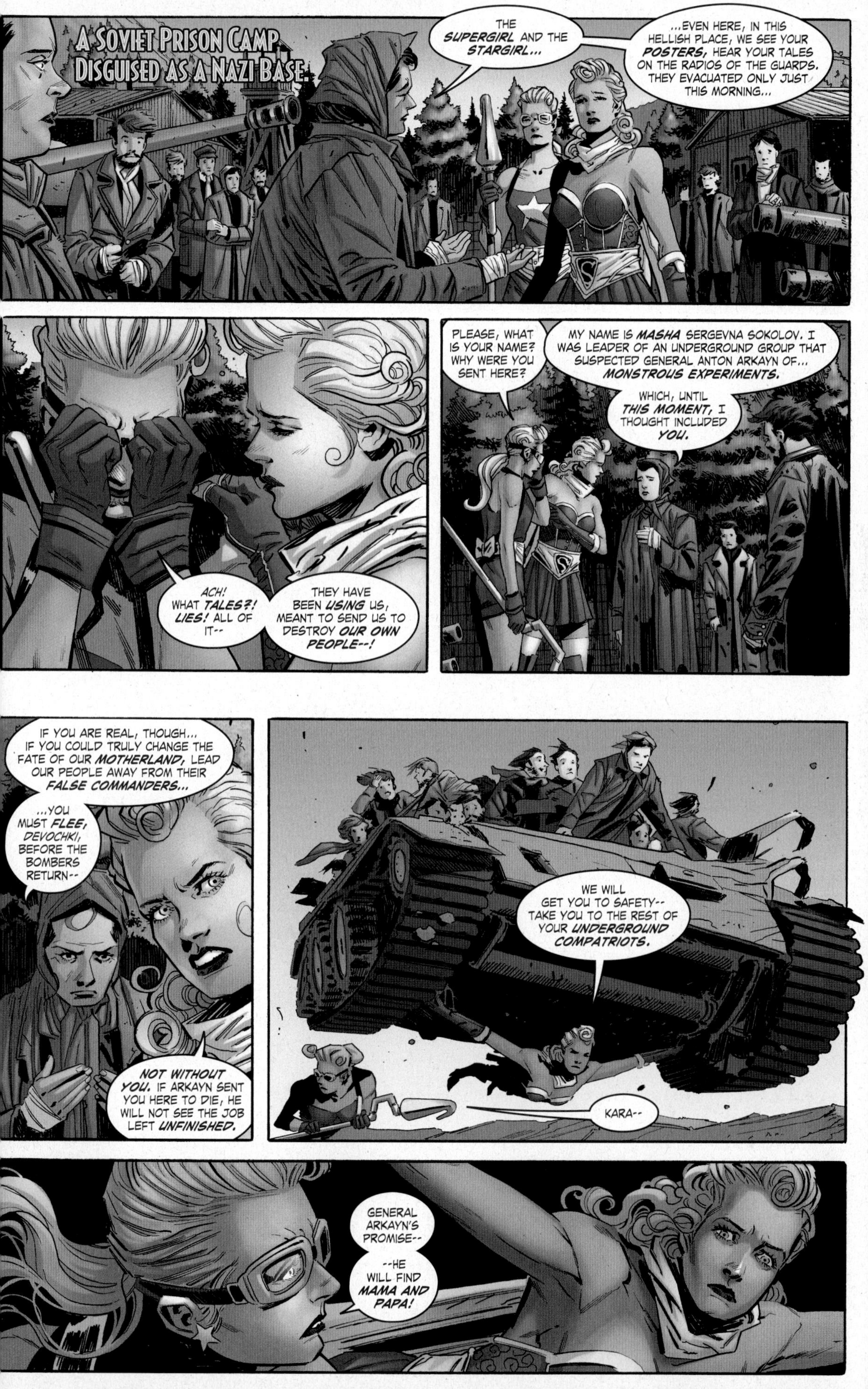
A SOVIET PRISON CAMP DISGUISED AS A NAZI BASE.
THE SUPERGIRL AND THE STARGIRL...
...EVEN HERE, IN THIS HELLISH PLACE, WE SEE YOUR POSTERS, HEAR YOUR TALES ON THE RADIOS OF THE GUARDS. THEY EVACUATED ONLY JUST THIS MORNING...
ACH! WHAT TALES?! LIES! ALL OF IT--
THEY HAVE BEEN USING US, MEANT TO SEND US TO DESTROY OUR OWN PEOPLE--!
PLEASE, WHAT IS YOUR NAME? WHY WERE YOU SENT HERE?
MY NAME IS MASHA SERGEVNA SOKOLOV. I WAS LEADER OF AN UNDERGROUND GROUP THAT SUSPECTED GENERAL ANTON ARKAYN OF... MONSTROUS EXPERIMENTS.
WHICH, UNTIL THIS MOMENT, I THOUGHT INCLUDED YOU.
IF YOU ARE REAL, THOUGH... IF YOU COULD TRULY CHANGE THE FATE OF OUR MOTHERLAND, LEAD OUR PEOPLE AWAY FROM THEIR FALSE COMMANDERS...
...YOU MUST FLEE, DEVOCHKI, BEFORE THE BOMBERS RETURN--
NOT WITHOUT YOU. IF ARKAYN SENT YOU HERE TO DIE, HE WILL NOT SEE THE JOB LEFT UNFINISHED.
WE WILL GET YOU TO SAFETY-- TAKE YOU TO THE REST OF YOUR UNDERGROUND COMPATRIOTS.
KARA--
GENERAL ARKAYN'S PROMISE--
--HE WILL FIND MAMA AND PAPA!

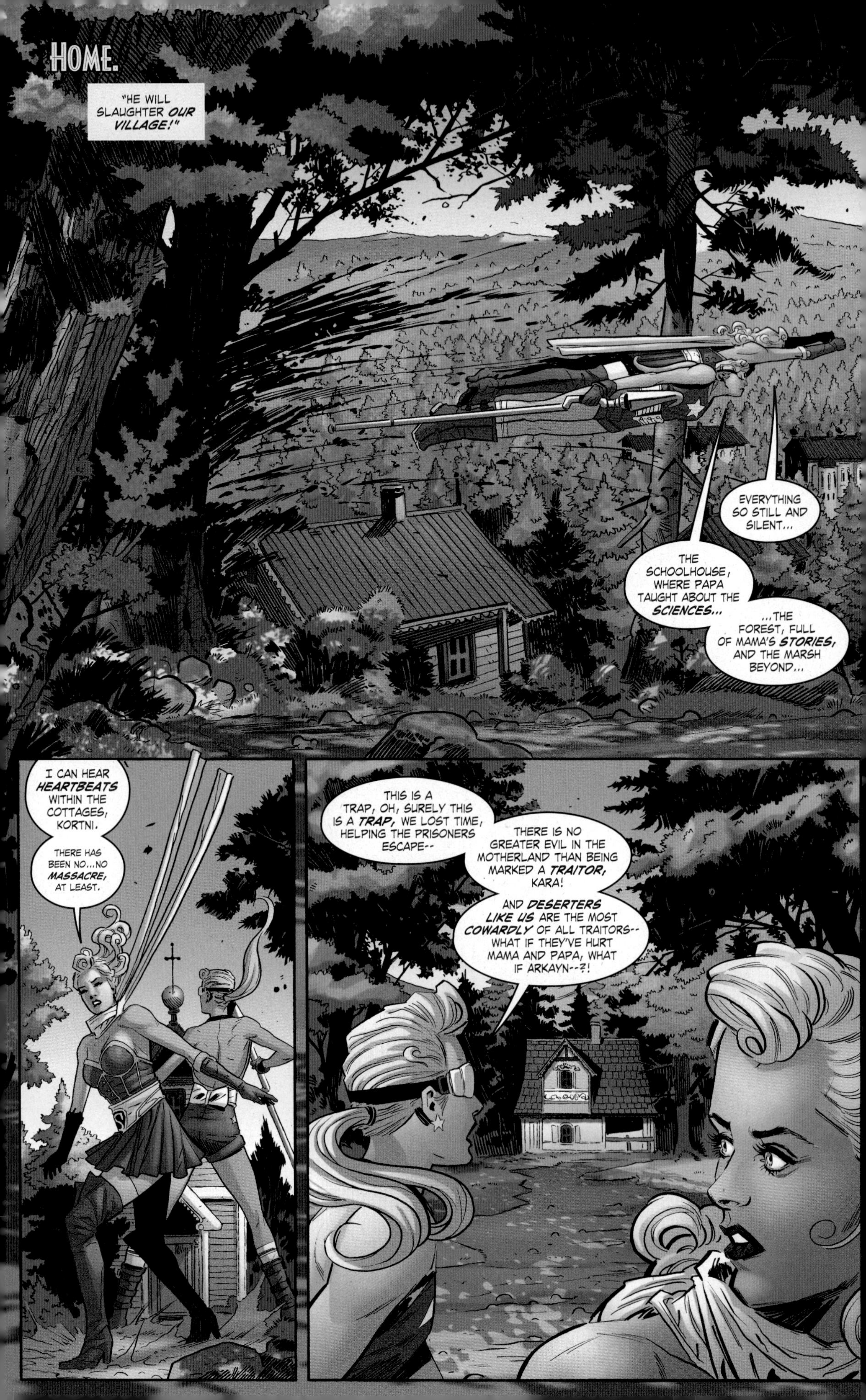

HOME.
"HE WILL SLAUGHTER OUR VILLAGE!"
EVERYTHING SO STILL AND SILENT...
THE SCHOOLHOUSE, WHERE PAPA TAUGHT ABOUT THE SCIENCES...
...THE FOREST, FULL OF MAMA'S STORIES, AND THE MARSH BEYOND...
I CAN HEAR HEARTBEATS WITHIN THE COTTAGES, KORTNI.
THERE HAS BEEN NO...NO MASSACRE, AT LEAST.
THIS IS A TRAP, OH, SURELY THIS IS A TRAP, WE LOST TIME, HELPING THE PRISONERS ESCAPE--
THERE IS NO GREATER EVIL IN THE MOTHERLAND THAN BEING MARKED A TRAITOR, KARA!
AND DESERTERS LIKE US ARE THE MOST COWARDLY OF ALL TRAITORS--WHAT IF THEY'VE HURT MAMA AND PAPA, WHAT IF ARKAYN--?!

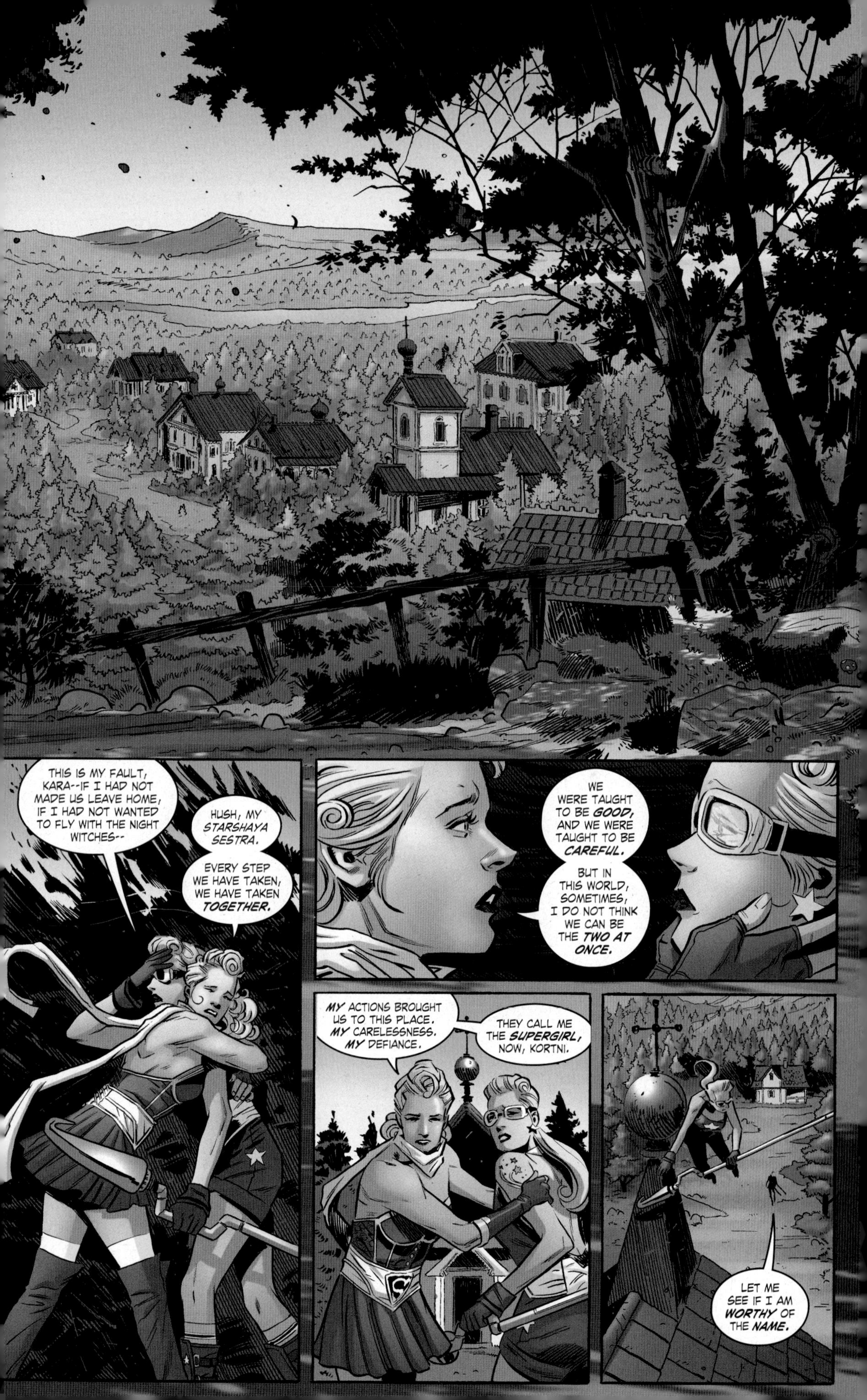

THIS IS MY FAULT, KARA--IF I HAD NOT MADE US LEAVE HOME, IF I HAD NOT WANTED TO FLY WITH THE NIGHT WITCHES--
HUSH, MY *STARSHAYA SESTRA.*
EVERY STEP WE HAVE TAKEN, WE HAVE TAKEN ***TOGETHER.***
WE WERE TAUGHT TO BE ***GOOD,*** AND WE WERE TAUGHT TO BE ***CAREFUL.***
BUT IN THIS WORLD, SOMETIMES, I DO NOT THINK WE CAN BE THE ***TWO AT ONCE.***
***MY*** ACTIONS BROUGHT US TO THIS PLACE. ***MY*** CARELESSNESS. ***MY*** DEFIANCE.
THEY CALL ME THE ***SUPERGIRL,*** NOW, KORTNI.
LET ME SEE IF I AM ***WORTHY*** OF THE ***NAME.***

MAMA, PAPA--

IPATI DUGIN, A DISGRACED INVENTOR FROM THE COSMONAUT PROGRAM, AND HIS LITTLE WIFE, VARVARA.

THEY ARE NOT *BLOOD KIN* TO YOU, *KARA STARIKOV.*

SURELY YOU WILL HAVE NO QUALMS ABOUT BETRAYING THEM AS EASILY AS YOU BETRAYED *ME.*

YOUR TRANSFORMATION FROM *"DISAPPOINTING PILOT"* TO *"EMBLEM OF THE PEOPLE,"* TO *"TRAITOR TO THE MOTHERLAND"* SHOWS--

--YOU LACK *PATIENCE,* LITTLE GIRL.

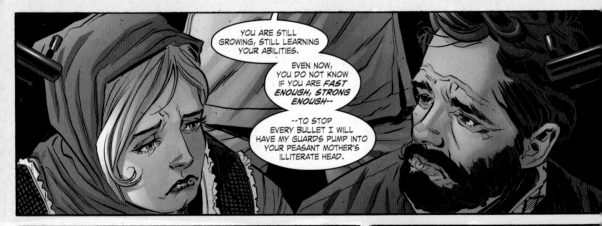

YOU ARE STILL GROWING, STILL LEARNING YOUR ABILITIES.

EVEN NOW, YOU DO NOT KNOW IF YOU ARE *FAST ENOUGH, STRONG ENOUGH*--

--TO STOP EVERY BULLET I WILL HAVE MY GUARDS PUMP INTO YOUR PEASANT MOTHER'S ILLITERATE HEAD.

I WARNED MY COMRADES THAT YOU WERE *UNTRUSTWORTHY,* AND *GENERAL KHULUN* IS NOT HERE TO *PROTECT YOU.*

NOW THE SOVIET COMMAND HAS GIVEN ME LEAVE TO PROVE A FEW *OTHER* HYPOTHESES I HAVE REGARDING YOU AND YOUR *LESS EXTRAORDINARY SISTER.*

YOU WILL AID OUR GLORIOUS UNION FAR BETTER AS *MEDICAL EXPERIMENTS...*

...ONCE I FIND A WAY TO TRANSFER THOSE ABILITIES OF YOURS TO *LOYAL SOVIET SOLDIERS.*

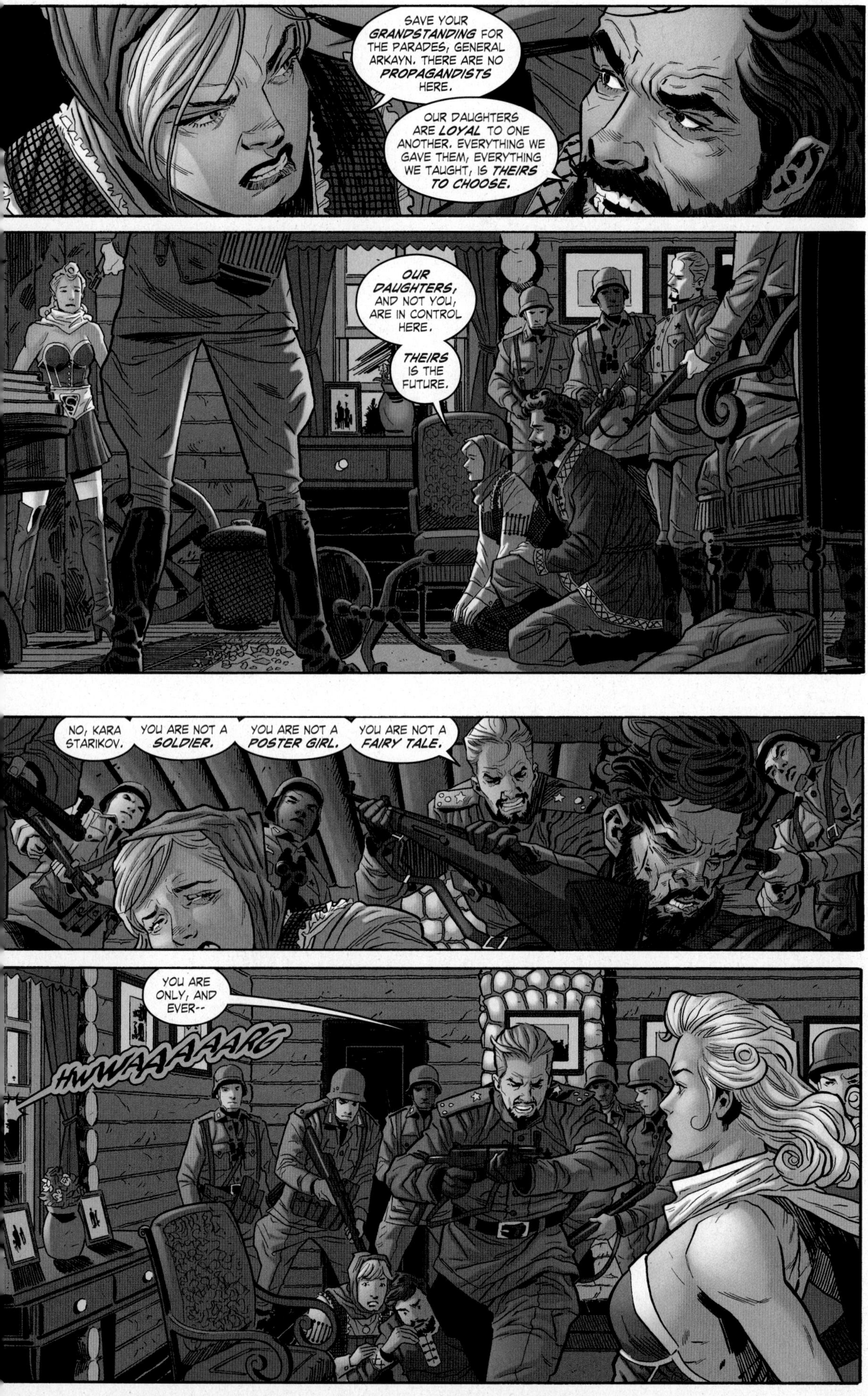
SAVE YOUR GRANDSTANDING FOR THE PARADES, GENERAL ARKAYN. THERE ARE NO PROPAGANDISTS HERE.
OUR DAUGHTERS ARE LOYAL TO ONE ANOTHER. EVERYTHING WE GAVE THEM, EVERYTHING WE TAUGHT, IS THEIRS TO CHOOSE.
OUR DAUGHTERS, AND NOT YOU, ARE IN CONTROL HERE.
THEIRS IS THE FUTURE.
NO, KARA STARIKOV.
YOU ARE NOT A SOLDIER.
YOU ARE NOT A POSTER GIRL.
YOU ARE NOT A FAIRY TALE.
YOU ARE ONLY, AND EVER--
HWAAAAAARG

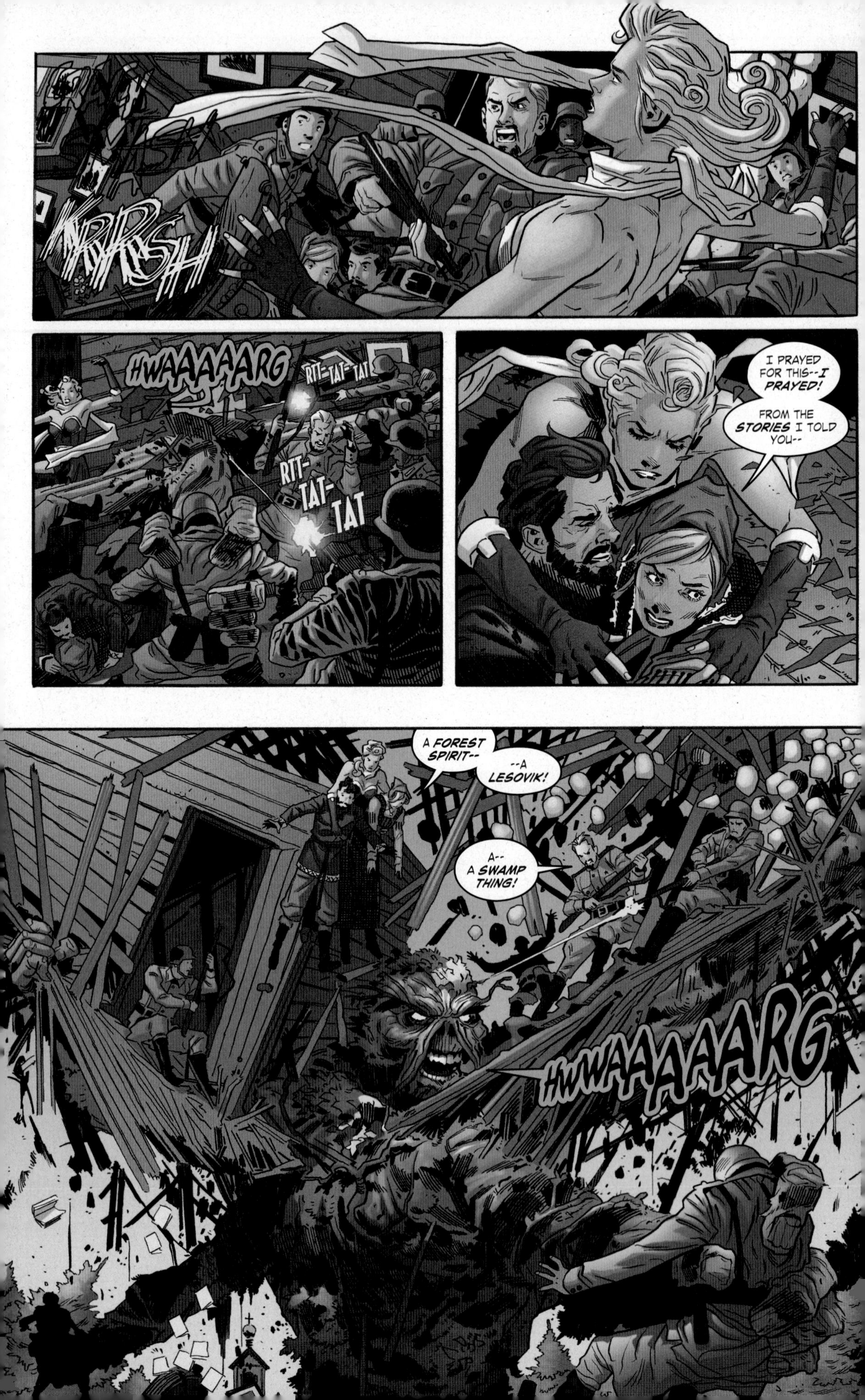
KRRASH
HWAAAAARG
RTT-TAT-TAT
RTT-TAT-TAT
I PRAYED FOR THIS--I PRAYED!
FROM THE STORIES I TOLD YOU--
A FOREST SPIRIT--
--A LESOVIK!
A-- A SWAMP THING!
HWAAAAARG

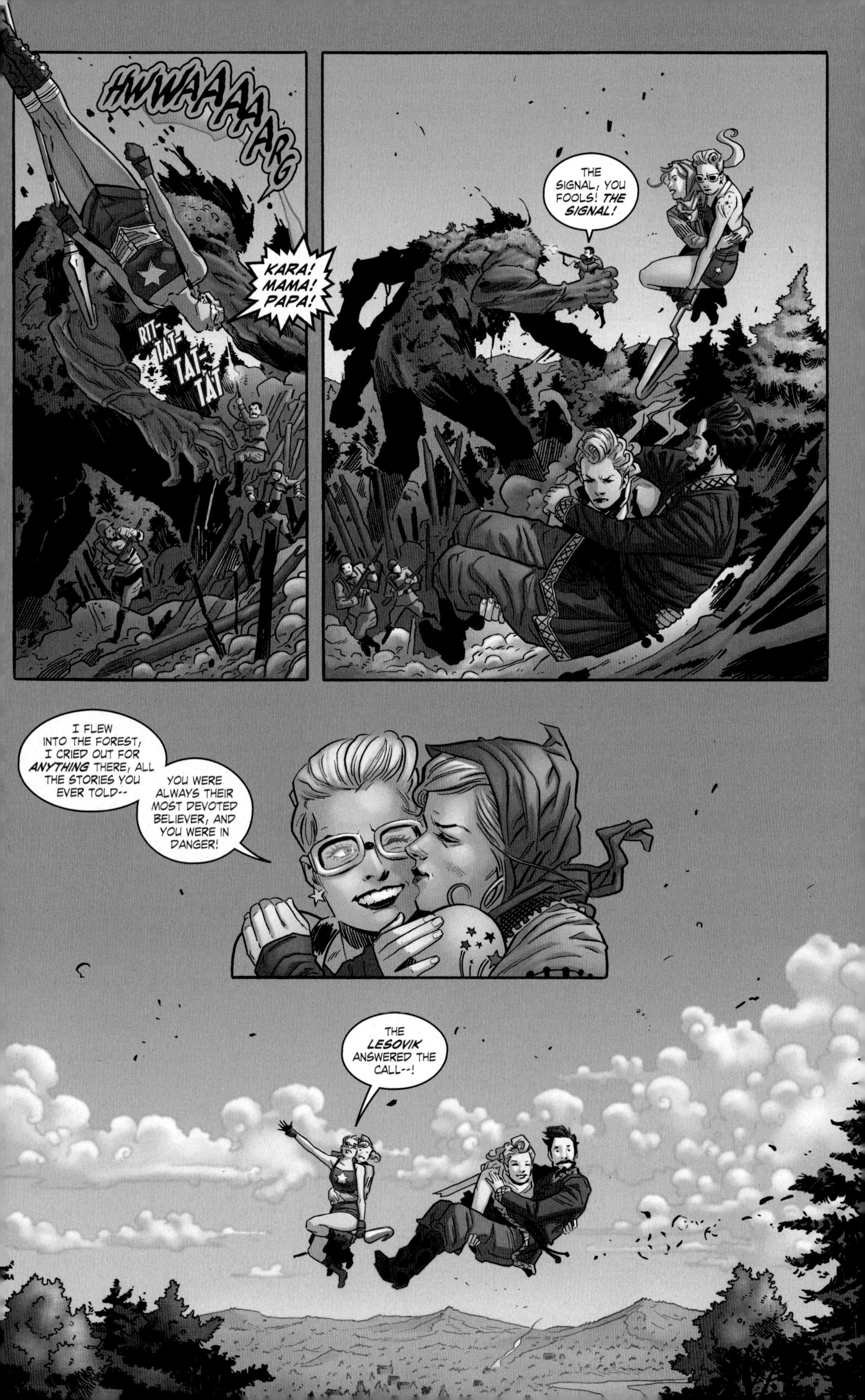
HWWAAAAAARG
KARA! MAMA! PAPA!
RTT-TAT-TAT-TAT
THE SIGNAL, YOU FOOLS! THE SIGNAL!
I FLEW INTO THE FOREST, I CRIED OUT FOR ANYTHING THERE, ALL THE STORIES YOU EVER TOLD--
YOU WERE ALWAYS THEIR MOST DEVOTED BELIEVER, AND YOU WERE IN DANGER!
THE LESOVIK ANSWERED THE CALL--!

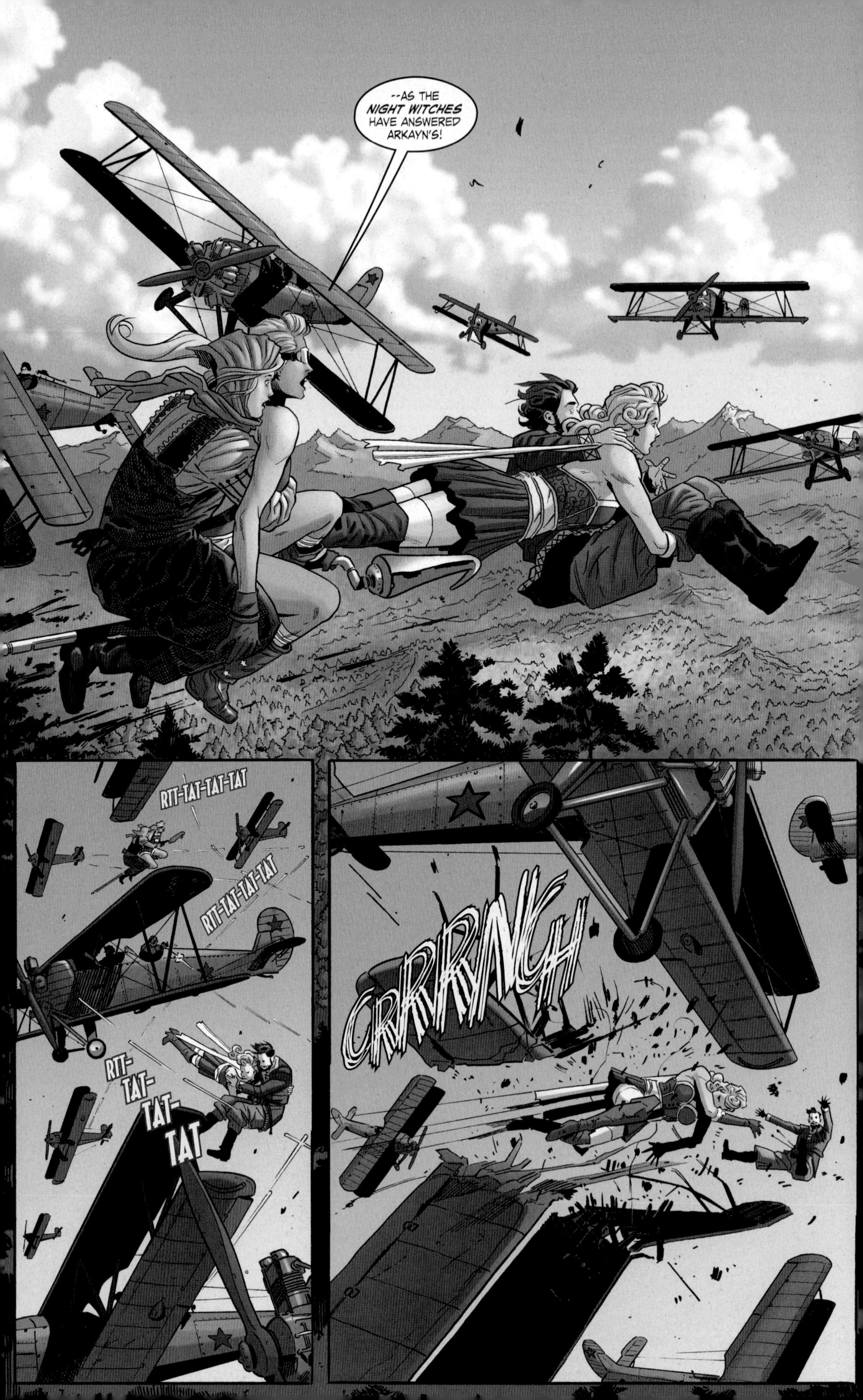
--AS THE NIGHT WITCHES HAVE ANSWERED ARKAYN'S!
RTT-TAT-TAT-TAT
RTT-TAT-TAT-TAT
RTT-TAT-TAT-TAT
CRRRNCH

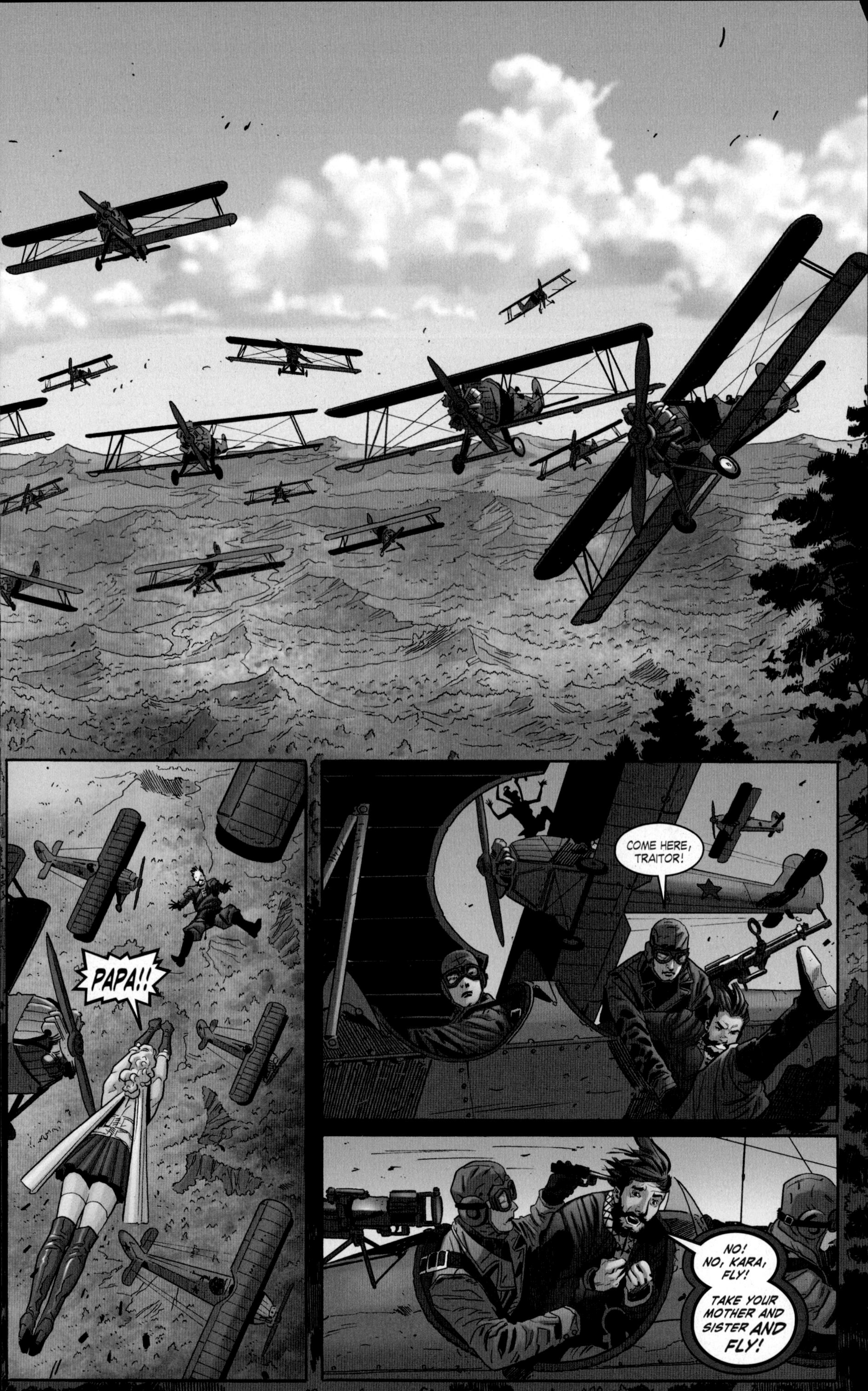
PAPA!!
COME HERE, TRAITOR!
NO! NO, KARA, FLY!
TAKE YOUR MOTHER AND SISTER AND FLY!

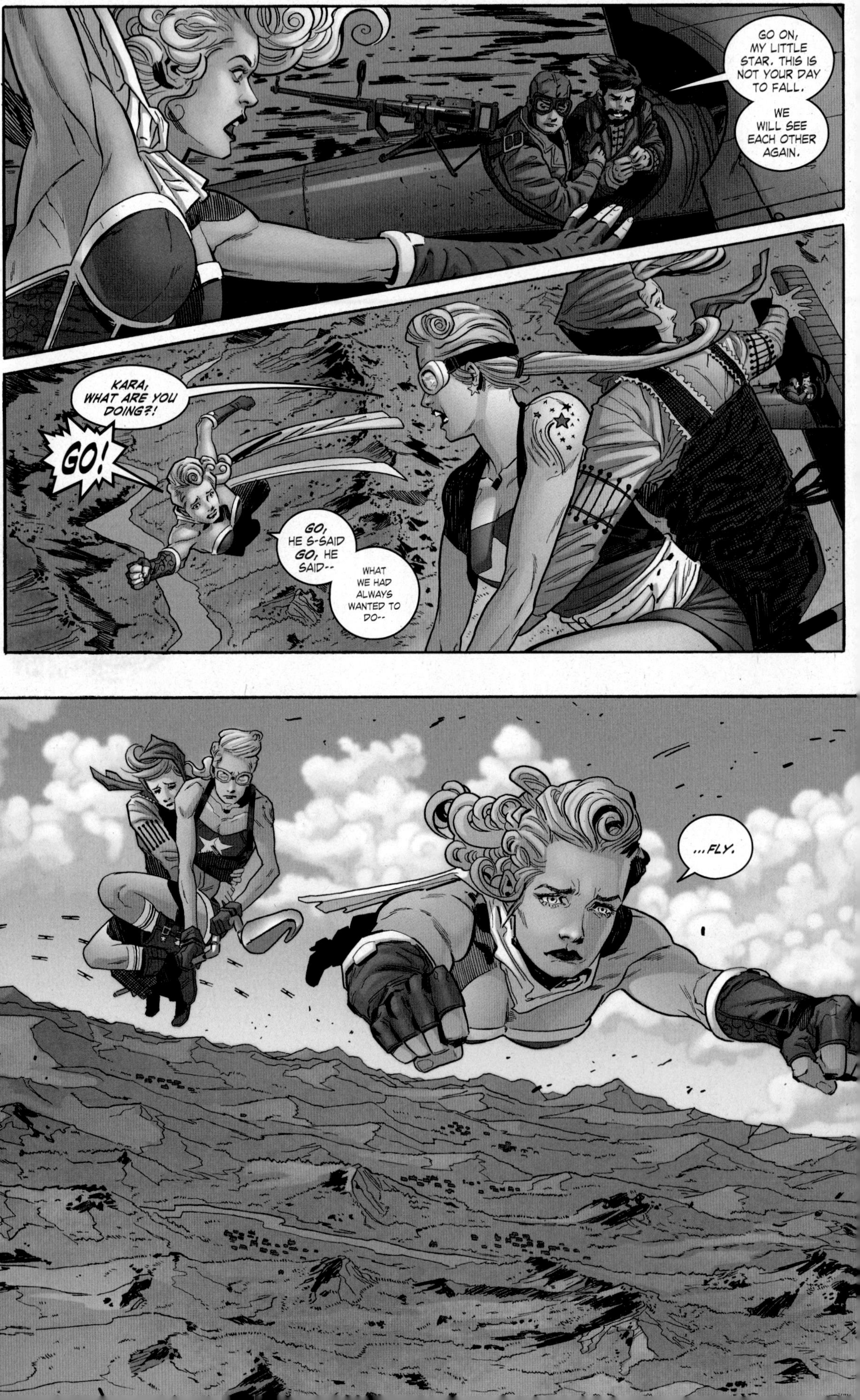
GO ON, MY LITTLE STAR. THIS IS NOT YOUR DAY TO FALL.
WE WILL SEE EACH OTHER AGAIN.
KARA, WHAT ARE YOU DOING?!
GO!
GO, HE S-SAID GO, HE SAID--
WHAT WE HAD ALWAYS WANTED TO DO--
...FLY.

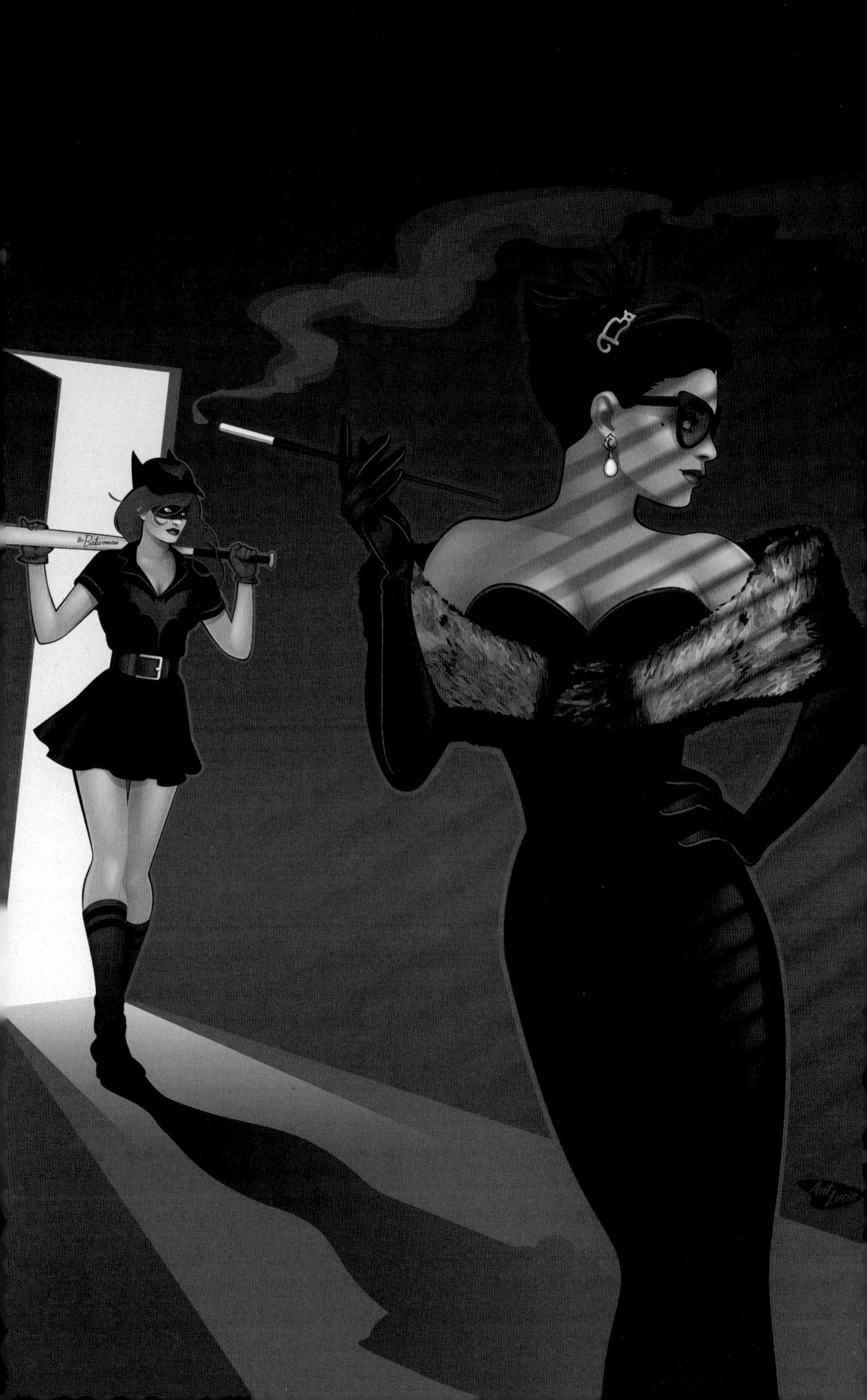
the Batwoman

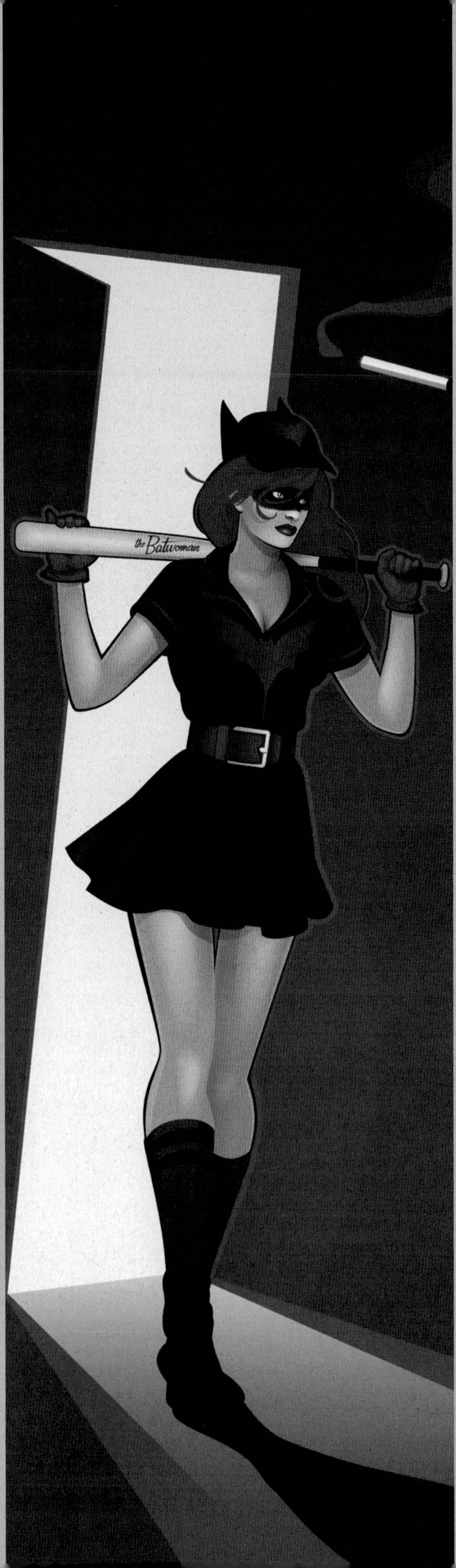
the Batwoman

# COMBAT
## *PART THREE*

MARGUERITE BENNETT
*Writer*

SANDY JARRELL
MING DOYLE
M.L. SANAPO
MARC DEERING
*Artists*

KELLY FITZPATRICK
DOUG GARBARK
*Colorists*

WES ABBOTT
*Letterer*

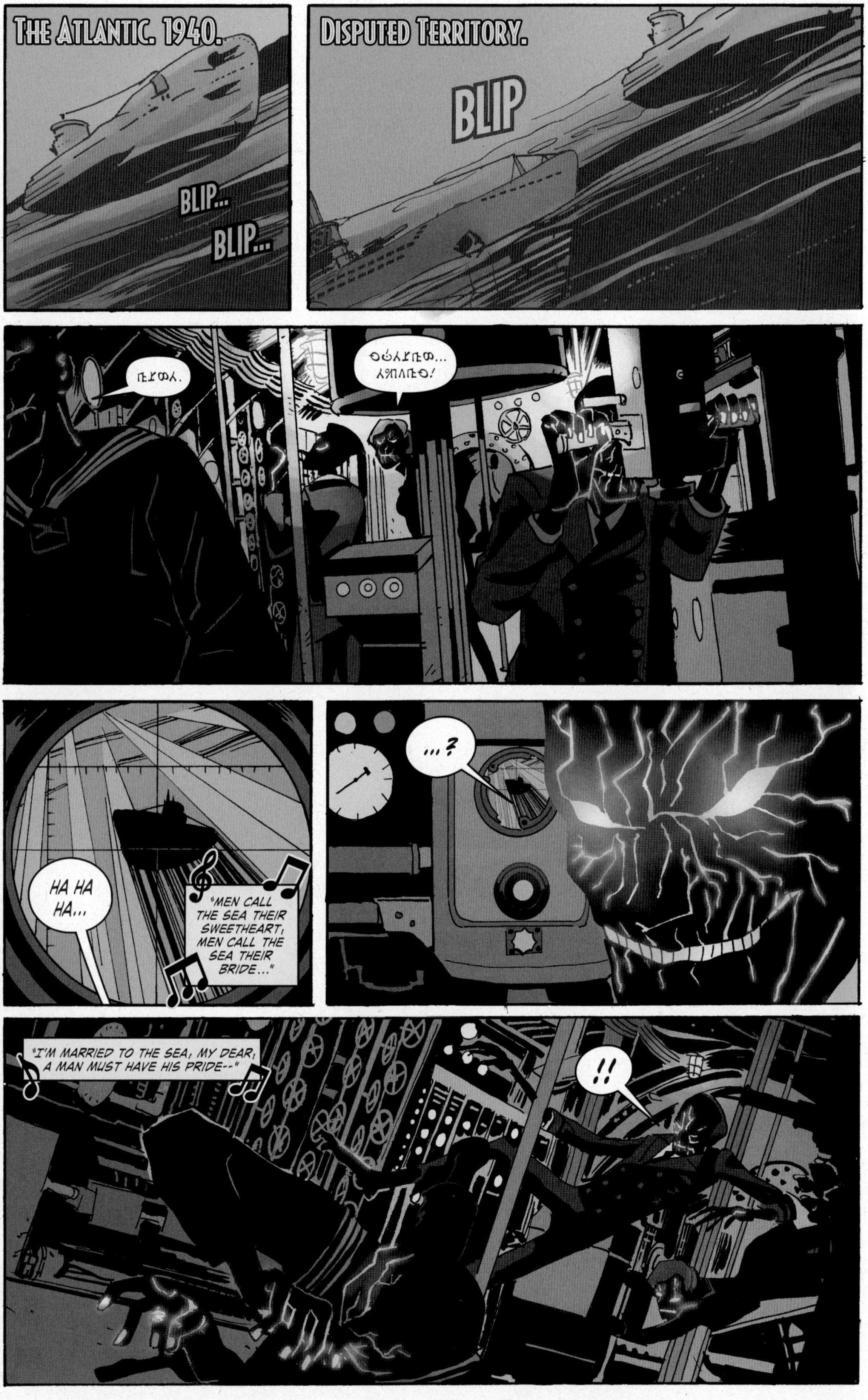
The Atlantic. 1940.
BLIP...
BLIP...
Disputed Territory.
BLIP
HA HA HA...
"MEN CALL THE SEA THEIR SWEETHEART, MEN CALL THE SEA THEIR BRIDE..."
...?
"I'M MARRIED TO THE SEA, MY DEAR, A MAN MUST HAVE HIS PRIDE--"
!!

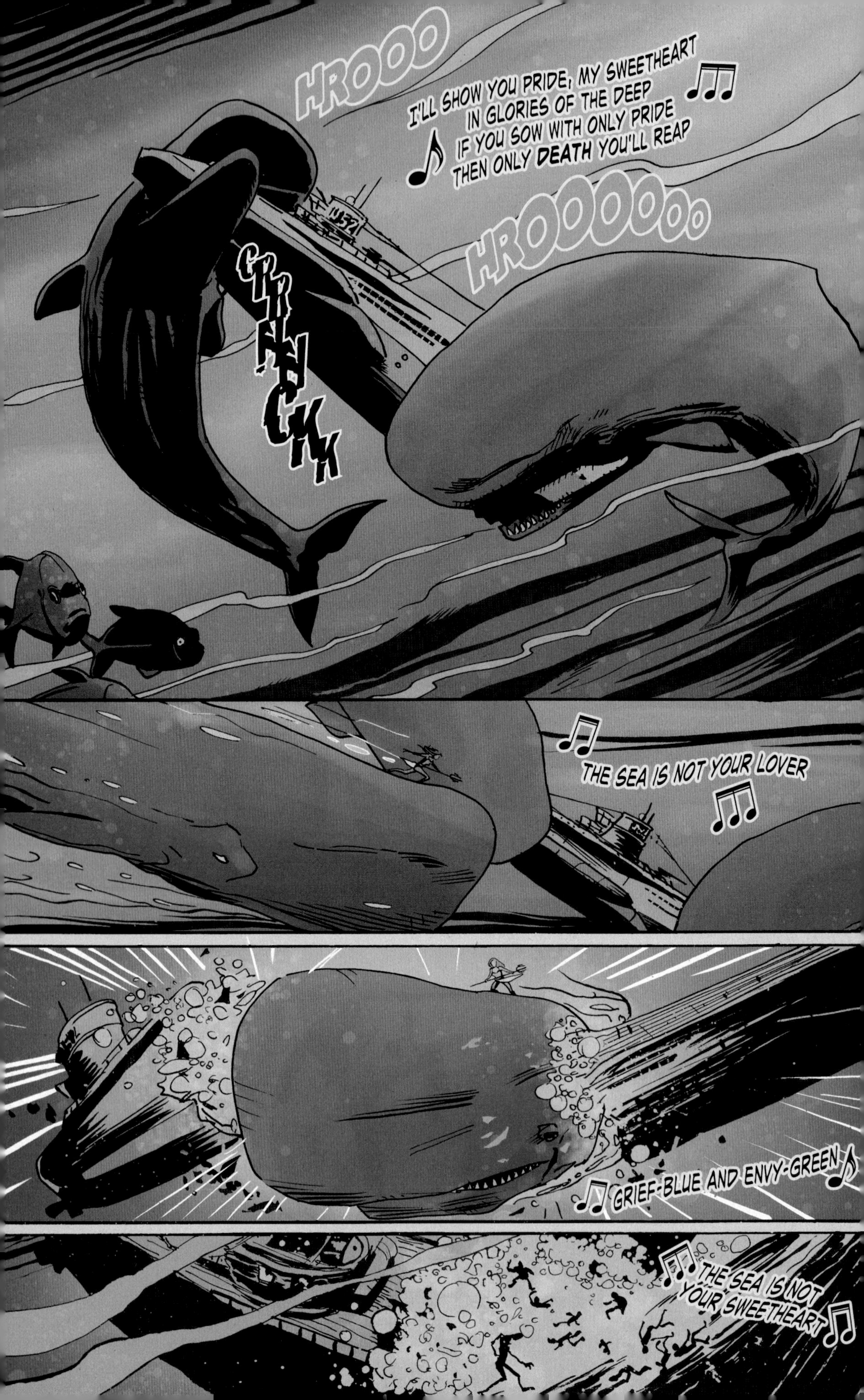
HROOO
I'LL SHOW YOU PRIDE, MY SWEETHEART
IN GLORIES OF THE DEEP
IF YOU SOW WITH ONLY PRIDE
THEN ONLY **DEATH** YOU'LL REAP
HROOOOOoo
THE SEA IS NOT YOUR LOVER
GRIEF-BLUE AND ENVY-GREEN
THE SEA IS NOT YOUR SWEETHEART

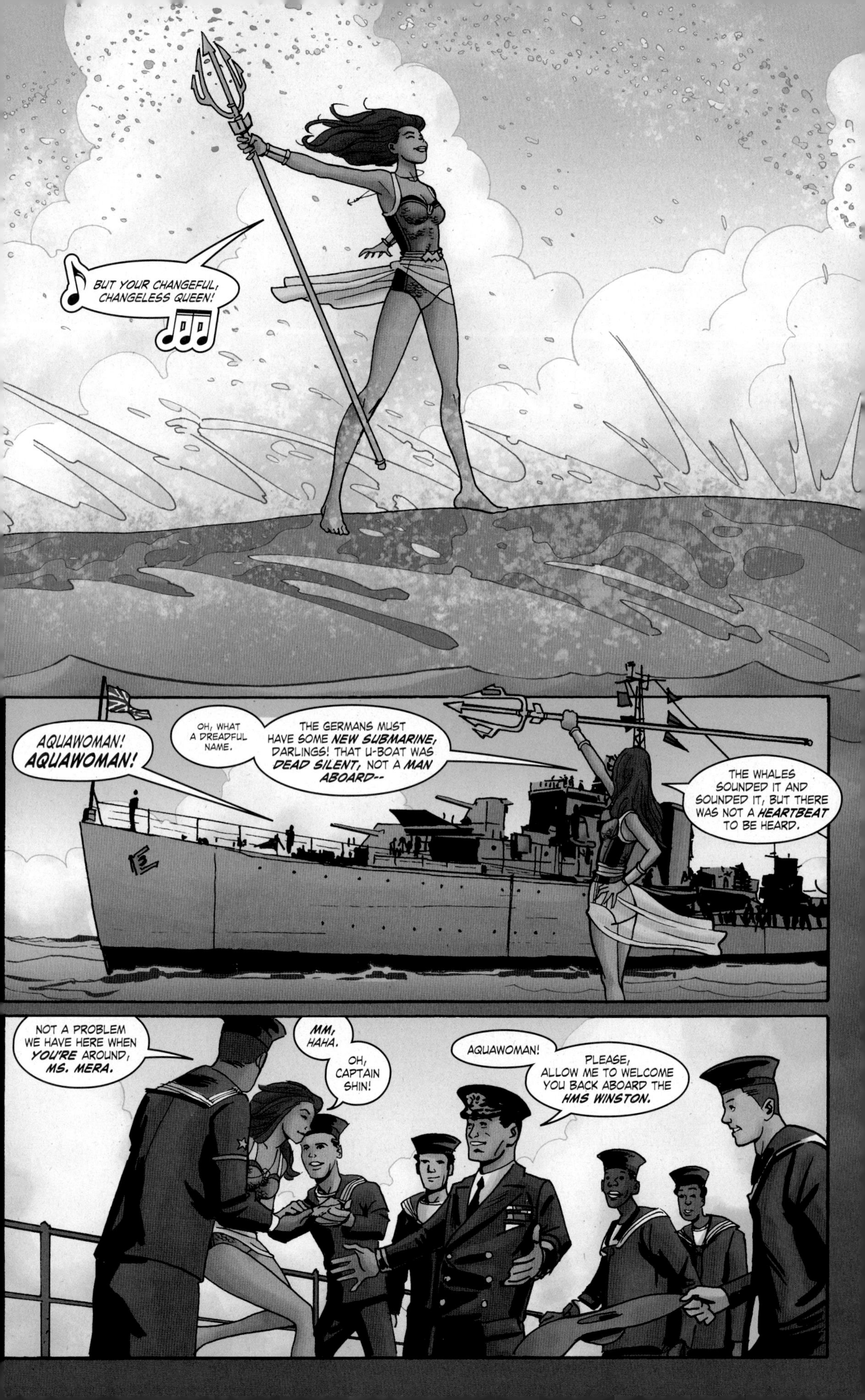
BUT YOUR CHANGEFUL, CHANGELESS QUEEN!
AQUAWOMAN! AQUAWOMAN!
OH, WHAT A DREADFUL NAME.
THE GERMANS MUST HAVE SOME NEW SUBMARINE, DARLINGS! THAT U-BOAT WAS DEAD SILENT, NOT A MAN ABOARD--
THE WHALES SOUNDED IT AND SOUNDED IT, BUT THERE WAS NOT A HEARTBEAT TO BE HEARD.
NOT A PROBLEM WE HAVE HERE WHEN YOU'RE AROUND, MS. MERA.
MM, HAHA.
OH, CAPTAIN SHIN!
AQUAWOMAN!
PLEASE, ALLOW ME TO WELCOME YOU BACK ABOARD THE HMS WINSTON.

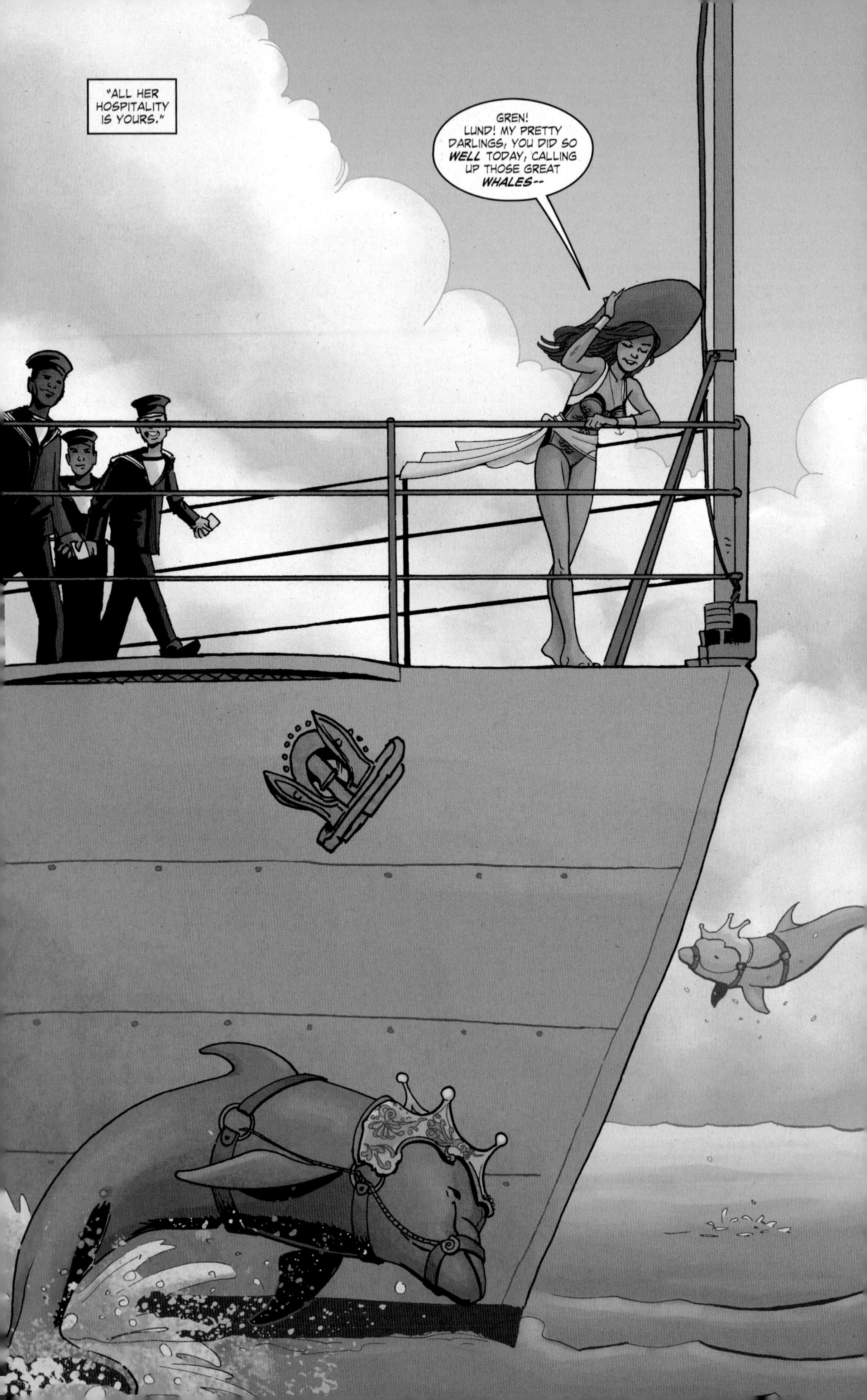
"ALL HER HOSPITALITY IS YOURS."
GREN! LUND! MY PRETTY DARLINGS, YOU DID SO WELL TODAY, CALLING UP THOSE GREAT WHALES--

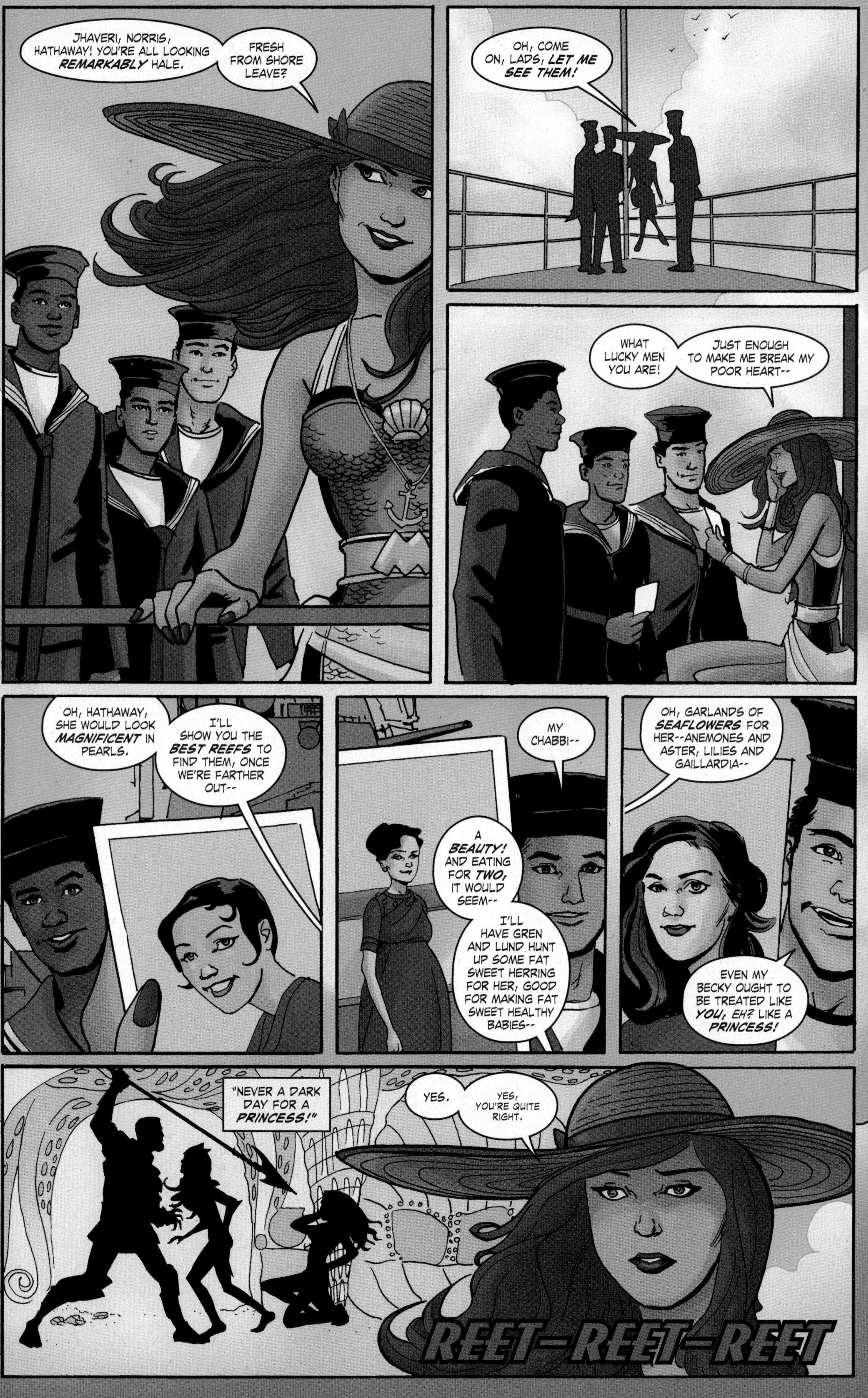
JHAVERI, NORRIS, HATHAWAY! YOU'RE ALL LOOKING REMARKABLY HALE.
FRESH FROM SHORE LEAVE?
OH, COME ON, LADS, LET ME SEE THEM!
WHAT LUCKY MEN YOU ARE!
JUST ENOUGH TO MAKE ME BREAK MY POOR HEART--
OH, HATHAWAY, SHE WOULD LOOK MAGNIFICENT IN PEARLS.
I'LL SHOW YOU THE BEST REEFS TO FIND THEM, ONCE WE'RE FARTHER OUT--
MY CHABBI--
A BEAUTY! AND EATING FOR TWO, IT WOULD SEEM--
I'LL HAVE GREN AND LUND HUNT UP SOME FAT SWEET HERRING FOR HER, GOOD FOR MAKING FAT SWEET HEALTHY BABIES--
OH, GARLANDS OF SEAFLOWERS FOR HER--ANEMONES AND ASTER, LILIES AND GAILLARDIA--
EVEN MY BECKY OUGHT TO BE TREATED LIKE YOU, EH? LIKE A PRINCESS!
"NEVER A DARK DAY FOR A PRINCESS!"
YES.
YES, YOU'RE QUITE RIGHT.
REET--REET--REET

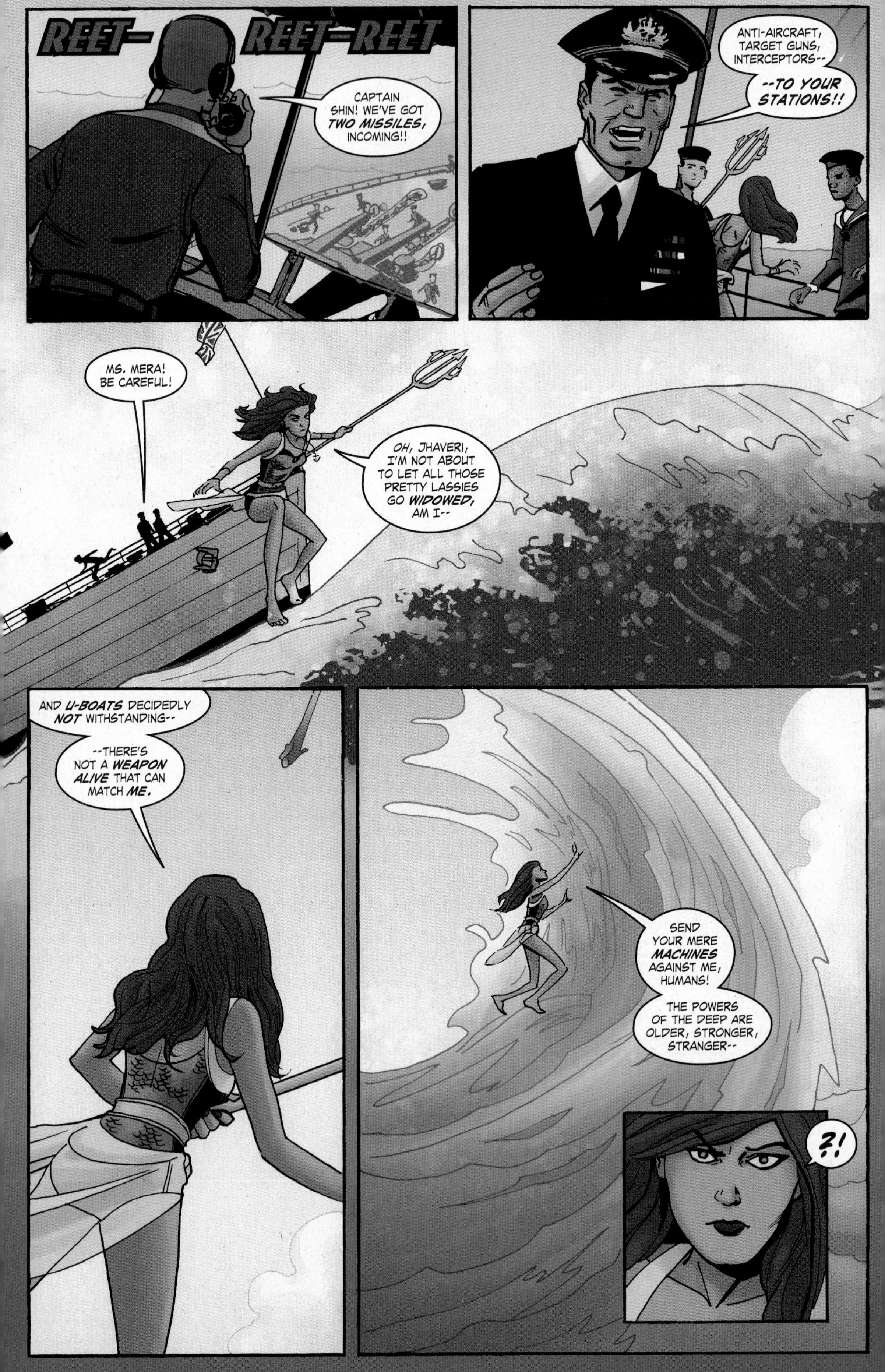
REET-REET-REET
CAPTAIN SHIN! WE'VE GOT TWO MISSILES, INCOMING!!
ANTI-AIRCRAFT, TARGET GUNS, INTERCEPTORS--
--TO YOUR STATIONS!!
MS. MERA! BE CAREFUL!
OH, JHAVERI, I'M NOT ABOUT TO LET ALL THOSE PRETTY LASSIES GO WIDOWED, AM I--
AND U-BOATS DECIDEDLY NOT WITHSTANDING--
--THERE'S NOT A WEAPON ALIVE THAT CAN MATCH ME.
SEND YOUR MERE MACHINES AGAINST ME, HUMANS!
THE POWERS OF THE DEEP ARE OLDER, STRONGER, STRANGER--
?!

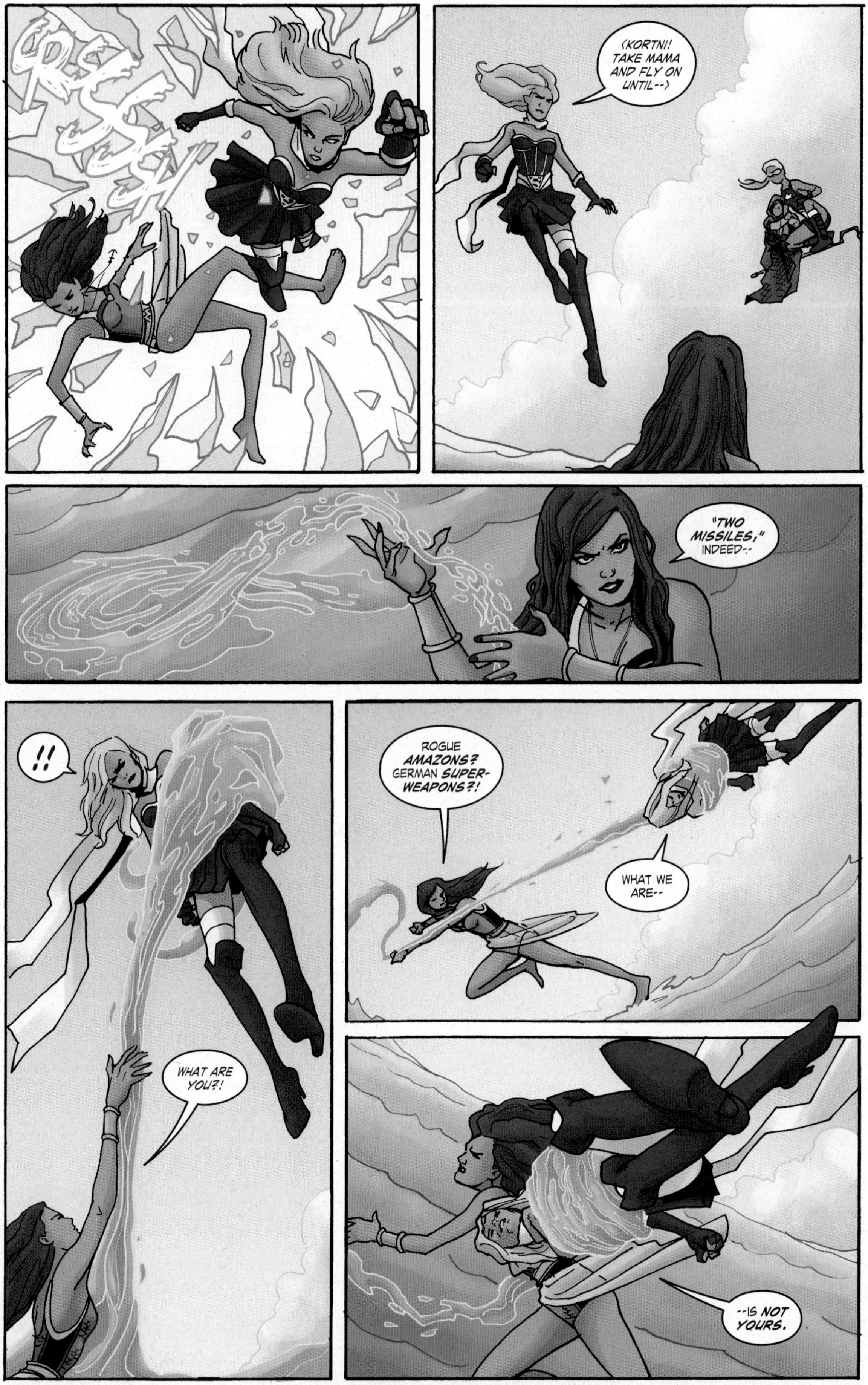

CRSSSH
‹KORTNI! TAKE MAMA AND FLY ON UNTIL--›
"TWO MISSILES," INDEED--
!!
WHAT ARE YOU?!
ROGUE AMAZONS? GERMAN SUPER-WEAPONS?!
WHAT WE ARE--
--IS NOT YOURS.

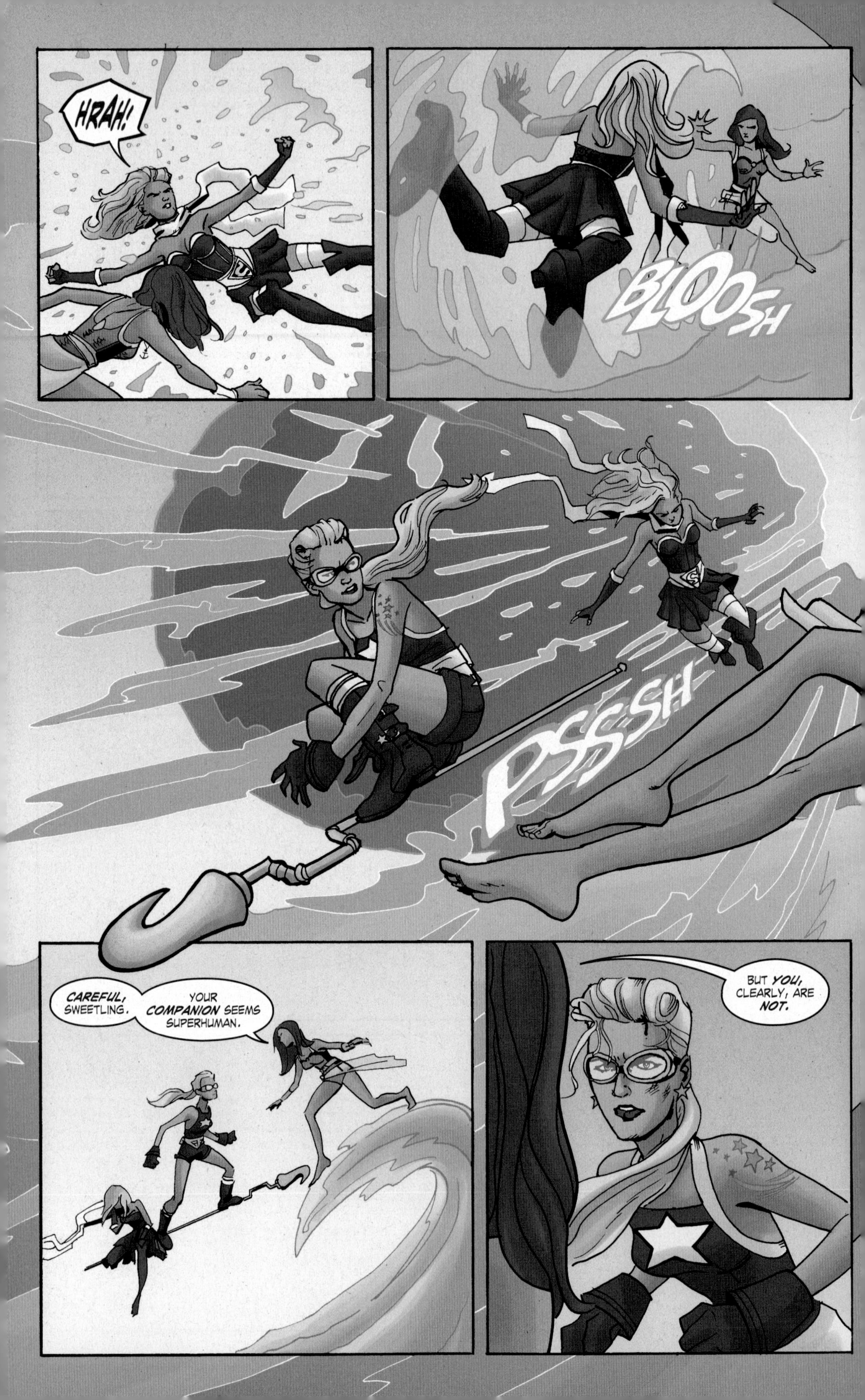

HRAH!
BLOOSH
PSSSSH
CAREFUL, SWEETLING.
YOUR COMPANION SEEMS SUPERHUMAN.
BUT YOU, CLEARLY, ARE NOT.

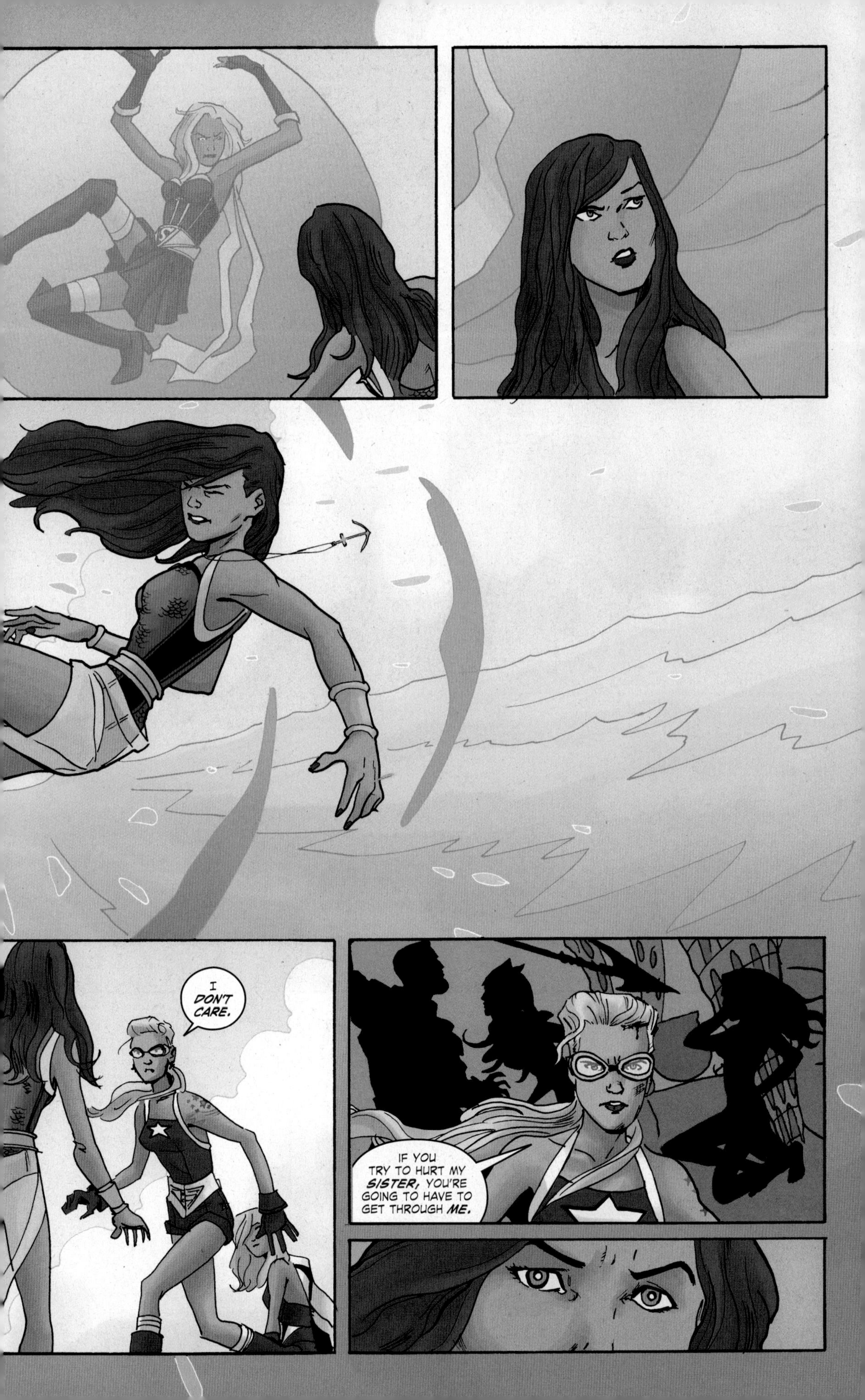
I DON'T CARE.
IF YOU TRY TO HURT MY SISTER, YOU'RE GOING TO HAVE TO GET THROUGH ME.

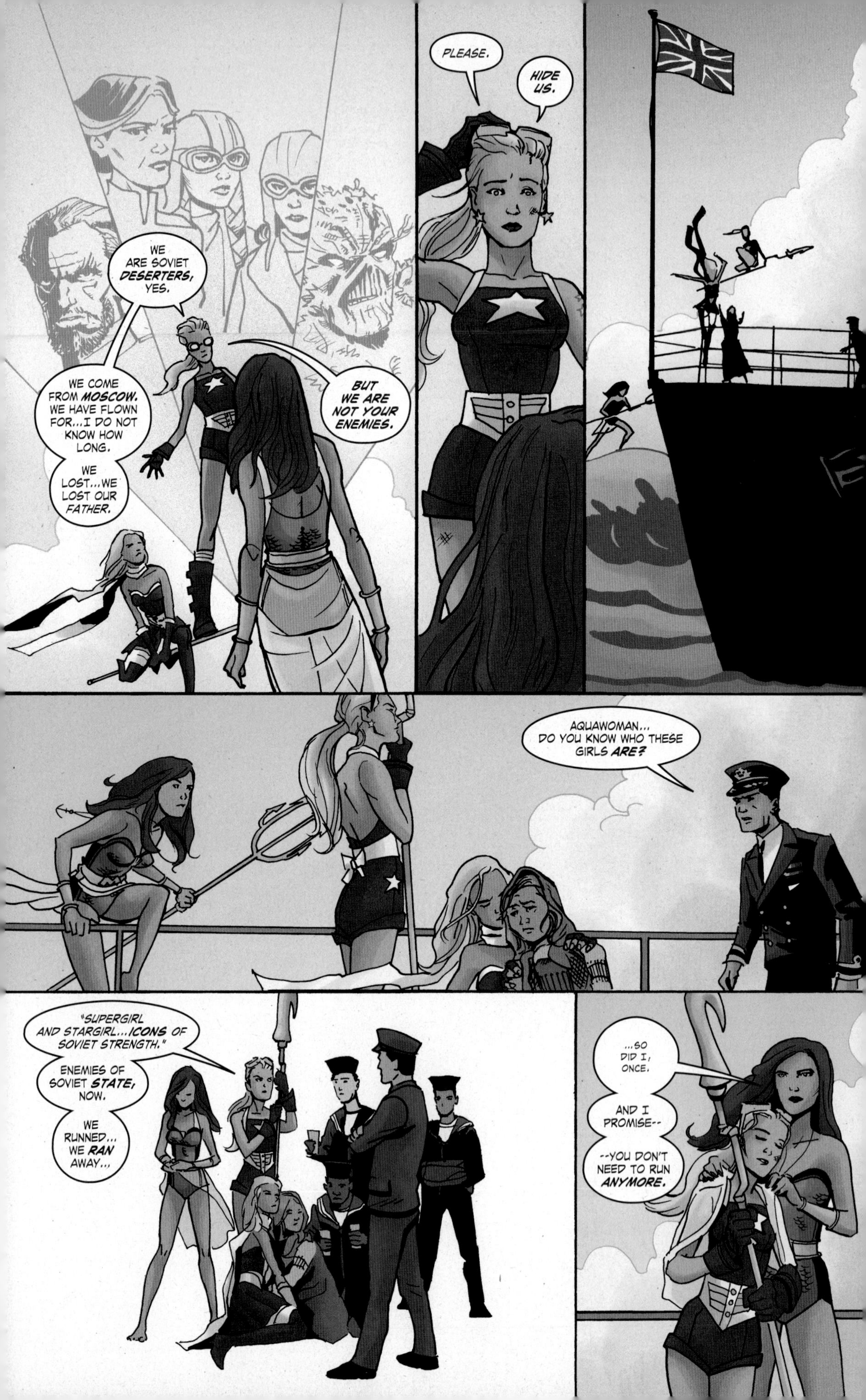
WE ARE SOVIET DESERTERS, YES.
WE COME FROM MOSCOW. WE HAVE FLOWN FOR...I DO NOT KNOW HOW LONG.
WE LOST...WE LOST OUR FATHER.
BUT WE ARE NOT YOUR ENEMIES.
PLEASE.
HIDE US.
AQUAWOMAN... DO YOU KNOW WHO THESE GIRLS ARE?
"SUPERGIRL AND STARGIRL...ICONS OF SOVIET STRENGTH."
ENEMIES OF SOVIET STATE, NOW.
WE RUNNED... WE RAN AWAY...
...SO DID I, ONCE.
AND I PROMISE--
--YOU DON'T NEED TO RUN ANYMORE.

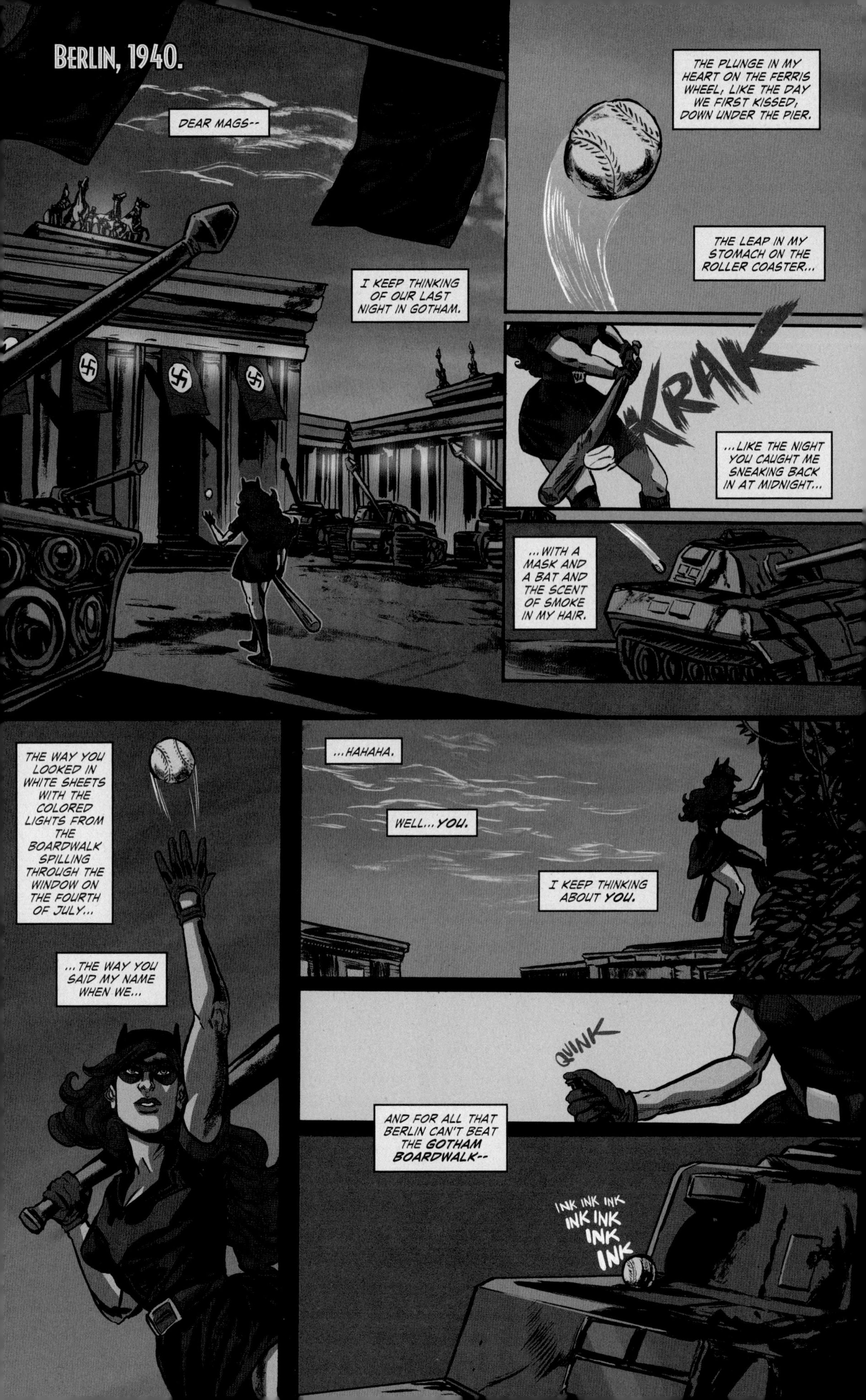

BERLIN, 1940.
DEAR MAGS--
I KEEP THINKING OF OUR LAST NIGHT IN GOTHAM.
THE PLUNGE IN MY HEART ON THE FERRIS WHEEL, LIKE THE DAY WE FIRST KISSED, DOWN UNDER THE PIER.
THE LEAP IN MY STOMACH ON THE ROLLER COASTER...
KRAK
...LIKE THE NIGHT YOU CAUGHT ME SNEAKING BACK IN AT MIDNIGHT...
...WITH A MASK AND A BAT AND THE SCENT OF SMOKE IN MY HAIR.
THE WAY YOU LOOKED IN WHITE SHEETS WITH THE COLORED LIGHTS FROM THE BOARDWALK SPILLING THROUGH THE WINDOW ON THE FOURTH OF JULY...
...THE WAY YOU SAID MY NAME WHEN WE...
...HAHAHA.
WELL...YOU.
I KEEP THINKING ABOUT YOU.
QUINK
AND FOR ALL THAT BERLIN CAN'T BEAT THE GOTHAM BOARDWALK--
INK INK INK
INK INK
INK
INK

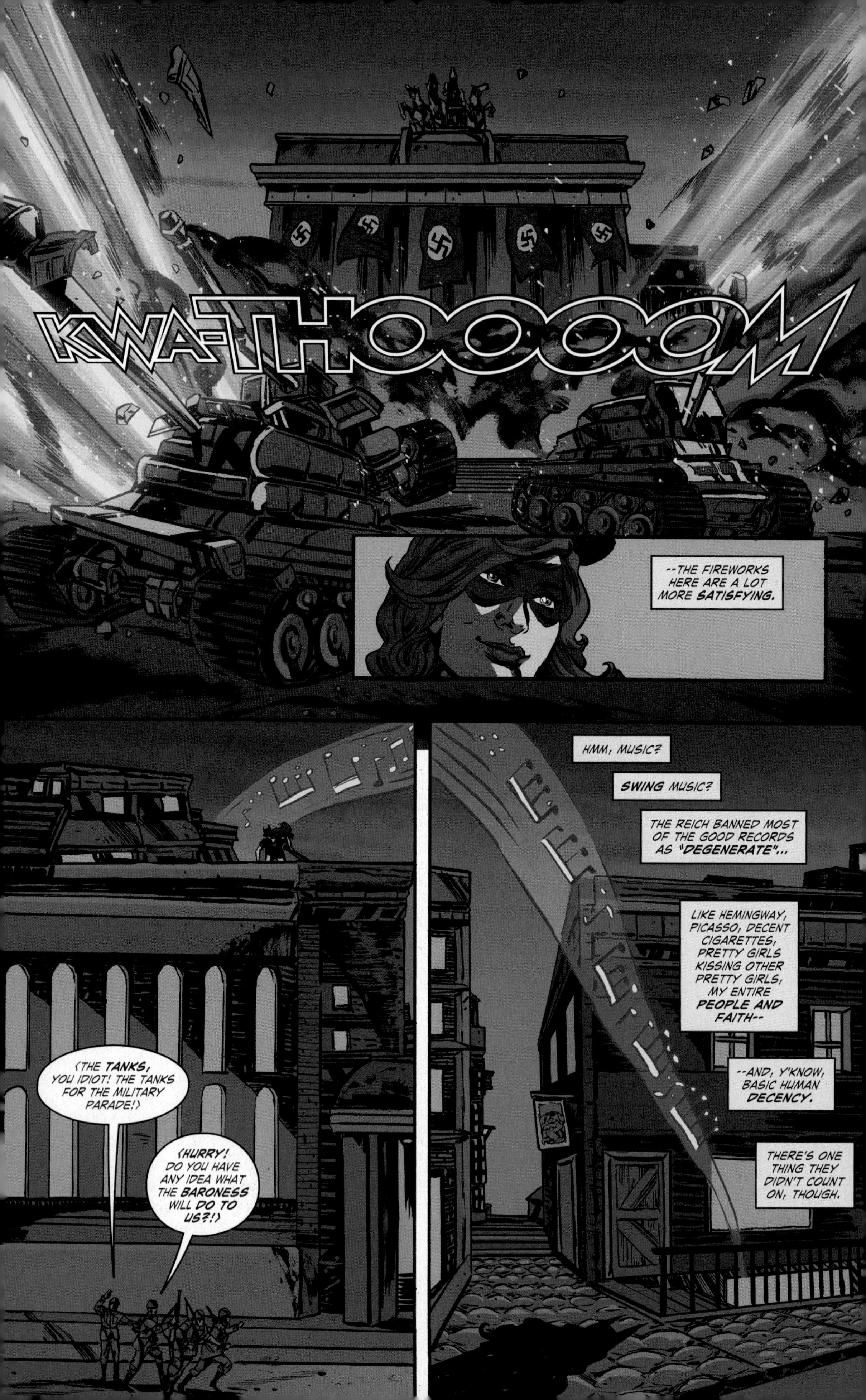
KWA-THOOOOM
--THE FIREWORKS HERE ARE A LOT MORE SATISFYING.
HMM, MUSIC?
SWING MUSIC?
THE REICH BANNED MOST OF THE GOOD RECORDS AS "DEGENERATE"...
LIKE HEMINGWAY, PICASSO, DECENT CIGARETTES, PRETTY GIRLS KISSING OTHER PRETTY GIRLS, MY ENTIRE PEOPLE AND FAITH--
--AND, Y'KNOW, BASIC HUMAN DECENCY.
‹THE TANKS, YOU IDIOT! THE TANKS FOR THE MILITARY PARADE!›
‹HURRY! DO YOU HAVE ANY IDEA WHAT THE BARONESS WILL DO TO US?!›
THERE'S ONE THING THEY DIDN'T COUNT ON, THOUGH.

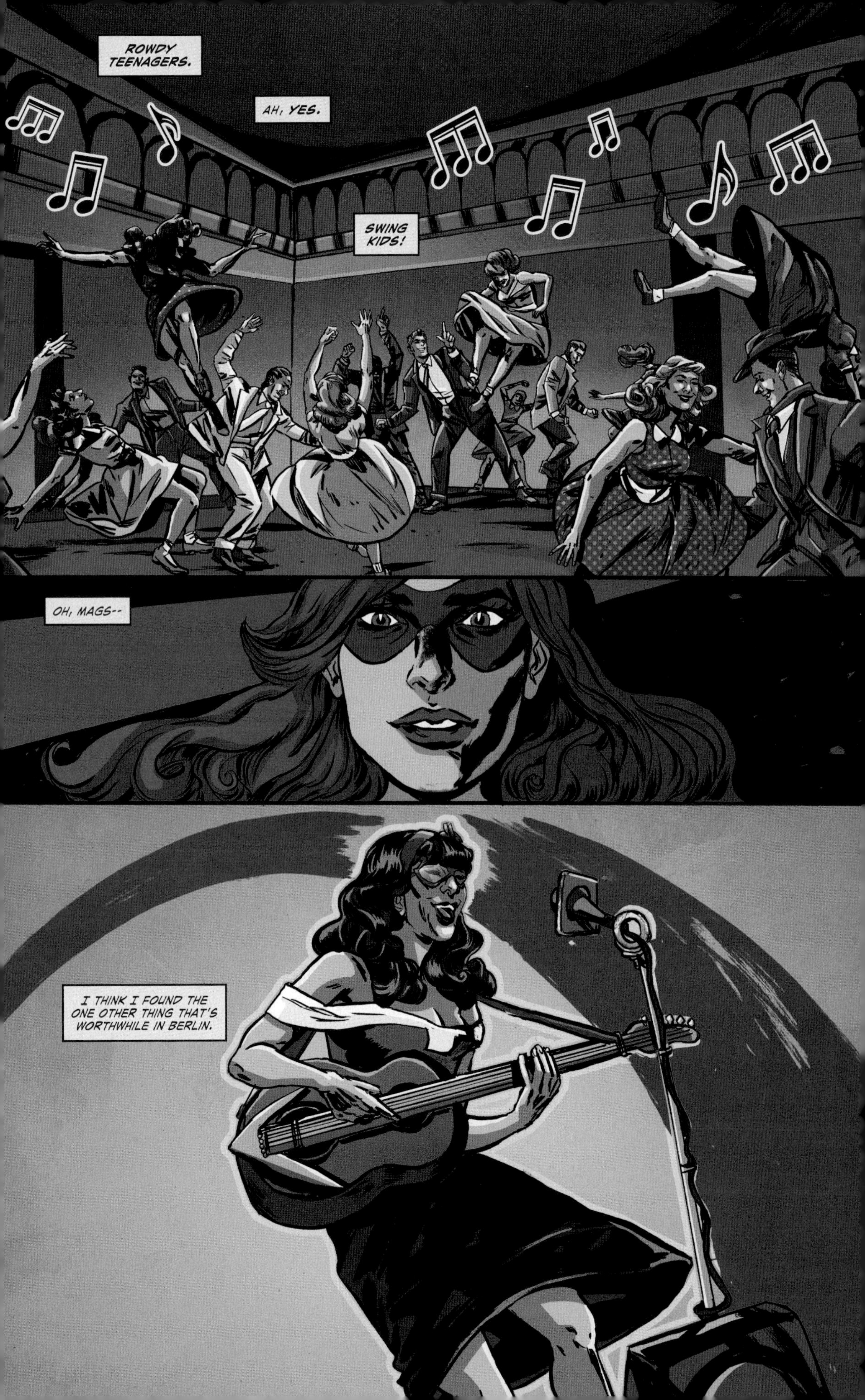
ROWDY TEENAGERS.
AH, YES.
SWING KIDS!
OH, MAGS--
I THINK I FOUND THE ONE OTHER THING THAT'S WORTHWHILE IN BERLIN.

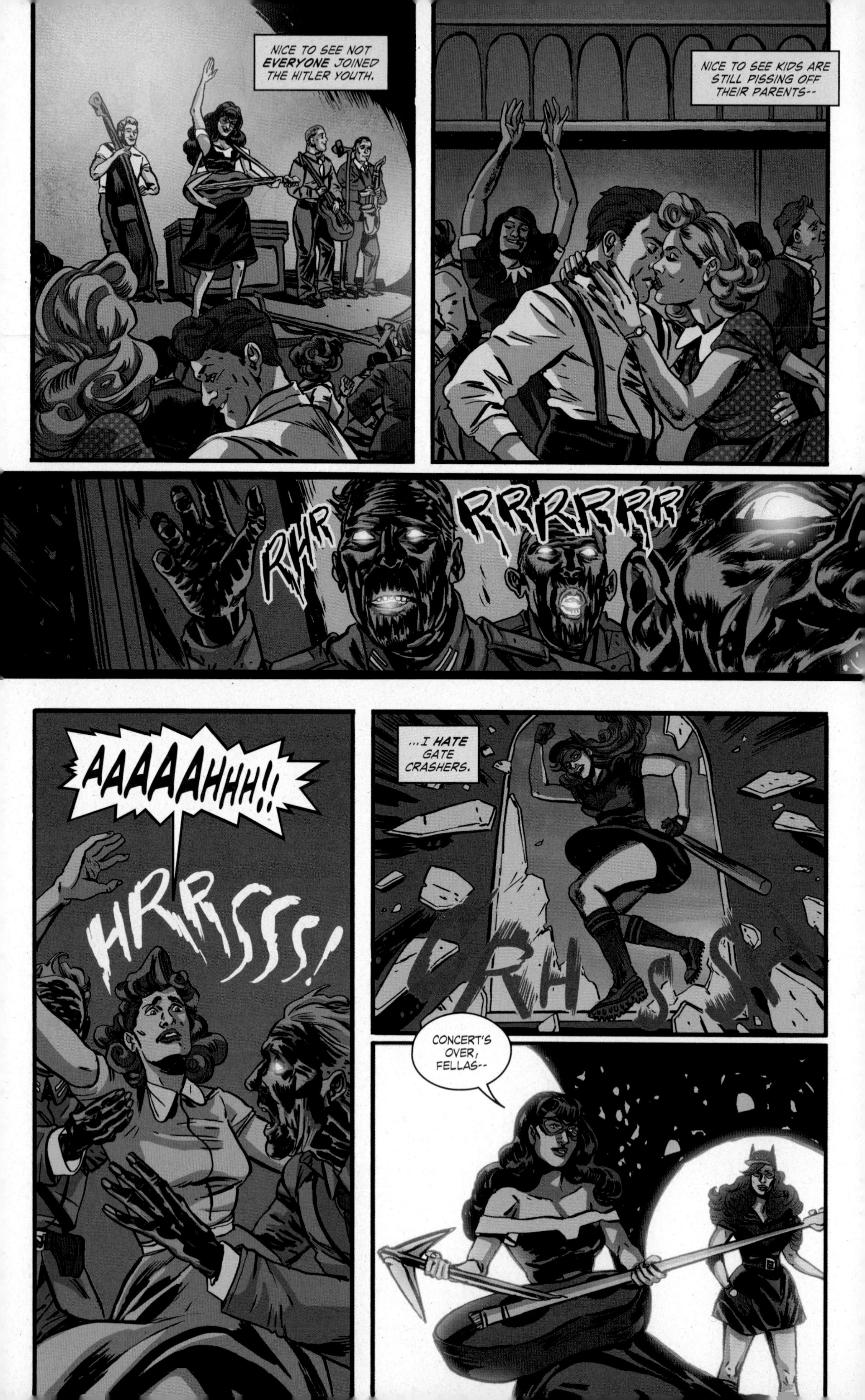
NICE TO SEE NOT **EVERYONE** JOINED THE HITLER YOUTH.
NICE TO SEE KIDS ARE STILL PISSING OFF THEIR PARENTS--
RHR
RRRRRRR
AAAAAHHH!!
HRRSSS!
...I **HATE** GATE CRASHERS.
RH
CONCERT'S OVER, FELLAS--

--EVEN AT THE END OF THE DAMN WORLD.

RHrrRr

HRRRR

CRNCH

BUT AS MUCH OF A HYPOCRITE AS IT MIGHT MAKE ME--

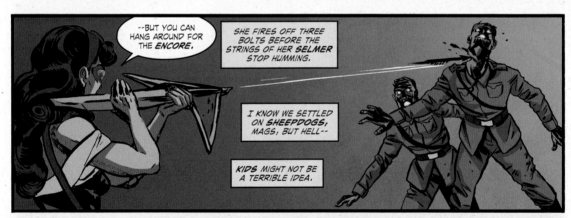

--BUT YOU CAN HANG AROUND FOR THE *ENCORE*.

SHE FIRES OFF THREE BOLTS BEFORE THE STRINGS OF HER *SELMER* STOP HUMMING.

I KNOW WE SETTLED ON *SHEEPDOGS*, MAGS; BUT HELL--

*KIDS* MIGHT NOT BE A TERRIBLE IDEA.

CAN WE ADOPT HER?

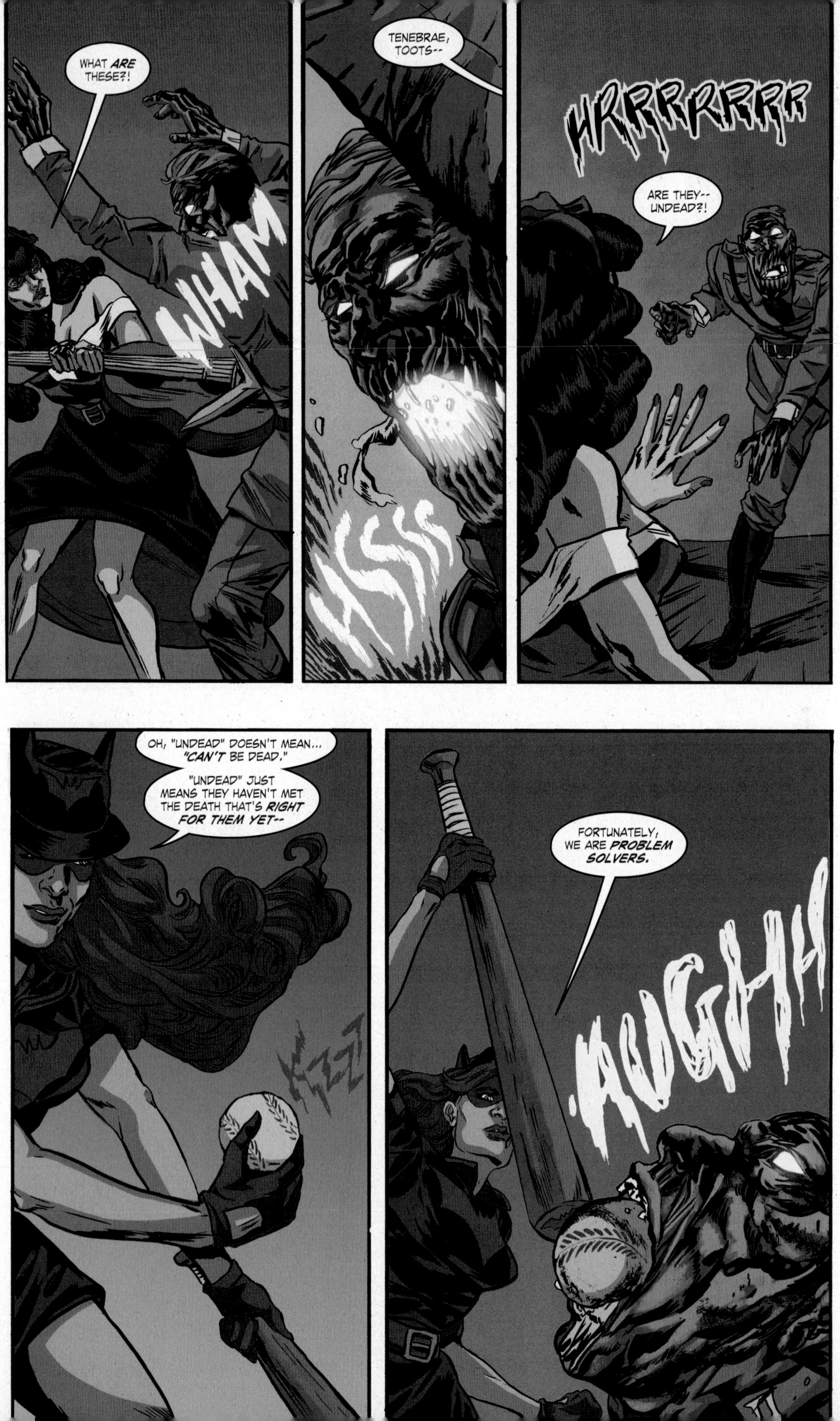
WHAT *ARE* THESE?!
WHAM
TENEBRAE, TOOTS--
HSSS
HRRRRRR
ARE THEY-- UNDEAD?!
OH, "UNDEAD" DOESN'T MEAN... *"CAN'T* BE DEAD."
"UNDEAD" JUST MEANS THEY HAVEN'T MET THE DEATH THAT'S *RIGHT FOR THEM YET--*
FORTUNATELY, WE ARE *PROBLEM SOLVERS.*
AUGHH

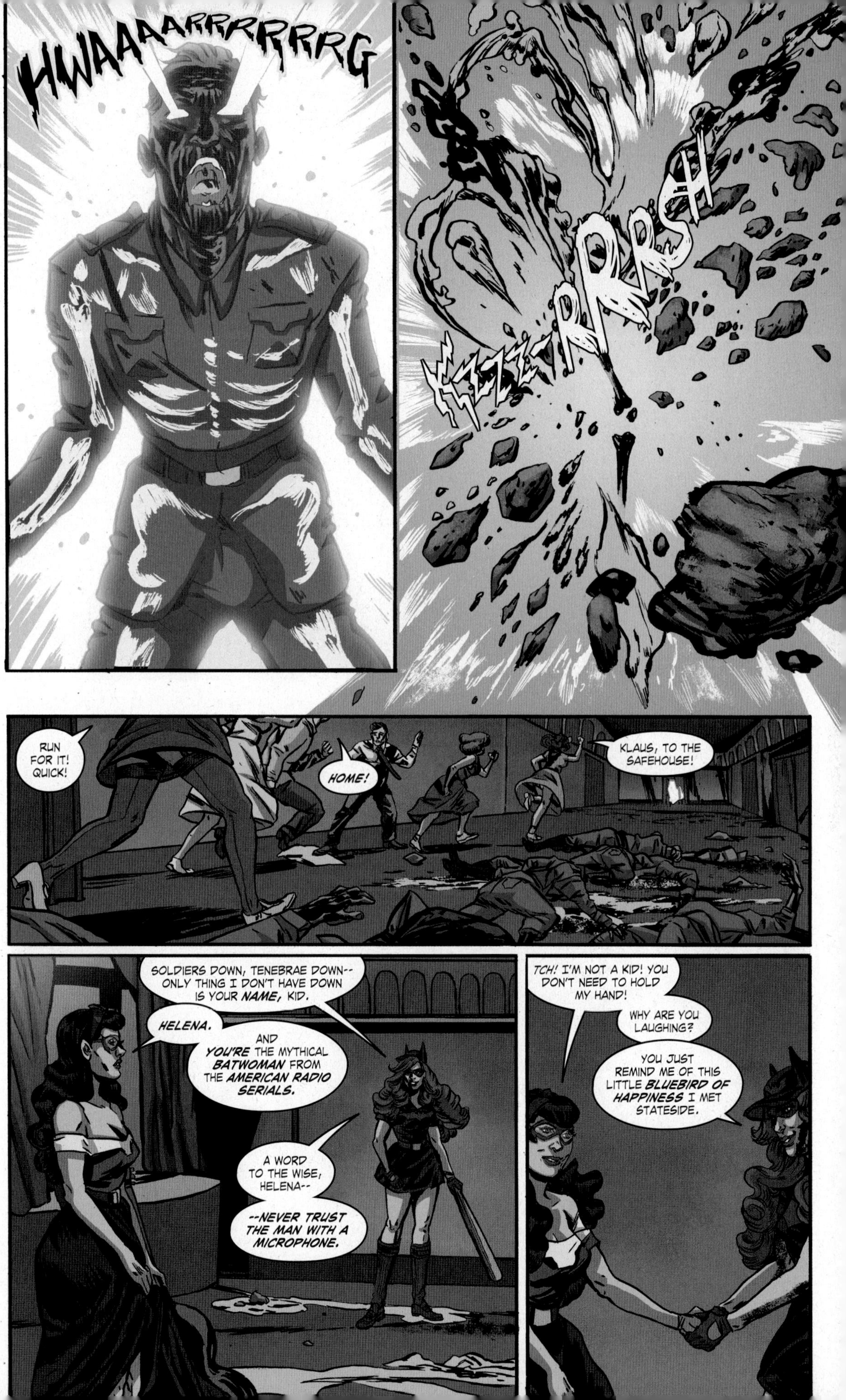
HWAAAARRRRRRG
KZZZZ-RRRRSH
RUN FOR IT! QUICK!
HOME!
KLAUS, TO THE SAFEHOUSE!
SOLDIERS DOWN, TENEBRAE DOWN-- ONLY THING I DON'T HAVE DOWN IS YOUR NAME, KID.
HELENA.
AND YOU'RE THE MYTHICAL BATWOMAN FROM THE AMERICAN RADIO SERIALS.
A WORD TO THE WISE, HELENA--
--NEVER TRUST THE MAN WITH A MICROPHONE.
TCH! I'M NOT A KID! YOU DON'T NEED TO HOLD MY HAND!
WHY ARE YOU LAUGHING?
YOU JUST REMIND ME OF THIS LITTLE BLUEBIRD OF HAPPINESS I MET STATESIDE.

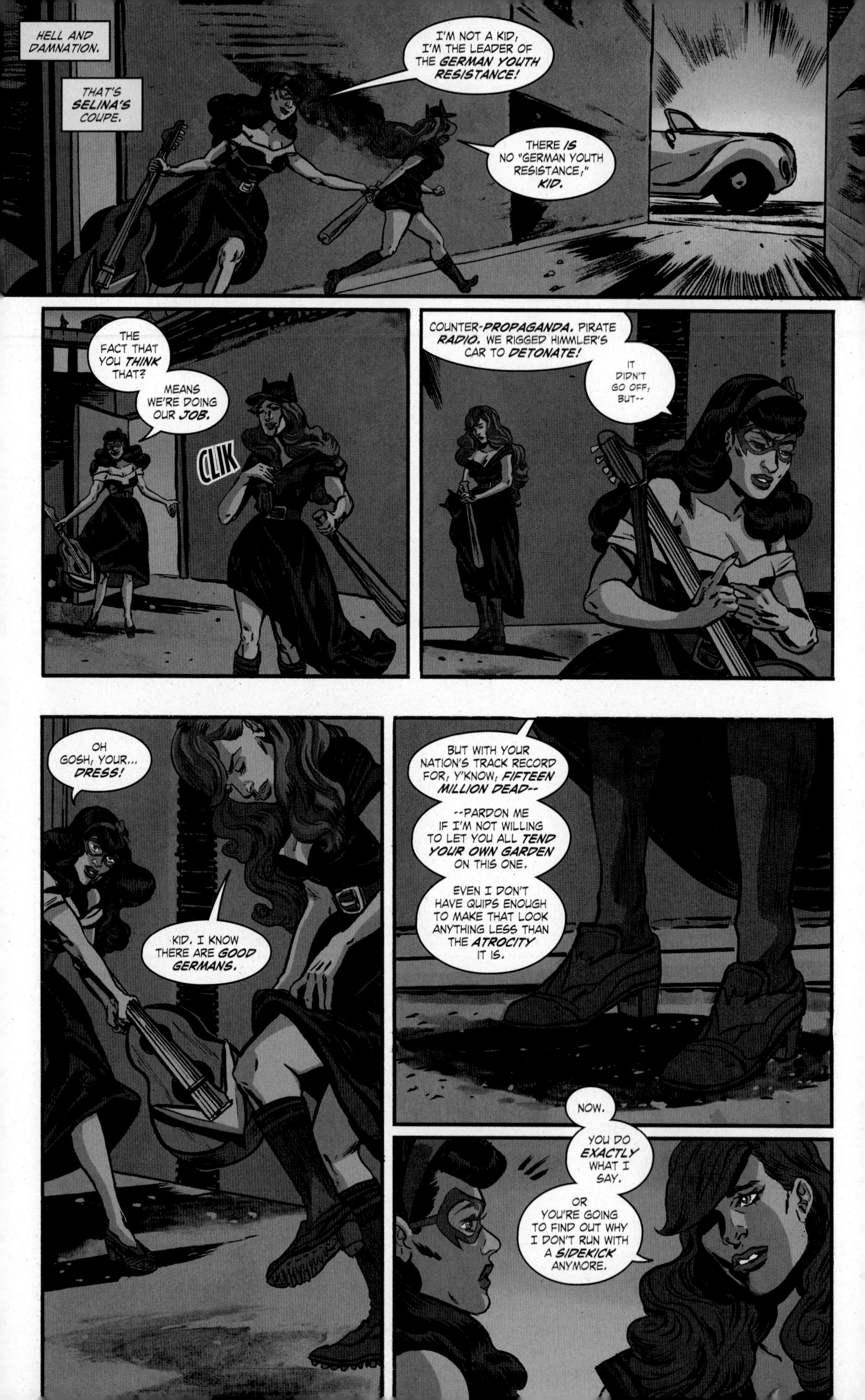
HELL AND DAMNATION.
THAT'S SELINA'S COUPE.
I'M NOT A KID, I'M THE LEADER OF THE GERMAN YOUTH RESISTANCE!
THERE IS NO "GERMAN YOUTH RESISTANCE," KID.
THE FACT THAT YOU THINK THAT?
MEANS WE'RE DOING OUR JOB.
CLIK
COUNTER-PROPAGANDA. PIRATE RADIO. WE RIGGED HIMMLER'S CAR TO DETONATE!
IT DIDN'T GO OFF, BUT--
OH GOSH, YOUR... DRESS!
KID. I KNOW THERE ARE GOOD GERMANS.
BUT WITH YOUR NATION'S TRACK RECORD FOR, Y'KNOW, FIFTEEN MILLION DEAD--
--PARDON ME IF I'M NOT WILLING TO LET YOU ALL TEND YOUR OWN GARDEN ON THIS ONE.
EVEN I DON'T HAVE QUIPS ENOUGH TO MAKE THAT LOOK ANYTHING LESS THAN THE ATROCITY IT IS.
NOW.
YOU DO EXACTLY WHAT I SAY.
OR YOU'RE GOING TO FIND OUT WHY I DON'T RUN WITH A SIDEKICK ANYMORE.

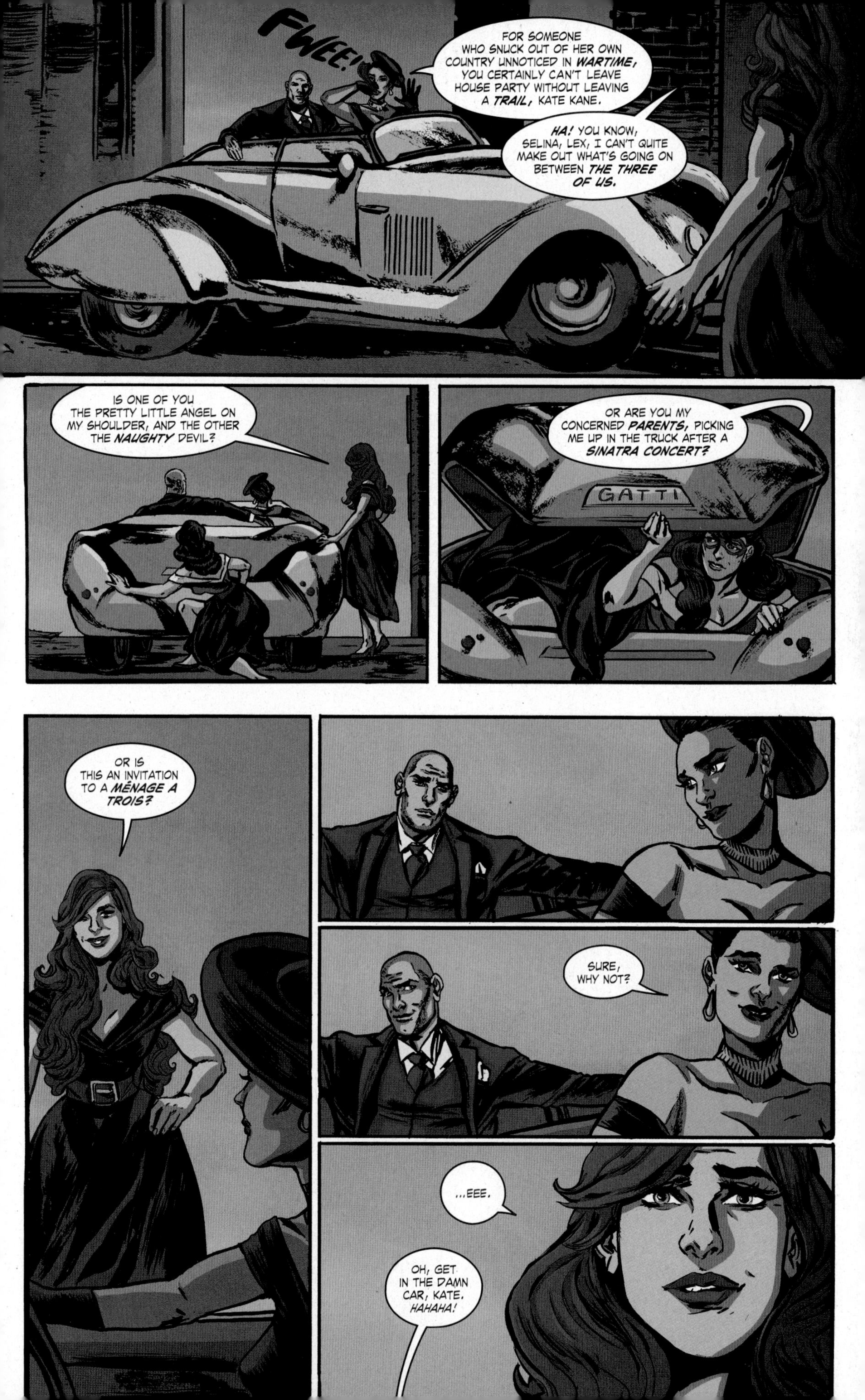
FWEE!
FOR SOMEONE WHO SNUCK OUT OF HER OWN COUNTRY UNNOTICED IN WARTIME, YOU CERTAINLY CAN'T LEAVE HOUSE PARTY WITHOUT LEAVING A TRAIL, KATE KANE.
HA! YOU KNOW, SELINA, LEX, I CAN'T QUITE MAKE OUT WHAT'S GOING ON BETWEEN THE THREE OF US.
IS ONE OF YOU THE PRETTY LITTLE ANGEL ON MY SHOULDER, AND THE OTHER THE NAUGHTY DEVIL?
OR ARE YOU MY CONCERNED PARENTS, PICKING ME UP IN THE TRUCK AFTER A SINATRA CONCERT?
GATTI
OR IS THIS AN INVITATION TO A MÉNAGE A TROIS?
SURE, WHY NOT?
...EEE.
OH, GET IN THE DAMN CAR, KATE. HAHAHA!

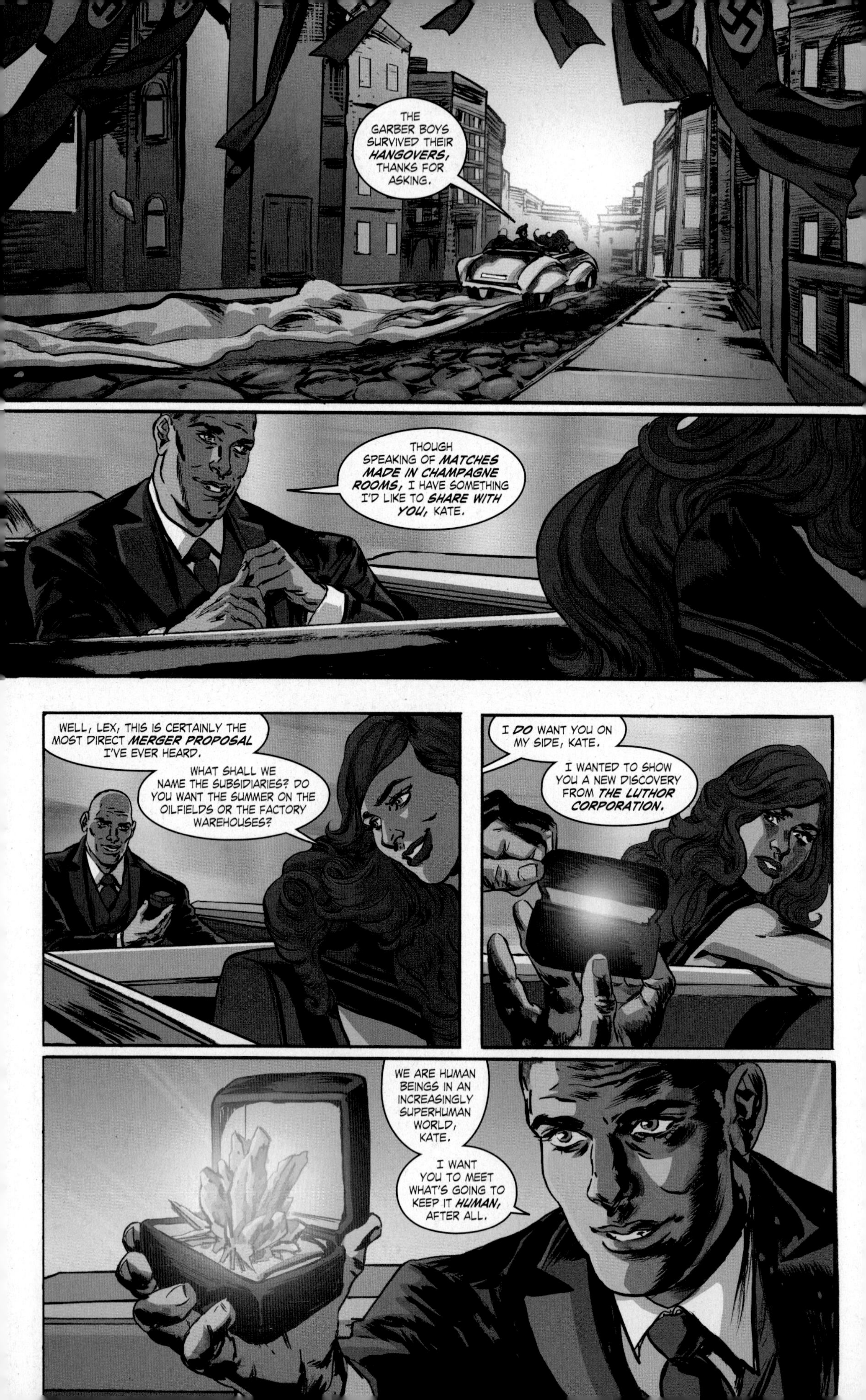
THE GARBER BOYS SURVIVED THEIR HANGOVERS, THANKS FOR ASKING.
THOUGH SPEAKING OF MATCHES MADE IN CHAMPAGNE ROOMS, I HAVE SOMETHING I'D LIKE TO SHARE WITH YOU, KATE.
WELL, LEX, THIS IS CERTAINLY THE MOST DIRECT MERGER PROPOSAL I'VE EVER HEARD.
WHAT SHALL WE NAME THE SUBSIDIARIES? DO YOU WANT THE SUMMER ON THE OILFIELDS OR THE FACTORY WAREHOUSES?
I DO WANT YOU ON MY SIDE, KATE.
I WANTED TO SHOW YOU A NEW DISCOVERY FROM THE LUTHOR CORPORATION.
WE ARE HUMAN BEINGS IN AN INCREASINGLY SUPERHUMAN WORLD, KATE.
I WANT YOU TO MEET WHAT'S GOING TO KEEP IT HUMAN, AFTER ALL.

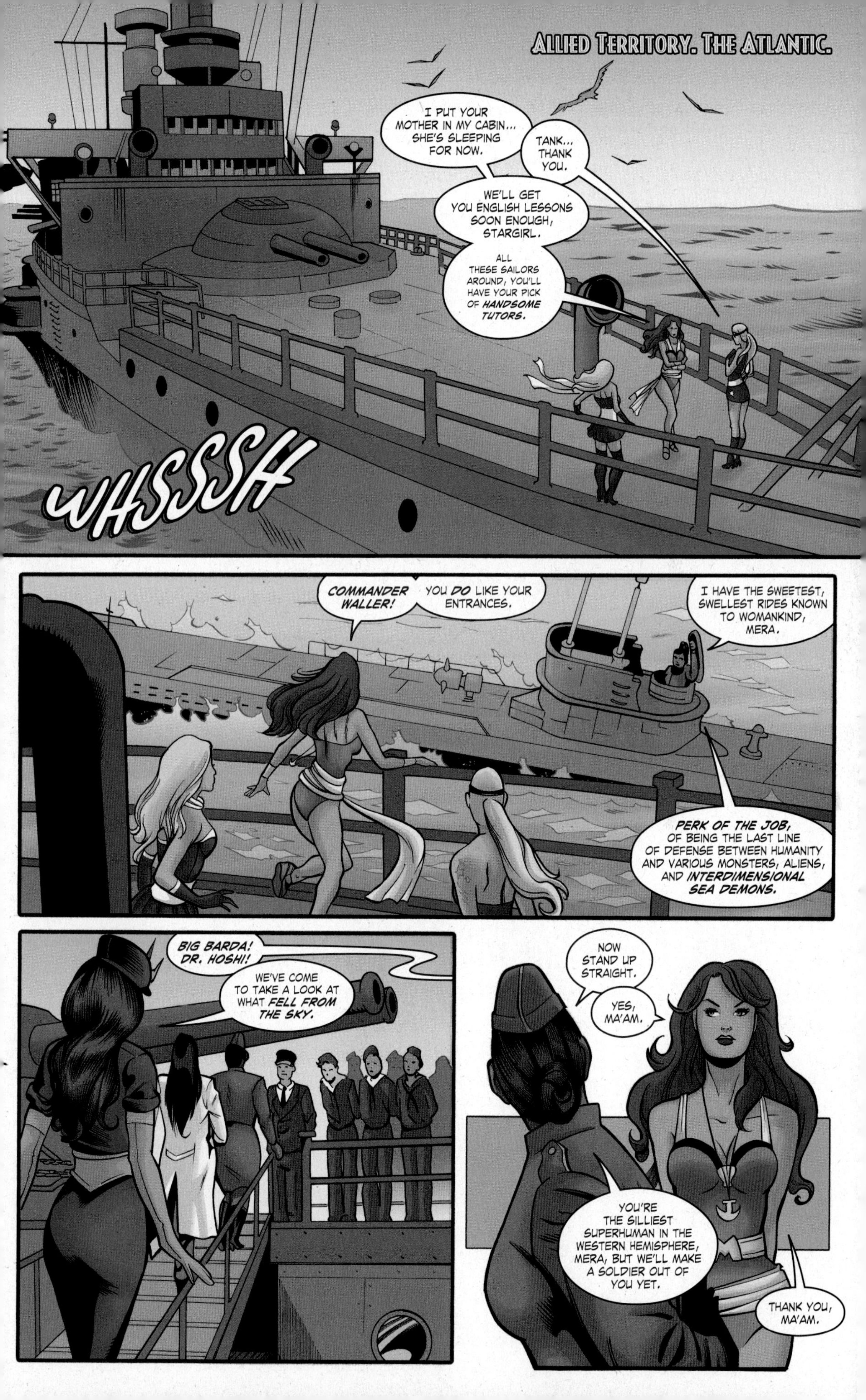
ALLIED TERRITORY. THE ATLANTIC.
I PUT YOUR MOTHER IN MY CABIN... SHE'S SLEEPING FOR NOW.
TANK... THANK YOU.
WE'LL GET YOU ENGLISH LESSONS SOON ENOUGH, STARGIRL.
ALL THESE SAILORS AROUND, YOU'LL HAVE YOUR PICK OF HANDSOME TUTORS.
WHSSSH
COMMANDER WALLER!
YOU DO LIKE YOUR ENTRANCES.
I HAVE THE SWEETEST, SWELLEST RIDES KNOWN TO WOMANKIND, MERA.
PERK OF THE JOB, OF BEING THE LAST LINE OF DEFENSE BETWEEN HUMANITY AND VARIOUS MONSTERS, ALIENS, AND INTERDIMENSIONAL SEA DEMONS.
BIG BARDA! DR. HOSHI!
WE'VE COME TO TAKE A LOOK AT WHAT FELL FROM THE SKY.
NOW STAND UP STRAIGHT.
YES, MA'AM.
YOU'RE THE SILLIEST SUPERHUMAN IN THE WESTERN HEMISPHERE, MERA, BUT WE'LL MAKE A SOLDIER OUT OF YOU YET.
THANK YOU, MA'AM.

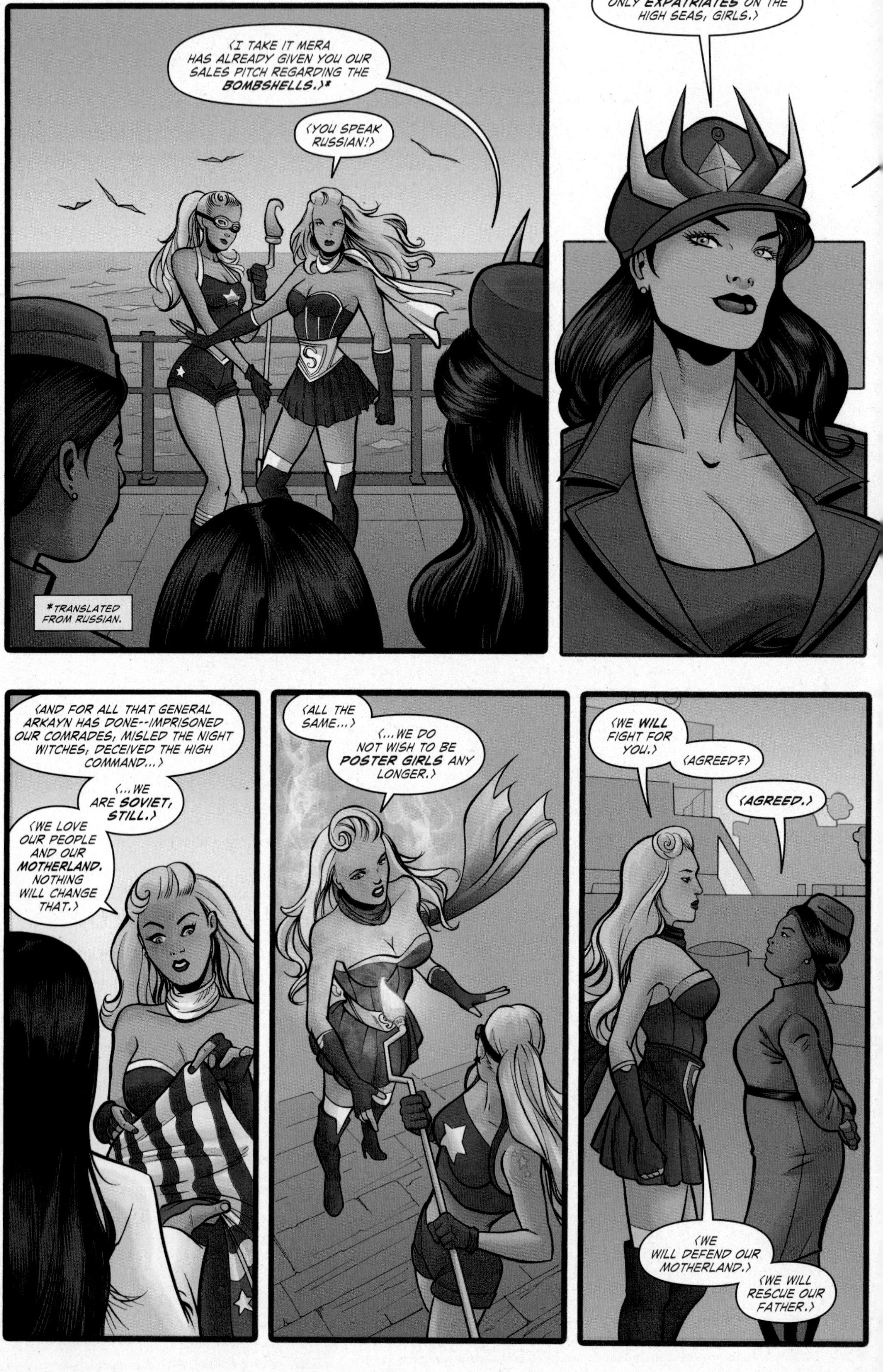
‹I TAKE IT MERA HAS ALREADY GIVEN YOU OUR SALES PITCH REGARDING THE BOMBSHELLS.›*
‹YOU SPEAK RUSSIAN!›
*TRANSLATED FROM RUSSIAN.
‹YOU'RE NOT THE ONLY EXPATRIATES ON THE HIGH SEAS, GIRLS.›
‹AND FOR ALL THAT GENERAL ARKAYN HAS DONE--IMPRISONED OUR COMRADES, MISLED THE NIGHT WITCHES, DECEIVED THE HIGH COMMAND...›
‹...WE ARE SOVIET, STILL.›
‹WE LOVE OUR PEOPLE AND OUR MOTHERLAND. NOTHING WILL CHANGE THAT.›
‹ALL THE SAME...›
‹...WE DO NOT WISH TO BE POSTER GIRLS ANY LONGER.›
‹WE WILL FIGHT FOR YOU.›
‹AGREED?›
‹AGREED.›
‹WE WILL DEFEND OUR MOTHERLAND.›
‹WE WILL RESCUE OUR FATHER.›

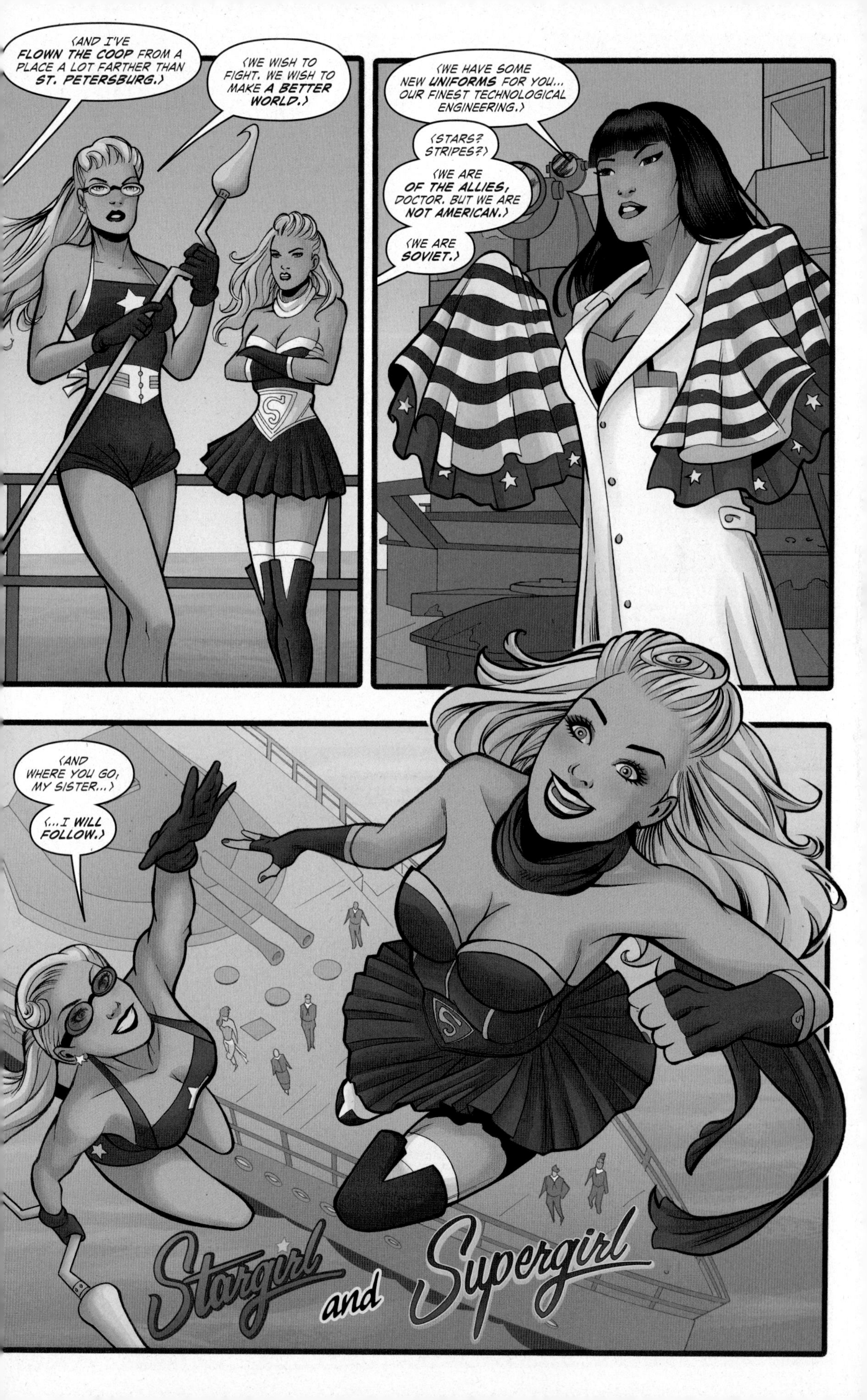

‹AND I'VE FLOWN THE COOP FROM A PLACE A LOT FARTHER THAN ST. PETERSBURG.›
‹WE WISH TO FIGHT. WE WISH TO MAKE A BETTER WORLD.›
‹WE HAVE SOME NEW UNIFORMS FOR YOU... OUR FINEST TECHNOLOGICAL ENGINEERING.›
‹STARS? STRIPES?›
‹WE ARE OF THE ALLIES, DOCTOR. BUT WE ARE NOT AMERICAN.›
‹WE ARE SOVIET.›
‹AND WHERE YOU GO, MY SISTER...›
‹...I WILL FOLLOW.›
Stargirl and Supergirl

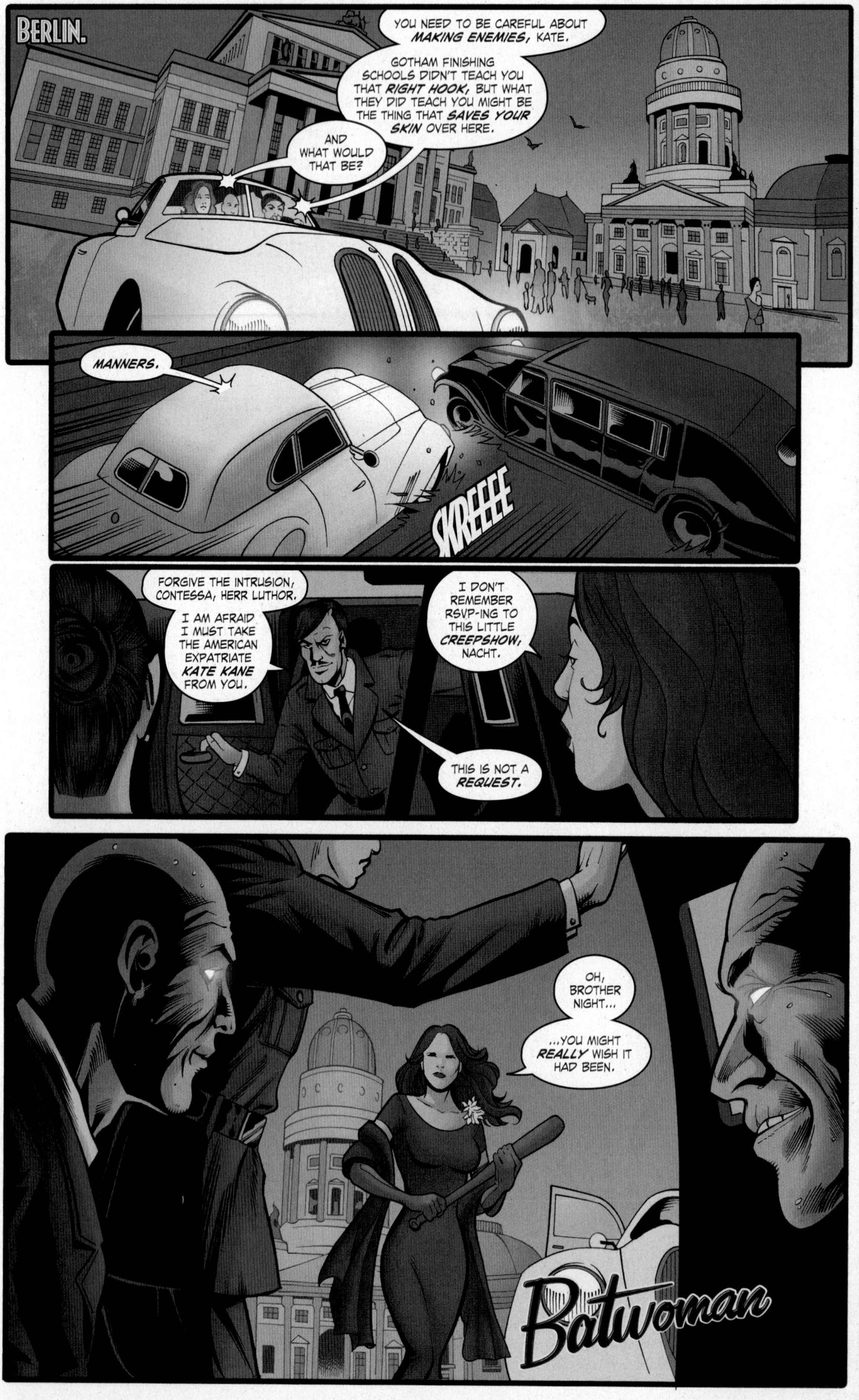
BERLIN.
YOU NEED TO BE CAREFUL ABOUT MAKING ENEMIES, KATE.
GOTHAM FINISHING SCHOOLS DIDN'T TEACH YOU THAT RIGHT HOOK, BUT WHAT THEY DID TEACH YOU MIGHT BE THE THING THAT SAVES YOUR SKIN OVER HERE.
AND WHAT WOULD THAT BE?
MANNERS.
SKREEEE
FORGIVE THE INTRUSION, CONTESSA, HERR LUTHOR.
I AM AFRAID I MUST TAKE THE AMERICAN EXPATRIATE KATE KANE FROM YOU.
I DON'T REMEMBER RSVP-ING TO THIS LITTLE CREEPSHOW, NACHT.
THIS IS NOT A REQUEST.
OH, BROTHER NIGHT...
...YOU MIGHT REALLY WISH IT HAD BEEN.
Batwoman

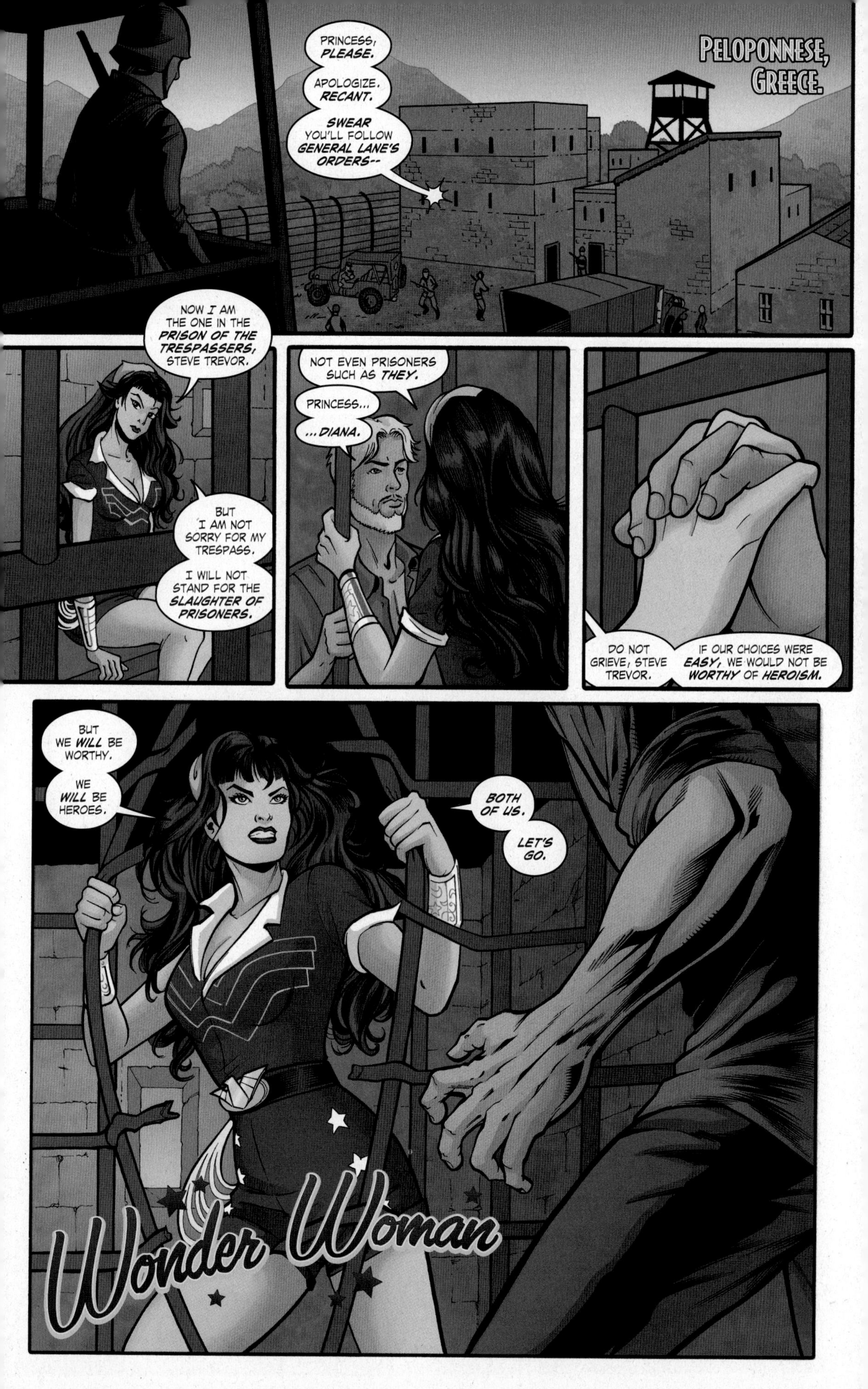
PELOPONNESE, GREECE.
PRINCESS, PLEASE.
APOLOGIZE. RECANT.
SWEAR YOU'LL FOLLOW GENERAL LANE'S ORDERS--
NOW I AM THE ONE IN THE PRISON OF THE TRESPASSERS, STEVE TREVOR.
BUT I AM NOT SORRY FOR MY TRESPASS.
I WILL NOT STAND FOR THE SLAUGHTER OF PRISONERS.
NOT EVEN PRISONERS SUCH AS THEY.
PRINCESS...
...DIANA.
DO NOT GRIEVE, STEVE TREVOR.
IF OUR CHOICES WERE EASY, WE WOULD NOT BE WORTHY OF HEROISM.
BUT WE WILL BE WORTHY.
WE WILL BE HEROES.
BOTH OF US.
LET'S GO.
Wonder Woman

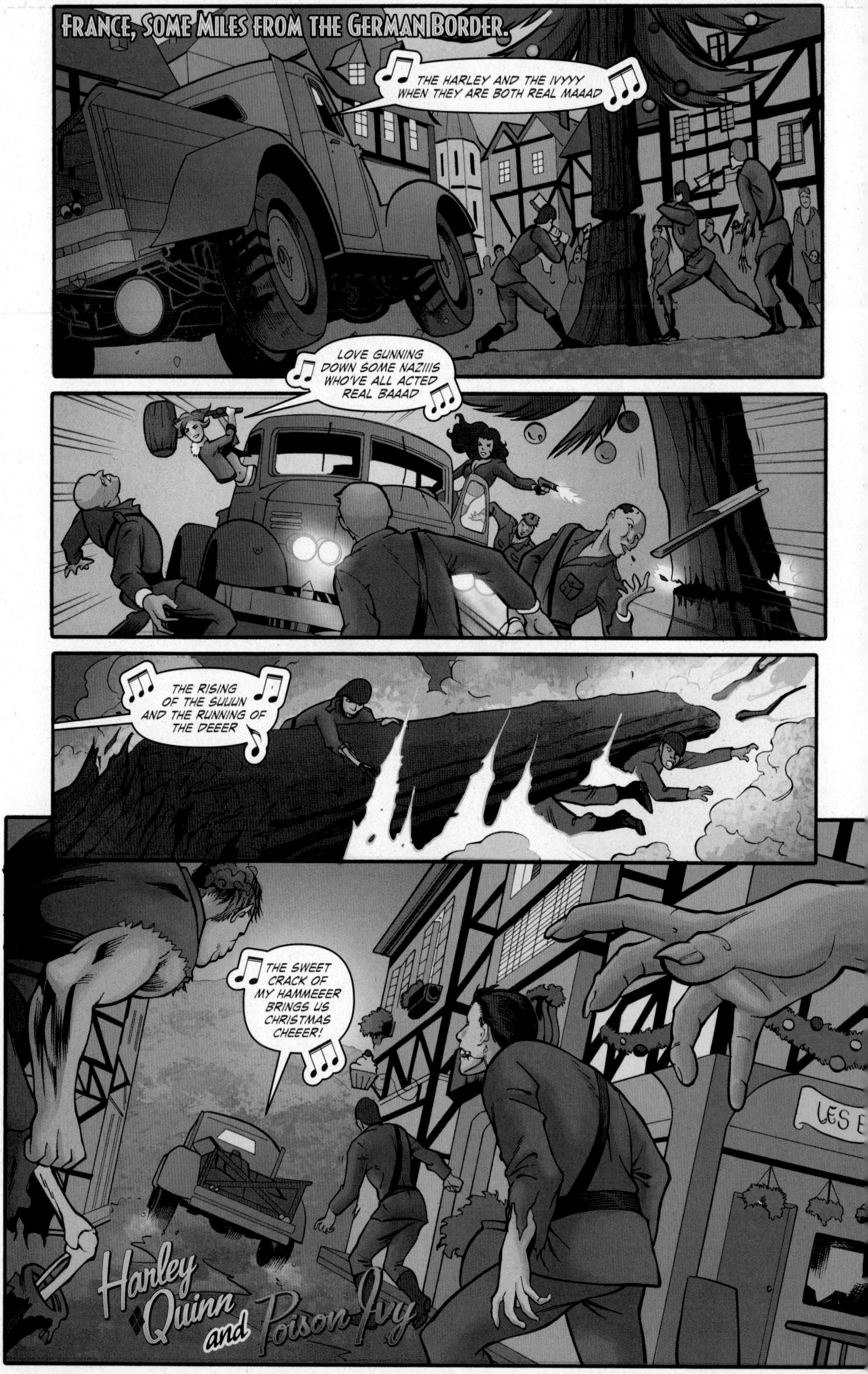
France, Some Miles from the German Border.
THE HARLEY AND THE IVYYY WHEN THEY ARE BOTH REAL MAAAD
LOVE GUNNING DOWN SOME NAZIIIS WHO'VE ALL ACTED REAL BAAAD
THE RISING OF THE SUUUN AND THE RUNNING OF THE DEEER
THE SWEET CRACK OF MY HAMMEEER BRINGS US CHRISTMAS CHEEER!
Harley Quinn and Poison Ivy

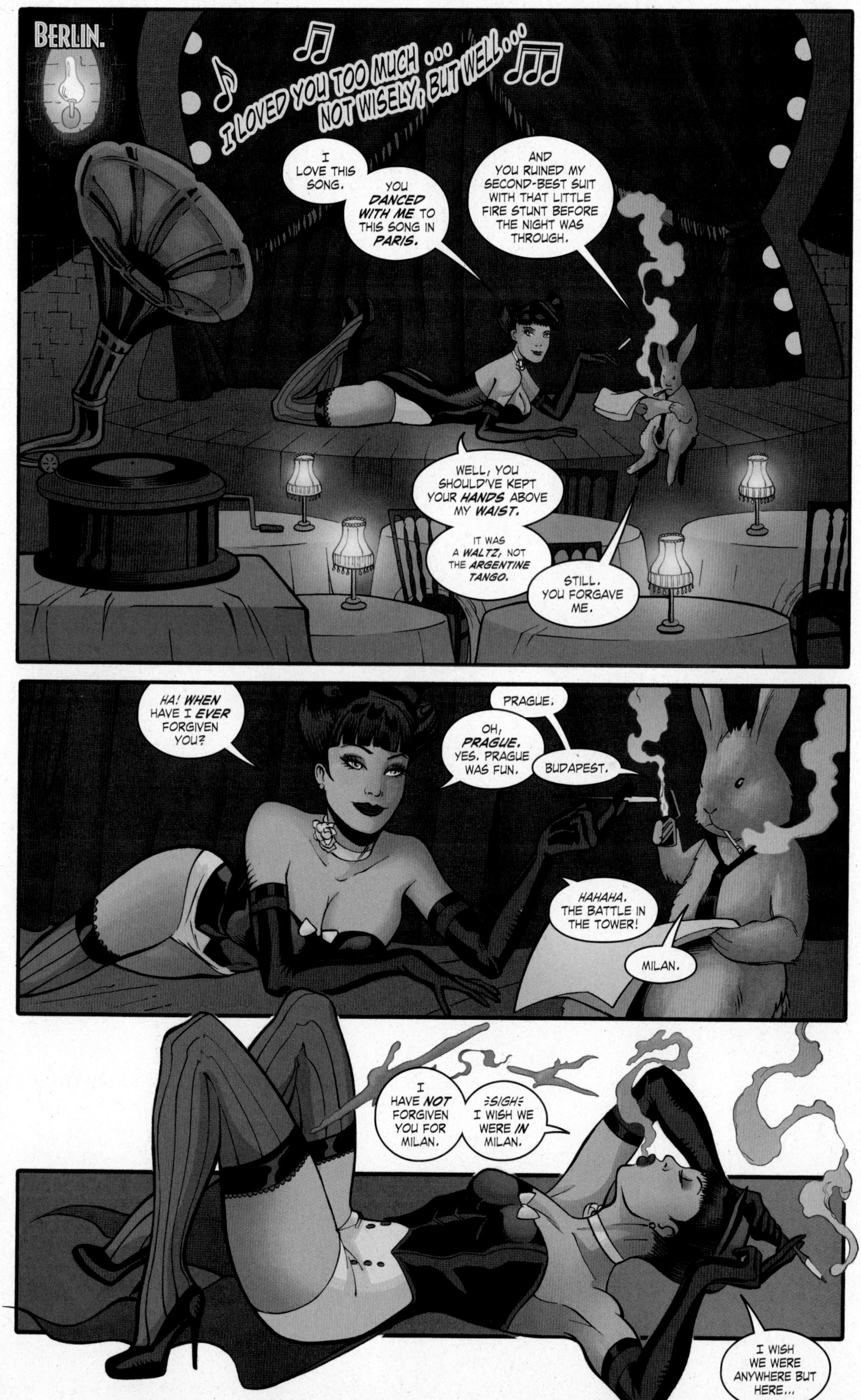

BERLIN.
I LOVED YOU TOO MUCH... NOT WISELY, BUT WELL...
I LOVE THIS SONG.
YOU DANCED WITH ME TO THIS SONG IN PARIS.
AND YOU RUINED MY SECOND-BEST SUIT WITH THAT LITTLE FIRE STUNT BEFORE THE NIGHT WAS THROUGH.
WELL, YOU SHOULD'VE KEPT YOUR HANDS ABOVE MY WAIST.
IT WAS A WALTZ, NOT THE ARGENTINE TANGO.
STILL. YOU FORGAVE ME.
HA! WHEN HAVE I EVER FORGIVEN YOU?
PRAGUE.
OH, PRAGUE. YES. PRAGUE WAS FUN.
BUDAPEST.
HAHAHA. THE BATTLE IN THE TOWER!
MILAN.
I HAVE NOT FORGIVEN YOU FOR MILAN.
≈SIGH≈ I WISH WE WERE IN MILAN.
I WISH WE WERE ANYWHERE BUT HERE...

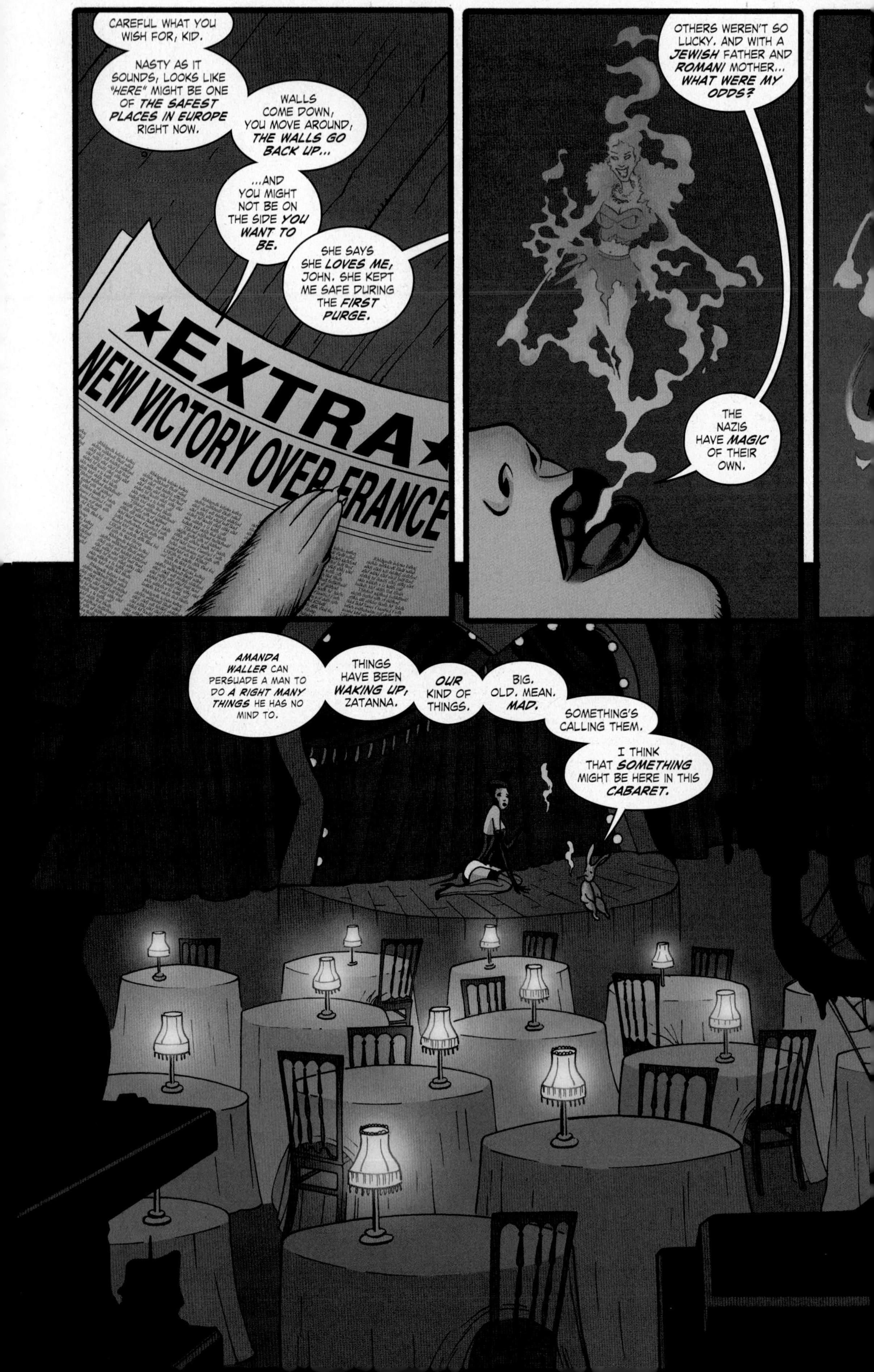
CAREFUL WHAT YOU WISH FOR, KID.
NASTY AS IT SOUNDS, LOOKS LIKE "HERE" MIGHT BE ONE OF THE SAFEST PLACES IN EUROPE RIGHT NOW.
WALLS COME DOWN, YOU MOVE AROUND, THE WALLS GO BACK UP...
...AND YOU MIGHT NOT BE ON THE SIDE YOU WANT TO BE.
SHE SAYS SHE LOVES ME, JOHN. SHE KEPT ME SAFE DURING THE FIRST PURGE.
★EXTRA★
NEW VICTORY OVER FRANCE
OTHERS WEREN'T SO LUCKY. AND WITH A JEWISH FATHER AND ROMANI MOTHER... WHAT WERE MY ODDS?
THE NAZIS HAVE MAGIC OF THEIR OWN.
AMANDA WALLER CAN PERSUADE A MAN TO DO A RIGHT MANY THINGS HE HAS NO MIND TO.
THINGS HAVE BEEN WAKING UP, ZATANNA.
OUR KIND OF THINGS.
BIG. OLD. MEAN. MAD.
SOMETHING'S CALLING THEM.
I THINK THAT SOMETHING MIGHT BE HERE IN THIS CABARET.

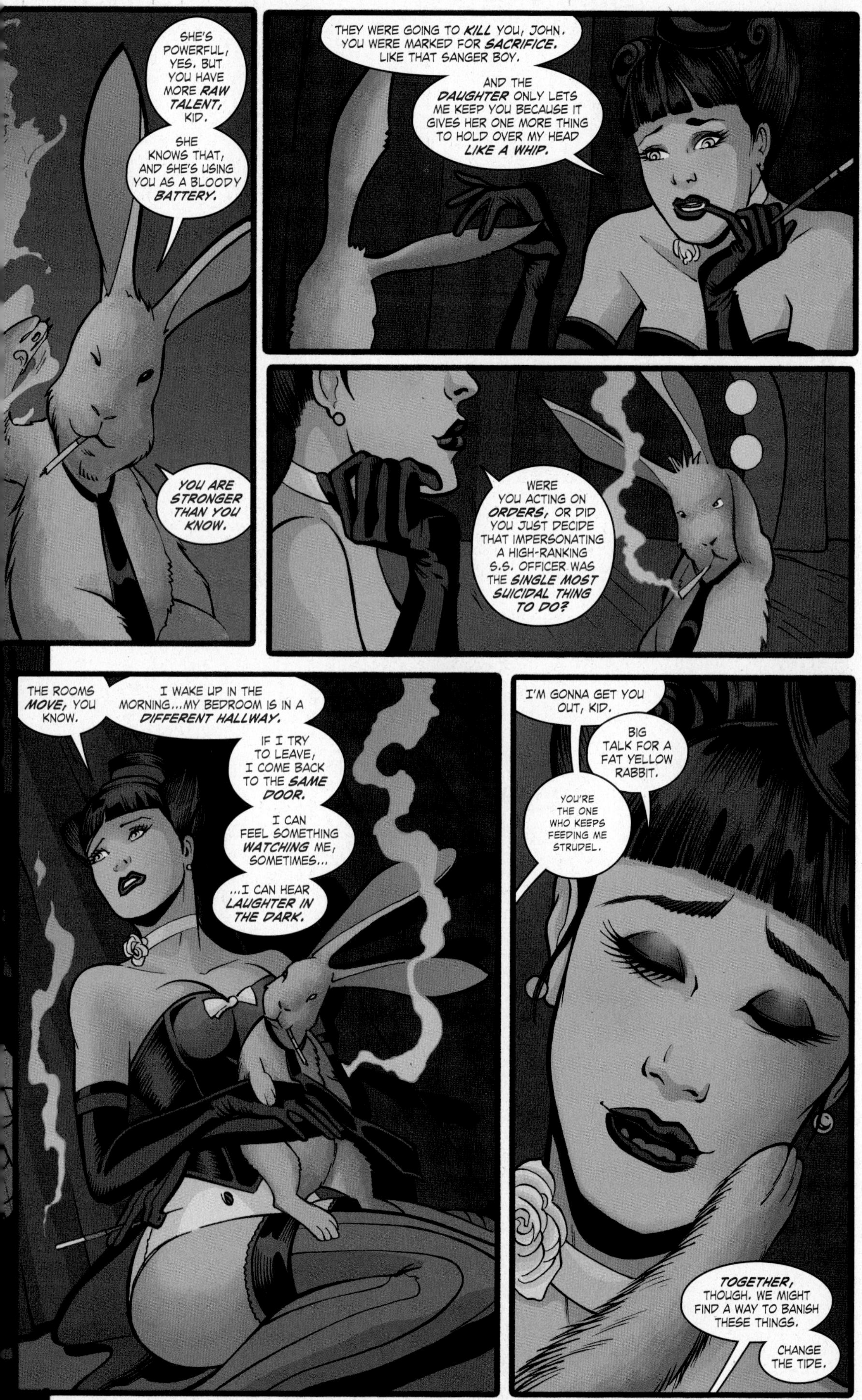
SHE'S POWERFUL, YES. BUT YOU HAVE MORE RAW TALENT, KID.
SHE KNOWS THAT, AND SHE'S USING YOU AS A BLOODY BATTERY.
YOU ARE STRONGER THAN YOU KNOW.
THEY WERE GOING TO KILL YOU, JOHN. YOU WERE MARKED FOR SACRIFICE. LIKE THAT SANGER BOY.
AND THE DAUGHTER ONLY LETS ME KEEP YOU BECAUSE IT GIVES HER ONE MORE THING TO HOLD OVER MY HEAD LIKE A WHIP.
WERE YOU ACTING ON ORDERS, OR DID YOU JUST DECIDE THAT IMPERSONATING A HIGH-RANKING S.S. OFFICER WAS THE SINGLE MOST SUICIDAL THING TO DO?
THE ROOMS MOVE, YOU KNOW.
I WAKE UP IN THE MORNING...MY BEDROOM IS IN A DIFFERENT HALLWAY.
IF I TRY TO LEAVE, I COME BACK TO THE SAME DOOR.
I CAN FEEL SOMETHING WATCHING ME, SOMETIMES...
...I CAN HEAR LAUGHTER IN THE DARK.
I'M GONNA GET YOU OUT, KID.
BIG TALK FOR A FAT YELLOW RABBIT.
YOU'RE THE ONE WHO KEEPS FEEDING ME STRUDEL.
TOGETHER, THOUGH. WE MIGHT FIND A WAY TO BANISH THESE THINGS.
CHANGE THE TIDE.

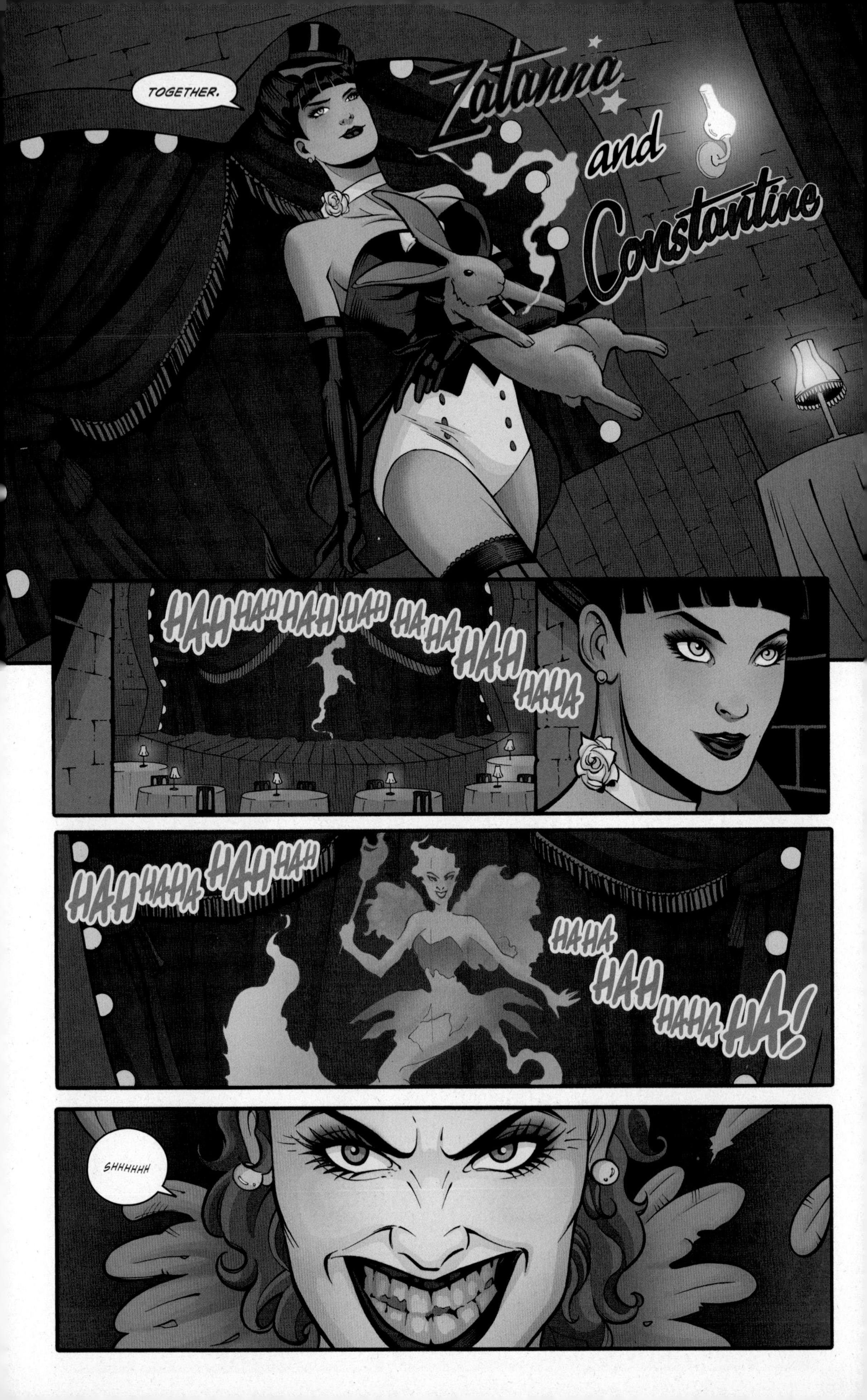
TOGETHER.
Zatanna and Constantine
HAH HAH HAH HAH HAHA HAH HAHA
HAH HAHA HAH HAH
HAHA HAH HAHA HA!
SHHHHHH

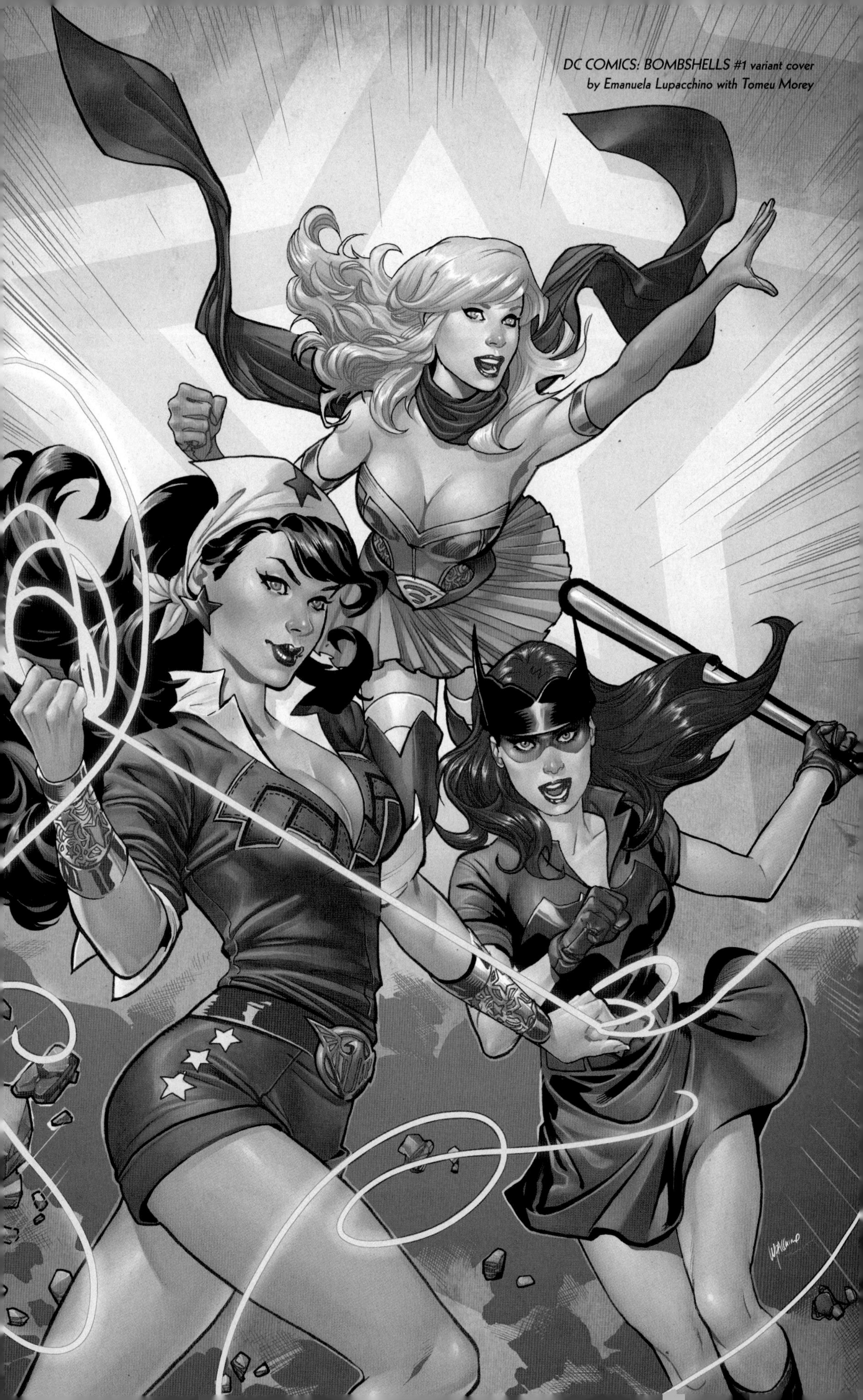

*DC COMICS: BOMBSHELLS #1 variant cover*
*by Emanuela Lupacchino with Tomeu Morey*

DC COMICS: BOMBSHELLS #2 variant cover by Kevin Wada

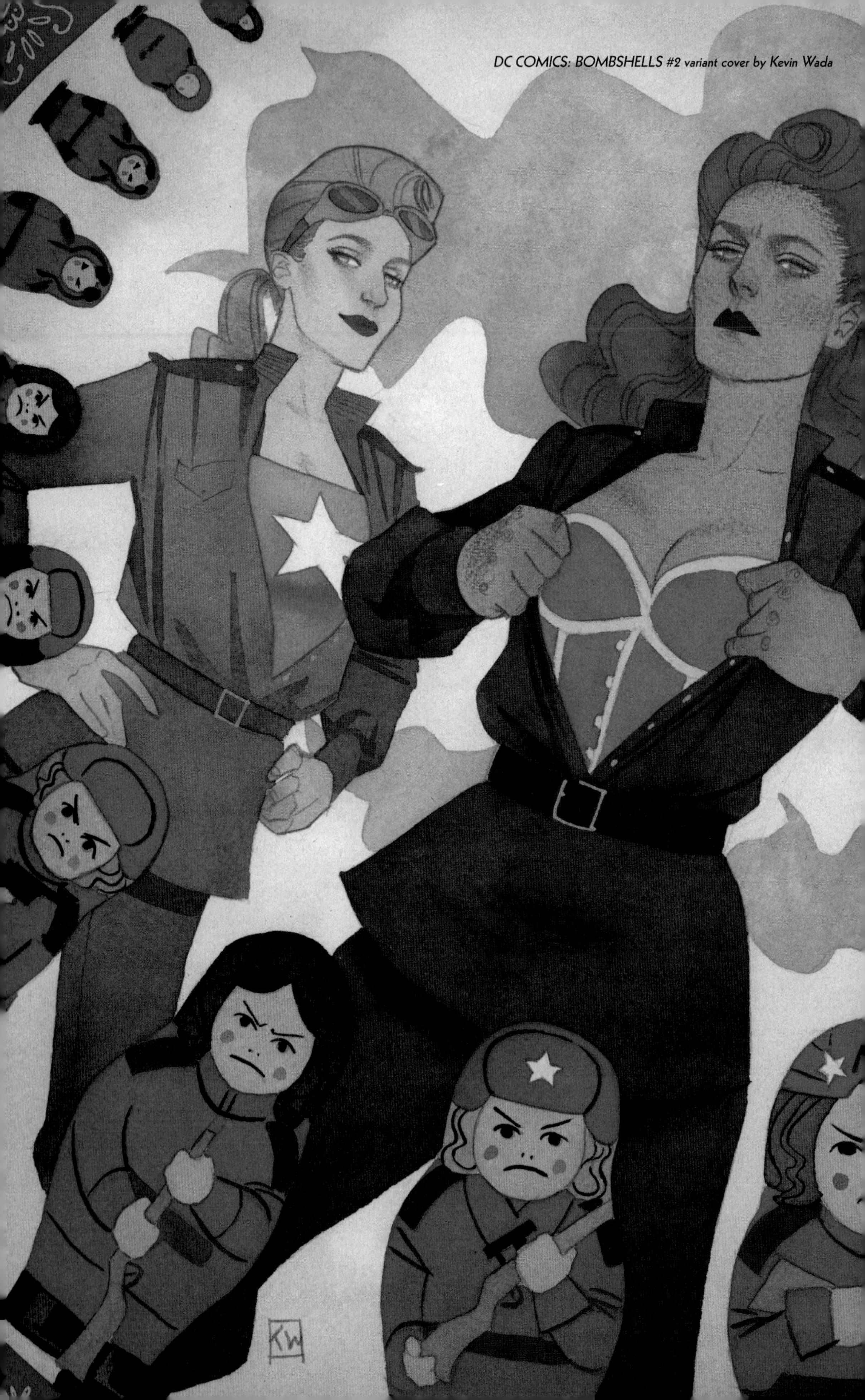
KW

*DC COMICS: BOMBSHELLS #3 variant cover*
*by Kate Leth with Paulina Ganucheau*

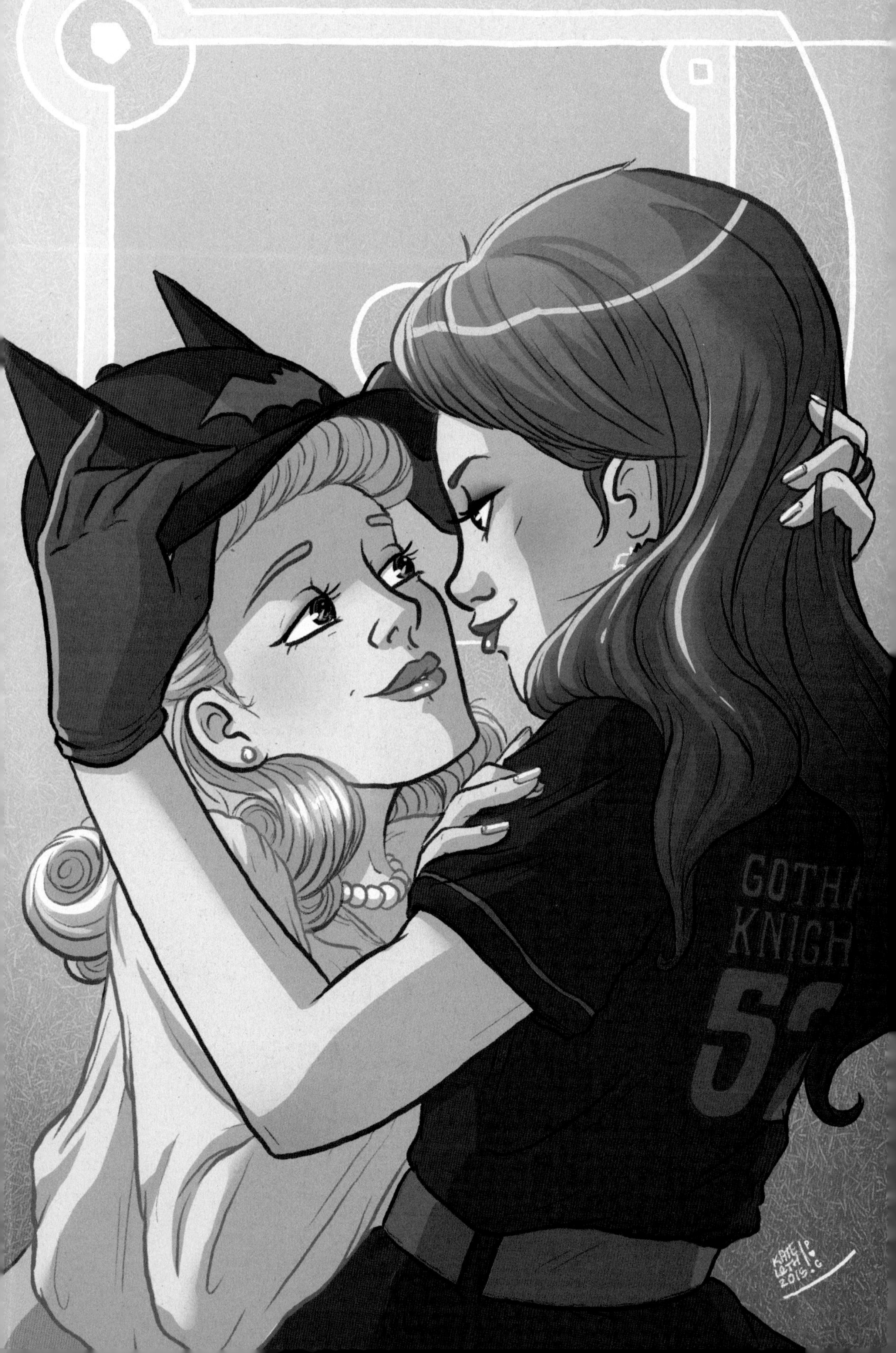
GOTH
KNIGH